6-19-74

Essays in Modern Economics

Essays in
Modern Economics

The Proceedings of the Association of University Teachers of Economics: Aberystwyth 1972

Edited by
Michael Parkin with A. R. Nobay

BOOKS
10 East 53d St., New York 10022
(a division of Harper & Row Publishers, inc.)

Published in the U.S.A. 1973 by
HARPER & ROW PUBLISHERS, INC.
BARNES & NOBLE IMPORTS DIVISION

ISBN 06 495395 5

Printed in Great Britain by
Adlard & Son Ltd, Bartholomew Press
Dorking, Surrey

List of contents

1808496

List of contributors

M. J. Artis	University of Wales, Swansea
A. B. Atkinson	University of Essex
M. Blaug	Institute of Education, University of London
C. J. Bliss	University of Essex
Frank Brechling	University of Essex and Northwestern University
I. C. R. Byatt	Department of the Environment
B. A. Corry	Queen Mary College, London
Avinash Dixit	Balliol College, Oxford
L. Fishman	University of Keele
Maxwell J. Fry	City University
Charles Goodhart	Bank of England
H. A. John Green	University of Toronto
F. H. Hahn	London School of Economics and Churchill College, Cambridge
P. J. Hammond	University of Essex
A. E. Holmans	Department of the Environment
Richard Jackman	London School of Economics
Elizabeth Johnson	London
P. N. Junankar	University of Essex
Malcolm Knight	University of Toronto
D. E. W. Laidler	University of Manchester
Richard Layard	London School of Economics
P. N. Mathur	University College of Wales, Aberystwyth
B. J. McCormick	University of Sheffield
David Metcalf	London School of Economics
J. S. Metcalfe	University of Manchester
J. A. Mirrlees	Nuffield College, Oxford
R. J. Nicholson	University of Sheffield
A. R. Nobay	University of Southampton
Michael Parkin	University of Manchester
D. L. Purdy	University of Manchester
A. Rayner	University of Canterbury, New Zealand

R. Rees   Queen Mary College, London
P. G. Sadler   University of Wales, Bangor
Robert M. Solow   Massachusetts Institute of Technology
Ian Steedman   University of Manchester
M. T. Sumner   University of Manchester
Neville Topham   Senior Lecturer, University of Salford
M. Wolfson   University of Durham and Oregon State University
G. Zis   University of Manchester

Essays in modern economics

Proceedings of the Conference of the Association of University Teachers of Economics held at the University College of Wales, Aberystwyth, March 1972.

AUTE executive committee

G. Clayton (Treasurer)	University of Sheffield
B. A. Corry (Secretary)	Queen Mary College, London
N. J. Gibson	New University of Ulster
H. G. Johnson	London School of Economics and University of Chicago
D. E. W. Laidler	University of Manchester
J. L. Carr	H.M. Treasury
E. T. Nevin (Chairman)	University of Wales, Swansea
A. R. Noaby (Ass. Secretary)	University of Southampton
D. C. Rowan	University of Southampton
J. Sproas	University College, London
R. Turvey	Scientific Control Systems, London
K. F. Wallis	London School of Economics
J. H. Williams	University of Warwick
J. M. Parkin (Ex officio)	University of Manchester

Editor's introduction

This collection of 'essays in modern economics' brings together papers presented to the Conference of the Association of University Teachers of Economics held at Aberystwyth in March 1972. Whilst the AUTE has been holding a regular annual conference for many years, this is the first time that the proceedings of the conference have appeared in a single volume. This has been made possible by generous support from the Royal Economic Society.

An AUTE conference programme is not drawn up on narrowly defined themes. This volume has, however, organised the papers presented under the broad headings of (i) microeconomics of the private sector, (ii) microeconomics of the public sector, (iii) on Keynes, and (iv) macro and monetary economics.

The programme committee invited contributions for the main evening sessions from distinguished scholars actively pursuing research in areas which seem important and promising. These papers lead off each of the sections.

Professor Robert M. Solow of the Massachusetts Institute of Technology, who is currently doing important theoretical work on urban economics, gave the first Frank W. Paish Lecture. He shows how relatively simple individual optimisation decisions lead to equilibrium urban locations which are, in broad qualitative terms, very much like the patterns observed in actual cities. While in many ways the analysis is a long way removed from the actual policy problems facing large urban communities, it represents (along with other work referred to by Solow) a very exciting and promising beginning to getting an analytical base from which to tackle some of those problems.

The second evening paper was presented by Professor A. B. Atkinson of the University of Essex. This appears as Chapter 6 and asks the basic question: 'How progressive should income tax be?' This is one of those questions which have been around a long time, and on which there has recently been a substantial revival of interest. Earlier work on this question (notably by Mirrlees) is presented in a very digestible form and Atkinson goes on, by considering a narrower class of questions than Mirrlees did, to provide clear answers as to what the optimal degree of progression depends on.

The third evening paper was given by Professor F. H. Hahn of Cambridge University. It deals with another question that has been around a long time—

namely: what is money; how does it come about that we use it; what are the *essential* differences between a money economy and a barter economy, and how might we model a money economy with the same degree of generality and rigour as Arrow and Debreu have modelled the barter economy? He presents a very useful account of the work which has been done in this area by himself and others, and helps considerably to clarify some of the issues.

The committee were pleased to be able to include a fourth specially invited paper in the programme. Elizabeth Johnson presented a personal and sensitive evaluation of, and reaction to, the Keynes that emerges from his professional papers. At a time when the profession is still trying to absorb the Clower–Leijonhufvud counter-revolution and increasingly prone to ask, 'what Keynes really meant', it is particularly timely to have this personal view as well as the more extensive treatment of the papers which Mrs Johnson (and others) are editing for the Royal Economic Society, and which are now beginning to appear.

The papers presented at the Conference, of course, generated a great deal of lively discussion from the floor. Space precludes us from including these in the volume. We have, however, included the comments of the primary discussant, and also, in many cases, authors have revised their papers for publication in the light of the general discussion following their papers.

We acknowledge the skilful secretarial and administrative help from Mrs Vicki Whelan, and from Mr Adrian Boucher who prepared the index.

October 1972   MICHAEL PARKIN
                                                                  A. R. NOBAY

I

Micro-economics of the Private Sector

On equilibrium models of urban location

1

Robert M. Solow

> What sort of rents do houses fetch?
> Within fairly clearly defined limits,
> it varies from area to area.
> A. J. Hodge in the *Irish Times*, from
> *Punch*, 5 January 1972.

1. Introduction[1]

I might as well begin, disarmingly, by calling attention to some weaknesses of all attempts to construct a theoretical urban economics, including this one. To begin with, nearly all economic theory is equilibrium theory. It proceeds by giving an appropriate definition of an equilibrium situation for the problem at hand, and then tries to discover the properties of equilibrium positions. Most especially, of course, one tries to analyse the characteristics of equilibrium positions as functions of the exogenous parameters.

To study the locational equilibrium of a city seems almost silly. Buildings, streets, subways are among the most durable objects we make, and it is very expensive to move them or even to remove them. Existing patterns of location must therefore have been determined in large part by decisions that were made and events that happened under conditions that ruled long ago. It seems far fetched to expect that what now exists will bear much relation to what would now be an equilibrium. Nevertheless, it turns out that the equilibrium states of simple models of urban location do actually reproduce some of the important characteristics of real cities. If this turns out to be more than mere coincidence, it is of some importance even for policy. In deciding what to do about urban 'problems', one could certainly use information about which 'symptoms' are equilibrium phenomena, and thus presumably subject to change only if basic underlying conditions change, and which are transitory disequilibrium phenomena, and thus presumably responsive to more super-

[1] Neither Martin Beckmann, nor Edwin Mills, nor Herbert Mohring, nor Richard Muth has seen this paper; but any reader of the literature will know how indebted I am to their work. I am grateful also to the National Science Foundation for financial support under Grant No. GS-33210.

ficial policy actions. To take a concrete example, it is useful to know whether 'suburbanisation' is a part of the pathology of urban life or a more or less normal aspect of the development of an urban economy. In either case, one can like or dislike suburbanisation, choose to encourage or discourage it; but it surely matters how the phenomenon fits into a general model of urban location.

There are at least two other important reasons—besides its long-run equilibrium character—why this sort of abstract theory must be handled in a very gingerly fashion. One of them is that the simplifying assumption is generally made that the city is 'monocentric' in the particular sense that everyone works in the central business district, and essentially all travel is radial travel to and from the centre. Real cities often have several centres of concentrated employment and quite a lot of local low-density employment. There are many trips taken for shopping, school, social and recreational purposes which are not radial. I think it will eventually be possible to capture some of these aspects of urban life in models still small enough to be thought of as theoretical; that is one of my purposes in this paper. In the meanwhile one must be aware that some theoretical results may not survive this generalisation.

The other big deficiency in abstract models is that they lack some of the very features that make cities happen, and make them something slightly different from merely denser concentrations of population and capital: I have in mind the variety of production externalities, local public goods, cultural enclaves, and segregated ethnic and racial neighbourhoods, whether voluntary or imposed. It is an open question how far economic theory can go in these directions without itself becoming something quite different. It is probably worth trying, but one must start with the simplest cases first, and that is my excuse.

I propose to describe a simple model of an abstract city. There is nothing very original about it: it is pieced together from elements to be found in the work of Alonso, Beckmann, Mills, Muth and others, though the arrangement is slightly different from what I have found in the literature. My hope is that even so simple a construct will be found to be interesting enough that others will be tempted to contribute to its elaboration.

2. Rent in the CBD

It is easy to rig assumptions that will lead to a central business district surrounded by a residential zone. Imagine then von Thünen's featureless plain with a single central point. Assume that the entire output of the single commodity produced in the city must be transported to the central point, whence it is exported or marketed for domestic use. The single commodity is produced under conditions of constant returns to scale,[1] using inputs of labour and land.[2]

---

[1] The assumption of constant returns to scale is particularly inappropriate here. The existence of some economies of scale is one of the reasons cities come into

The most convenient way to represent the technology is through the cost function that gives the least feasible unit cost of production as a function of the annual wage rate (w) and the annual rental of a unit of land (r). (Under constant returns to scale, the level of output is not an argument of the unit cost function.) A single wage rules in the CBD, but the annual rent of a unit of land depends on its distance (x) from the central point of the city. Our first task is to study the dependence of r on x, the rent profile within the CBD. Once $r(x)$ is determined, everything else follows easily.

Suppose that all producers are price-takers, and that p is the given 'national' price of the commodity delivered at the central market. Let $t(x)$ be the cost of shipping a unit of the produced commodity through a distance x to the centre. (Transportation is thus also carried on at constant returns to scale, and the symmetry of the situation permits us to regard transportation cost as depending only on distance and not on direction.) Competition for land will cause differential rent in equilibrium to absorb the difference between the price of the commodity net of transportation cost and the minimised cost of production. If $C[w, r(x)]$ is the cost function, then $r(x)$ satisfies

$$C[w, r(x)] = p - t(x). \qquad (1)$$

Since production cost is an increasing function of the factor prices and transportation cost an increasing function of distance, this equation yields $r(x)$ as a decreasing function[1] of x for given w and p.

As an illustrative special case with easy results, consider the fixed-proportions[2] production function, which has a linear cost function:

$$C = \lambda w + \mu r(x) = p - t(x)$$

where λ and μ are the labour and land requirements per unit of output. If, in addition, $t(x) = tx$, the competitive equilibrium rent gradient for business use of land must fall linearly with distance from the centre.

In general, rent per acre falls with increasing distance from the centre

---

[1] By differentiation, $C_r r' = -t'$; and again $C_r r'' + C_{rr} r'^2 = -t''$. For a well-behaved production function, the cost function is concave in its arguments, hence C_{rr} is non-positive. Thus r'' is certainly non-negative if t'' is non-positive, i.e. if the cost of a trip does not increase more than proportionally with distance. In this normal case, the rent gradient is a falling convex function of distance from the centre.

[2] This assumption has the disadvantage that it rules out the possibility of substitution of labour and especially buildings for land where rents are high, near the centre. In general, the abstract city will have tall buildings near the centre, as it should.

---

existence; otherwise most production could be dispersed, with no loss of efficiency and some saving of transport costs. I would gain very little from the extra trouble of allowing U-shaped cost curves, however, because I am not concerned with the number of cities, or with the number of concentrations of production within the single city. There is an excellent topic for research here, and David Starrett has already written a very interesting unpublished paper 'On the optimal degree of increasing returns'.

[2] As I shall point out later, it would be perfectly feasible to allow for a third input —call it 'producer goods', say—imported into the city at a given 'national' price and used in producing the export good, local services, and housing. This would add something to the model, particularly the ability to describe the varying ratio of buildings to land at different locations. I omit this generalisation only to avoid detail.

solely because of the transportation-cost advantage conferred by locations nearer the central market point.

3. Rent in the residential zone

The city is inhabited by a given number, N, of identical workers and their identical families, which makes for a dull city but a simple model. (I shall also assume that land is owned either by the government or by absentee landowners, so that none of the workers has any rental income. As soon as we have a two-class city, it will not be hard to suppose that land is privately owned; but not much is gained by that generalisation.) Each worker is employed in the central business district, where he earns an annual income of w. This income is spent in three ways: on a single consumption good, on housing, and on transportation. A family's annual consumption is c; I shall choose this commodity as the numeraire, so its price is 1. The consumption good may or may not be the same good as the one produced locally; if it is, then $p = 1$. For expository simplicity, I assume that the only cost of housing is the rental of land, so that a family consuming h units of housing at a distance x from the centre must spend $r(x)h$ per year on rent. Finally, a family living at radial distance x incurs commuting costs of $T(x)$ per year.

The identical families have a common utility function defined over c and h. One could suppose that x enters the utility function explicity, that families prefer to live close to the centre, other things being equal, or perhaps further from the centre, or perhaps neither too near nor too far. Presumably most real preferences for location are fundamentally preferences for the topographical or social character of a particular neighbourhood. Both considerations are excluded from the model, so I shall assume that choice of location matters only through the difference in transport costs (i.e. that x does not enter the utility function directly). This means, of course, that if the rent were the same at two distances from the centre, all families would choose the closer location, to save transportation costs. This could not be an equilibrium, because there is only a limited supply of residential land at any given distance from the centre.[1] Thus, in the residential ring as in the central business district, rent per acre falls with increasing distance from the centre, to offset the transport-cost advantage of location closer to the centre.

The choice problem of a typical family boils down to the choice of c, h, and x to maximise $U(c, h)$ subject to the budget constraint $c + r(x)h + T(x) = w$. Consider a family that chooses to live in the ring at distance x. The largest utility it can achieve obviously depends on its income net of transportation cost, and on the prices it must pay for consumer goods and housing. This dependence is called the indirect utility function, and it turns out to be the natural representation for this problem. Thus

$$U^* = U(c^*, h^*) = V[1, r(x), w - T(x)]$$

[1] Actually, with some utility functions, one could imagine a singular equilibrium in which some families consume zero space, i.e. live at 'infinite' density in high-rise flats.

where c^* and h^* are the optimal choices of c and h (i.e. the demand functions) for a family living at x, and V is the indirect utility function. (I have included the argument 1, the price of the numeraire commodity c, just to remind that it is there. Clearly V is homogeneous of degree zero in all three of its arguments, decreasing in the first two and increasing in the third.)

This is for a family choosing to live at x. Now consider all families with the same income w, gross of transportation cost. Either all those families choose the same x or they choose a variety of locations. In the latter case, an equilibrium rent profile must have the property that all families with income w achieve the same utility. If that were not so, every family living at x_2 and enjoying less utility than families with the same income living at x_1 could and would attempt to imitate the better-off families by moving to x_1. There would be excess demand for land at x_1, excess supply at x_2, $r(x_1)$ would rise, $r(x_2)$ would fall, until either everyone with income w lived at x_1 or rents were such as to equalise the net advantages at x_1 and x_2 for families with income w. If, as I have assumed, *everyone* in the city has income w, *everyone* must achieve the same utility, wherever he or she lives. An equilibrium rent profile must therefore satisfy

$$V[1, r(x), w - T(x)] = \bar{v} = \text{constant} \qquad (2)$$

The constant $\bar{v}$ is as yet undetermined.

As an illustrative special case for explicit calculation, consider a Cobb–Douglas direct utility function. For a consumer maximising $Az_1^\alpha z_2^\beta$ subject to $p_1 z_1 + p_2 z_2 = y$, it is easily calculated that

$$V(p_1, p_2, y) = A\alpha^\alpha \beta^\beta (\alpha+\beta)^{-(\alpha+\beta)} y^{\alpha+\beta} p_1^{-\alpha} p_2^{-\beta}$$

is the indirect utility function. Making the appropriate identifications, including $p_1 = 1$, we find

$$V[1, r(x), w - T(x)] = \gamma[w - T(x)]^{\alpha+\beta} r^{-\beta}$$

If every family has the same income, then everywhere that the city is actually occupied,

$$\bar{v} = \gamma[w - T(x)]^{\alpha+\beta} r^{-\beta}$$

or

$$r(x) = (\gamma/\bar{v})^{1/\beta}[w - T(x)]^{1+(\alpha/\beta)}$$

Thus, in the residential ring rent is an increasing convex function of income after transportation cost. If transport cost increases less than proportionally with trip distance [i.e. if $T(x)$ is concave], $r(x)$ is a decreasing convex function of distance from the centre throughout the residential ring.

4. The boundary of the CBD

For the next bit of the argument, it will be useful to distinguish notationally between the rent function $r_F(x)$ deduced for firms and that $r_H(x)$ deduced for households. (From (1), $r_F(x)$ depends on w; from (2) $r_H(x)$ depends on w and $\bar{v}$, which are still to be determined.) So far, it is only stage management that has placed the business district at the centre of the city and the residential ring around it. For that to be in actual fact an equilibrium configuration, it is necessary and sufficient that firms be prepared to outbid households for central land and households be prepared to outbid firms for peripheral land. That is to say, if x^* is to be the boundary of the CBD, it should be the case that $r_F(x)$ be greater or less than $r_H(x)$ according as x is less or greater than x^*. General economic reasoning is sufficient to establish the further result that, in equilibrium, $r_F(x^*) = r_H(x^*)$; the overall rent function is continuous at the boundary. If it were not so, clearly either firms or households could gain by penetrating across the boundary. For the special case, this gives the equation

$$p - t(x^*) - \lambda w = \mu(\gamma/\bar{v})^{1/\beta}[w - T(x^*)]^{1+\alpha/\beta}$$

satisfied by x^*.

In the Santa Claus case of a fixed coefficients technology, we can actually determine x^* explicitly from the condition of full employment of labour. Then this boundary condition helps to determine the two remaining unknowns, w and $\bar{v}$. Suppose a given fraction j_1 of the central disc is available for business use, the remainder being reserved for streets, public buildings, and such. Then the total business area is $j_1 \pi x^{*2} = \theta_1 x^{*2}$, where I have adopted the simplifying notation $j_1 \pi = \theta_1$. Since μ units of land are required per unit of output the capacity of the CBD is $\theta_1 x^{*2}/\mu$ units of output . This in turn requires $\lambda \theta_1 x^{*2}/\mu$ units of labour. Since there are N workers in the city, full employment requires that $\lambda \theta_1 x^{*2}/\mu = N$ or

$$x^* = \sqrt{\frac{\mu N}{\lambda \theta_1}}.$$

For this special case, the radius of the CBD can be determined directly from data. In the more general case, when labour, capital and land can be substituted for one another, the relation between aggregate output and aggregate land use, even for given total employment, will depend on factor prices. But the principle is the same, and full employment provides another equation to be solved simultaneously with the continuity equation.

A general treatment of the full employment condition proceeds from the cost function $C[w, r(x)]$. It is a well-known property of the cost function that its partial derivative with respect to any input price gives the cost-minimizing demand for the corresponding input per unit of output. Thus $C_w[w, r(x)]$ is the demand for labour per unit of output for production located at x; and C_r is the demand for land per unit of output if production is located at x. Therefore C_w/C_r is employment per unit of land at x. The land available for production in the ring with inner radius x and outer radius $x + dx$ is $j_1 2\pi x dx = 2\theta_1 x dx$, and employment in that ring is $2\theta_1 x C_w/C_r dx$. The condition of full employment of labour is thus

$$2\theta_1 \int_0^{x^*} x \frac{C_w[w, r(x)]}{C_r[w, r(x)]} \, dx = N \tag{3}$$

With a fixed-coefficients technology, $C[w, r(x)] = \lambda w + \mu r(x)$ so that

$C_w/C_r = \lambda/\mu$. It is trivial to check that use of the general formula leads to the solution for x^* that was derived directly earlier.

It is easy to give a partial picture of the economic mechanism that is supposed to be at work; it bears repeating that the picture is only partial, and anyhow it is hard to imagine this market mechanism actually working itself out in real time. A lower wage raises the whole rent function for firms, because there is more surplus over other costs for rents to absorb at any distance from the centre. A lower wage reduces the whole rent function for households, because the wage is the source of income, and housing is a normal good. Thus, if the wage were below equilibrium, the two branches of the rent function would intersect at a larger x^*; the CBD would be 'too large'. There would be excess demand for labour and the wage would be driven up toward equilibrium. The same story goes in reverse if the wage is above its equilibrium value.

We must still make precise the conditions that guarantee that firms will occupy the CBD and households the periphery. The global condition is as stated earlier, that $r_F(x)$ lie above or below $r_H(x)$ according as x is smaller or larger than x^*. A local necessary condition is that $r_F'(x^*) < r_H'(x^*)$.

Since $C[w, r_F(x)] = p - t(x)$, we have that $C_r r_F'(x) = -t'(x)$, and since C_r is the cost-minimising demand for land per unit of output—$h_F(x)$, say—it follows that

$$r_F'(x^*) = \frac{-t'(x^*)}{h_F(x^*)}.$$

Similarly, since in equilibrium $V[1, r_H(x), w - T(x)] = \bar{v}$, we have that $V_r r'(x)_H - V_w T'(x) = 0$. So

$$r_H'(x) = \frac{V_w}{V_r} T'(x)$$

The duality property of the indirect utility function is that $-V_r/V_w = h(x)$, the utility-maximising consumption of land per family. So

$$r_H'(x^*) = \frac{-T'(x^*)}{h(x^*)}$$

and the local necessary condition for the existence of a central business district is that

$$\frac{t'(x^*)}{h_F(x^*)} > \frac{T'(x^*)}{h(x^*)},$$

i.e. that moving an acre of business a bit further from the centre should add more to transport costs than would be saved by moving an acre's worth of commuters a bit closer. It follows that the centralised business pattern is likely to be the right one if an acre of business land tends to incur more transportation cost than an acre of residential land, and if those costs rise more sharply with distance. That corresponds to common sense. It is perhaps less obvious that the centralised pattern is more appropriate the smaller the business requirement of land per unit of output compared with the demand for housing space per household. But this does make sense; it is a concession to the fact that one can economise on transportation by packing the limited supply of central land with activities that are not very land intensive.[1]

5. Further equilibrium conditions

The equilibrium configuration is still not determinate. We have only two equations in the three unknown constants, w, x^*, and $\bar{v}$. Actually there is a fourth characteristic to be determined, the outer radius of the city, which I shall call x^{**}. So two more equilibrium conditions are needed.

One of them is easy to write down. The city will expand into any land that is more valuable in urban than in any alternative use. Let the residual use of land be agriculture, and suppose the annual rental of agricultural land is r_A. (Von Thünen would point out immediately that the agricultural value of land also depends on its distance from the market. True enough, but that merely makes r_A a function of x^{**}.) Then the outer radius of the city satisfies

$$r(x^{**}) = r_H(x^{**}) = r_A$$

if, in fact, the outer ring of the city is residential.

The final equilibrium condition comes from equalising the supply of residential land and the aggregate demand for it. The typical family maximises $U(c, h)$ subject to a budget constraint involving x. Out of this process comes a demand for housing space per family at distance x, say $h(x)$. For instance, in the special Cobb–Douglas case, the family spends the fraction $\beta/(\alpha+\beta)$ of its income after transportation cost on housing. The demand function is thus

$$h(x) = \frac{\beta}{\alpha+\beta} \frac{w - T(x)}{r(x)}$$

Let there be $n(x)\,dx$ families resident in the circular ring whose inner radius is x and whose outer radius is $x + dx$. Their aggregate demand for land in that ring is $h(x)n(x)\,dx$. The total area of the ring is $2\pi x\,dx$. Suppose only a fraction j_2 of that area is available for housing. Then the supply of residential land in the ring is $2\theta_2 x\,dx$. Supply and demand balance if $n(x) = 2\theta_2 x/h(x)$. This offers no problem: in equilibrium, families are indifferent about where they live—the rent gradient sees precisely to that. We need only make sure that supply and demand for space balance in the aggregate, i.e. that there is enough space inside the city limits to accommodate the whole population of N families. That will be so if

$$N = \int_{x^*}^{x^{**}} n(x)\,dx = 2\theta_2 \int_{x^*}^{x^{**}} \frac{x}{h(x)}\,dx = -2\theta_2 \int_{x^*}^{x^{**}} \frac{xV_w}{Vr}\,dx.$$

In the special case, this becomes

$$\frac{\alpha+\beta}{\beta} \left(\frac{\gamma}{\bar{v}}\right)^{1/\beta} \int_{x^*}^{x^{**}} x[w - T(x)]^{\alpha/\beta}\,dx = N$$

---

[1] This local condition is not sufficient in general, or in our special case. In the special case, because r_H is convex and r_F linear, it would be enough to verify that $r_F(0) > r_H(0)$.

which can be integrated in terms of elementary functions if $T(x) = Tx$. However, it yields nothing very transparent.[1]

6. Density patterns

The model does yield the unambiguous, but obvious, result that $h'(x) > 0$: households living further from the centre consume more space. This does not depend on any special case assumptions. Since $1/h(x)$ is the population density, we may say that density decreases with increasing distance from the centre. In fact, there appears to be a historical tendency for density gradients to flatten over time. That is to say, suburban population density, at a given distance from the centre, appears to rise relative to density nearer the centre. Mills has shown that this development can be deduced from an equilibrium model much like the present one. The density function will flatten as consumer income rises and commuter costs per mile fall over time, as indeed they do. The particular model Mills uses is, however, not fully general-equilibrium in character; so the result may be worth pursuing further.

I do not know if such a proposition is formally true in the model I have been using. I can, however, offer a heuristic argument that does indeed suggest that reduction of commuting cost and increase of income (with rising industrial productivity, say) will flatten the density function. Such an argument can be built on the formula for the slope of the household rent function:

$$r_H'(x) = -T'(x)/h(x).$$

The cheapening of transportation can be expected to reduce the numerator of the fraction. Since housing space is a normal good, one would expect the general rise in incomes to increase the denominator. On both counts, the rent gradient should flatten. This is not a rigorous argument, if only because the demand for housing space depends on the level of the rent function, which must itself change as transport costs and industrial productivity change. (It is worth remarking that if time costs bulk large in commuting costs, and the value of time spent in transportation increases sharply with the commuter's income, then the argument is further weakened.) Nevertheless, this and other heuristic considerations suggest that the rent function and the density function are very likely to flatten over time. In any concrete case, it is a routine exercise in total differentiation to find out.

---

[1] For the record

$$\left(\frac{\gamma}{\bar{v}}\right)^{1/\beta} \frac{1}{T^2} \left[\{(w - Tx^*)^{1 + (\alpha/\beta)} [w - \frac{\alpha + \beta}{\alpha + 2\beta} (w - Tx^*)]\} \right.$$

$$\left. - \{(w - Tx^{**})^{1 + (\alpha/\beta)} [w - \frac{\alpha + \beta}{\alpha + 2\beta} (w - Tx^{**})]\} \right]$$

$$= \frac{1}{(\alpha + 2\beta) T^2} \{r(x^*)[\beta w + (\alpha + \beta) Tx^*]$$

$$- r(x^{**})[\beta w + (\alpha + \beta) Tx^{**}]\}$$

$$= N$$

Suppose this general conclusion stands up. It then illustrates the possible value of equilibrium models. Many people deplore the phenomenon itself as one of the unattractive aspects of suburbanisation. I take it that this is roughly what is meant by 'surburban sprawl'. The city itself is at least relatively depopulated, and many of the specifically urban virtues are lost. Simultaneously, the suburbs become more densely populated, and they lose their charm too.[1] The kind of corrective action that is called for may well be different according as one believes the flattening of the density gradient to be an expectable consequence of higher incomes and improved transportation or the perverse result of defects in the housing market and the transportation system. (There is no implication here that undesirable but 'natural' evolutionary developments should be immune from deliberate corrective action, only that the policy prescription may be better if the nature of the phenomenon is understood.

7. Several income classes

I want to suggest a few ways one can generalise this model to correspond better with real cities. The first simplifying assumption that must be abandoned is the one that gives every worker the same income. To show how that can be done, it is enough to say what happens if there are two income classes, though I continue to suppose that all have the same tastes.

The basic principle to observe is that space is occupied by those who are prepared to pay the highest rent for it. In general there will be segregation by income: the residential ring will be subdivided into two rings, one occupied by the rich, the other by the poor. We can see what happens by considering the boundary between the two zones. On one side of it, the rent profile is given by $\bar{v}_1 = V[1, r(x), w_1 - T(x)]$, and on the other by $\bar{v}_2 = V[1, r(x), w_2 - T(x)]$, where w_1 is the lower CBD wage and w_2 the higher, and, of course $\bar{v}_2 > \bar{v}_1$ because it is better to be rich than to be poor. At the boundary, the two rent functions must cross, i.e. the combined rent function must be continuous. If it were not, whichever class had the discretely higher rent function at the boundary would want to move across the boundary into the other zone, because the discrete reduction in rent would more than compensate for any smooth increase in commuting cost. Moreover, at the boundary the inner rent function must be falling more steeply than the outer: otherwise the outer group would wish to move in across the boundary *and* the inner group would wish to move out across the boundary. (In each case the market rent lies below the continuation of the constant-utility rent function; in each case, therefore, there would be a gain from penetrating into the other zone.) Thus in equilibrium, the combined rent function must be convex if the component rent functions are.

Finally, one can show that the rich must be the outer suburban group and the poor must live nearer the CBD. This follows from the formula for the

---

[1] I have no wish to deny that there may be other socio-economic causes at work too.

slope of a rent function. At the boundary, $T'(x)$ is the same for both groups, and so are all the other prices. Since housing is a normal good, $h(x)$ must be higher for the rich than for the poor; hence they live on its outside. Here is another example of an equilibrium property that does in fact mimic real life.[1]

If there are given numbers of high-wage and low-wage workers (or if these numbers are determined inside the model), it is not hard to find the location of the boundary that equalises supply and demand for housing space in each zone.

8. A local service sector

Excessive centralisation of employment is another of the major deficiencies of this model city as an abstraction of a real city. As a partial step toward realism, then, I would like to introduce a 'local services' industry which generates employment not in the CBD, but in each residential ring. (The prototype of a 'local service' is small-scale retailing, but the notion extends easily to schools, film theatres, household services and the like.) I shall assum that local services must be consumed where they are produced. I shall also assume that workers in the local services industry live where they work, and incur no commuting costs. The first of these assumptions is natural enough; the second is at least a legitimate simplification.[2]

Let $m(x)$ be the number of local service workers who live (and work) at distance x from the centre. If the symbol $n(x)$ is retained for the number of commuters who live at x, then the total population of the ring is $m+n$. Let $a(x)$ be the area devoted to the production of local services at x. Land and labour are the only inputs in the industry. Together $m(x)$ workers and $a(x)$ land produce a flow of local services $s(x)$ in the ring at x under conditions of constant returns to scale, here quite natural. The price of a unit of local services is $q(x)$ units of numeraire. Since local services are not transportable, there is no constraint from the supply side on the spatial variation of their price.

Housing and the local services industry compete for land throughout the residential area, so the rent at x is $r(x)$ irrespective of the use to which the land is put. Suppose that workers are intrinsically indifferent as between work in the CBD and work in local services. Then the net wage (after commuting costs) must be equalised in each ring or the labour market in that ring can not be in equilibrium. This gives the condition

$$w(x) = w_0 - T(x), \qquad x^* \leqslant x \leqslant x^{**}$$

[1] It should be clear that this argument fails if time costs bulk large in commuting costs and if the rich value their time at a much higher figure than the poor. This may be one (though only one) factor helping to account for the existence of high-rent luxury apartments near the centre of any real city.

[2] The idea of introducing this sector came to me from Mr John Riley, a graduate student at MIT, who uses it in a different context in his PhD thesis. Muth also discusses local employment.

where $w(x)$ stands for the local-service wage at distance x and w_0 is the CBD wage, with the subscript now appended for notational convenience.

The technology of the local services industry is represented by its cost function $D[w(x), r(x)]$. Competition in the input and output markets insures that

$$q(x) = D[w(x), r(x)] = D[w_0 - T(x), r(x)] \qquad (4)$$

By the fundamental property of the cost function under constant returns to scale:

$$m(x) = s(x)D_w[w_0 - T(x), r(x)] \qquad (5a)$$

$$a(x) - s(x)D_r[w_0 - T(x), r(x)] \qquad (5b)$$

Equilibrium in the land market now requires that the supply of rentable land in each ring equal the sum of the residential and commercial demands in that ring. In the notation already established,

$$2\theta_2 x = a(x) + [n(x) + m(x)]h(x) \quad \text{for all } x^* \leqslant x \leqslant x^{**} \qquad (6)$$

The demand side of the model has to be expanded to allow for the new commodity. Let b represent a single family's consumption of local services. Then a typical family chooses, c, h, b, and x to maximise $U(c, h, b)$ subject to the budget constraint $c + r(x)h + q(x)b = w_0 - T(x)$. The first order conditions are routine. In the usual way, we define the indirect utility function $V[1, r(x), q(x), w_0 - T(x)]$ and, as before, locational equilibrium requires that all families achieve the same level of utility:

$$V[1, r(x), q(x), w_0 - T(x)] = \bar{v} \qquad (2')$$

By itself, this equation is insufficient to determine the equilibrium rent profile, because it contains a second unknown function, $q(x)$. But it can be combined with the earlier equation giving $q(x)$ in terms of the cost function D, and together they do the trick. It can be shown that the rent profile falls, as it did in the simpler model. It then follows that the price of local services, $q(x)$, is lower at greater distance x.

Now we have the residential rent function $r_H(x)$ in terms of the CBD wage w_0 and the known function $T(x)$. The boundary of the CBD is determined, as before, so that $r_F(x^*) = r_H(x^*)$. Also as before, the outer radius is determined to satisfy $r_H(x^{**}) = r_A$.

The remaining modifications are less straightforward. The full employment condition is a little more complicated because there are two sources of employment. The earlier formula (3) will still do for CBD employment. Local service employment in the ring at x has been designated $m(x)$. To get a closer grip on $m(x)$, we can add to (5a), (5b) and (6) one more equation

$$s(x) = [m(x) + n(x)]b(x) \qquad (7)$$

which merely says that the total consumption of local services at x is equal to the number of families living at x multiplied by the consumption of a typical family. The latter, $b(x)$, can be expressed in terms of the prices $r(x)$ and $q(x)$ via the indirect utility function:

$$b(x) = \frac{-V_q[1, r(x), q(x), w_0 - T(x)]}{V_w[1, r(x), q(x), w_0 - T(x)]}$$

Now by successive substitution we can derive that

$$m(x) = \frac{2\theta_2 x b(x) D_w}{h(x) + b(x) D_r}$$

Thus $m(x)$ is expressed entirely in terms of the prices (since, as already pointed out, $h(x) = -V_r/V_w$, and D_r and D_w are functions of w and r). Putting everything together, we get the full employment condition in the form

$$2\theta_1 \int_0^{x^*} x\, \frac{C_w[w, r(x)]}{C_r[w, r(x)]}\, \mathrm{d}x + 2\theta_2 \int_{x^*}^{x^{**}} \frac{x V_q D_w}{V_r + V_q D_r}\, \mathrm{d}x = N \qquad (8)$$

The last piece of bookkeeping that remains is the balancing of demand and supply for residential and commercial land outside the CBD. For this, it is sufficient to insure that there is house room for the whole population in the residential zone. It can be calculated that $m(x) + n(x) = 2\theta_2 x/[h(x) + b(x) D_r]$. Thus we need

$$\int_{x^*}^{x^{**}} [n(x) + m(x)]\, \mathrm{d}x = 2\theta_2 \int_{x^*}^{x^{**}} \frac{x}{h(x) + b(x) D_r}\, dx \qquad (9)$$

$$= -2\theta_2 \int_{x^*}^{x^{**}} \frac{x V_w}{V_r + V_q D_r}\, \mathrm{d}x = N$$

By construction, it is guaranteed that each ring of the residential zone is divided properly between residential and commercial uses of land.

The model is now complete. We know how to put everything in terms of the prices $q(x)$ and $r(x)$, and we know how to find them in terms of the CBD wage w_0 from (2′) and (4). Finally we have the two rent continuity conditions at x^* and x^{**}, and the two aggregate supply–demand balances in the land and labour markets (8) and (9), to determine the structural constants x^*, x^{**}, w_0 and $\bar{v}$. From these, we know how to calculate equilibrium values for the physical variables.

We can now ask more complicated questions about the pattern of land use. For example: how does the division between residential and commercial land use change with distance from the centre? Of course we can ask these questions, as Owen Glendower could call spirits from the vasty deep. But will the model answer? Clearly one can calculate the answer for any particular specification of the raw material of the model; and I have it in mind to do such experiments. But it seems unlikely that one can give a general answer.

In the first place, although I know that the rent, the net wage, and the price of local services all fall with increasing distance from the centre, there seem to be few general statements one can make about their ratios.[1] If the ratio of rent to wage as input prices and the ratio of rent to the price of local services as final output prices can rise or fall (even though they will rise or fall together), then not very much can be said about variation in land use. More uncertainty is contributed by the variety of price- and income-elasticities of demand that must be compatible with the basic choice of a utility function that will yield empirically realistic values of precisely those elasticities.

In the special case that both the direct utility function and the production function for local services are of the constant-elasticity Cobb–Douglas type, it is easy to prove that land use in the residential zone is invariant with distance from the centre: the proportion of land area devoted to housing and the complementary proportion devoted to localized production are constant. This is not an implausible description (I simply don't know what the stylised facts are), I quote it mainly to suggest that if the invariant pattern can come out of assumptions that are not extreme, then other cases must be quite possible.

9. Possible directions of research

Let me conclude by mentioning a few possible directions in which this model can be generalised. I have already said that it would be easy to introduce another factor of production—think of it as 'producer goods' or even 'capital' —which is imported from outside the city and is available at the same price everywhere in it. One could regard 'producer goods' as an input used with labour and land in the CBD to produce the single commodity; and one could suppose that land and producer goods together produce something called 'housing services' in the residential zone. The consumer pays a price for housing services, which can be decomposed into a land rent and an annualised cost of producer goods. The advantage of this extension is that one can begin to talk about the substitution of producer goods (i.e. buildings) for land in the production sector at locations very near the centre, and a similar substitution of residential land for housing at residential locations far from the centre. (Mills and Muth have worked with models of this kind; they are not complicated.)[2]

Another improvement would be the introduction of further income differences among households. For example, one could assume, as I showed earlier, the existence of several grades of labour, employed in the CBD at

[1] Because the cost function for local services is increasing, concave, and homogeneous of degree one, it follows that $q(x)/r(x)$ is an increasing concave function of $w(x)/r(x)$.

[2] (Added in proof.) Since the paper was written, I have carried out that generalisation. It turns out to be very simple to do so using the dual formulation introduced here. At the suggestion of Mr Malcolm Getz of Yale University I have also extended the model to include workers' travel costs inside the CBD. I hope to spell all this out in a later paper.

different wages. Or else one could make room for a property-owning or land-owning class. In most models of this kind, we know that the richer class will live further from the CBD, the poorer class nearer. I am curious to know if this conclusion survives the introduction of a local service sector. There are some tentative indications that it may, if not in general, then for plausible parameter values at least. But there are difficulties with the simple formulation of such a model. Generally only one income class lives in a given residential ring. There is, so to speak, segregation by income class (assuming all tastes are the same). How can this be squared with the simplifying assumption that local service workers live where they work? It seems altogether too artificial to require that local services be produced by high-wage workers in high-income residential zones, and by low-wage workers in low-income zones. This difficulty worsens when there are many income classes. I haven't thought of a good way to deal with it.

Finally, I come to the sort of question that actually got me interested in these models of urban structure. One would like to understand the dependence of the equilibrium structure on the layout of the transportation system. At a minimum, one could study the consequences of devoting different amounts of urban land to transportation uses, especially different amounts in different parts of the city. Sooner or later, in this context, it will have to be recognised that transportation costs are not merely a function of distance travelled, but also of the quality of the transportation network at each point and the volume of traffic using it. In other words, congestion costs will have to be reckoned into the model, and that does involve a mean increase in complexity. I have sparred a little with this problem and made a small amount of progress. But I would like to get to the point where one could say something about the socially best patterns of land use in transportation, and I am still some way from that.[1]

I hope some of you will find this class of problems interesting enough to tackle them. Anybody who likes economic theory and calculus, and has ever been caught in a traffic jam, could do worse.

[1] And this is on the assumption that all traffic is radial. As soon as one recognises that there is a certain amount of non-radial traffic, and that the choice of route for such traffic has to be analysed within the model, problems arise of a whole higher order of complexity. Some of them have been studied by Avinash Dixit and Marvin Kraus.

Announcement effects of profits taxation[1]

2

M. T. Sumner

1. Introduction

In terms of the 'traditional view' enshrined in the principles course, the title of this paper is a gross misnomer. A profit-maximising firm will not change its behaviour in either the short or long run when faced with a tax on pure profits: $(1-t)$ per cent of maximum pre-tax profits corresponds to maximum post-tax profits.

The traditional view has often been contrasted with the results of alternative assumptions about business objectives, but it is not clear that the special nature of the profit maximisation postulate has been fully appreciated. This point is developed in the next section, where the certainty assumption is discarded and the impact of a profits tax on a risk averter is considered; it will be shown that in such a case behaviour is not invariant with respect to changes in the rate of profits tax. Furthermore, the results are very different from those obtained when a conventional alternative to profit maximisation, such as constrained sales maximisation, is adopted.

It has frequently been stated, at least since 1927 [16]*, that the base of observed taxes seldom corresponds exactly to the appropriate theoretical magnitude; hence in practice announcement effects are to be expected. In the present context, particular reference is made to the inclusion of the opportunity cost of shareholders' funds in the base of the profits tax (e.g. [13]), and to the tax treatment of fixed capital expenditure. Moreover, profits taxes are confined to the corporate sector; in consequence it has been argued, most notably by Harberger [10], that profits taxation imposes an excess burden by reducing the relative size of the corporate sector.

The second strand of this paper attempts to provide a comprehensive analysis of the discrepancies between observed and hypothetical taxes on

* Numbers in square brackets relate to References on p. 31.

[1] I am indebted to Nigel Duck, Malcolm Gray, Michael Parkin, Will Peters and Clive Stones for advice and encouragement during the preparation of this paper. Substantial changes have been made in response to the insistence of Frank Brechling, the conference discussant, that the analysis should be made more explicit. Remaining errors and omissions are my own property.

business income, and their effects on resource allocation. On the conventional assumption of profit maximisation, it will be shown that an increase in the corporate tax rate may make investment in the corporate sector more attractive, and that within the corporate sector both the capital/labour ratio and the level of output may rise or fall.

2. Utility maximisation

It has been a favourite pastime among economists to replace profit maximisation by an alternative objective, and to deduce the consequences for price and output and the response of the model firm to exogenous changes. In the present paper, however, the empty box of the subheading is filled by supplementing instead of supplanting the traditional assumption: the firm's objective is to maximise a utility function

$$U = U(\bar{\pi}, \sigma_\pi^2) \qquad U_{\bar{\pi}} > O, \, U\sigma_\pi^2 < 0$$

where $\bar{\pi}$ represents expected post-tax profits and σ_π^2 the variance of profits; the subscripts indicate partial derivatives.

To reduce the problem to its simplest form by eliminating inventory decisions, the firm is assumed to choose output, Q, and to sell for what it can get. Uncertainty enters the problem via a stochastic demand curve

$$P = f(Q) + \epsilon;$$

initially it is assumed that $E[\epsilon] = 0$ and $E[\epsilon^2] = \sigma_p^2$. The arguments of the utility function may therefore be written as

$$\bar{\pi} = (1-t)[Qf(Q) - C(Q)]$$

and

$$\sigma_\pi^2 = Q^2(1-t)^2\sigma_p^2$$

where t is the rate of profits tax and $C(Q)$ the cost function; nothing is lost by assuming the latter to be known with certainty.

The first-order condition for a maximum is written in conventional notation as

$$U_Q = (1-t)[U\bar{\pi}(\bar{MR} - MC) + U\sigma_\pi^2 2Q(1-t)\sigma_p^2] = 0$$

where $\bar{MR}$ is the expected value of marginal revenue and MC is marginal cost. Two conclusions follow immediately: the risk averter (and for that matter the risk lower) will not operate at the level of output at which expected profits are maximised; and, more significantly in the present context, his behaviour is not independent of the profits tax rate, irrespective of the time period allowed for adjustment. The standard result emerges only as a special case, when uncertainty is absent or when the utility function is linear.

The risk averter will clearly produce a lower output than the profit maximiser in the presence of uncertainty: if by some mischance he chose the profit maximising output, U_Q would be negative and a reduction of output would follow from the second-order requirement that U_{QQ} be negative. Hence, in a perfectly competitive industry in which risk aversion predominates, price must exceed marginal and average cost even in long-run equilibrium. The interesting question in the present context concerns the response of a firm to a change in the tax rate.

It will be argued that an increase in the profits tax will raise output, at least in the perfectly competitive case. Suppose an initial utility-maximising equilibrium is disturbed by a tax change; setting the total differential of the first-order condition at zero yields

$$\mathrm{d}U_Q = \mathrm{d}Q.\,U_{QQ} + \mathrm{d}t.\,U_{Qt} = 0,$$

or

$$\frac{\mathrm{d}Q}{\mathrm{d}t} = -\frac{U_{Qt}}{U_{QQ}}$$

Since stability requires a negative value of U_{QQ}, the relation between tax changes and output changes takes the same sign as U_{Qt}. The latter is given by

$$U_{Qt} = -U_Q/(1-t) - U\sigma_\pi^2 2 Q\sigma_p^2(1-t)$$

$$- U_{\bar\pi\bar\pi}(\bar{M}\bar{R} - MC)\bar\pi - U\sigma_\pi^2\sigma_\pi^2 4 Q^3\sigma_p^4(1-t)^3$$

$$- U_{\bar\pi}\sigma_\pi^2 2(1-t)^2\, Q\sigma_p^2[Q(\bar{M}\bar{R} - MC) + (\bar{T}\bar{R} - TC)]$$

If the initial position is an equilibrium the first term can be ignored; $U\sigma_\pi^2$ is strictly negative, and $U_{\bar\pi\bar\pi}$ and $\sigma_\pi^2\sigma_\pi^2$ are non-positive; finally, the assumption that the marginal utility of (in this case) profit is independent of risk, hence $U_{\bar\pi}\sigma_\pi^2 = 0$, is hallowed by tradition[1] and is also a property of widely used forms of the utility function. Thus U_{Qt} is indeed positive, and so the impact effect of a tax increase is to disturb the equilibrium condition in such a way as to call forth an increase of output.[2] The opposite conclusion would require that the marginal disutility of risk decreases as expected profit increases ($U_{\bar\pi}\sigma_\pi^2 > 0$), and to do so sufficiently rapidly to offset the other terms.

It may be helpful to illustrate this result by postulating a particular form of utility function. Two examples are given here, the exponential

$$U = 1 - ae^{-b\pi} \qquad a, b > 0$$

and the quadratic

$$U = c\pi - \mathrm{d}\pi^2 \qquad c, d > 0;$$

in spite of its well-known defects (e.g. [1]), the latter remains widely used in the literature. In the case of the exponential, provided the probability

---

[1] See, for example, Domar and Musgrave [7]. Their measure of risk differs from that used here.

[2] The writer's confidence in this result was increased by the *ex post* discovery of a paper by Baron [2], who provides a rigorous proof of the proposition that output is an increasing function of the profits tax rate in the case of a risk-averse competitive firm with rising marginal cost. The treatment in the text is considerably simpler than Baron's, and as his analysis is confined to perfect competition he does not examine the effect of heteroscedastic disturbances.

density function of profits is normal, then maximising the expected value of utility is equivalent to maximising

$$\bar{\pi} - \frac{b\sigma_\pi^2}{2}$$

the resulting value of the crucial expression is

$$U_{Qt} = -(\bar{MR} - MC) + 2bQ\sigma_p^2(1-t)$$
$$= -U_Q/(1-t) + bQ\sigma_p^2(1-t)$$

For the quadratic

$$U_{Qt} = -c(\bar{MR} - MC) + 4\mathrm{d}\,(\bar{MR} - MC)\,\bar{\pi} + 4\mathrm{d}\,(1-t)Q\sigma_p^2$$
$$= -U_Q/(1-t) + 2\mathrm{d}\,[(\bar{MR} - MC)\,\bar{\pi} + (1-t)Q\sigma_p^2]$$

In both cases, U_{Qt} must clearly be positive if the initial position is assumed to be an equilibrium ($U_Q = 0$), since the added expressions are unambiguously positive.

Although the above argument had focused on perfect competition, there is no obvious reason why it should not be applied, *mutatis mutandis*, to other market structures. The *mutandis* are likely to include the specification of the stochastic term in the demand function: while a homoscedastic disturbance may reasonably be assumed in the competitive case, this assumption is much less plausible in other cases. A less restrictive formulation would be to redefine the stochastic term as

$$\epsilon = Q^\alpha \eta$$

where $E(\eta) = 0$, $E(\eta^2) = \sigma_\eta^2$, and presumably α is negative, i.e. price fluctuations are absolutely larger the higher is expected price. This modification does not change the principal conclusion, that behaviour is not independent of a pure profits tax, except where $\alpha = -1$; in that instance, the variance of profit reduces to

$$\sigma_\pi^2 = (1-t)^2\,\sigma_\eta^2$$

and hence is independent of output; the first-order condition becomes

$$U_Q = U\pi(1-t)(\bar{MR} - MC) = 0$$

and so utility maximisation yields the same predictions as profit maximisation. However, in other cases the nature of the solution changes radically. In particular, if $\alpha < -1$ then $\partial\sigma_\pi^2/\partial Q$ is negative, and from the first-order condition it follows that the firm will produce more than the profit-maximising output, since $\bar{MR} < MC$. Moreover, the response to an increase in the tax rate is a decrease in output. The general proposition which emerges is that the higher the rate of profits tax, the smaller the absolute discrepancy between utility and profit-maximising output.

The interrelationship between market structure and the effect of a change in the tax rate on output weakens any temptation to draw normative conclusions from the analysis, even when uncertainty is hypothesised to be purely 'secondary' and hence the contentious issue of the appropriate attitude to social risk does not arise. Assessment of the allocative effects of an increase in the profits tax hinges on whether all firms attempt to raise output or competitive outputs are increased and 'monopolistic' outputs reduced. In any case, there remains the important positive problem of determining whether the results obtained from this very simple model continue to apply in more complex situations, where the risk-averting firm chooses a price, an output and a planned change in inventories.

3. Profits and the tax base

In the remainder of the paper the economic effects of differences between profits and the base of the profits tax are examined. It will prove convenient to ignore initially the limited coverage of the profits tax, and to consider inter-sectoral shifts of resources in response to tax changes at a later stage.

Three 'imperfections' in the taxation of profits have been widely noted: the FIFO method of valuing inventories, the absence of any allowance for the opportunity cost of shareholders' funds, and the treatment of depreciation. Since nothing new is to be said about the first of these, it will be ignored. Indeed, it is dubious whether anything new will be said at all; many of the components of the analysis which follows are to be found in the literature, but an adequate synthesis is less easy to find. The implication of most existing discussions appears to be that the profits tax necessarily raises costs and makes investment less attractive; this conclusion will be contested in the following sections. In the interests of brevity the discussion will be based on the conventional assumption that the firm's objective is to maximise post-tax profits.

4. Taxation and the cost of capital

The firm seeks to maximise over the relevant time horizon the present value, discounted at the net-of-tax rate of return required by its shareholders, of net cash inflows. If equity funds were the sole source of finance net revenue in any period would consist simply of sales revenue minus factor payments minus tax payments; however, the firm may also incur debt: interest payments to bondholders constitute an additional outflow and net receipts from new bond issues an additional inflow. The objective may therefore be stated as maximisation of

$$W = \sum_{i=0}^{\infty} (1+\rho_i)^{-i} [p_i Y_i - w_i L_i - q_i I_i - T_i + \Delta D_i - r_i D_i]$$

where ρ = rate of return net of profits taxes required by shareholders.
  p = price of output
  w = wage-rate
  q = price of fixed capital
  T = tax payments

2

Y = output
L = labour input
I = gross investment
r = bond rate
D = value of debt outstanding
Δ = first-difference operator

The discount rates of both shareholders and bond-holders are assumed to be non-decreasing functions of leverage, defined as D_i/q_iK_i.

Taxes are levied on the difference between sales revenue and the sum of the wage bill, interest payments and depreciation; the latter depends in principle on the entire history of investment. More formally, tax payments can be expressed, given the postwar structure of capital allowances in the UK, as

$$T_i = t[p_iY_i - w_iL_i - r_iD_i - (a+b+c)q_iI_i$$

$$- \sum_{j=0}^{i\neq 1} q_jI_jc(1-b-c)(1-c)^{t-j-1}]$$

where t = profits tax rate
a = investment allowance
b = initial allowance
c = annual allowance on declining balance basis; balancing allowance ignored.

The expected tax and allowance rates are assumed constant.

The maximisation process is constrained by a production function

$$Y_i = F(K_i, L_i)$$

and by the identity between gross investment and the sum of replacement and net investment. Assuming that economic depreciation is a constant proportion of last period's capital stock, this identity can be expressed as

$$\Delta K_i = I_i - \delta K_{i-1}$$

where δ = true depreciation rate
K = capital stock

Finally, to obviate the possibility of a variable discount rate, the firm is assumed to maintain a constant leverage ratio, β; hence

$$D_i = \beta q_iK_i$$

and

$$\Delta D_i = \beta(q_{i-1}\Delta K_i + K_{i-1}\Delta q_i)$$

The adoption of an infinite horizon renders a debt repayment constraint otiose.

The constraints can now be substituted in the objective function to yield the maximand

$$W = \sum_{i=0}^{\infty} (1+\rho)^{-i}[(1-t)(p_i F(K_i, L_i) - w_i L_i)$$
$$- q_i(K_i - (1-\delta)K_{i-1}) + t(a+b+c)q_i(K_i - (1-\delta)K_{i-1})$$
$$+ t\sum_{j=0}^{i\neq1} q_j(K_j - (1-\delta)K_{j-1})\, c(1-b-c)(1-c)^{i-j-1}$$
$$+ \beta(q_{i-1}\Delta K_i + K_{i-1}\Delta q_i) - (1-t)\, r\beta q_i K_i]$$

The necessary conditions for a maximum are that labour and capital inputs be optimal in each period: in other words, for any (interior) period, n,

$$\frac{\partial W}{\partial L_n} = (1+\rho)^{-n}[(1-t)(p_n \frac{\partial Y}{\partial L} - w_n)] = 0$$

and

$$\frac{\partial W}{\partial K_n} = (1+\rho)^{-n}\left[(1-t)\, p_n \frac{\partial Y}{\partial K} - q_n + t(a+b+c)\, q_n\right.$$
$$\left. + \beta q_{n-1} - (1-t)\, r\beta q_n\right]$$
$$+ (1+\rho)^{-(n+1)}[q_{n+1}(1-\delta) - t(a+b+c)\, q_{n+1}(1-\delta)$$
$$+ tq_n c(1-b-c) - \beta(q_n - \Delta q_{n+1})]$$
$$+ (1+\rho)^{-(n+2)}[tq_n c(1-b-c)(1-c)$$
$$- tq_{n+1}(1-\delta)\, c(1-b-c)]$$
$$+ (1+\rho)^{-(n+3)}[tq_n c(1-b-c)(1-c)^2$$
$$- tq_{n+1}(1-\delta)c(1-b-c)(1-c)]$$
$$+ \ldots\ldots\ldots = 0$$

The first condition can be expressed directly in the more familiar form

$$\frac{\partial Y}{\partial L} = \frac{w_i}{p_i} \qquad i = 0, 1 \ldots \infty$$

but the second requires some tedious though trivial manipulation before it emerges in a recognisable form. The process is facilitated by defining the present value of depreciation allowances, discounted at the equity rate, as

$$Z = (a+b+c) + (1+\rho)^{-1}c(1-b-c)$$
$$+ (1+\rho)^{-2}c(1-c)(1-b-c) + \ldots;$$

and by introducing the approximations

$$(1+\rho)^{-1} \simeq (1-\rho)$$
$$q_{n+1}/q_n \simeq (1+\dot{q}_n)$$
$$q_{n-1}/q_n \simeq (1-\dot{q}_n)$$

Then, ignoring second-order terms, the condition for capital input reduces to

$$\frac{\partial Y}{\partial K} = \frac{q_i[(\rho + \delta - \dot{q}_i)(1 - tZ) - \beta\rho + (1 - t)\beta r]}{p_i(1 - t)} \quad i = 0, 1 \ldots \infty$$

$$= (\text{say}) \frac{q_i}{p_i} F$$

Alternative derivations of the equality between the marginal product of capital and the implicit rental of capital services have been presented by Hall and Jorgensen ([9], *inter alia*[1]) and Coen [4], who incorporate fiscal parameters but not debt financing. The discrete-time formulation adopted here was first used by Brechling [3].

The possibility of debt financing introduces an additional choice variable, and hence an additional necessary condition, viz.

$$\frac{\partial W}{\partial \beta} = \sum_{i=0}^{\infty} (1 + \rho)^{-i} \left[q_{i-1} \Delta K_i + K_{i-1} \Delta q_i \right.$$

$$\left. - (1 - t)\left(r + \beta \frac{\partial r}{\partial \beta} \right) q_i K_i \right]$$

$$- \frac{\partial \rho}{\partial \beta} \sum_{i}^{\infty} i(1 + \rho)^{-(i+1)} [p_i Y_i - w_i L_i - q_i I_i - T_i$$

$$+ \beta(q_{i-1} \Delta K_i + K_{i-1} \Delta q_i - (1 - t) r q_i K_i] = 0.$$

No obvious interpretation of this condition suggests itself. A more tractable formulation is to choose that value of β which minimises the implicit rental of capital services. The assumed constancy of the inflation rate and the fiscal parameters, and of the relationships between leverage and the bond and equity rates ensures that the optimal value of β is constant over time. Minimising the rental is equivalent to minimising F, and the appropriate necessary condition is

$$\frac{\partial F}{\partial \beta} = (1 - t)^{-1} \left[\frac{\partial \rho}{\partial \beta} \left(1 - tZ - t \frac{\partial Z}{\partial \rho} (\rho + \delta - \dot{q}) - \beta \right) - \rho \right.$$

$$\left. + (1 - t) \left(r + \beta \frac{\partial r}{\partial \beta} \right) \right] = 0$$

The problem which now arises is to evaluate

$$\frac{\partial F}{\partial t} = (1 - t)^{-2} [(\rho + \delta - \dot{q})(1 - Z) - \beta\rho] + \frac{\partial \beta}{\partial t} \frac{\partial F}{\partial \beta}$$

since the sign of this expression determines the direction of response to a change (or more accurately a difference) in the rate of profits tax. In particular, if $\partial F/\partial t$ takes on a negative value then a tax increase raises the profit-maximising stock of capital; the extent of any such increase depends, of

---

[1] In Jorgenson's earlier work, e.g. [12], a different formulation was used.

course, on the form of the production function as well as the magnitude of the tax-induced change in relative prices.

In the light of the preceding argument that $\partial F/\partial\beta=0$ in equlibrium, the expression for $\partial F/\partial t$ can be approximated as

$$\frac{\partial F}{\partial t} \simeq \frac{(\rho+\delta-\dot{q})(1-Z)-\beta\rho}{(1-t)^2}$$

for appropriately small variations in the tax rate. The direction of any bias which results is easily determined: $\partial\beta/\partial t$ is positive since the higher the tax rate, the more attractive, *ceteris paribus*, is tax-deductible debt financing;[1]

$$\frac{\partial^2 F}{\partial\beta\partial t} = \frac{\partial F}{\partial\beta}(1-t)^{-1}-(1-t)^{-1}\left[\frac{\partial\rho}{\partial\beta}\left(Z+\frac{\partial Z}{\partial\rho}(\rho+\delta-\dot{q})\right)\right.$$
$$\left.+\left(r+\beta\frac{\partial r}{\partial\beta}\right)\right]$$

is unambiguously negative. Hence, the approximation serves to overstate the (algebraic) value of $\partial F/\partial t$. It is immediately apparent that a sufficient condition for $\partial F/\partial t$ to be negative is $Z>1$. The practical relevance of this condition and the formulation of necessary conditions for $\partial F/\partial t<0$ are empirical issues which will be considered below. First, however, some aspects of the theoretical framework require closer scrutiny, particularly its relationship to earlier work on this topic, and the effects of inflation.

5. Existing literature

As noted above, the general question of the effects of fiscal policy on investment behaviour have been explored within the neoclassical framework by Hall and Jorgenson [9] and by Coen [4]. Debt financing is ignored in both studies, but while Coen obtains results corresponding to those derived above for the special case $\beta=0$, Hall and Jorgenson propose a weaker (sufficient) condition for $\partial F/\partial t=0$. The difference in results stems from their assumption that the pre-tax rate of return demanded by shareholders is constant,[2] whereas the post-tax rate is held constant in the above discussion. They conclude:

> Thus the condition for neutrality of changes in the tax rate depends on whether the burden of the tax is borne by the firm ... or shifted. ... To resolve the controversy surrounding the incidence of the corporate income tax requires a general equilibrium analysis based on an econometric model including saving as well as investment. Here it is assumed that the burden of the tax is borne by the firm, that is, that the before-tax rate of return is unaffected by changes in the tax rate.

[1] Miller [15] concludes from his examination of US experience that $\partial\beta/\partial t$ is close to zero.

[2] On this assumption, with $\beta=0$, the condition for $\partial F/\partial t=0$ is equality of economic and tax-allowable depreciation, i.e.

$$Z=\frac{\delta}{1+\rho(1-t)}+\frac{\delta(1-\delta)}{[1+\rho(1-t)]^2}+\cdots$$

Their argument ignores the question under discussion here, viz. the discrepancy between a profits tax and existing taxes on business income in respect of their treatment of the opportunity cost of equity. Shareholders, at least individually, have the option of switching into other assets in the event of a *ceteris paribus* fall in the corporate rate of return, induced by an increase in profits tax. Parenthetically, Hall and Jorgenson's necessarily inconclusive reference (not quoted) to econometric assessments of corporate tax incidence compounds their error; this literature purports to examine the extent of *short-run* shifting, and includes frequent caveats about the largely unexplored problem of long-run shifting, which stems precisely from the inclusion of cost elements in the tax base.

It must be admitted that Hall and Jorgenson's call for a general equilibrium model to be used in the analysis of corporate tax incidence applies equally to the question under discussion here, viz. whether an increase in the rate of profits tax may raise the capital stock of the taxed sector. The corporate sector is not so small that an increase in its demand for capital would have no effect on the rate of return achievable elsewhere, and hence there would be repercussions on the rate of return required by the marginal shareholder. However, the outcome would be an *increase* in the net discount rate in the case where $\partial F/\partial t < 0$. Thus Hall and Jorgenson's model is internally inconsistent.

Economists investigated the effects of fiscal policy on investment long before the rediscovery of the neoclassical model. Indeed, a close relation of the expression obtained above for $\partial F/\partial t$ can be obtained directly, using the insights of Domar [6], Eisner [8] and Schiff [18].

The base of a tax on business income consists of pure profits plus any excess of economic costs over allowable costs. The latter consists of the opportunity cost of shareholders' funds, $\rho(1-\beta)q_nK_n$, plus true depreciation, δq_nK_n, minus depreciation allowances on present and past gross investment.[1] Total depreciation deducations in period n are, in a UK context,

$$(a+b+c)q_nI_n+c(1-b-c)q_{n-1}I_{n-1}+c(1-c)(1-b-c)$$

$$\times q_{n-2}I_{n-2}+c(1-c)^2(1-b-c)q_{n-3}I_{n-3}+...$$

Suppose that capital stock grows at a constant rate,

$$\frac{K_{n+1}-K_n}{K_n}=\gamma;$$

then

$$I_n=K_{n+1}-K_n(1-\delta)=K_n(\gamma+\delta)$$

Suppose also that the (proportional) rate of change of the price of capital

[1] The same symbols are used as in the previous section, but it is now convenient to date stocks at the beginning of the period.

goods, q, is constant. Then the expression for total depreciation deductions reduces to

$$q_n K_n(\gamma+\delta)\left[a+b+c+\frac{c(1-b-c)}{\gamma+\dot{q}+c}\right]$$

$$=q_n K_n(\gamma+\delta)\,Z_{\gamma+\dot{q}}$$

where $Z_{\gamma+\dot{q}}$ denotes the present value of depreciation deductions on an investment of £1 discounted at rate $\gamma+\dot{q}$. Economic costs minus tax-allowable costs may therefore be written as (say)

$$C_n=q_n K_n[\rho(1-\beta)+\delta-(\gamma+\delta)\,Z_{\gamma+q}]$$

If this takes on a negative value, the 'imperfections' in the taxation of profits involve a partial subsidy instead of a partial tax on costs; the magnitude of the tax or subsidy depends, given the other assumptions, on the tax rate and the value of capital. Hence the profit-maximising firm will operate at a higher level of output and a higher capital-labour ratio, relative to its position in a no-tax world.

In the special case characterised by a constant price of capital goods and a growth rate of capital equal to the shareholders' discount rate, C corresponds exactly to $\partial F/\partial t$. However, while the parallel between early and recent discussions of fiscal influences on investment may be of some interest to *cognoscenti*, the forward-looking view of the neoclassical formulation is a surer guide for the aspiring profit-maximiser than the apparent stress on bygones in the earlier literature, especially when conditions do not approximate to those of a golden age.

6. The effects of inflation

In the absence of profits taxation, the emergence, or an increase in the rate, of inflation would have no effect on the profit-maximising output and input choices, provided distributional effects are excluded from the analysis. In other words, input and output prices are assumed to be equally affected by the inflation, which is perfectly anticipated, with the result that both the bond and equity rates change sufficiently to maintain the corresponding real rates constant. Even under these ideal conditions, however, inflation is not neutral in a world in which 'profits' are taxed, except in special cases.

While the condition for labour input is unaffected by variations in the perfectly-anticipated inflation rate, the implicit rental of capital services is not. Assuming

$$\frac{\partial\rho}{\partial\dot{q}}=\frac{\partial r}{\partial\dot{q}}=1$$

then, ignoring variations in β,

$$\frac{\partial F}{\partial\dot{q}}=-t(1-t)^{-1}\left[\frac{\partial Z}{\partial\rho}(\rho+\delta-\dot{q})+\beta\right]$$

Since $\partial Z/\partial \rho$ is clearly negative, this expression cannot be signed *a priori*. Its intuitive interpretation is that the tax authorities share that part of the nominal cost of inflation which results from a higher borrowing rate, but on the other hand depreciation allowances are based on historical cost. Discussions of the effects of inflation on the firm have usually stressed the second element to the exclusion of the first.

It also follows that the possibility of $\partial F/\partial t$ taking on negative values is not independent of the inflation rate for

$$\frac{\partial^2 F}{\partial \dot{q} \partial t} = \frac{\partial F}{\partial \dot{q}} [t^{-1} + (1-t)^{-1}]$$

This expression is in general non-zero.

7. Empirical relevance of the results

It is already evident that in principle a tax increase may raise rather than lower the profit-maximising capital stock. It remains to consider whether this somewhat paradoxical outcome is or ever has been anything more than a possibility. Attention has been drawn elsewhere [19] to the fact that the UK allowances on plant and equipment (i.e. machinery) satisfied the sufficient condition for $\partial F/\partial t < 0$, i.e. $Z > 1$, during the period 1962–66: in other words, even in the case of purely equity financing, a tax increase would have provided an incentive to substitute machinery for other factors at discount rates within the relevant range. Here the broader question of capital-labour substitution is examined for the same period.

Because the tax allowances on different classes of assets differed markedly, an assumption regarding the appropriate weighting procedure is required. The calculations which follow are based on the wholly inappropriate assumption that the four types of asset distinguished by the Inland Revenue (viz. machinery, industrial buildings, cars and other vehicles) are perfect complements. The weights used are those implied by the composition of manufacturing investment in 1964.[1] This assumption contrasts sharply with that of perfect substitutibility, which underlies the concept of aggregate capital. Obviously, *any* possibility of substitution makes negative values of $\partial F/\partial t$ more likely, but in the present state of knowledge it is hardly possible to refine the calculations in this respect.[2]

The calculations are confined to the industrial sector, represented by manufacturing, on account of two special features of fiscal legislation. First, no depreciation deduction from taxable income is permitted for non-industrial (i.e. commercial) buildings. Second, expenditure on non-mobile industrial

[1] Source: *Monthly Digest of Statistics*. The 7 per cent of expenditure devoted to vehicles is assumed to be divided between cars and other road vehicles in a 3 : 4 ratio. The quantitative limitations on car allowances instituted in 1961 and amended in 1963 are ignored.

[2] For an estimate of the substitution elasticity between equipment and structures in the US see Sato [17].

equipment qualified for 'free depreciation' from April 1963;[1] this provision, together with the investment allowance, meant that the present value of depreciation allowances on qualifying equipment amounted to 130 per cent of the asset's costs. Information on the proportion of equipment spending thus affected is not available, but it is known that of 43·3 million sq. ft of industrial building approved by the Board of Trade in the first nine months of 1964, 11·5 million sq. ft was located in development districts;[2] hence, it was assumed that 26 per cent of expenditure on equipment qualified for this special treatment. For equipment outside development areas the median annual allowance of 20 per cent was used.

The final requirement is an estimate of the depreciation rate. Dean's frequency distribution of plant and equipment lives in manufacturing and construction [5] implies a mean life of thirty-four years, equivalent to a depreciation rate of 0·127 on the declining-balance basis. It will be noticed that this is markedly lower than any of the rates permitted for tax purposes from November 1962. The same authority's estimate of the life of industrial buildings is eighty years, so that the weighted average depreciation rate, assuming a 3 : 1 ratio of equipment to buildings, is approximately 0·11.

Table 2.1, constructed on the basis of these assumptions, shows for various values of the real rate of return demanded by shareholders ($\bar{p}$) and the inflation rate ($\dot{q}$) the present value of depreciation allowances discounted at the corresponding nominal rate ($\rho = \bar{p} + \dot{q}$). It also shows the critical values of the gearing ratio (β^*) at which the implicit rental of capital services is unaffected by tax changes; at higher values than those tabulated $\partial F/\partial t$ would be negative.

TABLE 2.1. *Combinations of real equity rate ($\bar{p}$), inflation rath ($\dot{q}$) and gearing ratio (β^*) for neutral tax change ($\partial F/\partial t = 0$)*

$\bar{p}$	$\dot{q}=0$		$\dot{q}=0\cdot 05$		$\dot{q}=10$	
	Z	β^*	Z	β^*	Z	β^*
0·05	1·088	—	0·987	0·023	0·925	0·080
0·10	0·987	0·027	0·925	0·105	0·882	0·124
0·15	0·925	0·130	0·882	0·153	0·850	0·156
0·20	0·882	0·183	0·850	0·186	0·829	0·177

These results require little comment. β^* approaches but never reaches a value of 20 per cent, which approximates the marginal gearing ratio during the period in question.[3] The contemporary discussions of prominent financial analysts, e.g. [14], suggest that even this marginal figure was well below the

---

[1] In addition, investments which generated 'adequate' employment were eligible for grants of 10 per cent in the case of machinery and 25 per cent for buildings; the latter provision was not confined to the industrial sector. Zero rates of grant are assumed in the calculations.

[2] *Board of Trade Journal*, 26 November 1965.

[3] More specifically, long term debentures issued by quoted manufacturing companies in 1964 represented 20 per cent of their total cash issues plus retentions. Source: *Financial Statistics*.

optimal level, which was said to correspond to a value of β in the 25–30 per cent range. In view of the results reported by Whittaker [20], particular attention should be given to values of $\bar{\rho}$ around 5 per cent[1] for which β^* is always less than the *average* degree of gearing (see [14]).

Thus it seems certain that an increase in the capital stock would have been a profit-maximising response to a tax increase in at least one particular period for the representative manufacturing business, provided of course that fiscal parameters were taken fully into account in appraisal of investment opportunities. The conclusion is hardly startling but fills a lacuna in the literature: when the tax base does not coincide with the theorist's convenient abstraction, the overall effect of the discrepancy hinges on precise institutional details.

TABLE 2.2. *Combinations of real equity rate* $(\bar{\rho})$, *inflation rate* $(\dot{q})$ *and gearing ratio* (β^{**}) *for neutral inflation-rate change* $(\partial F/\partial \dot{q} = 0)$

$\bar{\rho}$	$\dot{q}=0$ β^{**}	$\dot{q}=0\cdot05$ β^{**}	$\dot{q}=0\cdot10$ β^{**}
0·05	0·397	0·240	0·160
0·10	0·315	0·210	0·149
0·15	0·260	0·185	0·139
0·20	0·220	0·166	0·130

The effects of inflation on the implicit rental of capital services, given the tax system of the early 1960s, are illustrated in Table 2.2, which shows critical values of the gearing ratio (β^{**}) at which changes in the inflation rate have no effect on the rental $(\partial F/\partial \dot{q} = 0)$. For plausible values of the real discount rate, it is clear that the transition from stable prices to inflation would reduce the profit-maximising capital stock. As the inflation rate rises, however, the critical values approach the empirically relevant range, and further increases in the inflation rate therefore reduce the rental.

8. Intersectoral allocation

The incomplete coverage of the profits tax has been neglected so far, but this point can now be dealt with summarily. If a net expansion of corporate capital results from a tax increase, this must imply at least a relative contraction in the size of the sector not subject to the profits tax. In general, the required rate of return will be increased in the process.

Although the direction of adjustment may be opposite to that predicted by Harberger, the more fundamental point, that in the absence of other distortions differential taxation involves a welfare cost, is not, of course, altered by the foregoing analysis. It follows from the above discussion that, *ceteris*

---

[1] The thirteen pension fund managers who responded to Whittaker's survey in 1967 required on average a minimum nominal return on equities, after corporate but before personal taxes, of 8·2 per cent, on the assumption of a 3 per cent inflation rate.

paribus, different rates of taxation of corporate and non-corporate business income involve differences in marginal rates of substitution,[1] and hence shift the transformation surface inwards (see [11]). In other words, the form of excess burden may be changed, in that an increase in the profits tax may make the corporate sector 'too large', but not the substance.

It may be worth adding that other differences in the fiscal treatment of different taxpayers have the same effect. For example, it was noted above that a substantial difference existed between 'industrial' and 'commercial' companies (and partnerships etc.) in respect of capital allowances.[2] A more obvious instance was the restriction of cash grants to 'manufacturing' in the period 1966–70, a measure which was only partially offset in its effects on optimal factor proportions by the selective employment tax. Whatever may have been the merits of the case for shifting resources from the tertiary to the secondary sector, the means adopted involved an unnecessary source of inefficiency.

The significance of such departures from fiscal neutrality depends, obviously, on economic parameters, notably substitution elasticities. At the empirical level there is little sign of a consensus as to their magnitudes in particular cases, but even less evidence that they are typically close enough to zero for the excess burdens entailed in discriminatory factor taxation to be safely ignored.

9. Qualification and conclusions

It remains only to make explicit the assumption, employed throughout the paper, of perfect loss offsets. Theoretical completeness would require a lengthy analysis, but at the empirical level provisions for carry-forward and, more recently, carry-back of losses seem sufficiently well developed to justify this simplification.

The arguments presented in this paper can now be summarised very briefly. Unless the utility function is linear, in which case the tax base coincides with the firm's maximand, even a tax on pure profits will affect price and output in both the short and long run. In practice, however, the base of the profits tax is not pure profits, so that even a linear utility function does not preclude announcement effects. The response of a utility maximiser to a change in the pure profits tax is indeterminate *a priori*; so is the response of a profit maximiser to a change in the actual imperfect profits tax.

References

1. ARROW, K. J. *Aspects of the Theory of Risk-Bearing*, Helsinki, Yrjö Johnssonin Säätiö, 1965.
2. BARON, D. P. 'Price uncertainty, utility, and industry equilibrium in pure competition', *International Economic Review*, 11 (1970).

[1] Except in the special case where $Z=1$ and $\beta=0$ in each sector.
[2] Discrimination in the tax treatment of expenditure on plant and equipment in development areas was abolished in July 1971, but discriminatory cash grants were reintroduced in March 1972.

3. BRECHLING, F. P. R. *Investment and Employment Decisions*, Manchester University Press, (forthcoming).
4. COEN, R. M. 'Effect of tax policy on investment in manufacturing', *American Economic Review*, **58** (May 1968).
5. DEAN, G. A. 'The stock of fixed capital in the UK in 1961', *Journal of the Royal Statistical Society*, Series A, **127** (1964).
6. DOMAR, E. D. 'Depreciation, replacement and growth', *Economic Journal*, **63** (1953).
7. DOMAR, E. D. and MUSGRAVE, R. A. 'Proportional taxation and risk-taking', *Quarterly Journal of Economics*, **58** (1944).
8. EISNER, R. 'Depreciation allowances and growth', *American Economic Review*, **42** (1952).
9. HALL, R. E. and JORGENSON, D. W. 'Application of the Theory of Optimum Capital Accumulation', *Tax Incentives and Capital Spending*, ed. G. Fromm, Washington D.C., Brookings Institution, 1971.
10. HARBERGER, A. C. 'Efficiency effects of taxes on income from capital', in *Effects of Coporation Income Tax*, ed. M. Krzyzaniak, Wayne State University Press, 1966.
11. JOHNSON, H. G. 'Factor market distortions and the shape of the transformation curve', *Econometrica*, **34** (1966).
12. JORGENSON, D. W. 'Anticipations and investment behaviour', in *The Brookings Quarterly Model of the U.S.*, ed. J. S. Duesenberry, G. Fromm, L. R. Klein and E. Kuh. North Holland, Amsterdam, 1965.
13. KRZYZANIAK, M. and MUSGRAVE, R. A. *The Shifting of the Corporation Income Tax*, Baltimore, Johns Hopkins University Press, 1963.
14. MERRETT, A. J. and SYKES, A. *The Finance and Analysis of Capital Projects*, Longmans, 1963.
15. MILLER, M. H. 'The corporation income tax and corporate financial policies', in *Stabilisation Policies*, Commission on Money & Credit Research Studies, Prentice-Hall, 1963.
16. ROBERTSON, D. H. 'The Colwyn Committee, the income tax and the price level', *Economic Journal*, **37** (1927).
17. SATO, K. 'A two-level C.E.S. production function', *Review of Economic Studies*, **34** (1967).
18. SCHIFF, E. 'A note on depreciation, replacement and growth', *Review of Economics and Statistics*, **36** (1954).
19. SUMNER, M. T. 'Recent changes in fiscal investment incentives', *Manchester School*, 1971.
20. WHITTAKER, J. 'What level for share price?', *Lloyds Bank Review*, **87** (1968).

Announcement effects of profits taxation: Discussion*

Frank Brechling

The contents of Mr Sumner's paper can be subdivided conveniently into three parts. In the first part, he illustrates the possibility that if firms maximise utility which is determined by both the mean and the variance of profits then their behaviour is, in general, not independent of a tax on pure profits. Such firms will typically produce less than risk-neutral firms and a rise in the profits tax will raise the slope of their constraint (that is $d\bar{\pi}/d\sigma^2$) to which they react by raising their equilibrium output. In recent years a large number of comparative static propositions of firm behaviour under uncertainty have been published. Mr Sumner's point is an interesting addition to this literature. Perhaps he should be encouraged to pursue this subject further and to study the influence of business taxation on firm behaviour under more general conditions of uncertainty and market structure.

The second part of Mr Sumner's paper contains a model of a long-run profit maximising firm (without uncertainty) in which (*a*) the profits tax is not levied on pure profits and (*b*) there is both equity and debt financing and the firm can borrow at a rate different from its shareholders' rate of discount. Three important results are implied by his model: First, even if the firm has no debt ($\beta = 0$), a *rise* in the profits tax may *lower* the rental of capital when the total discounted depreciation allowances (Z) exceed 100 per cent of the investment. The crucial expression is $g = (1 - tZ)/(1 - t)$, where t is the proportionate tax rate. Suppose that initially $Z = 1\cdot2$ and $t = 0\cdot75$, then $g = 0\cdot4$. Superficial analysis might suggest that a lowering of the profits tax would induce more investment; consider a government policy which *raises* the depreciation allowances to $Z = 1\cdot4$ and *lowers* the profits tax to $t = 0\cdot25$, then $g = 0\cdot87$ and *the rental of capital has more than doubled*. Hence, it is important to bear in mind the possibility of a negative influence of the profits tax upon the rental of capital. Second, even if the profits tax is levied only on pure profits (so that $Z = 1$) but there is some debt financing ($\beta > 0$), a rise in the profits tax lowers the rental on capital; the strength of this effect depends on the ratio of debt to total capital (β). This negative effect stems from the fact

---

* This is an amended version of my original comments, some of which have become irrelevant because of changes in Mr Sumner's paper.

that interest payments on debt are not taxed while returns to equity capital are taxed. Third, because of the profits tax, a rise in the expected rate of increase in all prices does have an influence on the rental of capital in spite of the fact that both interest rates are fully adjusted. But the direction of this influence cannot be determined. All three implications of Sumner's long-run profit maximisation model are important both for theoretical analysis and for purposes of economic policy.

It is interesting to note that Mr Sumner has obtained results which are richer in predictive power than those of more conventional models. Moreover, his discrete time period approach requires no more than simple calculus. It would appear that this model can now be easily extended to incorporate, say, non-linear adjustment costs or possibly even uncertainty.

In the third part of this paper, Mr Sumner presents some evidence on the likely relationship between the rental of capital and the profits tax or inflation rate. It would appear that, on plausible assumptions, a rise in the profits tax would always lower the rental on capital, given the British tax structure and gearing ratios ruling in recent years. Moreover, moderate inflation tends to raise and severe inflation to lower the rental of capital. These results are clearly extremely important and should not be ignored in future studies of the efficacy of government policy in controlling investment expenditure.

Mr Sumner should be congratulated on a paper which contains many relevant and intriguing ideas. Each of the three parts of his paper could (and, hopefully, will) be developed into a full paper. His results are extremely important for economic policy decisions, because governments adjust both allowances and the profits tax rate in attempts to affect both total investment and, perhaps more importantly, its regional distribution. His analysis indicates that superficial theorising may easily lead to mutually offsetting policy measures, which, apart from involving administrative costs, would not have much impact on the economy.

Comparative dynamics from the point of view of the dual[1]

3

Avinash Dixit

1. Introduction

Many problems of capital theory concern comparisons between paths of proportional growth. The structure common to such discussions is a model of general equilibrium with constant returns to scale in production. The inputs are labour and a vector of capital goods and the outputs are a consumer good and a vector of capital goods. Outputs become available one unit of time after inputs are used. At equilibrium prices, no feasible plan has a higher value than the equilibrium plan, which has zero value. On paths of proportional growth, all quantities increase through time at a common rate (the natural rate of growth) and all prices in present value terms fall through time at a common rate (the rate of interest). Of two such plans with the same natural growth rate, each has zero value at its own prices and non-positive value at the prices of the other. All comparative dynamic results that are valid at this level of generality can be derived from these two equations and two inequalities.[2]

As we should expect from our experience of competitive equilibrium theory, there are very few such results, the Golden Rule being almost the only one of any importance. Further results depend on special assumptions about the number of goods distinguished and on particular features of the technology beyond convexity and constant returns to scale. In the simplest model only one good is distinguished, or equivalently all goods are perfect substitutes as outputs. For this model, comparing proportional growth paths, we find that a lower interest rate, a higher wage rate, higher consumption per head and a higher amount of the capital good per head all go together. Practically none of these associations remain valid in the most general model, but some of them survive longer than others as we admit complications in stages. Both for theoretical and for empirical work, we need different levels of generality for

[1] I am very grateful to Peter Hammond, who corrected a major error in the first draft of this paper.

[2] The most general and yet the clearest discussion of this model known to me is by Bliss [1]. I have benefited a great deal from having had access to parts of a draft of his manuscript.

different purposes. It will therefore be useful to have on hand a classification
of the comparative dynamic associations by the level of generality to which
they remain valid. I hope to provide the beginnings of such a catalogue here.

There is a related purpose of the paper that I would like to stress. It is to
illustrate the usefulness in capital theory of a technique which is becoming
increasingly popular in other branches of economics. This approach specifies
the technology in terms of a cost function, an equivalent and dual concept to
the usual transformation function.[1] As it involves prices, comparative
dynamics necessarily relies on duality. But a much greater role for the dual
brings several advantages. Special restrictions on technology are much easier
to express using cost functions. Even the mechanical steps of algebra retain
much of the economic content of the problem. I hope to illustrate these
advantages here. Of course there are times, especially if convexity is the only
restriction on the technology, when the basic inequalities mentioned earlier
are the best way to do comparative dynamics.

I shall base the discussion on the two-good model. This allows a variable
price of the capital good relative to the consumer good, and so brings in
complications of valuations and interest rates. On the other hand, it does not
involve problems of aggregation of a variety of capital goods. Thus the
knowledge of which associations remain valid for the two-good model helps us
pinpoint the reasons for the breakdown of different associations. At this level
of aggregation, I shall start with the most general technology compatible with
general equilibrium, and introduce special cases later. This will show how
the validity of different associations can depend on special features of the
technology.

2. The cost function approach

To study proportional growth paths, we can focus attention on any one stage
in the production sequence. For the two-good model, suppose two inputs
l_0 and k_0 applied at date 0 produce two outputs c_1 and k_1 available at date 1.
The technology is usually described by a transformation function

$$c_1 \leq f(k_1, l_0, k_0) \tag{1}$$

where f is concave, non-increasing in k_1, and non-decreasing in l_0 and k_0.
With constant returns to scale, it is homogeneous of degree one. For an
efficient production plan, we can find prices w_0, p_0 for the inputs and q_1, p_1
for the outputs so that at these prices, the plan in question maximises
$q_1 c_1 + p_1 k_1 - w_0 l_0 - p_0 k_0$ subject to (1). With constant returns to scale, the
maximum value is zero.

[1] This method has been applied to the principles and practice of estimating production relations by McFadden *et al.* [6]. Essentially the same idea in a simpler model
has been used with great success by Jones in the theory of international trade, in [4]
and a number of recent papers. A related approach using the revenue function is
employed for equilibrium dynamics by Hahn [2].

The dual approach uses the efficiency prices more directly by means of the cost function:[1]

$$\phi(c_1, k_1, w_0, p_0) = \min\{w_0 l_0 + p_0 k_0 \,|\, c_1 \le f(k_1, l_0, k_0)\} \tag{2}$$

This function has the following properties:

1. It is non-decreasing in all arguments.
2. For any given (w_0, p_0), it is convex in (c_1, k_1). With constant returns to scale, it is homogeneous of degree one in these two. This convexity arises from the usual diminishing marginal rate of transformation.
3. For any given (c_1, k_1), it is concave and homogeneous of degree one in (w_0, p_0). The concavity arises from the usual diminishing marginal rate of substitution of inputs; the homogeneity is obvious.
4. The cost-minimising choices of l_0 and k_0, i.e. the factor demands, are given by the partial derivatives[2] ϕ_w and ϕ_p respectively, when these exist. This is a standard envelope theorem type result. In addition, I shall assume that ϕ is twice differentiable.

Equilibrium conditions are now evident. In factor markets, we simply equate the demands ϕ_w and ϕ_p to the respective supplies l_0 and k_0. In output markets, the supplies of c_1 and k_1 will be chosen to maximise the profit, $q_1 c_1 + p_1 k_1 - \phi$. The marginal costs ϕ_c and ϕ_k will therefore equal the respective prices q_1 and p_1.

For proportional growth paths, it is convenient to write these in a special form. By choice of units, we can set

$$l_0 = 1, \quad q_1 = 1 \tag{3}$$

Let the growth factor be α and the interest factor β, so that

$$k_1 = \alpha k_0, \quad p_0 = \beta p_1. \tag{4}$$

Now the equilibrium conditions become

$$\phi_c(c_1, k_1, w_0, p_0) = 1$$
$$\phi_k(c_1, k_1, w_0, p_0) = p_1 = p_0/\beta$$
$$\phi_w(c_1, k_1, w_0, p_0) = 1 \tag{5}$$
$$\phi_p(c_1, k_1, w_0, p_0) = k_0 = k_1/\alpha$$

Given α and β, these serve to define c_1, k_1, w_0 and p_0. There is an evident symmetry between the effect of the growth factor on the quantity variables

---

[1] For a detailed discussion of the cost function, see McFadden [5]. I should add that the cost function is only a partial dual. The full dual would use all prices to define a profit function

$$\pi(q_1, p_1, w_0, p_0) = \max\{q_1 c_1 + p_1 k_1 - w_0 l_0 - p_0 k_0 \,|\, c_1 < f(k_1, l_0, k_0)\}$$

This cannot be used here owing to constant returns to scale. The other partial dual—the revenue function—could be used, but interesting restrictions on the technology are easier to express using the cost function.

[2] For typographical convenience, I shall omit the date subscripts on the letter subscripts of ϕ. This is not likely to cause any confusion.

and that of the interest factor on the price variables. This is in essence the famous Bruno–von Weizsäcker type of duality relationship.

With constant returns to scale, ϕ is homogeneous of degree one in (c_1, k_1) and in (w_0, p_0) separately, and therefore

$$c_1\phi_c + k_1\phi_k = \phi = w_0\phi_w + p_0\phi_p \tag{6}$$

Using (5), this can be expressed in the alternative forms:

$$c_1 + p_1k_1 = w_0 + p_0k_0 \tag{6'}$$

$$c_1 = w_0 + (\beta - \alpha)\,p_1k_0 \tag{6''}$$

The first of these is the familiar equality between the national product and the national income. The second says that consumption equals the wages plus the excess of interest income over the requirements for maintaining growth. This form is often useful, and I shall carry out much of the comparative dynamics in terms of these variables, namely c_1, k_0, w_0 and p_1.

To study the effects of a change in β alone on the equilibrium values of these variables, the easiest method is to take total logarithmic differentials of (5). Let $\hat{x}$ denote a small proportional change dx/x in a variable x, and let $\eta_{xy} = y\phi_{xy}/\phi_x$, the partial elasticity of ϕ_x with respect to y, evaluated at the equilibrium. Then

$$\eta_{cc}\hat{c}_1 + \eta_{ck}\hat{k}_1 + \eta_{cw}\hat{w}_0 + \eta_{cp}\hat{p}_0 = 0$$
$$\eta_{kc}\hat{c}_1 + \eta_{kk}\hat{k}_1 + \eta_{kw}\hat{w}_0 + \eta_{kp}\hat{p}_0 = \hat{p}_0 - \hat{\beta} \tag{7}$$
$$\eta_{wc}\hat{c}_1 + \eta_{wk}\hat{k}_1 + \eta_{ww}\hat{w}_0 + \eta_{wp}\hat{p}_0 = 0$$
$$\eta_{pc}\hat{c}_1 + \eta_{pk}\hat{k}_1 + \eta_{pw}\hat{w}_0 + \eta_{pp}\hat{p}_0 = \hat{k}_1$$

These can be greatly simplified using the homogeneity properties of ϕ. Note that Euler's theorem can be stated in the form: If a function is homogeneous of degree n in a set of variables, then its partial elasticities with respect to them add up to n. Now ϕ is homogeneous of degree one in (c_1, k_1), so ϕ_c is homogeneous of degree zero in these two, and therefore $\eta_{cc} + \eta_{ck} = 0$. Moreover, ϕ being convex in (c_1, k_1), $\eta_{cc} \geq 0$. Let me write τ_1 for η_{cc} and $-\tau_1$ for η_{ck}. Similarly, I can write τ_2 for η_{kk} and $-\tau_2$ for η_{kc}. Note that τ_1 and τ_2 are not quite independent, for we can use $\phi_{ck} = \phi_{kc}$ to get

$$\tau_1/\tau_2 = p_1k_1/c_1 \tag{8}$$

the relative composition of the national product. This dependence does not really matter for comparative dynamics, but it and other similar relations will prove useful in simplifying some expressions.

The same argument can be applied to (w_0, p_0), and I can set

$$\eta_{ww} = -\sigma_1 = -\eta_{wp}$$

and

$$\eta_{pp} = -\sigma_2 = -\eta_{pw}$$

Also,

$$\sigma_1/\sigma_2 = p_0k_0/w_0 \tag{9}$$

the relative factor shares.

The σ's have an immediate economic significance. For example, σ_1 is the numerical value of the elasticity of ϕ_w, the labour demand, with respect to the wage rate. Changes in factor use in response to changes in factor prices reflect substitution possibilities in production. If there are no such possibilities, the cost of producing any desired combination of outputs can be found simply by multiplying the fixed factor requirements by the corresponding factor prices and adding. This is linear in factor prices, so $\sigma_1 = \sigma_2 = 0$. The more the substitution possibility, the higher will be σ_i.

The τ's can be interpreted along similar lines. They will be zero if the cost function is linear in (c_1, k_1), that is,

$$\phi = c_1 \phi^c(w_0, p_0) + k_1 \phi^k(w_0, p_0) \tag{10}$$

If ϕ^c and ϕ^k are themselves increasing, concave and homogeneous of degree one in (w_0, p_0), then as far as the economics of production is concerned, the situation is as if there were separate 'industries' for producing the consumer good and the capital good, with ϕ^c and ϕ^k as the respective unit cost functions. In other words, production is essentially non-joint.[1]

We have seen that if production is non-joint, then $\tau_1 = \tau_2 = 0$. Thus the τ's being positive indicates essential jointness in the technology. It seems that jointness in production is a dual concept to substitution in inputs, and we could define an index of jointness dual to the elasticity of substitution. For my present purpose, such a measure would not shed any great light.

If the technology is non-joint, we can solve the first two equations in (7) immediately for w_0 and p_0, and then substitute for these in the last two to get the full solution. This is the case studied by Jones [4], who also derives explicit expressions for σ_1 and σ_2 in terms of the elasticities of substitution in the two industries.

Let us turn to the remaining cross-elasticities involving both inputs and outputs. As ϕ is homogeneous of degree one in (w_0, p_0), so is a partial of ϕ with respect to any argument other than these two. Then Euler's theorem applied to ϕ_c as a function of (w_0, p_0) gives $\eta_{cw} + \eta_{cp} = 1$. I shall write θ_1 for η_{cw} and $(1 - \theta_1)$ for η_{cp}. Similarly, $\eta_{kw} = \theta_2$ and $\eta_{kp} = 1 - \theta_2$, $\eta_{wc} = \lambda_1$ and $\eta_{wk} = 1 - \lambda_1$, $\eta_{pc} = \lambda_2$ and $\eta_{pk} = 1 - \lambda_2$.

The λ's and the θ's have a ready interpretation in the non-joint case. From (10), we have $\phi_c = \phi^c$, and so $\phi_{cw} = \phi^c{}_w$. As ϕ^c is the unit cost function for the consumer good industry, so $\phi^c{}_w$ is the amount of labour demanded for producing one unit of the consumer good. We have already seen that in equilibrium, ϕ_w is the overall demand for labour in the economy, and ϕ_c equals the price of the consumer good. Then $\lambda_1 = c_1 \phi_{cw}/\phi_w$ is the proportion of the labour force that is employed in the consumer good industry, and $\theta_1 = w_0 \phi_{cw}/\phi_c$ is the distributive share of labour in the consumer good in-

---

[1] The dual specification of non-jointness is discussed by Hall [3]. The condition for the transformation function (1) to be derivable from separate industry production functions is much more complicated; it is that the matrix (f_{ij}) of second order cross partials should be of rank one. (Under constant returns to scale alone it would be of rank two.) See Samuelson [7].

dustry. Similarly, we can interpret all the λ's as factor allocation ratios and all the θ's as distributive shares. This is also discussed by Jones, who shows that $(\lambda_1 - \lambda_2)$ and $(\theta_1 - \theta_2)$ have the same sign, and the common sign is positive if the consumer good industry is more labour intensive.

When there is joint production, we cannot split unit costs or factor uses in this way. In fact, there is in general no guarantee that all these cross elasticities will be positive, and some λ's or some θ's may correspondingly lie outside the interval [0, 1]. Let us see what this means. If ϕ_{wc} is negative, for example, ϕ_w decreases as c_1 increases, other arguments being held constant. In other words, an increase in the amount of the consumer good with the amount of the capital good and the input prices held constant lowers the demand for labour, so that at the margin, labour is an inferior input for producing the consumer good. Normally, constant returns to scale would rule out inferior inputs. With joint production, constant returns to scale for the vector of outputs are consistent with there being some inferior inputs at the margin for some of the outputs. I shall later give an example of such a cost function. I feel, however, that there is quite strong presumption against this even for joint technologies.

Once again, we can use the equality of cross-partials of ϕ to get connections between one λ and one θ. The ratios will now equal a mixture of product and income terms. I shall need only two of these:

$$\lambda_1/\theta_1 = c_1/w_0, \quad \lambda_2/(1-\theta_1) = c_1/(p_0 k_0) \qquad (11)$$

Using all this notation, (7) can be written in the form

$$
\begin{bmatrix}
\tau_1 & -\tau_1 & \theta_1 & 1-\theta_1 \\
-\tau_2 & \tau_2 & \theta_2 & -\theta_2 \\
\lambda_1 & 1-\lambda_1 & -\sigma_1 & \sigma_1 \\
\lambda_2 & -\lambda_2 & \sigma_2 & -\sigma_2
\end{bmatrix}
\begin{bmatrix}
\hat{c}_1 \\
\hat{k}_1 \\
\hat{w}_0 \\
\hat{p}_0
\end{bmatrix}
=
\begin{bmatrix}
0 \\
-\hat{\beta} \\
0 \\
0
\end{bmatrix}
\qquad (12)
$$

Even though this set of equations looks formidable, it is relatively easy to solve.[1]

3. Comparative dynamic results

The solutions to (12), expressed in terms of chosen variables, are

$$\hat{c}_1 = -[\sigma_2\lambda_1 + \sigma_1\lambda_2 - \sigma_2]/[\sigma_2\tau_2 + \lambda_2\theta_2]\,\hat{\beta}$$

$$\hat{k}_0 = -[\sigma_2\lambda_1 + \sigma_1\lambda_2]/[\sigma_2\tau_2 + \lambda_2\theta_2]\,\hat{\beta} \qquad (13)$$

$$\hat{w}_0 = -[\lambda_2(1-\theta_1) + \sigma_2\tau_1]/[\sigma_2\tau_2 + \lambda_2\theta_2]\,\hat{\beta}$$

$$\hat{p}_1 = [\lambda_2(\theta_1 - \theta_2) - \sigma_2(\tau_1 + \tau_2)]/[\sigma_2\tau_2 + \lambda_2\theta_2]\,\hat{\beta}$$

[1] The best way is to group terms in $(\hat{c}_1 - \hat{k}_1)$ and $(\hat{w}_0 - \hat{p}_0)$ where possible, and then use successive substitutions.

Some fundamental results can be derived from these. Using (9) and (11), we find

$$\hat{c}_1/\hat{k}_0 = 1 - w_0/c_1 \tag{14}$$

or, substituting from (6″)

$$dc_1/dk_0 = (\beta - \alpha)\, p_1 \tag{14'}$$

Thus, except when the rate of interest is less than the rate of growth, i.e. excluding the Phelps–Koopmans inefficient region, a greater quantity of the capital good is associated with a higher level of consumption. Further, (14) shows that consumption increases less than proportionately when capital increases.

There is a positive association between capital and wages as well. For

$$\hat{w}_0/\hat{k}_0 = [\lambda_2(1 - \theta_1) + \sigma_2\tau_1]/[\sigma_2\lambda_1 + \sigma_1\lambda_2] \tag{15}$$

Although we cannot be sure that all the λ's and the θ's are in the range $[0, 1]$, we know from (11) that λ_2 and $(1 - \theta_1)$ have the same sign, so their product is non-negative. Also, (9) and (11) show that the denominator in (15) is positive, being equal to $\sigma_2 c_1/w_0$.

These two results are true for the general two-good model. If there are no inferior inputs in the sense explained earlier, then the one-good associations of the interest rate continue to hold: a lower interest rate goes with a greater quantity of capital, and hence with a higher wage rate and—except in the Phelps–Koopmans inefficient region—a higher level of consumption. So it seems that while consumption and capital perversities and an upward sloping factor price frontier are all possible in the general two-good model, we should not expect them to be common occurrences. Of course, the value of capital can move in either direction, but that is not a perversity in any sense.[1]

We have seen that non-jointness of the technology is sufficient to ensure that all the λ's and the θ's lie in $[0, 1]$, which in turn is sufficient to ensure the validity of the one-good associations. In spite of being only indirectly sufficient, non-jointness is an interesting condition. I shall comment on its theoretical relevance in the fifth section. Its empirical relevance has been studied by Hall [3], whose findings support it strongly. The test does not reject the hypothesis of non-jointness by a long way. What is more, the assumption greatly increases the tightness of the estimates of the relevant coefficients.

It will be useful to state and examine some of the results for the non-joint case. We have

$$\hat{w}_0 = -(1 - \theta_1)/\theta_2 \ \hat{\beta}$$
$$\hat{p}_1 = (\theta_1 - \theta_2)/\theta_2 \ \hat{\beta} \tag{16}$$

The first of these gives an expression for the elasticity of the factor price frontier: it is the ratio of capital's share in the consumer good industry to

---

[1] 'The Wicksell effect is nothing but an inventory revaluation', Swan [8].

labour's share in the capital good industry. This is a simple generalisation of the result for the one-good model. The second equation says that a low-interest economy, i.e. one with more capital, has a lower price of capital if the consumer good industry is more labour intensive, i.e. if the capital good industry is more capital intensive. This has a simple explanation. With a fixed growth rate, the demand for capital on a proportional growth path increases in the same proportion as the quantity of the capital good. When the capital good industry is more capital intensive if output prices were unchanged, then by Rybczynski's theorem (see Jones [4]) the supply of capital would increase by a greater proportion. To maintain proportional growth, therefore, production of capital goods has to be discouraged, which requires a lower relative supply price of capital.

Another special restriction often imposed on the technology is that of separability. This requires that the inputs and the outputs in the transformation function can be separated in the form

$$F^o(c_1, k_1) = F^i(l_0, k_0) \tag{17}$$

where o stands for outputs and i for inputs. This means that the marginal rate of transformation between outputs is independent of input composition and the marginal rate of substitution between inputs is independent of output composition, which seems theoretically undesirable. Also, the empirical work of Hall contradicts separability quite strongly. I shall quickly mention the consequences of separability for comparative dynamics for sake of completeness. Hall has shown that (17) is equivalent to the following restriction on the cost function:[1]

$$\phi = \phi^o(c_1, k_1)\, \phi^i(w_0, p_0) \tag{18}$$

Now it is easy to see that

$$\theta_1 = \theta_2 = w_0 \phi^i_w / \phi^i = \theta$$

say, and similarly

$$\lambda_1 = \lambda_2 = c_1 \phi^o_c / \phi^o = \lambda$$

say. As both ϕ^o and ϕ^i are increasing in their respective arguments, both λ and θ lie in [0, 1]. This ties in with the discussion of inferior inputs. We can look at a separable technology as one in which (l_0, k_0) produce a single output F^o, which is then divided into (c_1, k_1) appropriately. Now an increase in one of these outputs can only be secured by an increase in the amount of F^o being produced. As this is produced under constant returns, neither input can be inferior.

Hall has shown that if we impose non-jointness and separability together, the outputs become perfect substitutes and the model essentially a one-good model. Thus, if we put $\theta_1 = \theta_2$ in (16), we see that all proportional growth

---

[1] The corresponding condition for the transformation function (1) to be expressible in the form (17) is not simple: it can be shown to be $f_{12}/f_2 = f_{13}/f_3$. This illustrates the superiority of the dual approach once again.

paths have the same relative price of capital, and the one-good result on the elasticity of the factor price frontier emerges, for we can now regard θ and $(1-\theta)$ as the distributive shares in production of either good, or indeed in production of F^o.

4. Problems of generalisation

The cost function approach works equally well for several capital goods, and leads to equations exactly like (5). For given α and β, these define the outputs $(c_1, \mathbf{k}_1)$ and prices $(w_0, \mathbf{p}_0)$ on proportional growth paths. Comparative dynamics can be studied in the same way, and many of the characteristics of (12) will carry over. The solutions may be worth calculating in specific cases. I shall only make some general comments on the new problems that can arise.

First, $\mathbf{k}_1$ (or $\mathbf{k}_0 = \mathbf{k}_1/\alpha$) is part of the solution to the set (5). Regarded as a function of β, it will trace out a curve in n-dimensional space where n is the number of capital goods. Only points on this curve will be possible proportional growth capital compositions with the given growth factor α. Thus it may be meaningless to ask questions such as in what direction the wage will change in response to an increase in the quantity of only one of the capital goods, for there may be no two proportional growth paths which differ in this manner.

Next, in the general form of (12), we cannot be sure that all the off-diagonal elements in the matrix of the σ's will be positive, or that those in the matrix of the τ's, negative. This is the problem of complementarity that can arise when there are three or more inputs in all. This can, for example, destroy any general relation between $\mathbf{k}_0$ and w_0. In a suitable index number sense, we still have an association between c_1 and $\mathbf{k}_0$ outside the inefficient region.

Finally, in the non-joint case of the two good model, the change in the price of capital depended on a factor-intensity condition. With more than two inputs, a large number of possible factor-intensity combinations can arise, and it is not usually possible to get any sensible set of conditions.

5. Some examples

A simple example of an essentially joint cost function which has an upward sloping factor price frontier is

$$\phi = (c_1 + a k_1) p_0 + [(c^2_1 + k^2_1)^{1/2} - k_1] w_0 \qquad (19)$$

Provided $\beta > (1/a) > \alpha$, this has a proportional growth equilibrium. The factor price frontier can be shown to be (with A, B independent of β):

$$w_0[A + \beta B/(\beta a - 1)] = 1 \qquad (20)$$

and it is easy to verify that $dw_0/d\beta > 0$ for this.

Of course non-jointness is only sufficient and not necessary for ruling out such behaviour; an example to show this is

$$\phi = c_1 p_0 + [(c^2_1 + k^2_1)^{1/2} - c_1] \, w_0 \tag{21}$$

This has a proportional growth equilibrium whenever $\beta \geq \alpha$, and a downward sloping factor price frontier. I shall omit the details. In both (19) and (21) I have taken the cost function linear in prices for ease of computation; as a result the amounts of the consumer good and the capital good are both independent of the interest rate.

These are contrived examples. One which is economically much more interesting is the standard two-sector model with durable capital. As some of the capital input to each sector survives to the next period, each sector 'produces' such capital as well as consumer goods or new capital goods. Thus the technology has joint production. I shall now use the cost function approach to study the economic consequences of this.

Consider first the case where there are fixed coefficients in each sector. Call the capital and labour inputs required for production of a unit of consumer goods a_c, b_c respectively, and those required for the production of a unit of new capital goods a_k, b_k respectively. Let the survival ratios (one minus the depreciation ratios) for capital allocated to the two sectors be γ_c and γ_k, both in the range $[0, 1]$.[1]

There is still some freedom in choosing inputs to minimise cost. Clearly, if $k_1 \leq \gamma_c a_c c_1$, then all the capital that is required to be made available at date 1 can be obtained as a byproduct of the consumer good sector, and no resources need be put into production of new capital goods. The cost function in this case is

$$\phi = (w_0 b_c + p_0 a_c) \, c_1 \tag{22}$$

When $k_1 > \gamma_c a_c c_1$, we must make available more capital than what would survive in course of production of c_1. This can be done either by letting additional capital lie idle in the consumer good sector, or by producing new capital goods. The relative profitability of these will depend on the factor prices.[2] Some simple algebra shows that new capital goods should not be produced if

$$\gamma_c w_0 b_k \geq p_0 [1 - (\gamma_c - \gamma_k) \, a_k] \tag{23}$$

and then

$$\phi = w_0 b_c c_1 + p_0 k_1 / \gamma_c \tag{24}$$

Otherwise, both sectors must operate and

$$\phi = (w_0 b_c + p_0 a_c) \, c_1 +$$
$$(k_1 - \gamma_c a_c c_1)(w_0 b_k + p_0 a_k)/(1 + \gamma_k a_k) \tag{25}$$

---

[1] The possibility of different survival ratios in the two sectors is allowed for sake of generality, and I know of no strong reason to assume either to be greater than the other.

[2] The relative cost calculation made here assumes that capital survives at the same rate even when it is not accompanied by its complement of labour.

We see that the cost function is piecewise linear in (c_1, k_1) and in (w_0, p_0), being linear in each set in each of the regions defined by the three cases.

I shall confine my discussion of comparative dynamics to the third of these cases, for the first two can be equilibria of proportional paths only if the population is decaying sufficiently rapidly, i.e. $\alpha \leq \gamma_c$, which seems an uninteresting case.

From (25), we see that ϕ_{kw} and ϕ_{kp} are clearly positive. Also,

$$\phi_{cw} = b_c - \gamma_c a_c b_k / (1 + \gamma_k a_k)$$

$$\phi_{cp} = a_c [1 - \gamma_c a_k / (1 + \gamma_k a_k)] \tag{26}$$

We see from (23) that for operation of both sectors, we must have $1 - (\gamma_c - \gamma_k) a_k > 0$, and this ensures $\phi_{cp} > 0$.

The sign of ϕ_{cw} is in doubt, and hence so are the signs of γ_1 and θ_1. In the present case, however, $\sigma_1 = 0 = \sigma_2$, and (13) shows that this ambiguity does not matter.

Some generalisation to allow substitution in production is possible. Suppose the input coefficients in each sector are chosen from isoquants $a_c = g_c(b_c)$ and $a_k = g_k(b_k)$ to minimise unit cost. Now we must ask if new capital goods are worth producing, and this will lead to equations (22)–(25), with the input coefficients regarded functions of factor prices. Now the second order derivatives of ϕ should involve derivatives of these functions. At this point an envelope argument comes to the rescue. The coefficients having been chosen optimally, their derivatives cancel out and (26) remains valid. I shall omit the details.

In this case, $\tau_1 = 0 = \tau_2$, but σ_1 and σ_2 are non-zero. The factor-price frontier must slope downward and the relative price of capital depends on relative factor intensities as before. The expression for $\hat{k}_0$ involves λ_1, but (9) and (11) show that $(\sigma_2 \lambda_1 + \sigma_1 \lambda_2)$ must be positive irrespective of the sign of λ_1. Thus the negative association between the amount of capital and the interest rate remains valid as well.

6. Summary of conclusions

In this paper I have used a dual specification of technology to analyse comparative dynamics of the general growth model with one consumer good and one capital good. It seems that we should expect the results for a fully aggregated model to carry over, i.e. a proportional growth path with a lower interest rate should have a higher wage, a greater quantity of capital and, except for the Phelps–Koopmans inefficient region, more consumption per head. For this, it is sufficient to rule out inferior inputs, for which in turn it is sufficient to rule out jointness in production. One specific but important instance of jointness arising from durability of capital is shown not to matter. Standard results like the Golden Rule and the dependence of the relative price change on the relative factor intensity are simple corollaries of the analysis.

I hope I have illustrated the ease and elegance with which the dual approach leads to all these results. I also hope the readers will be able to discover for themselves many more applications of the method.

References

1. BLISS, C. J. *Capital Theory and the Distribution of Income*, North-Holland Publishing Co., forthcoming.
2. HAHN, F. H. 'On some equilibrium paths', in *Theory of Economic Growth*, ed. J. A. Mirrlees and N. H. Stern, Macmillan, forthcoming.
3. HALL, R. E. 'The specification of technology with several kinds of output', in [6], abstract in *Econometrica*, 39, no. 4 (1971), 244.
4. JONES, R. W. 'The structure of simple general equilibrium models', *Journal of Political Economy*, 73, no. 6 (1965), 557–72.
5. MCFADDEN, D. 'Cost, revenue and profit functions', in [6].
6. MCFADDEN, D. *et al. The Econometric Approach to Production Theory*, North-Holland Publishing Co., forthcoming.
7. SAMUELSON, P. A. 'The fundamental singularity theorem for non-joint production', *International Economic Review*, 7, no. 1 (1966), 34–41.
8. SWAN, T. W. 'Economic growth and capital accumulation', appendix, *Economic Record*, 32, no. 2 (1956), 343–61.

Comparative dynamics from the point of view of the dual: Discussion

P. J. Hammond

The major achievement of this paper is to provide another instance of the helpfulness of cost functions in deriving certain economic theorems, and this is brilliantly done. I propose to start the discussion with an attempt to explain why this might be, and then to suggest further possible uses of the dual approach.

The common approach to finding cost minimising factor demands is to write down a lot of first-order conditions involving first derivatives of the production function. These first-order conditions are a set of simultaneous equations in the factor inputs, and the solution is difficult to analyse. But, if the cost function is known, cost minimising factor demands can be derived immediately by partial differentiation alone. Of course, there remains the problem of determining equilibrium output and factor prices, but, given the solution to that problem, the rest is formally very much easier.

A close parallel arises in demand theory, where cost or expenditure function and expenditure minimising compensated demand vector can be defined as follows:

$$C(\mathbf{p}, \bar{U}) = \min\{\mathbf{px} \,|\, U(\mathbf{x}) \geq \bar{U}\}$$
$$= \mathbf{px}(\mathbf{p}, U)$$

This reformulation of the consumer's problem is extremely useful for deriving some results, e.g. the Slutsky results.[1]

It is also this parallel which brings out the appropriateness of the term 'inferior input'. An inferior input is one for which cost minimising demand falls as the output of some commodity increases. This is a precise analogy of an inferior good-one for which cost minimising demand falls as utility increases.

Apart from the analytical simplifications, there are a number of other advantages in using cost functions.

One is pedagogic. First year economics students meet cost functions (or cost-curves) and learn the use of concepts such as marginal and average cost. Later, their microeconomic courses use mostly production functions.

---

[1] See, for example, Arrow and Hahn [1], ch. 4, p. 81 and p. 105, or McKenzie [2].

The sudden transition which seems to be common may cause unnecessary difficulties.

A second advantage is that it may be a way out of endless debates over production functions and marginal productivity theory—particularly where capital is concerned. It is hard to see how any economist can deny the existence of cost functions.

A third advantage is simply that cost minimisation is a more general hypothesis than profit maximisation. Managers of 'managerial' firms may have non-neoclassical objectives, but it seems hard to deny that managers will minimise the cost of production, given their output decisions and the state of their factor markets.

A fourth advantage is that the cost-function approach seems to be more suited for empirical work.

Let me now turn to problems which are nearer to comparative dynamics. In the first place, the methods of this paper can be applied directly to a more general problem and they yield very similar results. Indeed, I know that Dr Dixit has started some work in the direction I am about to indicate.

The problem I have in mind is that of Hicks's temporary equilibrium. All agents have rationally based plans for a single period and, in equilibrium, all these single period plans are realised. In particular, firms will want to minimise costs for the single period—so we have 'temporary cost minimisation'. For this problem, it is more appropriate to consider the rental on capital—r—rather than the rate of interest—β. The cost function is now $\phi(c_1, k_1; w_0, r)$, where c_1, k_1 are outputs of consumption and capital, respectively, at the end of the period, and w_0 is the wage. The equilibrium conditions are obvious modifications of equations (5) of the paper. To determine equilibrium, the model has to be closed by household demand equations— these can be regarded as determining the price of new capital p_1 and the supply of labour l_0—cost minimisation does the rest. But, even without demand being specified, many two sector results can be derived very easily using just cost minimisation. However, one problem has been overlooked— in a temporary equilibrium economy, that capital is not shiftable can matter.

Another dynamic problem to which this sort of method may be suited is that of optimal growth—or, indeed, efficient growth. Given the stream of consumption goods, and the opportunity costs of using factors, an efficient growth path must minimise the intertemporal factor cost of producing the consumption stream. The intertemporal cost is the discounted present value of a stream of temporal costs. Each temporal cost has to be minimised, given the consumption output and factor prices that period—and given also the capital stock required for the following period. The intertemporal cost minimisation problem can be solved by working backwards and solving a sequence of one-period problems. This approach involves a kind of dual Hamiltonian, it seems.

The above remarks have all been fairly general. Very few specific comments seem called for. But I do wonder whether it is not possible to give meanings

Comparative dynamics from the point of view of the dual

to more of the elasticities featured in equations (12) of the paper—even in the joint case.

For example, $-\tau_1$ is the (negative) elasticity of the marginal cost of consumption with respect to the output of capital goods. Put this way, it is clear why τ_1 is zero in the non-joint case.

When there is non-joint production, average cost and marginal cost of consumption (say) will be identical. So, in splitting up average cost into labour's share and capital's share, we are also splitting up marginal cost. When there is joint production, splitting up average cost is no longer helpful. But if we split up *marginal* cost into *marginal* labour's share and *marginal* capital's share, we find that these shares are precisely θ_1 and $1 - \theta_1$.

The λ's are not so easy to interpret in the joint case. But they still depend only on the ratio of factor prices and the ratio of outputs of consumption and capital. And, if we were forced to classify labour as being either consumption-producing or capital-producing, we would probably regard $c\phi_{cw}$ as consumption-producing labour, and $k\phi_{kw}$ as capital-producing labour. Then λ_1 is the proportion of labour which is consumption-producing, and the other terms in λ have similar interpretations.

The examples in the final section of the paper are of some interest. The first seems to be a simpler case than Samuelson's [3] of the non-existence of a genuine factor price frontier (i.e. a downward sloping factor price relation).

In the standard two-sector model with durable capital, there is, *a priori*, joint production. The question then is whether this jointness is essential—in particular, whether the factor price relation is downward sloping, and whether any input can be inferior. As is shown in the paper, the factor price relation must in fact be downward sloping. The only possible inferior factor is labour in the production of consumption. It may be worth noting that this inferiority is possible even if capital depreciates at the same rate in both sectors.

I look forward to further work by Dr Dixit in this area.

References

1. ARROW, K. J. and HAHN, F. H. *General Competitive Analysis*, Holden-Day, 1971; Oliver & Boyd, 1972.
2. MCKENZIE, L. W. 'Demand theory without a utility index', *Review of Economic Studies*, 24 (1956–57), 185–9.
3. SAMUELSON, P. A. 'Parable and realism in capital theory: the surrogate production function', *Review of Economic Studies*, 29 (1962), 193–206.

4 Heterogeneous capital and the Heckscher–Ohlin–Samuelson theory of trade[1]

J. S. Metcalfe and Ian Steedman

1. Introduction

While many objections have been raised as to the validity of the assumptions underlying the Heckscher–Ohlin–Samuelson theory of trade, that theory is widely regarded as immune from criticism of its internal logic, once the assumptions are granted. If the theory is to be useful in the understanding of real world trade, however, the assumption that each country has a given endowment of capital must be interpreted in such a way that the heterogeneity of capital goods can be allowed for. Such an interpretation is indeed possible but it immediately raises doubts as to whether recent results from the controversy over capital theory might not show the internal logic of the HOS analysis to be open to criticism. The object of the paper is to suggest that the existence of heterogeneous capital goods does lead to a breakdown of the logic of the HOS theory and hence to that of its major conclusions.

2. The assumptions

In order to focus attention explicitly on the role of capital in HOS trade theory we shall make the normal assumptions of the *two* consumption commodity, *two* factor, *two* country model of trade. Thus we assume that:

(a) two countries, A and B, produce the same two consumption commodities, 1 and 2,

(b) each country has a given endowment of factors, identical with respect to the quality of the factors but different with respect to relative quantities,

(c) productive techniques are identical between countries and are of the constant returns to scale type everywhere,

(d) the two consumption commodities are produced with different and uniquely ordered factor intensities. There are thus no 'factor intensity reversals',

[1] We should like to thank C. J. Bliss and J. M. Parkin for helpful comments on earlier versions of this paper.

(e) All consumers in the two country world have identical homothetic preference maps,

(f) perfect competition rules in all markets, transport costs are absent and there is free trade in consumption commodities (unless otherwise stated).

It is to be stressed that we make all the above assumptions and that our analysis is in no way concerned with the usual objections to HOS theory based on the rejection of one or more of the above assumptions. We are thus solely concerned with the internal logic of the argument.

Assumption (b) requires further consideration. It is assumed that a country's factor endowment consists of given supplies of two homogeneous resources, one of which is taken to be labour. If the other were taken to be an endowment of a single homogeneous capital good, then the HOS analysis would be logically unassailable[1] but would be of limited interest until it were known that the results could be extended to systems in which there are many different capital goods. The object of this paper is to question the possibility of such an extension.

It might be thought that one way of allowing for the heterogeneity of capital goods would be to relax the assumption that there are only two factors and to interpret a country's 'endowment of capital' as a given *set* of physically specified capital goods.[2] (The simple analysis with two factors and two commodities could then be presented as a useful first step toward the full analysis.) Such an interpretation of capital endowment would, however, be out of place in a theory of comparative advantage, since the latter 'would seem properly to be a long-run theory'[3] and, by definition, in a long-run equilibrium analysis, the stocks of physical capital goods are not given but have been so chosen (by profit-maximising capitalists) as to yield a uniform rate of return. The normal concern of HOS trade theory has always been the comparison of long-run equilibria and in such analyses the assumption of given sets of capital goods can have no place.[4]

Assumption (b) can, however, be given an alternative interpretation which is quite consistent with the existence of many different capital goods, namely, that the capital endowment consists of a given equilibrium value of capital in terms of some standard of value.[5] The physical composition of the capital

[1] The HOS theory is also *logically* unassailable if the second resource is taken to be homogeneous land.

[2] Since our objection to such a procedure does not turn on the well-known problems which arise when the number of factors is different from the number of commodities, the reader may assume that the number of commodities is assumed to increase *pari passu*.

[3] Robinson [13, p. 23].*

Cf. Kenen's statement; 'Because trade theory is concerned with long-run phenomena, it must treat capital as a stock of "waiting", not as a collection of tangible assets' [9, p. 438]. It may also be noted that with given *sets* of capital goods a distinctive feature of HOS theory, the comparison of the countries' relative capital endowments, would be lost.

[4] To avoid a possible ambiguity, it should be noted that the usual HOS analysis is, in the sense given by Robbins [12], a static and not a stationary analysis.

[5] Cf. Caves [4, pp. 94–6] and the references there given to Ohlin and   *(contd.)*

* Numbers in square brackets relate to References on pp. 59–60.

stock is then free to vary in accordance with the variations in the pattern of consumption commodity output, provided only that the value of the stock is constant and equal to the given capital endowment. Since a central feature of HOS trade theory is that no-trade factor prices are related to factor endowments we can, indeed, say that, with heterogeneous capital goods, we *have* to interpret the capital endowment as a value of capital. If there are many different capital goods then the 'price of capital' can only mean the rate of interest and the only 'factor quantity' to which a rate of interest can be related is, ultimately, a value of capital.[1]

That the 'capital endowment' has been taken to be a value aggregate is strikingly confirmed by the discussion of the Leontief paradox.[2] In both his papers, Leontief measured 'capital' in value units and while the ensuing discussion of his tests of HOS theory has been both long and highly critical, no one has ever questioned, so far as we know, the appropriateness of using a value measure of capital when testing the HOS theory. (Indeed those who have sought to remove the paradox by taking account of 'human capital' have done so precisely by summing human and non-human capital in value terms.) We would suggest that anyone wishing to argue that the capital endowment has *not* been taken to be a value aggregate is obliged to explain why, in that case, Leontief's work has been thought to constitute a test of HOS theory.

In this paper we shall therefore assume that each country has a given endowment of 'capital value' measured, let us say, in terms of the first consumption commodity.[3] We not only ignore the possibility of international transfers of 'free' capital but also rule out the possibility of trade in produced means of production; the latter assumption is made simply in order to confine our attention to the normal static HOS analysis, in which only consumption commodities are traded.

3. Two crucial relationships

The HOS analysis depends crucially on the properties of two relationships;

1. The consumption commodity price ratio is monotonically related to the rate of interest;

[1] We say 'ultimately' because, of course, theories have been constructed in which the rate of interest is related to the value of capital only indirectly, there being one or more intervening variables, such as an average period of production or a number of absolute periods of production. Note that in his discussion of trade theory Wicksell assumed explicitly that the available quantity of capital in a country is a sum of value in terms of some standard [18, p. 198].

[2] For references, see the section on The Leontief Paradox, below.

[3] Since the no-trade commodity price ratio will differ between the two countries, it follows that the country ranking by 'capital'-labour ratio may depend on the choice of value standard. While this would appear to be rather awkward for HOS trade theory, it is not important for our argument.

Haberler. This interpretation of capital endowment appears, often implicitly, in much of the HOS literature. It has recently been given quite explicitly by Acheson [1, pp. 565–6], who also discusses the frequent implicit use of this interpretation.

2. The rate of interest is monotonically related to the capital-labour ratio in the production of each commodity.

These relations are displayed in Fig 4.1

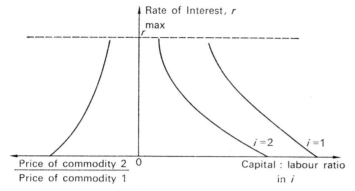

FIG 4.1

The righthand side of Fig 4.1 illustrates the relationship between the rate of interest and the capital : labour ratios in the two consumption commodity industries, industry one being the more capital intensive at each rate of interest. Notionally higher rates of interest are associated with more labour intensive processes of production in each industry and with a lower relative price of commodity two, as shown in the lefthand side of Fig 4.1. That there is no objection to using the rate of interest on the vertical axis, rather than a rent/wage ratio, has been shown by Samuelson.[1] It will be clear that this formulation with the rate of interest has to be used in a discussion of the multi-capital good world, since in such a world, in long-run equilibrium, the rate of interest must be uniform on the value of all capital goods while the rentals on different capital goods will, in general, differ.

Now if assumption (b) is interpreted to mean that the non-labour resource is a single homogeneous capital good, then the relationships 1 and 2 do indeed follow from assumptions (b) to (d). However, if assumption (b) is interpreted in terms of homogeneous labour and a given *value* of capital, then these two crucial relationships are *not* entailed by assumptions (b) to (d). The next section of this paper will be devoted to a proof of this assertion by means of a numerical example. In the subsequent sections we shall discuss the implications of this assertion for the fundamental theorems in HOS trade theory.

4. A numerical example

In this section we present a numerical example of an economy in which net output consists of quantities of two consumption commodities. Each

---

[2] See [14], p. 43, figure 2. Note that this presupposes the reproducibility of the capital good(s); cf. Kemp [8], pp. 82–3.

consumption commodity is produced in its own integrated sector, a sector, that is, which produces the consumption commodity in question by means of labour and a machine and also produces that machine by means of labour and further machines of the same type. The *kind* of machine used will vary as the rate of interest varies but at any given interest rate the same kind of machine is used in the production of machines and of the consumption commodity.[1] We are able to refer to the use of machines, rather than machine services, in production since all machines in our example are fully used up (worn out) within one year. In both sectors there is an infinite number of alternative constant-returns-to-scale methods of producing the consumption commodity; thus we make the normal assumptions about the available methods of production.

Since production is by means of labour and *heterogeneous* capital goods, we mean the *value* of capital per worker when we refer to the capital intensity in either sector and if we are to compare the capital intensities in the two sectors, as we need to, we must value the capital in the two sectors in terms of a common standard. We use as our common standard of value the first consumption commodity. Our example has been so constructed that, in the sense just explained, production of the first consumption commodity is more capital-intensive than that of the second at every interest rate. There is, in other words, *no* 'factor-intensity-reversal' in our example and we may unambiguously refer to the first consumption commodity as the more capital-intensive commodity.

We take as our first integrated sector, the sector producing the first consumption commodity, the sector for which the relevant data are set out in Table II of the Appendix to Garegnani's paper [6], p. 429. This table gives, for thirteen alternative values of the interest rate, r, the value of the wage in terms of the first consumption commodity, w_1 say, and the value of capital per worker, in the integrated sector, in the same standard, k_1 say. We take as our second integrated sector, producing the second consumption commodity, a sector which belongs to the family of sectors discussed by Garegnani [6, pp. 431–2]. In this second sector, the wage in terms of the *second* consumption commodity, w_2, is given by

$$w_2 = 1 - r - 20r^2$$

and the value of capital per worker, in terms of the *second* consumption commodity, k_2' is given by

$$k_2' = 1 - 10r + 50r^2$$

For each of the interest rates appearing in Garegnani's Table II we can calculate w_2 and k_2'; the price ratio of the two consumption commodities, (p_2/p_1), is then calculated[2] from $(p_2/p_1) = (w_1/w_2)$ and the capital-intensity

---

[1] There is no relation between the kinds of machine used in the two, different, integrated sectors at a given interest rate.

[2] At $r = 20$ per cent, $w_1 = w_2 = 0$ and in calculating (p_2/p_1) we therefore replaced (w_1/w_2) by the limit of (w_1/w_2) as r tends to 20 per cent.

in sector two, in terms of the *first* consumption commodity, k_2, is calculated from $k_2 = (p_2/p_1)k_2'$. We thus obtain our Table 4.1.

TABLE 4.1

$r\%$	(p_2/p_1)	k_1	k_2
0	0·200	1·080	0·200
2·6	0·182	0·635	0·141
4·1	0·183	0·393	0·123
6·1	0·184	0·257	0·106
8·3	0·194	0·184	0·100
10·5	0·213	0·148	0·107
12·9	0·240	0·179	0·130
14·4	0·238	0·379	0·142
15·1	0·211	0·552	0·133
15·9	0·182	0·715	0·123
16·9	0·158	0·850	0·117
17·5	0·122	0·947	0·095
20·0	0·103	1·000	0·103

On plotting the price ratio and the two capital-intensities as functions of the interest rate, in the usual way, we obtain Fig 4.2.

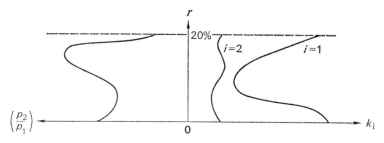

FIG 4.2

It will be seen at once that Fig 4.2 is strikingly different from Fig 4.1. On the righthand side we find that in neither sector is there an inverse, monotonic relation between the interest rate and the capital-intensity of the technique used. On the lefthand side we find that, despite the complete absence of 'factor-reversal' on the righthand side, there is not a monotonic relation between the consumption commodity price ratio and the rate of interest. Thus both the crucial relations on which HOS trade theory rests are, in general, invalid when there are heterogeneous capital goods, even when all the normal linear process assumptions are made about the available methods of production.[1]

5. The basic theorem

We now use the results of the last section to discuss the fundamental propositions of the Heckscher–Ohlin–Samuelson analysis; we naturally start with the basic theorem relating the pattern of trade to the relative 'factor endowments' of the two countries. This basic theorem may be stated in two alternative forms, corresponding to 'price' and to 'quantity' interpretations of relative factor endowment. When the two factors are 'capital' and labour and their relative 'prices' are expressed by the rate of interest, these two forms of the theorem become:

1. The country with the lower *no-trade* rate of interest will export the capital-intensive consumption commodity;
2. The country with the higher ratio of capital to labour will export the capital-intensive consumption commodity.

We have shown in our example that, when capital goods are heterogeneous, the usual assumptions (*a*) to (*f*) do not entail the existence of a monotonic relation between the rate of interest and the consumption commodity price ratio. It follows immediately that the basic theorem in form 1, the 'price' form, is not of general validity when capital goods are heterogeneous. (This is easily seen from the lefthand side of Fig 4.2.)

The failure of the basic theorem in its 'price' form leads, in turn, to the conclusion that it is not of general validity in its 'quantity' form, form 2 above, even if the country with the higher ratio of capital to labour has the lower no-trade interest rate.[2] All that would be guaranteed by an inverse relation between relative capital–labour ratios and relative no-trade interest rates would be that the theorem either gave a correct prediction in both forms or gave a false prediction in both forms. If there is not such an inverse relation then the basic theorem could give a correct prediction in one form and a false prediction in the other form. More important, however, is the simple result that, with heterogeneous capital goods and endowments of 'value capital', neither form of the basic theorem is of general validity; the assumptions (*a*) to (*f*) do not lead to any predictions about the pattern of trade.

---

[1] We have not asserted, it may be noted, that in the presence of heterogeneous capital goods both the crucial relations *inevitably* break down. One can, at will, construct numerical examples in which both relations hold, in which neither holds or in which one holds but the other does not; all that is necessary for our argument is that the two relations do not *necessarily* hold good. While most of our argument will turn on the non-monotonicity of the interest-rate/price ratio relation, it must be remembered that the conditions for the possibility of incomplete specialisation are generally discussed in terms of the righthand side of the standard diagram.

[2] It should not be taken for granted that there would be an inverse relation between relative capital–labour ratios and no-trade interest rates.

6. The Stolper–Samuelson theorem

The Stolper–Samuelson theorem states, essentially, that an increase in the domestic relative price of a consumption commodity will raise the real return to the factor used relatively intensively in the production of that commodity. Since this result depends on there being a monotonic relationship between the consumption commodity price ratio and the interest rate, our example shows that it is not of general validity in a world with heterogeneous capital goods.

Consider country B and suppose that it is importing consumption commodity two, the labour intensive commodity, at international terms of trade p. In Fig 4.3 these terms of trade are consistent with interest rates of r_1, r_2 and r_3 in B.

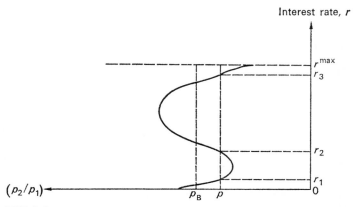

FIG 4.3

Suppose now that a tariff is imposed on B's imports and that, as in the original Stolper–Samuelson analysis [16], the imposition of the tariff leaves the international price ratio, p, unaltered. The domestic consumption commodity price ratio will increase to, say, p_B but whether the interest rate will rise or fall it is impossible to say. If, for example, the no-tariff interest rate were r_2 then, even if the tariff led to the smallest of the three possible interest rate changes in Fig 4.3, the with-tariff interest rate would be higher than r_2.[1] Now in any system of production involving no joint products, the interest rate is inversely related to the real wage rate, no matter what (single or composite) commodity the latter is measured in terms of:[2] a rise in the interest rate would then imply a fall in the real wage. Since, as we have seen, a tariff on the labour-intensive import can *raise* the interest rate, it follows that such a tariff can *lower* the real wage. With heterogeneous capital goods, there is no *a priori* relation between the consumption commodity price ratio and the real

---

[1] Of the two with-tariff interest rates involving 'larger' interest rate changes in Fig 4.3, one would be above r_2 and the other below it.
[2] With joint production, the interest rate may be positively related to the real wage in terms of certain commodities (see Sraffa [15, pp. 61–2]) but such a relation would not, of course, serve to restore the validity of the Stolper–Samuelson theorem.

wage, even in the absence of 'factor reversal', and hence the HOS analysis tells us nothing about the effect of a tariff on income distribution, even when the terms of trade are unaffected by the tariff.

7. Equalisation of the interest rate and real wage

As we have shown by means of our numerical example, in a world with heterogeneous capital goods there need not be a one-to-one relation between the consumption commodity price ratio and the rate of interest. It follows immediately that free trade in the two consumption commodities does *not* guarantee that both countries have the same interest rate and real wage when they trade with one another, even if specialisation is incomplete in both countries.[1]

8. The Leontief paradox

We consider, finally, Leontief's statistical findings [10, 11] that the ratio of value capital to labour in the production of US exports was less than the corresponding ratio for competitive US imports. Since the USA is generally considered to be abundantly endowed with capital per worker relative to its major trading partners, these findings appeared to contradict the basic HOS theorem in its 'quantity' form.[2] A common response to this 'paradox' was to modify the assumptions (a) to (f) so as to obtain predictions consistent with Leontief's findings.[3] We have shown above, however, that, in the presence of heterogeneous capital goods, there is no need to modify any of the assumptions in order to remove the 'paradox'; it is sufficient to recognise that when the endowment of capital means the value of capital, the HOS analysis gives no prediction whatever concerning the pattern of trade and thus neither Leontief's findings nor any other empirical findings relating to the pattern of trade can be regarded as 'paradoxical'.

9. Conclusion

The Heckscher–Ohlin–Samuelson analysis of trade has always been concerned with the comparison of static long-run equilibria. In such a comparison, in a world of heterogeneous capital goods, the assumption that each country has a given endowment of capital must be interpreted to mean that it has a given value of capital. It then follows, from recent work in the theory of capital, that there is no rational basis for the existence of the two crucial relations on which HOS analysis turns. It follows that the basic HOS theorem (in either

[1] This result might appear to conflict with Samuelson's conclusion [14], p. 49, but in fact, as Bliss has pointed out [3], pp. 342–3, Samuelson's 'conclusion' is quite empty, in effect stating that equalisation will occur when conditions are such as to make it occur.
[2] See Bhagwati [2], pp. 24–5, for a discussion of similar studies relating to Canada, East Germany, India and Japan.
[3] e.g. Clemhout [5], Jones [7], Valavanis-Vail [17].

form), the Stolper–Samuelson theorem and the interest-rate equalisation theorem all cease to hold. For an analysis of real-world trade the HOS analysis is therefore of somewhat limited use.

Recent arguments in the theory of capital, value and distribution have not only undermined the theoretical foundations of the HOS analysis, i.e. the neoclassical analysis of value and distribution: they have also suggested that the work of the classical economists, such as Ricardo, may prove to be a valuable starting point for the analysis of capital, value and distribution.[1] This suggests that it may be fruitful for trade theorists to return to Ricardo's approach to the analysis of trade. In saying this, we do not suggest that no-trade price ratios should be assumed to be equal to embodied labour ratios, for the essential features of Ricardo's approach can be retained without that assumption. Nor do we suggest that the role of capital and interest should be glossed over, as it is in much analysis described as 'Ricardian'; on the contrary, we suggest first that trade theorists might follow Ricardo in regarding the theory of distribution as a major concern of economic theory and second that the production of and trade in produced means of production should be placed at the centre of trade theory.

References

1. ACHESON, K. 'The aggregation of heterogeneous capital goods and various trade theorems', *Journal of Political Economy*, **70** (1970), 565–71.
2. BHAGWATI, J. 'The pure theory of international trade: a survey', *Economic Journal*, **74** (1964), 1–84.
3. BLISS, C. J. 'Collected scientific papers of Paul Samuelson', *Economic Journal*, **77** (1967), 338–45.
4. CAVES, R. E. *Trade and Economic Structure*, Harvard University Press, 1960.
5. CLEMHOUT, S. 'Production function analysis applied to the Leontief scarce-factor paradox of international trade', *Manchester School*, **31** (1963), pp. 103–14.
6. GAREGNANI, P. 'Heterogeneous capital, the production function and the theory of distribution', *Review of Economic Studies*, **37** (1970), 407–36.
7. JONES, R. 'Factor proportions and the Heckscher–Ohlin theorem', *Review of Economic Studies*, **24** (1956–7), 1–10.
8. KEMP, M. C. *The Pure Theory of International Trade and Investment*, Prentice Hall, 1969.
9. KENEN, P. B. 'Nature, Capital and Trade', *Journal of Political Economy*, **73** (1965), 437–60.
10. LEONTIEF, W. 'Domestic production and foreign trade: the American capital position re-examined', *Proceedings of the American Philosophical Society*, **97** (1953), 332–49.
11. LEONTIEF, W. 'Factor proportions and the structure of American trade: further theoretical and empirical analysis', *Review of Economics and Statistics*, **38** (1956), 386–407.
12. ROBBINS, L. 'On a certain ambiguity in the conception of stationary equilibrium', *Economic Journal*, **40** (1930), 194–214.
13. ROBINSON, R. 'Factor proportions and comparative advantage: Part I', *Quarterly Journal of Economics*, **70** (1956), 169–92.
14. SAMUELSON, P. A. 'Equalization by trade of the interest rate along with the real wage', in *Trade, Growth and the Balance of Payments; Essays in Honour of Gottfried Haberler*, ed. R. E. Baldwin, *et al.* North Holland, 1965.
15. SRAFFA, P. *Production of Commodities by Means of Commodities*, Cambridge University Press, 1960.

[1] We have in mind particularly, of course, the work of Sraffa [15].

16. STOLPER, W. F. and SAMUELSON, P. A. 'Protection and real wages', *Review of Economic Studies*, **9** (1941), 58–73.
17. VALAVANIS-VAIL, S., 'Leontief's Scarce Factor Paradox', *Journal of Political Economy*, **62** (1954), 523–8.
18. WICKSELL, K., *Lectures on Political Economy*, Vol. 1, Routledge & Kegan Paul, 1934.

Heterogeneous capital and the Heckscher–Ohlin–Samuelson theory of trade: Discussion

C. J. Bliss

The authors should be thanked for bringing to our attention a subject of great importance and one badly neglected in the published literature: the implication for trade theory of produced capital goods. The subject has suffered here from overspecialisation in that trade theorists too seldom know much about the theory of capital and have sometimes treated the problems that it raises rather roughly. Metcalfe and Steedman have studied their capital theory but have perhaps exaggerated the extent to which it is the peculiarities of capital theory that are responsible for the results at which they arrive.

The conclusions of the paper could be viewed in a very different light from that chosen by the authors, as follows. If we introduce produced capital goods that are not traded, then we are introducing non-traded intermediate goods (which in this case are also capital goods in that they earn a common rate of return on their value). Is there a factor–price equalisation theorem for an economy with more than one-traded intermediate good? There is no such result. Thus heterogeneous capital in this case brings no new feature not already involved in allowing produced goods to be used as productive inputs but not enter into trade. Suppose on the other hand that we assume every produced good to be traded: then it is not difficult to show that any condition sufficient for the factor–price equalisation theorem without capital goods will suffice with capital goods. Furthermore, it is clear that much weaker conditions would do for the capital good case, although these conditions have not yet been derived. A result which can be used to reach a factor–price equalisation conclusion in the usual type of discussion, not recognising capital goods, is the theorem due to D. Gale and H. Nikaidô [2]. As it happens the Gale–Nikaidô result is rather unsatisfactory, being a formal result devoid of the kind of economic interpretation that is available in the two-by-two case. But to say this is to say that we really have not got a usable factor–price equalisation theory beyond the two-good case, and this is true without capital goods, and the introduction of capital goods will certainly not make this situation worse—if the conditions of the Gale–Nikaidô theorem are satisfied we will get factor–price equalisation anyway given the usual postulates—

no specialisation, etc. However, we might dispense with such a stringent condition by exploiting the extra information provided by the knowledge that some goods used as inputs must have a price structure identical to that pertaining to those same goods produced as outputs. Far from concluding that a factor–price equalisation theory will demand even more stringent assumptions when capital goods are admitted; when the capital goods are traded we reach precisely the opposite conclusion.

To see why a Heckscher–Ohlin argument will fail when non-traded intermediates are included, consider an economy in which labour and land are used to produce at least two[1] intermediate goods which are then used together with labour to produce two final traded outputs. Assume that one of these goods is labour-intensive relative to the other good at all factor prices, here meaning that the share of labour in the value of output exceeds that of the other good. This is no guarantee that a rise in the wage rate will raise the relative price of the labour-intensive good, for such a change will also change the costs of production of the intermediate goods. Where the latter are capital goods this corresponds to the 'Wicksell Effect'. The resulting cost changes may dominate the direct effect of a wage change at given intermediate-good prices, which effect can be evaluated from intensity conditions. In short, relative intensity in the direct use of labour is no key to determining how relative costs will respond to a wage change, and this is equally true whether the indirect use of labour attracts an interest cost or whether it does not.[2]

It is a pity that the authors have given the impression by their emphasis on currently fashionable *curiosa* of capital theory that the observation that capital per man may not decline as the rate of interest rises has anything to do with the type of factor–price equalisation theory that they are seemingly considering. Whatever the importance of the observation for capital theoretic discussion as such, the theorem presently under consideration fails because of the existence of 'Wicksell Effects'—full stop. It fails whether these Wicksell Effects arise in an example which is 'traditional', 'well-behaved', 'regular', or whatever; or whether the example exhibits every feature to which Professor Garegnani would like to draw our attention. These particular issues of capital theory are simply not germane to the present discussion.

What happens if capital goods are traded? Perhaps one could regard this assumption as closer to the spirit of the early factor–price equalisation investigations without entering into meaningless discussions about what early writers held about questions that they did not consider. If labour is the only non-produced good, and if the conditions for the generalised non-substitution theorem held,[3] then all goods prices will be the same if the wage

[1] With one intermediate good there is no difficulty. A rise in the wage rate of labour must raise the cost of labour relatively to the intermediate good if any land is used to produce the latter. If then one final output is relatively labour-intensive an increase in the wage rate will increase its relative price. Similarly, with one capital good (a two sector model) no important new consideration is introduced: on this see Bhagwati [1].

[2] This point is obscured by Samuelson's discussion in [5] where he neglects to detail the conditions that would give rise to a monotonic relation between the interest rate and the relative price of two trade goods.

[3] On this theorem see Mirrlees [4].

rate is equalised between countries and all goods are produced in all countries. This last condition is most unlikely to be satisfied and a satisfactory theory would integrate with the discussion of price determination the problem of determining the pattern of international specialisation. The worst feature of the stress laid on the traditional discussion of factor–price equalisation in many expositions of international trade theory is that it mitigates against just this desirable integration. One might say further that if wage rates are not equalised then relative goods prices will very probably differ (one cannot quite say that they *must* differ) and this could be seen as the basis for specialised production and trade. I have seen an unpublished note by none other than Metcalfe and Steedman [3] making just this point.

Now we have here the beginnings of a factor–price equalisation discussion.[1] If relative prices are equalised when real wage rates are equalised, can we not conclude conversely that real wage rates will be equalised if relative goods-prices are equalised? Well, we certainly can reach no such conclusion immediately; we have to consider the possibility that the same structure of relative goods-prices might arise from two different values of the real wage. However, one sufficient condition to rule out this last possibility is immediately to hand. If the technical transformation possibilities satisfy the condition of Gale–Nikaidô we know that we go back from a structure of goods-prices to a unique structure of input costs, and hence in particular to a unique real wage rate. Furthermore this observation is only one example of the general observation that any condition sufficient to invert the mapping from input prices to output costs, which is what we are looking for in the usual factor–price equalisation investigation, will give us a unique wage rate in the present case.

It remains to note that this approach to the problem, which parallels the discussion of the case where inputs and outputs are distinct goods, throws away valuable information. Consider by way of example the case in which all capital goods are perfectly durable. Then we know that the vector of input prices of the services of capital goods (the capital rentals) must be proportional to the output price vector for those goods. This means that even if the mapping from input prices to output costs cannot be inverted, yet we may be able to identify a unique admissible inverse image because only one vector of input prices would both produce the required vector of output costs and also satisfy the proportionality condition for the produced goods. In principle then we should be able to produce a factor–price equalisation theorem for the problem proposed by the authors, but allowing trade in capital goods, with sufficient conditions much weaker than the Gale–Nikaidô condition. Far from making this particular academic exercise more difficult the introduction of produced capital goods should make it somewhat easier.

It seems that the factor–price equalisation theory is less vulnerable to the

---

[1] Which is surely the one that Samuelson had in mind when he embarked upon the penultimate section of his paper [5]. How else could the references to the non- substitution theorem be explained when that theorem is nowhere used and nowhere relevant to what he actually does?

64   C. R. Bliss

introduction of capital goods than the authors have maintained. However-any assumption which expands the number of goods that have to be considered will tend to undermine the assumption (which is not only unrealistic but is also illegitimately postulated prior to the economic analysis of the solution for world equilibrium) that there is no specialisation in production. On this ground alone the consideration of heterogeneous capital goods by Metcalfe and Steedman is to be welcomed.

References

1. BHAGWATI, J. 'The pure theory of international trade: a survey', *Economic Journal*, **74** (March 1964), 1–84.
2. GALE, D. and NIKAIDÔ, H., 'The Jacobian matrix and the global univalance of mappings', *Matematische Annalen*, **159** (1965), 81–93.
3. METCALFE, J. S. and STEEDMAN, I. 'The non-substitution theorem and international trade theory', unpublished note.
4. MIRRLEES, J. A. 'The dynamic non-substitution theorem', *Review of Economic Studies* (1969), 67–76.
5. SAMUELSON, P. A. 'Equalization by trade of the interest rate along with the real wage', in *Trade Growth and the Balance of Payments: Essays in Honour of Gottfried Haberler*, ed. R. E. Baldwin *et al.*, Rand McNally, 1965.

Income and the demand for housing: some evidence for Great Britain[1,2]

5

I. C. R. Byatt, A. E. Holmans and D. E. W. Laidler

1. Summary

This paper reports the results of some econometric work on the income elasticity of demand for housing in Great Britain. These results are, however, partial in three senses. First, they are derived from analysis of the behaviour of owner-occupiers and, as far as this is possible, of tenants in non-controlled private tenancies. Second, in the circumstances of the British housing market, many households probably increase their consumption of housing by switching between sectors, notably from being tenants to becoming owner-occupiers. Third, these results make no allowance for the effect of income on the rate household formation—or on the demand for a second house.

The studies show that this partial income elasticity for owner-occupiers is unlikely to exceed unity by any large amount; it could well be somewhat lower, perhaps as low as 0·75. For private renters it appears to be lower than for owner-occupiers.

The analysis of the cross-sectional data provided a highly consistent pattern of results, and taken at face value results seem very well based. But there is reason to suspect a downward bias in parameter estimates coming from our regressions and the figures just quoted allow for some correction to this bias —corrections which are unfortunately speculative.

Considering the innumerable factors which influence people's expenditure

[1] This paper reports on work carried out in the Department of the Environment (and formerly in the Ministry of Housing and Local Government). The first two authors are Director of Economics and Senior Economic Adviser respectively; the third is Professor of Economics in the University of Manchester and was acting as consultant to the Department. We are especially indebted to Mrs Yvonne Thresh, who took charge of all the data handling for the main bulk of the work. We are also indebted to numerous colleagues in the Department who have been involved in the work; in particular to Andrew W. Evans, David Stanton, and K. Wallis (a former consultant to MHLG). Computations were made by HMSO and IBM; an early pilot study was analysed at the National Physical Laboratory. We wish to thank the Department for permission to publish these results.

[2] Editor's Note: The discovery of a computer programming error during the proof stage led to this paper and the discussion by Professor Nicholson undergoing major last minute changes.

on housing, and given the very large sample sizes, these studies were successful in 'explaining' a large amount of the variance found in practice. The R^2s emerging from the studies were typically of the order 0·5 to 0·6. This is an encouraging result and should prove useful in forecasting work. But much is still to be done to improve our understanding of the relationship between income and the demand for housing, in particular to deal adequately with the role of income in moves between tenures and to separate the effects of occupation and income on choice of tenure and expenditure on housing within the owner-occupied sector.

2. The background to the quantitative work

Most of the literature (surveyed in [7]* and [4]) on the income elasticity of demand for housing relates to the United States. British work has been sparse [11], and not until 1971 was there published a monograph on income elasticities of demand for housing in Great Britain [1], although the subject was previously mentioned in the course of analyses of consumers' expenditure generally [10, 8]. The contrast with the United States may partly be explained in terms of the data available, though this can only be a superficial explanation since data can almost always be collected if the need is thought to be sufficiently great.

Of equal importance is probably the structure of the British housing market, and in particular the importance since World War I of rent control and building by public authorities for letting at subsidised rents. Within these sectors of the housing market, the relationship between the occupier's income and his expenditure on housing is determined in a very different way from the relationship in the owner-occupied and non-controlled sector. Moreover, since 1919 a substantial amount of new investment in housing in Britain has been made by public authorities, which makes time series analysis of the relationship between gross fixed investment, or the value of the total housing stock, and national income virtually meaningless as a way of measuring the income elasticity of demand for housing. If the dependent variable is to be gross fixed investment in housing by the private sector, then there is a complex problem to be solved about the cross-relationship between public and private investment [2].

The implications of the foregoing paragraph are:
(a) It is not appropriate to use evidence from controlled private lettings or from the public sector in order to estimate income elasticities of demand for housing. Such a measure can only be estimated (and as will be seen, only in part) from data relating to owner-occupied houses and non-controlled private lettings. A significant but seldom commented on fact is that unless one goes back to before 1915, only for a few years in the 1930s and since around 1960 have more than one half of all British households lived in that part of the housing stock where the relationship between housing expenditure and income

are even in principle market determined, and hence susceptible to analysis in terms of the standard theory of consumer demand.

(b) The number and direction of moves between tenures and new households' choice of tenure, are important ways in which higher incomes affect the aggregate demand for housing. The influence of income on the choice between housing tenures, both by newly formed households setting up house and by continuing households who move, is—in British circumstances—a very important way in which higher income affects the demand for housing. Under present conditions in Britain, particularly both financing and tax arrangements, owner-occupation seems in general to be the preferred form of tenure for houses of otherwise similar characteristics. But it normally is also the most expensive in terms of initial outlay. Income and ownership of liquid assets impose constraints on the choice between tenures, as well as on expenditure on housing within the owner-occupied sector.

(c) A move from privately rented housing to owner-occupation adds to effective demand in the owner-occupied sector, and subject to qualifications about the number and quality of vacant houses on offer for sale there, to new building. But there is no offsetting reduction in building for renting in the private sector, because there is very little building there to reduce. The main effect of outward moves by former tenants becoming owner-occupiers is to reduce sharing or to increase vacancies; since so many private lettings are parts of houses or old houses in poor repair, it is not to be expected that many of them will be sold for owner-occupation. If all rents were market rents and money could be borrowed—at a price—to purchase any kind of living accommodation, market adjustments in rents, selling prices, and interest rates would probably prevent moves from privately rented accommodation to owner-occupation affecting the number of new houses built. But the British housing system is very different from such a hypothetical situation, and likely to remain so.

(d) Moves from local authority tenancies to owner-occupation have a similar effect on the demand for new houses for private owners, but a less predictable effect on total new building. The way in which local authorities respond to an increase in the number of vacancies, due to more tenants leaving to become owner-occupiers, will vary according to circumstances. Some may reduce their rate of building, particularly if they do not have many new applicants for tenancies; others may continue to build at the same rate in order to make greater inroads into their waiting lists or to enlarge their slum clearance programme.

Prima facie one would also expect that higher incomes would influence the rate of increase in the number of households. The tendency towards earlier marriage, the rise in proportion of newly married couples who set up on their own straight away instead of sharing temporarily with parents, and the increase in the number of young unmarried men and women who live as separate households, probably owes something to rising incomes. So may the tendency for elderly widowed householders to carry on longer in their own households rather than go and live as part of another household (usually that of a son or daughter) or in an institution. But the quantitative nature of the relationship between headship rates and income has yet to be investigated successfully. In addition, it would be surprising if the demand for second homes was not influenced by income levels.

3. Data

These various aspects of the effect of income on the demand for housing have been discussed at some length, in order to set in context the results of the cross-sectional studies reported in the following sections—studies which examine exclusively the relationship between household income and household expenditure on housing within the owner-occupied sector and in the non-controlled part of the privately rented sector.

This relationship may, however, be investigated using two distinct sets of data: one may estimate the relationship for the whole household population, or defined subclasses of it: e.g. an age group or family type; alternatively one may estimate the relationship solely for those households that move.

Cross-section studies of whole populations have been extensively used in income elasticity work, especially in the United States. The US Census reports market value of owner-occupied houses (as returned by households) by Census Tract, along with data on income and household type. The Census in Britain does not report such information and for such studies it would be necessary to rely on survey data. We relied on such data in making the estimate of the income elasticity of demand for housing by tenants of non-controlled private lettings. But for owner-occupiers there would be serious problems involved in using the expenditure data collected by household surveys to measure consumption of housing services, as the most important element of expenditure—mortgage payments—is a poor proxy for consumption of housing services. Because of changes in house prices, in the proportion of the purchase price which can be borrowed, in interest rates, and in repayment periods, a householder who bought his house two years ago and a neighbour who bought an identical house seven years ago, would normally be making very different mortgage payments, even though the standard of housing they enjoy is the same.

Clark and Jones [1], avoided this problem by using rateable values as a measure of the standard of housing an owner-occupier enjoys. Rateable values could be used for this purpose with considerable effect if it could be shown that they were a suitable proxy for market prices. Further studies are needed in this area, but work carried out so far in the Department of the Environment does suggest that rateable values (probably gross rather than net) may be good enough as proxies for market value to be used in income elasticity work.

There are, however, important reasons for preferring to estimate the income elasticity from the data for households who move. Although housing quality can be increased by improvements, renovations and extensions, in general households are better able to vary their consumption of housing services by moving. For owner-occupiers, particularly with families, the financial costs and disruptive effects of moving are such as to be a strong dis-incentive to frequent moves. There are likely to be long lags (and on occasion long leads) in the adjustment of housing to changes in income and other circumstances. A move is an opportunity to adjust housing consumption to income, among other variables, and thus provides a particularly suitable opportunity for observing households' underlying behavioural relationships. Thus if the relationships are estimated from data relating to movers, the coefficients ought to be much better determined. On the other hand, if movers have different characteristics from householders generally, it would be possible to introduce bias by sampling movers only. However, the estimates of the income elasticities of demand for different groups in terms of age and region were not significantly different, so that sampling errors in the distribution by age or by region could not have a material effect on the elasticities.

The results reported here on the income elasticity of demand for housing for owner-occupiers came from analyses of transactions financed by mortgages from building societies. There might be some advantage if the data used could be extended to cover transactions financed in other ways, but at the time the material drawn from building society sources was all that was available. Since 1966, the Government has carried out a 5 per cent sample survey of building society mortgages,[1] recording the price paid, the amount, term and rate of interest on the mortgages, some characteristics of the house, the purchaser's income, his age and sex, and (since April 1968) his previous tenure. In addition, a special survey was undertaken in February 1970 to collect additional information, including the family circumstances of the purchaser and, for those selling one house and buying another, the price received for the house being sold.

Although building societies financed about three-quarters of all sales of new houses, and something close to two-thirds of other house sales during the period studied (1967–68 and February 1970), these transactions were probably not representative of all transactions. Building societies do not often finance the purchase of the poorest and cheapest houses; they play a relatively less prominent part in financing the purchase of the most expensive houses. They lend at standard rates and tend to reject risky business, rather than accept it at an enhanced interest rate. They have a body of custom and practice about what may be lent in relation to income, in which not all kinds of income confer the same borrowing power. There is a possibility therefore that a study using data derived from building society transactions will analyse not so much the economic behaviour of house purchasers as the lending policy of the building societies. But examination of the data, in particular comparison of the relationship of average mortgage to income in areas where house prices are low with areas where house prices are high, shows that households tend to borrow less in relation to income where prices are relatively low. Also, in the income elasticity analysis, the influence of the availability of building society funds—as reported later in this paper—was shown to have only a

[1] A description is given in [3].

very minor influence on the measured income elasticity. It is probably safe to conclude that data on housing transactions drawn from building society sources does show something about the economic behaviour of house purchasers, and not merely about building society practice.

The conventional procedure for estimating the income elasticity of demand for housing would be to regress the logarithm of housing expenditure on that of income, using a model of the form:

$$\log P = a + b \log Y + c_1 z_1 + \ldots + c_n z_n + u \qquad (1)$$
where P = house price, or rent where relevant
and Y = income and $z_1 \ldots z_n$ are dummy variables

so that the estimate of b, $\hat{b}_1$ is a direct estimate of the income elasticity. However, before we can take such an estimate at face value, we must consider the question of whether or not it is likely to be biased. There are a number of reasons why some bias—in an upward as well as a downward direction—may be present. In this paper we can only concentrate on what we consider to be the more important ones. One important source of such bias is measurement error in the independent variable.

It is to be expected that housing expenditure decisions are related to the income which a household expects to have over a fairly long period of time. The existence of significant monetary and non-monetary movement costs is a sufficient justification for this view. A particular version of this view is the hypothesis that housing expenditure is determined by a household's 'permanent income'—in Friedman's sense of the term. Because current income is an imperfect measure of permanent income, the permanent income hypothesis predicts the existence of downward bias in the marginal propensity to consume measured in cross-sectional consumption function studies, and in income elasticities estimated from cross-sectional housing demand studies [5, 6, 9]. It is not necessary to argue the details of the matter at any length here; it is sufficient to note that it seems inappropriate to expect that households will always act only on the basis of their present incomes when planning housing expenditures.

Quite apart from this theoretical problem, the income as recorded by the building societies is not necessarily the whole of the mortgagor's current income. There are believed to be some households who declare only what they have to declare to get the mortgage they want, putting in spouse's earnings, regular overtime pay, etc. only if this is needed to meet the society's requirements about the income necessary to carry a given mortgage. On the other hand, building societies, working through a complex set of conventions which give different weight to different components of income, are concerned to discount temporary income which is associated with but not identical to transitory income as defined in the permanent income hypothesis.[1] An

---

[1] The building society data show the 'basic income' of the first applicant, as well as the total income declared to support the mortgage application. Although 'basic' income in this sense is by no means the same as long run or permanent income, some regressions were run on the 1966 pilot data, using 'basic' income as the income

associated point is that householders with temporarily low incomes would almost certainly wait until their income had returned to normal before applying for a loan.

These two considerations suggest that there may be significant measurement errors in the data and hence downward bias in $\hat{b}_1$.

A procedure used in some American studies, to allow for measurement error in the independent variable, is to regress income on house prices, i.e. to fit an equation of the form:

$$\log Y = a + \frac{1}{b} \log P + c_1 z_1 + \ldots + c_n z_n + v \qquad (2)$$

If the relationship between income and housing expenditure is an exact one, the regression of $\log Y$ on $\log P$ would give the same income elasticity estimate as the regression of $\log P$ on $\log Y$. But if there is some stochastic element present, either because there are measurement errors in either of the variables, or because the relationship between them is influenced by omitted variables, the two estimates will differ. As we have already noted, the presence of measurement errors in income will ensure that the regression of $\log P$ on $\log Y$ provides an underestimate of the income elasticity. There are many good reaons, however, for supposing that the relationship between housing expenditure and income is influenced by other variables, and that the housing expenditure variable is itself measured with some error. Thus the regression of $\log Y$ on $\log P$ will inevitably give an upward-biased estimate of the income elasticity. Regressions based on equation (2) may be used to estimate an upper limit to the value of the income elasticity of demand for housing, but there can be no presumption about whether the estimates that these regressions provide are nearer to the true value than those yielded by more conventional procedures.

One may carry the analysis somewhat further. Let measured income, Y, be the sum of permanent income Y_p, where this is defined as the income which determines housing expenditure and transitory income Y_t, where Y_t includes both transitory income in Friedman's sense of the term and all other measurement errors. It follows that the income variable in the regression equations should be $\log Y_p$ and that by using $\log Y$ instead we incur a measurement error, say w. That is:

$$\log Y = \log Y_p + w$$

The error is related to the transitory income by:

$$w = \log \left(1 + \frac{Y_t}{Y_p} \right)$$

As a result of the measurement error, the estimate, $\hat{b}_1$, of b obtained by using

---

variable. This was not a success; the calculated elasticities were much less consistent than calculated from total income data. The influence of 'non-basic' income, although small, was statistically significant.

log Y is biased. Provided w is independent of log Y_p and the random error term, the limit of $\hat{b}_1$ in probability is:

$$\hat{b}_1 \frac{\text{var (log } Y_p)}{\text{var (log } Y)}$$

and hence a consistent estimate of b is:

$$\hat{b}_1 \frac{\text{var (log } Y)}{\text{var (log } Y_p)}$$

Because actual incomes are easier to think about than their logarithms, it is helpful to note that, with reasonable assumptions, var (log Y)/var (log Y_p) is approximately the same as var (Y)/var (Y_p); if Y_p and Y_t are independent, or nearly so, this in turn is approximately the same as $[1 + \text{var } (Y_t)/\text{var } (Y_p)]$. Hence a consistent estimate of b is approximately:

$$\hat{b}_1 \left[1 + \frac{\text{var } (Y_t)}{\text{var } (Y_p)} \right]$$

This relationship can be used to make plausible guesses about the likely 'true' value of the income elasticity of demand for housing, and we shall do so below when discussing the results based on building society data.

Another way of tackling the measurement error problem is to note that, according to the permanent income hypothesis, consumer expenditure is linearly related, with a zero intercept, to permanent income. For this and other reasons expenditure may be used as a proxy variable for permanent income. The Family Expenditure Survey provide such expenditure data for renters and we used them in the course of our study of the income elasticity demand for rented housing. For obvious reasons of lack of data, we were unable to follow this procedure when dealing with building society survey data on owner-occupiers.

Quite apart from the measurement error problem, is that of bias in the data themselves. De Leeuw [4] argues that an American study of owner-occupiers [12] using transactions financed by mortgages insured by the Federal Housing Administration, underestimates the true income elasticity of demand, on the ground that those low-income purchasers who obtained FHA-insured mortgages had to spend an untypically large amount on housing in relation to their income (since FHA does not insure mortgages on poor properties), and that because there is an upper limit to the size of a mortgage that FHA may insure, those high income households with FHA mortgage were buying house whose prices were untypically low in relation to the purchasers' incomes. Similar arguments would apply, *prima facie*, to building society mortgages in Britain, particularly in view of the under-representation of sales of the cheapest and most expensive houses in building society transactions. However, building society mortgages predominate to a much greater extent in Britain than do FHA-insured mortgages in the USA, the bias—if there is one—would probably be smaller than that alleged by De Leeuw of

Winger's estimates. Although there must be some doubt about the matter until estimates of income elasticities can be made independently of building society data, the authors believe this is a less important source of potential bias in our results than those discussed above.

As for tenants, inability to exclude all rent-controlled tenancies from the sample could also lead to bias, though the number of such tenancies in the sample is believed to be small and the bias therefore not substantial.

4. The quantitative studies: results

Owner-occupiers

The first study whose results are reported here used transactions included in the Department of Environment's sample survey of building society mortgages in the second half of 1967 and the second half of 1968. The periods chosen permit investigation of the effect of the availability of building society mortgage finance; in the second half of 1967, building societies had sufficient funds to meet most of demand from credit-worthy borrowers, whereas in the second half of 1968 there was fairly severe credit rationing.

In order to make the samples reasonably homogeneous, they were restricted to houses (with flats excluded) sold freehold with vacant possession and with bathroom and garage or garage space. They were further restricted to transactions where the mortgage was for a term of not less than twenty years or more than twenty-five years at the Building Societies' Association's recommended rate of interest. The building societies record income before tax, but one would expect expenditure on housing, like other consumers' expenditure, to be determined by income net of tax. The sample survey does not record the family circumstances of mortgagors and conversion to income net of tax was made by assuming, somewhat arbitrarily, that all mortgagors were married with one child, but entitled to no tax reliefs other than their personal reliefs and allowances and tax relief on mortgage interest, and that all their income attracted earned income relief.

A relationship of type (1) was fitted to the data: where P is the house price and Y is the recorded income of the purchaser, adjusted for income tax as described above. The reasons for logarithmic transformation were:

(a) the estimate coefficients, $\hat{b}_1$ yield elasticities direct;

(b) as long as the opportunity cost (imputed rent) of owner-occupied houses can be assumed to be a constant proportion of the price, for all buyers, the units of measurement do not affect the elasticity estimate.

An earlier small-scale study using data for a single month in 1966 showed that when the data were analysed separately by region, the individual income elasticities were less than that computed by using all the data for the country as a whole. A possible explanation for this is that an upward bias in the income elasticity estimate was introduced because of the regional correlation between high prices for housing of a given quality and high incomes. Also, assumption on (b) above may not hold on a sample of different age houses. Houses do not all have the same length of life and the (usual) appreciation in the value of the site may not be sufficient to offset the depreciation of the structure. In view of these results from the pilot study, equation (1) was fitted in the main study (whose results are summarised in Table 5.1) to the data for Great Britain as a whole and separately for Scotland, Wales and four sub-divisions of England, and separately for three age groups of house purchasers. Dummy

TABLE 5.1. *Initial estimates of income elasticities of demand for housing for owner-occupiers: building society samples*

	1967		1968	
	$\hat{b}_1$	R^2	$\hat{b}_1$	R^2
Great Britain	0·66 (0·01)	0·57	0·64 (0·01)	0·60
North	0·75 (0·02)	0·49	0·63 (0·02)	0·56
Midlands	0·64 (0·02)	0·41	0·64 (0·03)	0·53
South	0·63 (0·02)	0·44	0·65 (0·02)	0·54
Greater London	0·38 (0·04)	0·33	0·59 (0·05)	0·54
Scotland	0·67 (0·05)	0·47	0·46 (0·10)	0·44
Wales	0·55 (0·07)	0·38	0·68 (0·10)	0·55
Purchaser aged:				
30 and under	0·60 (0·02)	0·54	0·59 (0·02)	0·59
31–40	0·69 (0·02)	0·53	0·68 (0·02)	0·56
over 40	0·69 (0·02)	0·56	0·66) (0·03)	0·57

Full regression was of type (1):

$$\log P = a + b \log Y + c_1 z_1 + \ldots c_n z_n$$

where dummy variables were:

age of house—before 1919, 1919–39, postwar, new.
age of purchaser—30 and under, 31–40, over 40.
region—North, Midlands, South, Scotland, Wales.
previous tenure (1968 only)—previous owner-occupier, previous renter, others.

variables representing the age of houses (pre-1919—interwar, postwar and new) were used in all the equations; purchaser's age dummies were used in the regional and Great Britain analyses and regional dummies in the analysis for separate ages. The values of $\hat{b}_1$, the standard errors and R^2 are shown in Table 5.1.

TABLE 5.2. *'Maximum' measures of income elasticity of demand for housing: building society sample*

	$\hat{b}_2$	
	1967	1968
Great Britain	1·69	1·48
	(0·03)	(0·03)
North	1·69	1·43
	(0·04)	(0·05)
Midlands	1·79	1·47
	(0·07)	(0·06)
South	1·63	1·41
	(0·04)	(0·04)
Greater London	1·54	1·45
	(0·14)	(0·12)
Scotland	1·59	1·82
	(0·11)	(0·35)
Wales	2·23	1·76
	(0·25)	(0·22)
Purchaser aged:		
under 30	1·72	1·46
	(0·04)	(0·04)
30–39	1·74	1·50
	(0·05)	(0·05)
over 40	1·59	1·49
	(0·05)	(0·07)

Full equation was of type (2):

$$\log Y = a + \frac{1}{b} \log P + c_1 z_1 + \ldots + c_n z_n$$

where the dummy variables were the same as those shown below Table 5.1.
Standard errors were calculated from the formula:

$$\text{standard error of } \hat{b}_2 = \frac{\sigma}{(1/b)^2 + \sigma/b}$$

where σ is the standard error of $(1/b)$.

The results show a very consistent pattern over all regions and, with the exception of the under thirty age group—over all ages. The disparate values for Scotland and Wales are not surprising, given the high standard errors which are what would be expected from the small numbers in these samples. The low income elasticity values for London are significantly different from the other results. This probably results from the fact that the market prices of the lowest standard of house that the building societies will accept are much higher than elsewhere, so that the prices paid by the lowest income households in the sample will be higher in London than elsewhere. The residuals from these regressions were inspected and did not show any pattern that would suggest that the relationship was not log-linear.

When the 1967 coefficients are compared with those estimated from 1968 data, it will be seen that one of the values (for Greater London) is lower, two (the Midlands and South) are the same, and the rest are higher. But where the 1967 coefficients are higher than those for 1968, only in one instance (the North) is the difference statistically significant. Taking all the coefficients for the whole country, the regions, and the age groups together, the estimate of the income elasticity obtained from the 1968 data is not significantly lower than that obtained from the 1967 data, notwithstanding a reduction of 17 per cent in the number of advances by building societies between the second half of 1967 and the second half of 1968. That the measured income elasticity was so little affected by a sharp reduction in the availability of funds suggests that income elasticity estimates derived from building society data are not so vitiated by institutional factors as to be useless.

For reasons discussed above, the income elasticities reported in Table 5.1 cannot be taken at face value; they are certainly biased downward. We therefore obtained alternative estimates by fitting equation (2), using the same dummy variables. The resulting estimates of the income elasticity are shown in Table 5.2. Again, the pattern of the results is consistent, but the figures are greatly in excess of those given in Table 5.1. Further interpretation of these results is deferred until a later section of the paper.

The second study was an analysis of a special survey carried out in February 1970 with the assistance of the Abbey National Building Society. All offers of a mortgage advance in that month were accompanied by a questionnaire, and 2800 usable replies, a response rate of just under 50 per cent were received. Examination of the distribution of replies by income, previous tenure and price of houses purchased did not suggest any material bias resulting from the nature of the sample (one building society) or from non-response.

It was hoped that this survey would enable an improved estimate of the income elasticity to be made for the following reasons:

(a) because the data came from only one society, errors due to different societies adopting different conventions about what income should be recorded would be eliminated;

(b) the data on the composition of households could be used to derive a better

TABLE 5.3. *Initial estimate of income elasticity of demand for housing: special survey*

Income elasticity $\hat{b}_1$ 0·65 $R^2 = 0·69$
                 (0·01)

Significant dummy variables

Previous owner-occupier	House pre-1919	Regions				Purchaser under 30	Household composition			
		North	Midlands	Scotland	Wales		1 working adult	More than 2 adults	More than 2 working adults	Expected higher incomes
0·06	−0·06	−0·11	−0·07	−0·07	−0·07	−0·02	0·01	0·04	−0·05	0·02
(0·01)	(0·01)	(0·01)	(0·01)	(0·01)	(0·01)	(0·00)	(0·00)	(0·01)	(0·02)	(0·01)

estimate of tax liability by basing it on the actual number of children and their age; and so improve the estimate of income after tax;

(c) planned expenditure on improvements was added to the price paid, thereby getting a better measure of the expenditure variable; and

(d) for purchasers who were selling one house and buying another, a partial 'liquidity' measure was obtained by taking the price received for the house and deducting the outstanding mortgage on it.

The equations fitted to the data were of the same form as equations (1) and (2) above. No separate regional analyses were made, but dummy variables were used for age of purchaser, age of house, region, household composition and previous tenure. For the subsample of purchasers whose previous tenure was owner-occupier with mortgage, the 'liquidity' variable was included. The regressions were fitted using a stepwise procedure.

Table 5.3 shows the results of fitting equation (1) at the point in the stepwise regression, when all those variables which eventually became significant (at a 0·95 level) first appeared. The inclusion of dummy variables again reduced the income elasticity from 0·81 when house prices were regressed on income alone, to 0·65 when all eleven significant dummy variables were included in the regression. The dummies in question related to regional household compositions, pre-1919 house, purchaser under 30, previous owner-occupier, expected income higher.

The measured income elasticity, when the influence of dummy variables is allowed for, is not significantly higher than in the first study—which is rather surprising as it is to be expected that measurement errors in the income variable would be reduced. However, the fit was improved; the R^2s are higher. Equation (2), fitted without dummy variables, gave a 'maximum' income elasticity of 1·44.

TABLE 5.4. *Initial estimate of income elasticity of demand for housing previous owner-occupiers with mortgage special survey*

Income elasticity $\hat{b}_1$	0·75	$R^2 = 0·73$
	(0·02)	
Liquidity elasticity	0·19	
	(0·01)	

Significant dummy variables		
Age of house		Household composition
Pre-1919	1919–1939	2 adults in household
0·06	0·02	0·03
(0·02)	(0·01)	(0·01)

This analysis of the special survey therefore cast only limited light on the gap between the downward biased conventional estimates of the income elasticity derived from the building societies' 1967 and 1968 samples. An attempt was made to allow for different income expectations by including questions on previous and expected income and by inserting 'past income lower' and 'future income higher' dummies. Although the effect of an expectation of higher income was significant, and had the right sign, the inclusion of this dummy had no effect on the income elasticity itself. But it is possible that this resulted from the question being interpreted by respondents in terms of money income rather than real income.

The results of the analysis of the sub-sample of previous owner-occupiers with a mortgage, using equation (1) are shown in Table 5.4—again with all significant dummy variables included. Regional and age of purchaser dummies were not, however, used in this analysis. The results are interesting. The inclusion of a 'liquidity' variable results in an improved fit and a higher income elasticity. The 'maximum' income elasticity using equation (2), without the liquidity variable and without dummies, was 1·43.

The significance of the 'liquidity' elasticity is not surprising as casual observation suggests that capital gains on existing housing and saving on previous mortgages are important determinants of the amount that a household is prepared to pay for a new house. Given fixed interest borrowing, the value of the sale price of the house minus the mortgage will tend to increase much more rapidly than house prices. The analysis suggests that an increase of as much as 10 per cent in this amount will result in an increase of about 2 per cent in the price of a subsequent house purchased by the household. For the mean value of houses purchased in the survey (£6,200) this would be about £125. This result is consistent with the finding of both the 1967 and 1968 building society samples and the Special Survey that previous owner-occupiers spent significantly greater amounts on their housing, other things measured being equal, than did new and previously renting households. It is clear that further investigation of the influence of wealth and liquidity on house purchase promises to be illuminating.

Private tenants

Two sets of results are available from analyses of the Family Expenditure Survey; a preliminary analysis for the 1965 Survey and a more considered one for the 1968 one. Unfortunately for present purposes, the Family Expenditure Survey does not distinguish between controlled and non-controlled tenancies (many tenants do not know whether their lettings are controlled or not). However, a survey [13] undertaken in 1964 (there would have been further decontrol subsequently) showed that—in the privately rented sector —only 10 per cent of heads of households under 30 years old and only 20 per cent under forty lived in rent controlled accommodation. Thus all households with heads over forty were excluded. The inclusion of rent controlled properties would, of course, be likely to give some downward bias to the measured income elasticity; some small degree of such bias may still be present. On the other hand, the information on household composition enabled better adjustments to be made for tax. It was also possible to use household expenditure on non-durables as a proxy variable for permanent income. Dummies were used for regions (in the Great Britain analysis) and for household composition. The results, using equation (1), are shown in Table 5.5. The regional results have very high standard errors and very low R^2s. But the Great Britain results, especially where expenditure is used as a proxy for income, are in line with the results obtained for owner-occupiers. The 'maximum estimate', using equation (2), i.e. $\hat{b}_2$, are implausibly high; 4·8 when the expenditure proxy was used and 6·7 when recorded income was used.

TABLE 5.5. *Initial estimate of income elasticity of demand for housing private renters, 1968*

	Using measured post tax income		Using expenditure as a proxy for income	
	Income elasticity $\hat{b}_1$	R^2	Income elasticity $\hat{b}_1$	R^2
Great Britain	0·40 (0·09)	0·36	0·63 (0·09)	0·41
North	0·30 (0·18)	0·09	0·37 (0·17)	0·11
Midlands	0·60 (0·29)	0·33	0·67 (0·29)	0·35
South	0·19 (0·25)	0·21	0·43 (0·21)	0·25
Greater London	0·47 (0·15)	0·24	0·84 (0·17)	0·38

There were insufficient observations to make analyses for Scotland and Wales worth while.

In any case, the use of expenditure as a proxy for income ought, of itself, to deal with much of the measurement error bias when it is treated as the independent variable. Thus these 'maximum' estimates need not be regarded as being of importance. The reader will note from Table 5.5 that the use of expenditure as the independent variable systematically increases the income elasticity estimates.

The analysis of the 1965 *FES* data was essentially a pilot operation. Analyses were, however, made using rent plus rates, as well as rent only, as housing expenditure variables and distinguishing between the income of the head of the household and other household income where both elements were present. The analysis using household expenditure as an income proxy did not in this case exclude expenditure on durables. The results are shown in Table 5.6. They show:

(a) that the inclusion of rates makes no significant difference; and
(b) the apparently dominant importance of income of head of householder over other income;
(c) the use of expenditure as the independent variable significantly increases the income elasticity estimate.

TABLE 5.6. *Initial estimate of income elasticity of demand for housing private renters, 1965*

	$\hat{b}_1$			
	Household expenditure*	Household income†	Head of household income†	Other household income†
Rent only	0·89	0·79	0·46	0·16
	(0·16)	(0·19)	(0·21)	(0·04)
Rent plus rates	0·84	0·76	0·49	0·15
	(0·13)	(0·16)	(0·17)	(0·04)

* For all households, $N = 164$.
† For all households where not all income was that of the head, $N = 118$.

5. Interpretation of the results

A very clear pattern of results emerges from the three analyses. The use of conventional regression equations of type (1), results in an internally consistent measure of the income elasticity of demand for housing—for Great Britain of between 0·6 and 0·7. On the whole, the standard errors are low and the R^2s consistently high. (The *FES* analyses are of small samples of a population of all households, rather than movers.) Similar results have been obtained by all investigators—to the authors' knowledge—who have used data derived from building society transactions, and it is highly unlikely that further analysis of this type of data with similar statistical methods will yield significantly different results.

But, as we have stressed, there are reasons for suspecting bias. The principal use for which income elasticity estimates are required is to predict and explain the demand for housing over time. For many categories of consumers' expenditure, income elasticities estimated from cross-section data are liable to underestimate the longer run elasticities required for forecasting work. Moreover, values in the range 0·6 to 0·7 are materially lower than those reported in the United States [4] and Sweden [7]. The results of the regressions of type (2) suggest that the amount of bias *could* conceivably be as large as the measured income elasticity itself. Bias is unlikely to be so high, but the criticisms levelled against income elasticities of demand for housing which are well below unity [9] (Reid, 1962, and others) have *prima facie* application here.

In American work on housing demand, a method sometimes used to deal with the problem of measurement error is to take groups in which positive and negative transitory incomes offset one another, so that average measured income is a close approximation to average permanent income. In general, this has been done by isolating small geographical areas; but such data do not exist for Britain. Nor at the moment do British data allow analyses based on time series to be used to estimate the income elasticity of demand with respect to permanent (the term is used loosely) income. In these circumstances, perhaps the best that can be done is to consider the likely variance in the permanent and transitory components of income, and use such estimates to adjust the initial estimate of measured elasticity.

As was noted above that an unbiased estimate of b_1 the income elasticity of demand for housing is given by:

$$\hat{b}_1 \left[1 + \frac{\text{var}(Y_t)}{\text{var}(Y_p)} \right]$$

where $\hat{b}_1$ is the estimate obtained by regressing the log of housing expenditure on that of income.

Direct measures of var (Y_t) and var (Y_p) are not available, but some somewhat speculative conjectures may be made about their relative size. Some considerations that are relevant here are set out in the next paragraph, but since finality is not attainable from the evidence now available, it is useful to show what the true value of b would be on various assumptions about the value of the ratio var (Y_t)/var (Y_p).

One indication of the possible bias that can occur in estimating income elasticities from cross-sectional data is given by the results of work on the aggregate consumption function. Typically time series studies yield a marginal propensity to consume of around 0·9 compared with estimates of around 0·6 suggested by cross-sectional studies. But there would be obvious risks in applying to housing alone results derived from all consumers' expenditure. As the cost of varying the consumption of housing services is much greater than the cost of varying consumption of other goods and services, it would be reasonable to expect that the time horizon over which households plan their expenditure of housing services would be longer than for goods and services as a whole.[1] One way in which this longer time horizon could come into decisions on housing expenditure is through anticipating increases in income that accrue with age (e.g. through incremental salary scales). These considerations are likely to be most important for younger households, as in general incomes do not rise with age much beyond thirty.[2]

---

[1] There is little evidence on this. But Muth's (1962) results run counter to this hypothesis.
[2] See Table 77 of *New Earnings Survey 1970*, Department of Employment, 1971.

In Table 5.1 it is shown that the measured income elasticity is materially lower for households where the head is under the age of thirty, which tends to confirm the argument just advanced. Some of the bias arising from expenditure being related to anticipated income can be excluded by relying on an estimate of the income elasticity that excludes households where the head is aged under thirty. The results of our analyses for private renters also provides some evidence. The income elasticity estimated by using expenditure on non-durables as a proxy for normal income was some 50 per cent above that estimated from the same sample by using recorded income; this is consistent with a value of 0·55 for $\text{var}(Y_t)/\text{var}(Y_p)$ for renters. Finally, the fact that the sample of owner-occupiers is drawn from households who are buying houses with building society mortgages makes it unlikely that it will include many households whose incomes are untypically low. Since a prospective house buyer's income is an important determinant of how much a building society will lend to him, householders whose incomes are untypically low would generally wait until it had returned to normal before applying for a loan. This suggests that $\text{var}(Y_t)$ and hence perhaps $\text{var}(Y_t)/\text{var}(Y_p)$ is somewhat smaller for the population sampled in our surveys than for the total household population.

Another approach is to ask what value of $\text{var}(Y_t)/\text{var}(Y_p)$ would be necessary to yield the same estimated income elasticity of demand for housing with respect to permanent income as recent United States studies suggest, i.e. about unity, and then consider whether such a value is plausible. The answer, between 0·4 and 0·7, does not seem out of the question, but since nearly all the observations in our samples lay within the income range £1000 to £4000, and given the probability that it included very few households whose incomes are untypically low, we find it virtually impossible to believe that the variance of the transitory component of income could be any larger than that of its permanent component. These considerations lead us to the view that in the samples studied $\text{var}(Y_t)/\text{var}(Y_p)$ is most likely to lie within the range 0·25 to 0·75, and Table 5.7 was constructed on that basis.

TABLE 5.7. *Estimates of the 'adjusted' income elasticity of demand for housing in Britain: owner-occupiers*

$\dfrac{\text{var}(Y_t)}{\text{var}(Y_p)}$	Initial estimate of income elasticity of demand	
	0·6	0·7
0·25	0·75	0·9
0·50	0·90	1·05
0·75	0·98	1·23

6. Conclusion

To sum up, the work reported in this paper puts bounds on the likely value of the income elasticity of demand for owner-occupied housing in Great Britain, rather than giving any precise measure of that parameter. It is unlikely to be lower than 0·75, and also unlikely to exceed 1·25. Without further work on the relationship of measured to permanent income in the context of housing expenditure, or a new study in which the sample is so drawn as to reliably exclude households whose measured income includes a significant transitory component, it is not possible to be more precise than this. The estimates have a central tendency of 1·0; but since the upper values of the regression estimates exclude the households aged under thirty, these upper regression estimates and the upper value for var $(Y_t)/$var (Y_p) would seem to be somewhat a less probable combination. It would therefore not seem likely that the true value is much above unity, whereas 0·75 as a lower estimate does not require any unlikely combination of values. For private tenants, the elasticity estimation by using consumption as a proxy variable for normal income is probably as good an estimate as can be got, although it may have a slight downward bias because of the inclusion of a few rent controlled tenancies. This result, about 0·6, implies an income elasticity rather lower than that for owner-occupiers. This is in line with the American findings [4] and is what would be expected in Britain, since beyond a certain point a tenant who wishes to occupy better housing will switch to owner-occupation.

References

1. CLARK, C. and JONES, G. T. *The Demand for Housing.* Centre for Environmental Studies, London, 1971.
2. HOLMANS, A. E. 'A forecast of effective demand for housing in Great Britain in the 1970s', *Social Trends*, 1970, pp. 33–42.
3. 'Notes and definitions', *Housing Statistics*, now known as *Housing and Construction Statistics*, HMSO quarterly various issues.
4. LEEUW, F. DE. 'The demand for housing; a review of cross selection evidence', *Review of Economics and Statistics*, 1971, pp. 1–10.
5. MUTH, R. 'The demand for non-farm housing' in *The Demand for Durable Goods*, ed. A. E. Harberger, Chicago, 1960, pp. 29–96.
6. MUTH, R. 'Urban residential land and housing markets', in *Issues in Urban Economics*, ed. H. S. Perloff and L. Wingo, Baltimore, 1968.
7. PALDAM, M. 'What is known about the housing demand', *The Swedish Journal of Economics*, 1970, pp. 130–48.
8. PRAIS, S. J. and HOUTHAKKER, H. S. *The Analysis of Family Budgets*, Cambridge, 1955.
9. REID, M. G. *Housing and Income*, Chicago, 1962.
10. STONE, J. R. *The Measurement of Consumers' Expenditure and Behaviour in the UK 1920–38.* Cambridge, 1954 and 1966.
11. WILKINSON, R. K. with GULLIVER, S. 'The economics of housing; a survey', *Social and Economic Administration*, 1971, pp. 83–99.
12. WINGER, A. R. 'Housing and income', *Western Economic Journal*, 1968, pp. 226–32.
13. WOOLF, MYRA. *The Housing Survey in England and Wales, 1964*, HMSO, 1967.

Income and the demand for housing: some evidence for Great Britain: Discussion

R. J. Nicholson

The sample: measurement and conceptual problems

(*a*) The authors refer to the possibility of underestimation of the income elasticity of demand, resulting from the underrepresentation of sales of the cheapest and most expensive houses in building society transactions which could result in lower income purchasers incurring mortgages relatively high in relation to income, and high income purchasers incurring mortgages relatively low in relation to income. Unpublished data appears to support this possibility since it shows clearly that the ratio of mortgage to income falls as income increases, particularly at the lower end of the income scale. I wonder, therefore, if the authors have considered examining mortgages arranged by local authorities? These, though only a small proportion of the total, do cater for low income borrowers and cover cheaper types of houses, so that their inclusion might make possible a better analysis of income elasticity at the lower income end, and counterbalance the possible underestimation of income elasticity resulting from the exclusion of this type of mortgage from building society data.

(*b*) It is true, as the authors point out, that random variations in the income variable will bias results downward. But in one important respect error in the income variable as recorded by building societies is systematic. This is because at the lower end borrowers may include all possible income to bring themselves into the range acceptable to building societies, whereas at the upper end that may state only that income necessary to obtain a mortgage. Moreover, not all income is equally acceptable to the societies. Recorded income may, therefore, involve a squeezing of the *de facto* income range. Relation of house prices to the reduced range of income (assuming that *de facto* income is appropriate) will raise the estimate of income elasticity. This consequence is shown by the authors' results for renters when they use expenditure as a proxy for income (Table 5.6). Quite apart from whether expenditure is a good approximation to permanent income, the simple arithmetical fact is that expenditure forms a decreasing proportion of income as one moves from low to high income classes, so that the expenditure elasticity will always be greater than *de facto* income elasticity. If, of course, expenditure is the appropriate income indicator (for permanent income), then the restricted income range given by building societies' data will fortuitously make for a bias in the right direction. But it seems unlikely that different definitions of income will have much effect in closing the spread between lower and upper estimates as exemplified by the direct and reciprocal estimates of Tables 5.1 and 5.2, for the R^2 for the expenditure elasticities of Table 5.5 are only trivially greater than those for the post-tax income elasticities.

(c) The authors use current market value of the house as their indicator of expenditure on housing. De Leeuw has questioned whether this is appropriate, arguing that the variable should be expense per unit of time. He quotes American data showing that 'housing expenses per year is a smaller fraction of market value for high value homes than for low value homes' resulting from the slower rate of increase of insurance, maintenance, repairs, heating and utilities. Thus income elasticity measured from house prices will be biased upwards in relation to the appropriate housing expenses elasticity. One would, therefore, like to hear the authors' views on the appropriateness of the variable they take (and one appreciates that they had no option) for the economic relation they are examining.

Statistical procedure, and possible lines for development

(a) The authors' procedure assumes, in effect, that there is some 'quintessential' elasticity which is the same for all homogeneous groups of purchases and purchasers, but that the *level* of the ratio of house price to income varies between groups. The reasonableness of this assumption is shown by the broad consistency of the regional and age group elasticities given in Table 5.1. It follows, therefore, that if all the observations are put into one regression, the 'crude' income elasticity obtained by relating house prices to income will be greater than that for homogeneous subgroups. Account is taken of this by incorporating a number of dummy variables (as 'shift' variables) into the regressions to represent partitions of the population. The more of these partitioning variables, correlated with house price and income, which are introduced, the more will the 'quintessential' income elasticity be reduced. This is clearly shown in the results of the stepwise regression summarised in Table 5.3 where the income elasticity is gradually reduced from 0·81 to 0·65 as more, relevant, dummies are brought in.

There are two further classifications which may be relevant and which could be handled in this way. One is social class of purchasers: other consumers' expenditure studies suggest that this is relevant. The other is the different building societies themselves. I suggest this because differences between building societies may be a source of nonhomogeneity in the data. It would seem, also, that further analysis by differences in previous tenure might be rewarding. Certainly, Table 5.3 shows that whether or not a borrower is a previous owner-occupier is important, and in Table 5.4 the 'liquidity elasticity', though low relative to the income elasticity, is significant. For this class of borrower (i.e. one having previously sold a house) the consequence of movement between areas might be important: the liquidity pool would be likely to have a different implication for movement from a cheap to a dear area than for a movement from a dear to a cheap area.

(b) Price variation over the country is obviously important, and the authors have interpreted their regional dummies as taking account of this. In the main analyses they use four dummies for five regional areas. But the variation in house prices over the country is exceedingly complicated: there are substantial variations in house prices for houses near to towns and those some way out of towns, between those in urban and non-urban areas, etc., and it is unlikely that these will be adequately reflected by dummies for five broad regions: in any case the regional dummies may be measuring other regional differences besides prices. What I would like to ask, therefore, is whether some more sensitive price index could be compiled to deal more efficiently with this problem. I am tempted to make this suggestion since the authors say that 'data can almost always be collected if the need is thought to be sufficiently great', and certainly such indices do exist for America. Their use in the present analysis would save increasing the number of dummy variables, and would also make possible a better approach to the price elasticity instead of confounding it with regional differences.

The income elasticity and demand forecasting

There would seem to be not one, but a range of income elasticities; what I have called the crude one, obtained when house prices are related to income alone, and the lower ones relating to particular partitions of the population—indeed the 'quintessential' elasticity seems to get lower as more relevant partitioning classifications are introduced (though the authors' stepwise regression shows it to have stabilised at 0·65 for the set of classifications they have examined). If one is using a general elasticity for forecasting the demand for housing should one use the higher, crude, one, or the lower, more homogeneous, ones? Although the analyses for homogeneous groups are important in examining and accounting for behavioural characteristics, I am inclined to think that since, over time, there are movements between groups—between social groups, between regions; and changes in the balance between groups —e.g. by different previous tenures; then perhaps the crude figure is the more useful planning indicator since provision of housing has to meet changes in demand from all these different factors.

I am further persuaded of this by some matters raised by the authors at the start of their paper. With increasing real income there is a trend showing preference for owner-occupier tenure, and hence there may well be a growing desire to move from the non-market controlled sector to the market controlled sector—which itself may imply rising standards demanded by those remaining in the non-market controlled sector. Since barely one half of the population lives in that part of housing stock which is controlled by market forces, there is obviously a considerable 'reserve pool' which could move. In addition, as the authors have pointed out, increasing real income may itself stimulate the growth of households demanding separate housing accommodation. In other words increasing real income may be accompanied by a change of tastes which would lead to a greater demand for housing services. One might expect, therefore, that the national, average, income elasticity of demand for housing will rise over time. This implies that the elasticity calculated from a present day cross-section study will underestimate the effective income elasticity in future years which will govern the demand for housing. So for a future planning statistic, I would be inclined to settle for an elasticity somewhat in excess of the authors' conservative estimate of 0·75—something in the region of 1·0 as suggested by American studies.

II

Micro-economics of the
Public Sector

How progressive should income tax be?[1]

6

A. B. Atkinson

The moment you abandon . . . the cardinal principle of exacting from all individuals the same proportion of their income or their property, you are at sea without rudder or compass, and there is no amount of injustice or folly you may not commit. . . . Graduation is not an evil to be paltered with. Adopt it and you will effectively paralyse industry. . . . The savages described by Montesquieu, who to get at the fruit cut down the tree, are about as good financiers as the advocates of this sort of taxes.

J. R. McCulloch (1845)

1. Introduction

In Britain the marginal rate of income tax on earned income is zero initially, rises to 30 per cent for a very wide range of incomes and then increases quite sharply to a maximum rate of 75 per cent for surtax payers. Is this structure too progressive or insufficiently so? The aim of this paper is to explore some of the arguments that could be applied in the unlikely event of the Chancellor of the Exchequer asking economists for guidance on this question, and to see just what can be said about how progressive the income tax should be. The first half of the paper surveys the current state of knowledge: the traditional sacrifice theories and the more recent extensions of these by Mirrlees and others. The second half of the paper introduces a simple model designed to throw light on the way in which the aims of the government influence the optimal degree of progression and to bring out considerations which have been obscured in the earlier literature.

It should be made clear at the outset that the paper makes no attempt to provide a definite answer to the question posed in the title. Indeed one of the main conclusions is that such an answer cannot be given without further clarification of social objectives. Instead the paper attempts to illuminate the

[1] I am very grateful to C. J. Bliss, J. A. Mirrlees and J. M. Parkin for their comments on earlier versions of this paper.

basic structure of the problem and to provide insight into the kind of argument required to justify positions which are commonly taken on this question. Two other qualifications should also be entered. The paper is concerned only with the taxation of earned income and not with the taxation of investment income, which introduces quite different considerations. Second, the paper deals only with income taxes and does not consider the possibility that other forms of taxation (such as a wage tax) might be employed.

2. The minimum sacrifice theory

Those textbooks which discuss the question of the optimal degree of progression usually begin by referring to the theories of equal sacrifice. The statements by Adam Smith that subjects should 'contribute in proportion to their respective abilities' and by John Stuart Mill that 'whatever sacrifices [the government] requires . . . should be made to bear as nearly as possible with the same pressure upon all' were translated by later writers into more precise principles of equal sacrifice. These took a number of different forms, but the principle of equal marginal sacrifice put forward by Edgeworth, Pigou and others had the clearest rationale, being derived from the utilitarian objective of the maximisation of the sum of individual utilities.

Let us suppose that individuals differ in their earning ability and that this is denoted by n. The before-tax earnings of a person of type n are denoted by $z(n)$ and the tax paid by $T(n)$. The utility derived from the after-tax income is given by $U_n[z(n) - T(n)]$, so that if $f(n)$ is the frequency distribution of people of type n the sum of individual utilities is denoted by

$$W = \int_0^\infty U_n[z(n) - T(n)] f(n) \, dn \qquad (1)$$

The government is assumed to choose the tax rates to maximise W subject to the revenue constraint

$$\int_0^\infty T(n) f(n) \, dn = \bar{R} \qquad (2)$$

(where $\bar{R}$ denotes the net revenue to be raised and $T(n)$ may be negative). The solution is straightforward (on the assumption that U is concave):

$$U'_n[z(n) - T(n)] \text{ equal all } n \qquad (3)$$

and if an identical marginal utility of income schedule is assumed, the tax structure is such that after-tax incomes are equalised:[1] 'A system of equimarginal sacrifice fully carried out would involve lopping off the tops of all

---

[1] This will only, of course, ensure an equal level of utility where the origins of the utility functions are identical (they are fully comparable—see Sen [21]).

If $T(n)$ were constrained to be non-negative, we would have the solution described by Dalton: 'taxing only the largest incomes, cutting down all above a certain level to that level, and exempting all below that level' ([5], p. 59).

92 A. B. Atkinson

incomes above the minimum income and leaving everybody, after taxation, with equal incomes' (Pigou [18],* pp. 57–8).

The minimum sacrifice theory has come under a great deal of attack and is dismissed by most authors. Two main lines of criticism may be distinguished:

(a) that the minimum sacrifice theory takes no account of the possible dis-incentive effect of taxation ($z(n)$ may be influenced by the tax structure),
(b) that the underlying utilitarian framework is inadequate.

The next section of this paper examines the contribution made by the recent work of Mirrlees and others to overcoming the first of these objections. The second line of criticism is taken up later in the paper.

3. Income tax progression and work incentives

The importance of the possible disincentive effect of taxation was clearly recognised in the discussion by Sidgwick: 'It is conceivable that a greater equality in the distribution of produce would lead ultimately to a reduction in the total amount to be distributed in consequence of a general preference of leisure to the results of labour' (quoted in [6], p. 104). The proponents of the minimum sacrifice approach did not, however, make any attempt to arrive at a tax formula incorporating these considerations. One of the main contributions of the recent papers in this area has been to fill this gap and to derive optimal tax schedules taking account of the effects of taxation on work effort. This section describes the formulation of the problem and the principal results obtained.

The recent revival of interest in this area is largely attributable to the impor-tant paper by Mirrlees [14], where he considers the influence of taxation on the work/leisure choice. A person of type n determines the proportion of the day he spends at work ($y(n)$) so as to maximise his utility $U[x(n), y(n)]$ where $x(n)$ denotes his after-tax income and is given by

$$x(n) = z(n) - T[z(n)] \tag{4}$$

and

$$z(n) = ny(n) \tag{5}$$

(i.e. the parameter of earning ability, n, represents the wage per unit of time for a man of type n). Otherwise, the formulation is identical to that described in section 2. The government chooses the income tax function $T(z)$ to maxi-mise the sum of individual utilities (where it is assumed that all individuals have identical utility functions):[1]

$$W = \int_0^\infty U[x(n), y(n)] f(n) \, dn \tag{6}$$

subject to the revenue constraint (2).

With the introduction of the work/leisure choice, the problem becomes a

[1] No account is taken in this paper of differing needs and this problem clearly requires further analysis. For discussion of the variation of taxation with family size, see Mirrlees [15].

* Numbers in square brackets relate to References on p. 108.

considerably more difficult one than the simple minimum sacrifice theory. The first part of Mirrlees's paper is concerned with the derivation of general properties of the optimal tax function $T(z)$, but the results he obtains are limited to establishing that:

(a) the optimal marginal tax rate lies between zero and one,
(b) it will be optimal (in most interesting cases) for some of the population to remain idle (i.e. $y(n)=0$).

More than this cannot be said: 'The optimum tax schedule depends upon the distribution of skills within the population . . . in such a complicated way that it is not possible to say in general whether marginal tax rates should be higher for high-income, low-income, or intermediate income groups' ([14], p. 186).

In the later part of his paper, Mirrlees goes on, therefore, to consider the special case where

$$U = \log_e [x^a(1-y)]$$

and $f(n)$ is either the lognormal or the Pareto distribution. This special case is considered analytically in section 8 of his paper, and for a range of numerical calculations (with $a = 1$ and $f(n)$ lognormal) in section 9.

On the basis of his analysis, and in particular of the numerical calculations, Mirrlees draws a number of (qualified) conclusions. Two of the most important for policy purposes are that: (a) the optimal tax structure is approximately linear: i.e. a constant marginal tax rate, with an exemption level below which negative tax supplements are payable; (b) the marginal tax rates are rather low and tend to fall rather than rise with the level of income—see Table 6.1 for two illustrative cases. The second conclusion is an unexpected one. Mirrlees comments that 'I had expected the rigorous analysis of income taxation in the utilitarian manner to provide an argument for high tax rates,' and expresses surprise that it has not done so.

TABLE 6.1. *Optimal tax rates—Mirrlees Cases I and II*

	Case I		Case II	
	Average tax rate %	Marginal tax rate %	Average tax rate %	Marginal tax rate %
Bottom decile	−5	24	−38	20
Median	5	22	−12	19
Top decile	13	19	2	17
Top percentile	14	17	7	16

Source: Interpolated from [14], Tables I–IV. In Case I the revenue requirement is positive, in Case II it is negative (the government is disposing of the profits of public sector production).

It is clear that the conclusions drawn by Mirrlees rest heavily on the particular assumptions made. In his concluding section he draws attention to the fact that 'the shape of the optimum earned-income tax schedule is rather sensitive to the distribution of skills within the population and to the income–leisure preferences postulated'. The latter assumption is, as he says 'heroic' and may well overstate the sensitivity of labour supply to changes in the marginal rate of income tax. There is, however, an aspect of the special cases taken by Mirrlees to which he does not draw adequate attention—the effect of the choice of a particular functional form to represent given income/leisure preferences.

In the minimum sacrifice theory, the particular cardinalisation selected did not affect the tax structure (providing it was the same for all). If we replace U by $G[U]$ where $G' > 0$, $G'' < 0$ the first-order condition is

$$G'\{U'[z(n) - T(n)]\} \text{ equal all } n$$

giving the same solution. In the present case, however, this is no longer true. In order to clarify this point, let us consider the particular transformations of the utility function

$$\frac{V^{1-\rho}}{1-\rho}, \rho \geq 0 \tag{7}$$

where V is normalised so that for $\rho = 0$ it just satisfies the concavity requirement, which in the present case means that

$$V = x^A(1-y)^{1-A} \tag{8}$$

The case taken in Table 6.1 corresponds to $\log_e V$ or to $\rho = 1$.[1] If, however, we were to take a higher value of ρ; this would lead to the optimal tax structure being more progressive. As ρ rises, the marginal utility of income diminishes more rapidly and the 'cost' of inequality (in terms of the loss of aggregate utility) increases.

The effect of changes in ρ may be illustrated by the numerical examples given by Mirrlees where

$$G = -e^{-U} \tag{9}$$

which corresponds to the case $\rho = 2$. His results are not presented in such a way as to facilitate the comparison, since the amount of revenue to be raised is not held constant in the different cases. However, the optimal marginal tax rate tends to fall as the revenue to be collected falls, so that the comparisons shown in Table 6.2 will tend to understate the rise in the optimal tax rate as ρ increases. It is clear in fact that the increase in ρ leads to definitely higher marginal tax rates.

[1] Writing the social welfare function

$$\frac{1}{\epsilon}W^\epsilon = \int \left(\frac{1}{\epsilon}V^\epsilon\right)f(n)\,\mathrm{d}n$$

(where $\epsilon = 1 - \rho$), in the limit as $\epsilon \to 0$, $\log W \to \int \log Vf(n)\,\mathrm{d}n$. See Hardy, Littlewood and Polya [11], Ch. 2.

TABLE 6.2. *Effect of increase in ρ on optimal marginal tax rates*

	$\rho=1$	$\rho=2$
	Revenue 7% of income Marginal tax rate %	Revenue 2% of income Marginal tax rate %
Bottom decile	24	33
Median	22	30
Top decile	19	26
Top percentile	17	21
	Revenue -10% of income Marginal tax rate %	Revenue -20% of income Marginal tax rate %
Bottom decile	20	28
Median	19	26
Top decile	17	24
Top percentile	16	21

Source: Interpolated from [14], Tables I–VIII.

This conclusion leads one to ask how Mirrlees's results would be affected by taking still larger values of ρ. Is it possible that he would have found optimal tax rates of the order of 50 per cent or more if he had chosen higher values of ρ? One way in which we can test this is by taking the limit as $\rho \to \infty$

$$\frac{\min V(n)}{n} \tag{10}$$

i.e. we can obtain an upper bound on the effect of increasing ρ by examining the tax structure which maximises the utility of the worst-off person.

A second important recent contribution is that by Fair [8]. The model considered by him differs from that of Mirrlees in two important respects:

(*a*) hourly earnings are assumed to be a function not only of ability but also of the level of education. If we denote the proportion of working hours spent in education by E, earnings are

$$z(n)=y(1-E)\,g(n,E) \tag{11}$$

where $g(n,E)$ is the wage rate per working hour.

The individual utility function is the same as before—education is purely an investment and does not provide consumption benefits—and E is chosen to maximise $z(n)$.

(*b*) the range of tax schedules under consideration is restricted to

$$T'(z)=\alpha_0 \log_e [1+z]$$

or

$$T(z)=\alpha_0[(z+1)\log_e[1+z]]-\alpha-\alpha_0 z \tag{12}$$

where α represents a guaranteed minimum income (if $z=0$).

The results obtained by Fair are numerical ones only, and are based on a normal distribution of abilities and an approximated relationship $g(n, E)$. The conclusions are primarily summarised in terms of the Gini coefficient of concentration, but it is possible to calculate the average and marginal tax rates for two of his nine earnings functions for people at different points on the ability range.

TABLE 6.3. *Optimal tax rates—results of Fair*

	Earnings function 5		Earnings function 8	
	Average tax rate %	Marginal tax rate %	Average tax rate %	Marginal tax rate %
Individual's position in ability range				
1% from bottom	17	29	< 0	29
Median	23	32	19	41
1% from top	32	38	40	49

Source: Calculated from [8], Table VI (case where a constant).

The optimal rates of tax are rather higher than in the case of the results reached by Mirrlees. At the same time, the top rates (those on the man 1 per cent from the top of the ability range) are still a long way below those indicated by the Edgeworth–Pigou analysis. Again, the form of the utility function adopted is important. The results given all relate to a case where $\rho = 1$, and it may be expected that higher values of ρ would have led to a more progressive tax structure.[1]

4. Recent work—conclusions

The recent contributions by Mirrlees and Fair suggest that the introduction of efficiency considerations may lead to a considerably less progressive tax structure than that indicated by the minimum sacrifice theory. At the same time they do not adequately consider the sensitivity of their results to the specification of the government objectives. In particular, the precise cardinalisation adopted, which was not important in the Edgeworth–Pigou analysis, may significantly affect the optimal tax structure.

The work of these authors has demonstrated that the introduction of the work/leisure choice adds considerably to the complexity of the solution and that analytic results are very difficult to obtain. This means that we have to choose between strongly simplified models for which analytic solutions can be

[1] Fair does report briefly on the results obtained when $\rho = 0$ (p. 574) and comments that 'the results did not change much'. However, the results are given in terms of the after-tax Gini coefficient and it is hard to see what is implied for the marginal rates of taxation.

obtained and more realistic models solved numerically. While the latter will undoubtedly be necessary for the formulation of actual policy prescriptions, at the present time it seems more useful to concentrate on identifying the considerations which are likely to have a significant influence on the solution. In the remainder of this paper a model is developed which, while highly stylised, does serve this purpose.

5. A simple model

The model developed in this section is considerably simpler than that considered by Mirrlees and Fair, and in particular assumes:

(*a*) that attention is restricted to the case of linear tax schedules:

$$T(z) = (1 - \beta) z - \alpha \tag{13}$$

i.e. a guaranteed minimum income α combined with a proportional tax on all income at rate $(1 - \beta)$ (see Fig. 6.1). This is the simplest form of progressive tax to consider; and corresponds quite closely to the kind of tax schedule actually in force.[1]

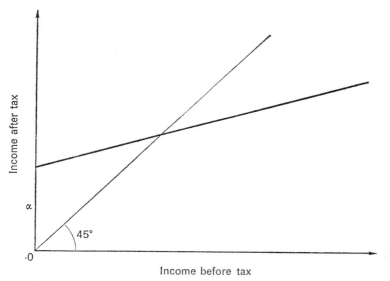

FIG 6.1.   Income tax schedule

(*b*) that the distribution of abilities is assumed to be Pareto in form:

$$f(n) = \mu n^{\mu} n^{-\mu - 1} \tag{14}$$

[1] The linear tax case is examined by Sheshinski [22], Wesson [26] and Atkinson [2]. It should be noted that Blum and Kalven [4] regard such a tax as being basically different from a general progressive tax with increasing marginal rates of tax, and that it does not allow us to consider the desirability of a 'surtax' or of a negative income tax rate different from that for the positive tax schedule.

where n represents the lowest value of n (see Fig. 6.2). (The exponent μ is assumed to be greater than or equal to 2.) This assumption is made primarily for its analytical convenience, and is one of the least satisfactory aspects of the model.[1]

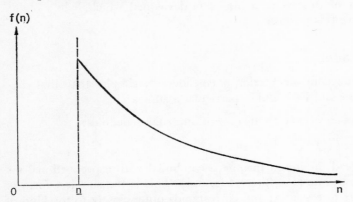

f(n)

0   n̲   n

FIG 6.2.   Pareto distribution

(c) that the individual's earnings are assumed to depend only on ability (n) and on the number of years of education received (S): i.e. hours of work (effort) are assumed to be fixed. While undergoing education the individual has zero earnings and is not eligible for the guaranteed minimum. He earns $z(n, S)$ when at work and retires after R years of work. He maximises the present value (at interest rate i) of his lifetime income:

$$I = \int_{S}^{R+S} [z - T(z)]\, e^{-it}\, dt$$

$$I = A[z - T(z)]\, e^{-iS} \tag{15}$$

where

$$A = \frac{(1 - e^{-iR})}{i}.$$

Finally we suppose (modifying a suggestion of Becker [3]), that $z(n, S) = nS^2$.

Combining the different elements of the model, we can see that the individual's choice of S will be determined by maximising

$$(\alpha + \beta nS)\, e^{-iS}$$

[1] Lydall [13], ch. 3 produces evidence that the upper tail of the earnings distribution approximately follows the Pareto law. It is also well known that the distribution of the number of scientific papers published per author is approximately Pareto in form (Simon [25])!

[2] This model owes a great deal to that of Sheshinski [23]. His formulation is, however, different:
$$I = z - T(z) - g(S)$$
and is rather more difficult to interpret.

which gives

$$S = \frac{1}{i} - \frac{\alpha}{\beta n}$$

for $n \geq i\alpha/\beta \equiv n_0$

$$S = 0 \text{ for } n \leq n_0 \tag{16}$$

The resulting level of I is given by

$$I = A\left(\frac{\beta n}{i}\right) e^{(\alpha i/\beta n - 1)} \tag{17}$$

for $n \geq n_0$. For $n \leq n_0$, $I = A\alpha$.

It may be noted that in the absence of taxation everyone would choose the same level of S; the effect of taxation is to widen pre-tax income differentials while narrowing after-tax differentials.

From the individual supply functions we can derive the possibilities open to the government, as determined by the revenue constraint:

$$\int_0^\infty T(z) f(n) \, dn = 0 \tag{18}$$

where it is assumed that the population is constant in size (so that there are the same number of tax payers for each n) and that no net revenue is required ($\bar{R} = 0$). With the particular distribution chosen, the constraint may take one of two forms:

Case (A) $n_0 \leq n$

Case (B) $n_0 > n$

Attention is focused here on case (A) where the revenue constraint is

$$\left(\text{since } \int_n^\infty f(n) \, dn = 1\right)$$

$$\alpha = (1 - \beta) \int_n^\infty \left(\frac{n}{i} - \frac{\alpha}{\beta}\right) f(n) \, dn$$

Using the fact that $n_0 = i\,\alpha/\beta$, this can be written

$$n_0 \frac{\beta}{1 - \beta} = \bar{n} - n_0$$

where $\bar{n}$ denotes the mean value, and this gives

$$\beta = 1 - \frac{n_0}{\bar{n}} \tag{19}$$

Equation (19) gives the combinations of β and n_0 (which together determine the optimal tax structure) satisfying the revenue constraint (subject to $n_0 \leq n$).[1]

As a background to the problem faced by the government, it is interesting to examine the choice that would be made by an individual aiming to maximise $I(n)$, where we denote by $n_0^*(n)$ the value of n_0 satisfying (19) chosen by a man of type n. Given that $n_0^*(n) \leq n$, the person maximises $\beta\, e^{n_0^*/n}$, or (from 19),

$$\frac{n_0^*}{n} + \log_e \left[1 - \frac{n_0^*}{\bar{n}}\right]$$

The first-order condition is given by

$$\frac{\bar{n}}{n} = \frac{1}{\left(1 - \frac{n_0^*}{\bar{n}}\right)}$$

reducing to

$$1 - \beta = \frac{n_0^*}{\bar{n}} = 1 - \frac{n}{\bar{n}}$$

Since

$$\bar{n} = \left(\frac{\mu}{\mu - 1}\right) n$$

the tax rate chosen falls from $1/\mu$ to zero at $n = \bar{n}$. Those with above average n would choose a lump sum tax and subsidy on earnings ($\alpha < 0$, $\beta > 1$) if that were possible (see Fig. 6.3).[2]

The presentation in terms of individual choice about taxation allows us to consider the possibility of majority voting. Although it is unlikely that the precise details of the tax structure would be subject to voting, issues of broad policy regarding the degree of progression may well be settled by appeal to the electorate. This question has been discussed by Foley [10], who considers the stability of different tax structures against majority rule (i.e. whether there is a tax schedule for which there will always be a majority in favour versus any alternative). As he points out, where the class of tax schedules under consideration is unrestricted, no element is stable against majority rule, but if attention is restricted to the class of linear tax schedules (for example), this

---

[1] In case (B) the revenue constraint is

$$\alpha = (1 - \beta) \int_{n_0}^{\infty} \left[\frac{n}{i} - \frac{\alpha}{\beta}\right] f(n)\, dn$$

using the fact that $n_0 = i\alpha/\beta$,

$$n_0 \cdot \frac{\beta}{1 - \beta} = \mu \int_{n_0}^{\infty} \left(\frac{n}{n}\right)^{-\mu} dn - n_0 \left(\frac{n_0}{n}\right)^{-\mu}$$

or

$$\frac{\beta}{(1 - \beta)} = \frac{1}{(\mu - 1)} \left(\frac{n_0}{n}\right)^{-\mu}$$

[2] The solution for $n_0^*(n)$ is given by $n/(\mu - 1)$, which is less than or equal to n for $\mu \geq 2$, so thar the revenue constraint is of type A.

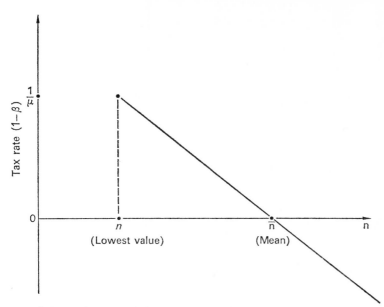

FIG 6.3.   Tax rate chosen by person of type n

will contain a stable element. Foley does not allow for the effect of taxation on the earnings of the individual, but his results can readily be extended to that case. In terms of the model set out above, an increase in n_0 ($=i\alpha/\beta$) will always be preferred by those for whom $n_0^* > n_0$ and opposed by those for whom $n_0^* < n_0$. It follows that the tax rate reached as a result of majority voting will be that given by $n_0^*(n_m)$ where n_m is the median, which can be calculated to be

$$1 - \beta = 1 - 2^{1/\mu}(1 - 1/\mu)$$

so that for $\mu = 2$ we obtain 29 per cent and for $\mu = 3$ we obtain 16 per cent. (Since the distribution is skew, $n_m < \bar{n}$, so this would always give a positive tax rate.)

6. Utilitarian and other objectives

Let us examine first the optimal tax structure where the government pursues the utilitarian objective of maximising the sum of individual utilities:[1]

$$W = \int_{n}^{\infty} U[I(n)] f(n) \, \mathrm{d}n \tag{20}$$

As we have seen in section 3, the solution depends on the precise form of the

---

[1] It is assumed here, as earlier, that an individual's utility depends only on his own income.

function $U(I)$. In order to explore this further, let us suppose that U can be written in the iso-elastic form

$$U = \frac{I^{1-\rho}}{1-\rho}$$

The case $\rho = 1$ corresponds to that taken by Mirrlees in the first of his examples and means that the maximand becomes

$$\log W = \int_n^\infty \log [I(n)] f(n) \, dn$$

$$= \log \beta + \int_n^\infty \log (An/i) f(n) \, dn$$

$$+ \int_n^\infty \left(\frac{n_0}{n} - 1\right) f(n) \, dn \tag{21}$$

Substituting from the revenue constraint and differentiating, we obtain the first-order condition

$$\int_n^\infty n^{-1} f(n) \, dn = \frac{1}{\beta \bar{n}} \tag{22}$$

From this it follows that

$$\beta = \frac{1+\mu}{\mu} \frac{n}{\bar{n}} = 1 - \frac{1}{\mu^2}$$

i.e. the optimal tax rate is $1/\mu^2$. If $\mu = 2$, this indicates a tax rate of 25 per cent; if $\mu = 4$, the tax rate is as low as 6·25 per cent.[1]

As ρ increases, the optimal rate of tax rises. This can be seen as follows. In the case where $\rho \neq 1$, we have

$$\frac{W^{1-\rho}}{1-\rho} = \left(\frac{\beta^{1-\rho}}{1-\rho}\right)\left(\frac{Ae^{-1}}{i}\right)^{1-\rho} \int_n^\infty n^{1-\rho} e^{n_0(1-\rho)/n} f(n) \, dn \tag{23}$$

Using the revenue constraint (19),

$$\frac{1}{W} \frac{\partial W}{\partial n_0} = \frac{1}{\beta} \frac{\partial \beta}{\partial n_0} + \frac{\int_n^\infty n^{-\rho} e^{n_0(1-\rho)/n} f(n) \, dn}{\int_n^\infty n^{1-\rho} e^{n_0(1-\rho)/n} f(n) \, dn} \tag{24}$$

[1] The data given by Lydall [13] for Britain, France, Germany and the United States suggest values of μ between 2·27 and 3·5.

giving a first-order condition

$$\beta = \frac{\int\limits_n^\infty n^{1-\rho} e^{n_0(1-\rho)/n} f(n) \, dn}{\int\limits_n^\infty \left(\frac{\bar{n}}{n}\right) n^{1-\rho} e^{n_0(1-\rho)/n} f(n) \, dn}$$

Writing

$$K(\mu, \rho) = [n_0(\rho-1)]^{\rho+\mu-1} \int\limits_n^\infty n^{-(\rho+\mu)} e^{n_0(1-\rho)/n} \, dn$$

this gives an equation for n_0

$$1 - \frac{n_0}{\bar{n}} = \frac{n_0(\rho-1)}{\bar{n}} \frac{K(\mu, \rho)}{K(\mu+1, \rho)} \tag{25}$$

The solution to this equation for different values of ρ and μ is given in Table 6.4.[1] As ρ increases above 1, the optimal tax rate rises quite significantly. For $\rho=2$ (the second case considered by Mirrlees), the tax rate is 33 per cent rather than 25 per cent (where $\mu=2$). Moreover, the limit as $\rho \to \infty$ can be

TABLE 6.4. *Optimal tax rates obtained from equation (25)*

	Value of μ		
	2·0	3·0	4·0
Value of ρ	%	%	%
1·0	25	11	6
2·0	33	18	9
4·0	36	21	14
6·0	39	24	15
8·0	40	25	18
16·0	43	28	21
Limit	50	33	25

[1] Substituting

$$m = n_0 \frac{(\rho-1)}{n}$$

gives the incomplete gamma function

$$K(\mu, \rho) = \int\limits_0^m e^{-m} m^{\rho+\mu-2} \, dm$$

where $m = n_0(\rho-1)/n$. The equation to be solved may be written as

$$\frac{K(\mu, \rho)}{K(\mu+1, \rho)} = \frac{1}{m}\left(\frac{\mu}{\mu-1}\right) - \frac{1}{(\rho-1)}$$

The left hand side is evaluated using the tables published by Pearson [17].

derived from the earlier analysis: as $\rho \to \infty$ the social welfare function tends to the maxi-min form

$$\max I(n)$$

and from the analysis of page 100 we can see that the optimal rate is $1/\mu$. As ρ increases, the optimal tax rate moves up along the line shown in Fig. 6.4. At the extreme point the optimal tax is considerably larger (by a factor of μ) than at $\rho = 1$.

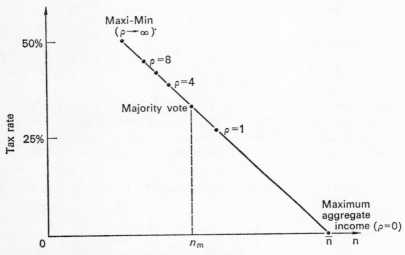

FIG 6.4.   Different solutions (for $\mu = 2$)

The results given in Table 6.4 suggest that the optimal rate of income taxation may depend quite sensitively on the particular cardinalisation adopted. At the same time it is not clear that we can obtain any firm estimate from individual behaviour of the value that is likely to be taken by ρ (the elasticity of the marginal utility of income). Moreover, we have to consider the possibility that ρ may reflect social values as well as individual utility. Mirrlees's formulation, for example, allows for the possibility that the objective function is

$$\int G[U] f(n) \, dn$$

where G is a social welfare function defined on individual utilities. In this case ρ represents the elasticity of the *social* marginal utility of income, which may be expected to be higher than the private elasticity. For these reasons there is no clear *a priori* expectation that the value of ρ would lie between 1 and 2 (the values taken by Mirrlees) and we should entertain the possibility that it may be considerably higher.

To this point the basic utilitarian framework has not been discussed. This framework does however suffer from well-known disadvantages, and these have led many authors to draw the conclusion that the equi-marginal or other sacrifice principles cannot provide a useful guide to policy. Prest, for example, writes that: 'It seems reasonable to conclude that sacrifice is not only unmeasurable and incapable of quantification for any one individual but also not comparable as between individuals. With such fundamental objections it would seem to be impossible to accept the conclusions derived from the theories of sacrifice' ([19], pp. 117–18).

In the same way, Johansen concludes that 'On the whole . . . the ability principle, in so far as attempts have been made to define and elaborate it with the aid of the theory of utility function, is mainly of abstract theoretical interest, and will not be able to play any significant role in the actual formulation of income taxation' ([12], p. 217).

If the utilitarian approach underlying the minimum sacrifice theories, and the recent extensions of these, is to be rejected, it is reasonable to ask what can be offered in its place. As Irving Fisher commented, 'philosophic doubt is right and proper, but the problems of life cannot and do not wait' ([9], p. 180). There are in fact two main alternative approaches which can be identified: (a) maximisation of the welfare of the worst-off individual; (b) considerations of income inequality.

(a) Fairness and 'maxi-min'

The first of these lines of argument has been developed by Rawls from considerations of the nature of the social contract. The foundation of this approach are the two basic principles of justice put forward by Rawls: 'first, each person engaged in an institution . . . has an equal right to the most extensive liberty compatible with a like liberty for all; and second, inequalities . . . are arbitrary unless it is reasonable to expect that they will work out to everyone's advantage' ([20], p. 61).

The second of these principles is interpreted by Rawls to mean the maximisation of the welfare of the worst-off individual (a 'maxi-min' criterion): 'The basic structure is just throughout when the advantages of the more fortunate promote the well-being of the least fortunate, that is, when a decrease in their advantages would make the least fortunate even worse off than they are' ([20], p. 66).

This formulation does not, of course, avoid all the difficulties of utilitarianism; at the same time the requirements are rather different (to apply the 'maxi-min' criterion, we require comparability of welfare levels, but not cardinality—see Sen [21]). Moreover, the maxi-min criterion does seem to capture some of the notions of 'fairness' which are current in public discussion and it is interesting to examine its implications.

If we can assume that individual utility is related to income in such a way that the worst-off individual is the man with the lowest n, the solution with this objective can be seen from the preceding analysis to be $1/\mu$. This tax rate may well seem surprisingly low. Although not much weight should be attached to the actual numerical values, it would indicate a tax rate of between

30 per cent and 45 per cent using the values of μ estimated by Lydall [13]. These rates are considerably higher than those given by Mirrlees, but nonetheless lower than one could expect from such an apparently egalitarian objective function. It is interesting to compare the maxi-min case with the egalitarian prescriptions of Pigou and Edgeworth, which led to 100 per cent marginal rate of tax. In the present case this does not happen because of the effects on the work decisions of the better-off groups. It is in the interests of the worst-off person to reduce the rate below 100 per cent to increase the revenue raised from those higher up the scale.[1]

(b) Income inequality

The second alternative approach is well described by Simons:

> Taxation must affect the distribution of income ... and it is only sensible to face the question as to what kinds of effects are desirable. To do this is to reduce the discussion frankly to the level of ethics or aesthetics. Such procedure, however, is certainly preferable to the traditional one of 'describing' the attributes of the good life in terms which simply are not descriptive. The case for drastic progression in taxation must be rested on the case against inequality—on the ethical or aesthetic judgment that the prevailing distribution of wealth and income reveals a degree (and/or kind) of inequality which is distinctly evil or unlovely ([24], pp. 18–19).

If, however, considerations of income inequality are to provide a guide to the rate of income taxation, they have to be more precisely formulated. A natural way in which this can be done is through one of the summary measures of inequality which are commonly employed in empirical studies of tax progression; we could, for example, choose the optimal income tax so as to minimise the Gini coefficient. This kind of procedure suffers, however, from two disadvantages:

(a) as I have argued elsewhere [1], the conventional summary measures have no inherent rationale and little interpretation can be given to them,
(b) the use of such measures implicitly involves a trade-off between inequality and some measure of the average level of incomes, and this trade-off has to be specified.[2]

One way of overcoming these difficulties is to follow the approach examined

[1] The extent to which this is worth while depends, of course, on the elasticity of the supply function. In this context it should be noted that the earnings function assumed here may well over-emphasise the effect of taxation on work incentives. The earnings function is in fact identical with that obtained from the utility function

$$U(x, y) = \log x - iy$$

where x denotes consumption and y hours of work. The fact that this corresponds to a perfectly elastic supply of effort suggests that the simple model used here may understate the optimal tax rate.

[2] The Gini coefficient would be minimised, for example, if all incomes were zero.

in [1] which assumes that we rank income distributions according to a social welfare function

$$J = \int_{n}^{\infty} H[I(n)] f(n) \, dn \tag{26}$$

where $H(I)$ denotes the social valuation of income accruing to an individual. The particular functional form explored is

$$H = \frac{I^{1-\rho}}{1-\rho} \quad \rho \geqslant 0$$

It appears at first sight that this is identical to the utilitarian approach discussed earlier. It is important to emphasise, however, that H represents the *social* valuation of income,[1] and that the choice of ρ is based on social values about inequality. The parameter ρ reflects in fact the degree of aversion to inequality in the society: $\rho = 0$ corresponds to maximising the sum of incomes, and increasing values of ρ mean that the society is more averse to inequality. The solutions obtained using this approach can be read off from Table 6.4. For $\rho = 0$ (zero inequality aversion), the optimal solution is a zero tax rate, and for higher values of ρ the optimal tax rate increases until it reaches the limiting case of maxi-min ($\rho \to \infty$).

The fact that the maxi-min solution represents the limiting case, and that, as we have seen, this does not necessarily lead to very high rates of taxation, may lead us to question whether the formulation (26) adequately captures our values about inequality. In particular it is not necessarily clear that the social welfare function is increasing in all its arguments: it is quite conceivable that a gift of £1 from Mars to the richest person in Britain may be considered to lower the level of social welfare. It is possible that we may attach particular weight to the distance between the top and the bottom. Fair [8] refers to the belief of Plato that no one in a society should be more than four times richer than the poorest member of society. If this is so, we may well choose tax rates higher than the maxi-min solution. Although this would reduce the lifetime income of the poorest man it would narrow the gap between him and those at the top. In the present model the after-tax income of the lowest man as a percentage of the average is (for $n_0 < n$)

$$(1 - 1/\mu) \, e^{t/\mu - 1}$$

The value of this ratio for different values of t (where $\mu = 3$) is given

$t = 0$	Ratio = 66 per cent
$t = 33\frac{1}{3}$ per cent (maxi-min solution)	Ratio = 79 per cent
$t = 50$ per cent	Ratio = 86 per cent
$t = 66\frac{2}{3}$ per cent	Ratio = 94 per cent

---

[1] This formulation is in effect that proposed by Musgrave: 'the concept of subjective utility is translated into one of social income utility. We may then postulate a marginal-utility schedule that seems proper as a matter of social policy. . . . If we proceed along these lines, the principle of ability to pay ceases to be the subjective matter that J. S. Mill had thought it to be. It becomes a question of social value' ([16], p. 109).

108 A. B. Atkinson

It is possible, therefore, that concern for income inequality may lead to the choice of a tax rate above that indicated by the maxi-min criterion. This would involve the government selecting a policy which in terms of individual lifetime incomes was Pareto-inferior.[1] If the tax rate is above $1/\mu$, all individuals would favour a tax reduction. The reason the government might choose such a policy is that the loss to the highest income groups is larger than to the lowest, and hence the gap between them would be narrowed.

7. Conclusions

The value of a model such as that discussed in this paper does not lie in the precise solutions obtained. It should indeed be obvious that the specification of the model is inadequate to provide any detailed prescriptions as to what the rate of income tax should be. The labour supply assumptions, for example, are highly stylised and leave out many important factors. The analysis may however have served to provide some insight into the structure of the arguments and to bring out the significance of considerations not discussed adequately in earlier contributions. In particular, I have tried to emphasise the role played by the formulation of the objectives of the government. This has been shown to be important at two levels. First, within the utilitarian framework underlying the minimum sacrifice theories and the recent work by Mirrlees and others, the results may depend sensitively on the particular cardinalisation adopted. Second, alternative approaches based on considerations of 'fairness' or 'inequality' may lead to very different results.

One point which emerges clearly as significant is the importance of the maxi-min solution. Not only does it have considerable intuitive appeal, but also it provides a limiting case for the utilitarian approach and an interesting watershed for those concerned about inequality. In further work in this area, with more complex models, it seems interesting therefore to consider first the maxi-min criterion. This will give an upper bound on the utilitarian solution, and we will only expect higher rates of tax to emerge from an inequality approach if the government attaches a negative weight to increases in income for well-off individuals.

References

1. ATKINSON, A. B. 'On the measurement of inequality', *Journal of Economic Theory*, September 1970, pp. 244–63.
2. ATKINSON, A. B. ' "Maxi-min" and optimal income taxation', *mimeo*, 1972.
3. BECKER, G. S. *Human Capital*, Columbia University Press, 1964.
4. BLUM, W. J. and KALVEN, H. *The Uneasy Case for Progressive Taxation* (Phoenix edition), University of Chicago Press, 1963.
5. DALTON, H. *Principles of Public Finance*, Routledge & Kegan Paul, 1954.
6. EDGEWORTH, F. Y. *Papers Relating to Political Economy*, Vol. ii, Royal Economic Society, London, 1925.

[1] It is important to emphasise at this point that no account has been taken of interdependencies (the possibility that a person's welfare may depend on the incomes of others). If such interdependencies exist, raising the tax rate above $1/\mu$ may still be Pareto-optimal in terms of individual utilities.

7. FAGAN, E. 'Recent and contemporary theories of progressive taxation', *Journal of Political Economy*, August 1938, pp. 457–98.
8. FAIR, R. C. 'The optimal distribution of income', *Quarterly Journal of Economics*, November 1971, pp. 551–79.
9. FISHER, I. 'A statistical method for measuring "marginal utility" and testing the justice of a progressive income tax', in *Economic Essays Contributed in Honour of John Bates Clark*, New York, 1927.
10. FOLEY, D. 'Resource allocation and the public sector', *Yale Economic Essays*, vol. 7, Spring 1967, pp. 45–98.
11. HARDY, G. H., LITTLEWOOD, J. E. and POLYA, G. *Inequalities*, 2nd edn., Cambridge University Press, 1952.
12. JOHANSEN, L. *Public Economics*, North-Holland, 1965.
13. LYDALL, H. F. *The Structure of Earnings*, Oxford University Press, London, 1968.
14. MIRRLEES, J. A. 'An exploration in the theory of optimum income taxation', *Review of Economic Studies*, April 1971, pp. 175–208.
15. MIRRLEES, J. A. 'Population policy and the taxation of family size', *Journal of Public Economics*, August 1972, pp. 169–198.
16. MUSGRAVE, R. A. *The Theory of Public Finance*, McGraw-Hill, 1959.
17. PEARSON, K. ed. *Tables of the Incomplete Γ-Function*, Cambridge University Press, 1965.
18. PIGOU, A. C. *A Study in Public Finance*, 3rd edn., Macmillan, 1947.
19. PREST, A. R. *Public Finance in Theory and Practice*, 3rd edn., Weidenfeld & Nicolson, 1967.
20. RAWLS, J. 'Distributive Justice', in P. Laslett and W. G. Runciman, *Philosophy, Politics and Society*, Third Series, Blackwell, 1967.
21. SEN, A. K. *Collective Choice and Social Welfare*, Oliver & Boyd, 1970.
22. SHESHINSKI, E. 'The optimal linear income tax', *Review of Economic Studies*, forthcoming, 1972.
23. SHESHINSKI, E. 'On the theory of optimal income taxation', *Journal of Public Economics*, forthcoming.
24. SIMONS, H. *Personal Income Taxation*, University of Chicago Press, 1938.
25. SIMON, H. A. 'On a class of skew distribution functions', *Biometrika*, **42**, 1955, pp. 425–40.
26. WESSON, J. 'On the distribution of personal incomes', *Review of Economic Studies*, forthcoming, 1972.

Public sector resource allocation under conditions of risk[1]

7

R. Rees

This paper is concerned with the theoretical basis for the analysis of optimal public enterprise pricing and investment policies under risk. The first section gives a brief survey of the theory of public sector pricing and investment under certainty, in order to clarify exactly what a satisfactory theory of resource allocation under risk must achieve. Part 2 shows that the existing contributions to the risk problem fall short of providing us with a satisfactory theory and the remainder of the paper, section 3, develops a model of resource allocation in conditions of risk, designed to permit the analysis of as wide a range of problems as has been treated on the restrictive assumption of certainty.

1. Criteria for a theory of public sector resource allocation

The analytical part of public enterprise economics has typically been concerned with finding necessary conditions for an optimal allocation of resources. These conditions then yield pricing and investment rules, the implementation of which is seen as a decentralised way of bringing about allocative efficiency.

In the context of the neoclassical first-best general equilibrium model under certainty, the theoretical problem of deriving optimal rules for public enterprises is, I would argue, almost trivial. An equilibrium allocation in such a model is Pareto-optimal, and either the government is content with the associated income distribution, or it can make the lump-sum redistributions required to maximise its Bergsonian social welfare function (s.w.f.). It follows that if certain industries supplying a subset of markets in the economy happen to be state-owned, their optimal policies are to conform to the necessary conditions for a Pareto-optimum. This implies marginal cost pricing, and use of the market rate of interest as the cost of public sector capital. This latter rule follows because the capital market is perfect, and therefore rates of time preference and marginal productivities of capital are all equal to each other

[1] This paper has benefited from discussions with A. H. Vanags, H. Gravelle and H. Thonemann. Responsibility for remaining shortcomings is my own.

and to the market interest rate, and presumably the government can make lump-sum redistributions over time to achieve any desired intertemporal distribution of income. Thus, the problem of optimal public enterprise resource allocation is hardly a separate area of study at the general equilibrium level.

Remaining with the first-best economy, the problem begins to acquire some interest at the partial equilibrium level, at which one deals with such problems as peak-load pricing, plant indivisibilities, and the precise calculation of certain opportunity costs. There are two possible approaches to the formulation of problems at this level. The first involves defining an appropriate partial equilibrium welfare function, and basing on it an explicit optimisation problem. The main issue here concerns the validity of the welfare function, and this usually requires a more general analysis to establish the conditions under which the function is appropriate.

The second approach takes the *general* form of the solution to the problem as known, and then attempts to apply this to the variables and relationships involved in the partial equilibrium problem. For example, in the peak-load pricing problem, one may take as maximand the sum of consumers' and producers' surpluses, and set up the problem as one of constrained maximisation.[1] Alternatively, one can simply take it as given that the optimal solution is marginal cost pricing, and all that is then necessary is to define the relevant cost and demand functions.[2] This is essentially a problem of defining correctly the time dimension of output.

The important point to note for subsequent analysis is that it is rarely possible in practice to implement general allocation rules without modifying them to take account of particularities of products, technologies, and distribution systems, and these modifications make it necessary to descend to the partial equilibrium level. It follows that any analysis of optimal allocation rules should try to derive a *consistent* set of general and partial equilibrium rules.

The general equilibrium analysis of optimal public enterprise resource allocation, may reacquire interest when we concede the existence of the second-best. If we ignore for the moment problems of uncertainty and information costs, the second-best problem arises in one or both of two ways. It is not feasible to finance provision of non-marketed public sector outputs, meet the deficits of marketed outputs subject to increasing returns, and achieve distributional aims, by lump sum taxes. Hence we have income and output taxes which affect things at the margin. Second, imperfections of competition and externalities will imply that private sector markets will not achieve Pareto-optimal allocations. One approach to these problems would be to find the necessary conditions for an optimum in an appropriately characterised second-best economy, with respect not only to outputs and inputs, but also to some set of policy instruments, e.g. taxes and subsidies, on the

[1] For example, see O. E. Williamson [21].
[2] This was the approach adopted by the earlier writers on the subject.

assumption that the government would adopt both the implied instruments and their optimal values.[1]

It should be stressed that there are two problems, which may well be interdependent. The first is that of defining the optimal set of instruments given the institutional nature of the economy, the administrative mechanism, and the costs of implementation. There is no reason why this optimal set should not be larger or smaller than that currently considered by economists and administrators. The second problem is to find the optimal values of this optimal set. Under this general approach, the public enterprise problem would again have no separate interest, except in so far as the different possibilities of intervention, as compared to the private sector, led to a different choice of instruments. As long as interest is confined to tax/subsidy policies, not even this latter qualification would hold: the question of the optimal way for a nationalised industry to meet a financial target, for example, would simply be a part of the general indirect taxation policy problem (as would the question of the size of the target itself[2]), and would require no separate solution.

The alternative to this general approach would be the so-called 'piecemeal' approach, under which we optimise only for the public enterprise sector. The resource allocation in the private sector is regarded as non-optimal, but alterable only through the interdependence of the public and private sectors. The piecemeal approach has characterised both the general second-best literature,[3] and that concerned more specifically with public enterprise problems.[4] In the former, the problem was simply used to illustrate the important general issues of the second-best. In the latter, the piecemeal approach resulted from the historical development of the subject. The question initially posed was that of determining optimal pricing and investment policies for public enterprises, and this was at first answered in first-best terms. Market imperfections, financial targets, etc., were then seen as impediments to the implementation of the first-best policies, and things which somehow had to be taken account of in the rules, but which could not themselves be changed. The piecemeal approach could perhaps be defended on the grounds that those institutions which control activities of public enterprises may be more amenable to influence of economists, and that the general approach would be infeasible,[5] but this is not entirely satisfactory.

In effect this is assuming, without explicit investigation, the solution to the question of the choice of the optimal set of instruments for allocative

[1] The paper by W. J. Baumol and D. Bradford [3] provides an illuminating discussion of the relation between optimal taxation policy and public enterprise pricing. P. A. Diamond and J. Mirrlees [8] adopt the general approach described here to the optimal taxation problem.

[2] Thus, the financial target becomes simply the amount of profit/loss implied by the imposition of the optimal tax/subsidy on the outputs of the industry. This does not conflict with the role of targets in stimulating managerial efficiency, since, in my view, it is the existence of targets rather than their levels which fulfil this.

[3] See, for example, R. G. Lipsey and K. Lancaster [12], and O. Davis and A. B. Whinston [6].

[4] For example, R. Rees [17].

[5] In fact I argued this in the paper cited in the preceding note.

policy in a second-best economy, and without proper analysis we cannot be sure that it is in fact optimal.

To summarise: although by no means complete, the theory of public enterprise pricing and investment under certainty can be regarded as well developed. The examination of this body of theory suggests criteria by which we would judge the theory of public sector resource allocation under risk to be satisfactory. To be so, it should analyse both pricing and investment policies, and the relation between them; it should provide a consistent set of partial and general equilibrium rules; and it should consider the problems arising out of the second-best, preferably from both the general and piecemeal points of view. The following section considers the extent to which the existing body of theory meets these criteria.

2. Public sector resource allocation under risk: the existing theory

Just as the development of the theory under certainty was closely related to the progress of welfare economics, so in the present case we are heavily dependent on the welfare economics of risk. The most well-developed body of theory in this area is, of course, that of Arrow [1]* and Debreu [7] who have formulated the state-contingent commodity approach. Let $T=\{t\}$ be a set of time periods of equal finite length, and let $S_t=\{s_t\}$ be a set of 'states of the world', one of which will prevail at time t. The elements of S_t are meant to be an exhaustive and mutually exclusive classification of the possible states at time t, where a state consists of a particular set of values of all those variables which are outside the control of a decision-taker, and which influence the outcome at t of at least one decision he may take at time 1, the present. Furthermore, it is usual to assume that all decision-takers in the economy have in mind the same S_t (this assumption has been relaxed by Radner [15] with interesting results, especially for the existence of equilibrium). This basic definition immediately raises problems in the present context, since many of the variables which private sector decision-takers will regard as environmental are actually within the control of the government, e.g. tax rates, the level of national income, etc. However, for most of this paper it is assumed that this problem does not exist.

Commodities are then defined not only in terms of their physical characteristics and the date and place at which they will be exchanged, but also the state of the world in which they will be exchanged. Thus, electricity supplied to your home on 20 December 1972 with warm weather is a different commodity to electricity at that place and date in cold weather. The number of such state contingent commodities may clearly be very large. If perfect markets exist in all state contingent commodities, where contracts are made at time 1, and prices are paid at time 1 for delivery of specified amounts of a given state-contingent commodity if and only if the specified state occurs, then

---

* Numbers in square brackets relate to references on p. 135.

Arrow and Debreu show that the resulting general equilibrium resource allocation will be Pareto-optimal.

Essentially, the device of the state-contingent commodity converts the economy to an expanded system of markets in each of which there is a price known with certainty, and the standard analysis of consumption and production choices applies directly to the state-contingent commodities; hence, known theorems can be applied.

The implications of this theory for public sector resource allocation are very similar to those of the first-best case under certainty. If a certain subset of the state-contingent commodities happen to be produced by state-owned industries, the Pareto-optimum will be achieved if those industries act as if they traded in perfectly competitive markets. Prices of state-contingent commodities will equal their marginal costs, and, as Hirshleifer [10] has shown, discount rates for new public sector investment projects can quite easily be derived. Indeed, the usual equivalence between long-run marginal cost pricing on the one hand, and the maximisation of net present value on the other, can be demonstrated to hold provided, of course, that the correct prices and discount rates are chosen. Thus, again, public sector resource allocation ceases to be a separate problem.

There are two questions which repeatedly occur in discussions of the appropriate public sector discount rate for risky projects. These are whether such discount rates should contain risk premia, and whether the state should intervene in the private sector to increase the allocative efficiency of risk-bearing. In the state-contingent commodity model, clearly the latter question loses interest; in relation to the former, Hirshleifer [10] has shown that in general the rate of discount on public sector investments should contain a risk premium, though it will vary with the project, and may be positive or negative. It is calculated from the prices for the state-contingent outputs which the investment will generate. Arrow and Lind [2] however, have proved a theorem which establishes conditions under which a *riskless* public discount rate should be used. This is further discussed below.

In the light of the similarity in implications between the Arrow–Debreu economy and the first-best economy under certainty, it might have been expected that the next step would have been to begin consideration of taxation, market imperfection, etc. However, a rather more fundamental difficulty arises, which is that we cannot assume the existence in fact of state-contingent commodities and their markets, and so the model loses some of its normative interest. An example will illustrate. The supply of electricity at some future point in time will depend on past forecasts of demand (which will have determined *planned* capacity), and the extent of plant availability. Demand at that point in time will depend on the weather. An excess of demand over available supply makes necessary disconnections of some consumers, i.e. complete cessation of supply for a period of time. Given probability distributions on forecasting errors, plant availability, and weather, an overall probability distribution of states could be constructed. We can regard a combination of particular values of these three variables as defining a state. Then, contracts for specified amounts of electricity in each possible state, at given prices, would be negotiated. Presumably, contracts in cold weather, low availability states would command high prices, while those in warm weather, high availability states would command lower prices. The effect would be that in each state, demand would equal supply, some consumers having decided to consume zero, or smaller amounts than they would otherwise have done, in the higher priced states. In addition, plant capacity will be optimally adjusted, since increments in plant which will yield known increments of output in each state can be evaluated at the given set of prices. Thus we would have the counterpart to the Arrow–Debreu economy. However, implementation of this system would require that the supply to each individual consumer can be continuously and finely controlled to match his contract. Although perhaps technically feasible, the cost of providing and maintaining the required metering equipment would be enormous. Thus we have the present system, in which some large industrial consumers do have crude state-contingent contracts (they pay a lower price for electricity in return for agreeing to disconnection at certain peak times), but, by and large, 'reliability of supply' is a public good. It is supplied to the system as a whole, in the form of a margin of plant capacity over and above that required to meet the expected value of demand, and no consumer can be excluded from 'consuming' the amount of reliability this provides. Given the well-known difficulties of estimating in practice the optimal supply of a public good, it is not surprising that decisions on the size of the plant margin are taken with little knowledge of consumer benefit.[1]

This example, then, illustrates a major difficulty in applying the Arrow–Debreu model; the costs of organising the required markets may be too high, and so the required markets do not exist. Rather than analysing this model further, therefore, it appears more fruitful to consider an alternative general equilibrium model under uncertainty.

Arrow and Lind [2] prove the theorem that in the Arrow–Debreu economy, with complete markets in state-contingent commodities, if the returns to a public sector investment project are uncorrelated with the value of national income (measured as excluding the returns to the project), then the relevant public sector discount rate does not contain a risk premium (cf. Hirshleifer's conclusions, described above). More important, given the inapplicability of that model, they prove that if all the benefits and costs of a public sector investment are recovered or borne by the government, which then determines its total taxation in the light of them, and if these net benefits are again uncorrelated with national income, then the total social costs of the riskiness associated with any individual investment tends to zero as the number of taxpayers tends to infinity, and so, for large populations, it can effectively be ignored. Hence, in this case the discount rate would not contain a risk premium. However, both the conditions of the theorem are necessary. If the

---

[1] For an application of the procedure in a context other than electricity supply, see J. A. Rees and R. Rees [16].

recipients of the outputs of the investment are risk-averse and retain net benefits, then these should be discounted for risk; and if the net benefits are correlated with income, a risk premium on the discount rate will be appropriate, and its sign will vary directly with the sign of the correlation in question.

The relevance of this theorem to public sector resource allocation is very much in doubt. The returns to most public enterprise investments are highly positively correlated with national income (it should be said that Arrow and Lind appear to have in mind small localised investments in non-marketed outputs, or at least those which have strong public good elements), while net benefits of public goods are certainly not recovered. In addition, the analysis neglects pricing policy, again because it is essentially concerned with the appropriate discount rate to be used in cost benefit analyses, rather than with public enterprise policies. Finally, it does not consider second-best problems, and thus meets few of the criteria set out above for a satisfactory theory of public sector resource allocation under risk.

A different and more fruitful approach was adopted by Malinvaud [13]. He analysed an economy consisting of two firms, one of which produced subject to uncertainties in production, the other of which faced no uncertainty. He was mainly interested in the question of the effect of increased riskiness of production in one firm on the optimal pattern of resource allocation, given that the overall s.w.f. exhibited risk-aversion. He showed, on special assumptions about the way in which randomness influenced the production function of the risky firm, that if both firms were producing the same good, the output of the risky firm varied inversely with the degree of risk; whereas if they produced different goods, the output of the risky firm could vary either directly or inversely with its riskiness. An intuitive reason for the positive relation is that, if the riskily produced good was very highly valued relative to the other, then more resources would be devoted to it in order to ensure enough of it as its riskiness increased. This bears a similarity to Hirshleifer's finding that, in the Arrow–Debreu model, a public sector good might require a negative risk premium if it paid off very highly in highly valued states, e.g. an investment to reduce the frequency of electricity plant breakdowns in the middle of winter (which may not pay off in warm winters at all).

Among several other important points raised by Malinvaud, is the desirability of government intervention in the private sector to improve the allocation of risk-bearing, particularly given a divergence between private risk (e.g. due to bankruptcy) and social risk.

Finally, in contrast to the general equilibrium approach of the papers discussed so far, Brown and Johnson [5] adopted a partial equilibrium approach to the question of optimal public utility pricing under stochastic conditions. Using a linear demand function, with an additive stochastic term in one case and a multiplicative one in the other, they showed that optimality required a lower price and a larger capacity than would apply under certainty, and that the utility operated at a loss, with operating costs covered but capacity costs not. Cost conditions were assumed known with certainty, and no discussion of the cost of capital under risk was offered. The maximand in the problem is expected value of consumers' and producers' surpluses.

There are several reasons for treating these results with caution. As Rothenberg and Smith [19] recently showed, in a model concerned with maximisation of expected value of profit, the result that output of a firm will be greater under risk may not hold when we take into account interaction among firms, e.g. expansion of one firm may raise input prices and costs which may then modify the partial equilibrium result. Indeed, the analysis by Malinvaud discussed above anticipated this point, at least for the production uncertainty case, and showed that in some cases optimal output of the public firm would be lower as risk increased. Furthermore, the authors do not justify their maximand, and yet can we necessarily assume that expected value of consumers' plus producers' surplus is appropriate? Do the special assumptions required to justify the corresponding maximand in the certainty case suffice here, or is it valid only under more restrictive assumptions? The problem really requires further analysis.

Although several other papers discuss the public sector problem, these tend to be *obiter dicta* by authors concerned primarily with some other aspects of risk (e.g. Diamond [8], Mossin [14]) though are none the less valuable for that. The general conclusion must be that, although there have been useful theorems and insights, nothing like a systematic body of theory which meets the criteria set out earlier has emerged. The rest of this paper is concerned with an attempt to establish a basis for the development of such a systematic body of theory.

3. A model of the economy under risk

If transactions costs are such that complete markets in state-contingent commodities are precluded, then it is natural to regard the following economy as the analogue of the first-best economy under certainty. There are three sectors, one of which produces capital goods, and the other two of which produce consumption goods. There are two points in time, time 1 and time 2. At time 1 production of capital and consumption goods takes place, but at time 2 production of consumption goods only takes place, i.e. the capital goods sector delivers its output to the two other sectors and then shuts down. The only constraints on production are production functions, fixed capital stocks at each time period, and the requirement that input demands and supplies be equal. The only constraints on consumption are that supplies and demands for consumption goods be equal. There are no externalities in production or consumption. So far, the model is simply a disaggregated version of the Fisher–Hirshleifer[1] two period model, where the degree of disaggregation is the minimum necessary to enable the model to be applied to the problem in hand.

Uncertainty is introduced in the following way. A continuous stochastic

---

[1] For a very thorough exposition of this model, see J. Hirshleifer [10].

state of the world parameter, θ, enters into all production and utility functions. Production and consumption at each point in time take place when the state of the world is known. However, the decision has to be taken at $t=1$ about how much capital to produce and install in each consumption good sector, and at that time the state of the world at $t=2$ is unknown. Thus, we have that short-run production and exchange decisions are taken under certainty, but that investment decisions are characterised by uncertainty. The uncertainty arises from future stochastic demand and cost functions. This last assumption effectively rules out what may be termed 'short-run uncertainty', and implies that the only uncertainty which prevails relates to the investment decision, and so may be termed 'long-run uncertainty'. This may be thought rather restrictive.

In production decisions, it rules out problems of the quality control kind. In exchange decisions, it implies that once θ is known, exchange takes place at known prices and the economy achieves a simultaneous equilibrium as envisaged in the Walrasian theory. Although of course it is important to study the consequences of the removal of each of these restrictions, for present purposes the most useful procedure would appear to be to concentrate on long-run uncertainty and its influence on the investment decision.

In this paper, the following two questions will be considered for this 'first-best economy':

(a) What are the necessary conditions for an unconstrained Pareto-optimal resource allocation?

(b) Are there conditions under which the equilibrium of a market economy will be a Pareto-optimum? What, if any, are the sources of failure to reach such an optimum, and how do we formulate the appropriate second-best problem?

The first question is answered by setting up an optimisation problem as if for some omniscient central planner who has complete information on utility and production functions, and probability beliefs. The second question is dealt with by setting up a model of the corresponding market economy, finding the conditions which will be satisfied at its equilibrium, assuming it exists, and then examining the correspondence between these and the solution of the planner's model.

The planner's economy

Let x_{it} be the output of the ith consumption good sector at time t, $i=2, 3$, $t=1, 2$, and let x_{11} be capital goods output. Denote the labour supply at time t by z_t. At time 1, each sector has fixed capital stock, $y^0{}_{i1}$, the result of past investment decisions, and a variable labour input, z_{it}. At time 2, the consumption good sectors have fixed capital stocks $x^0{}_{i11}$, it being assumed for simplicity that $y^0{}_{i1}$ is scrapped after use. Then:

$$\sum_{i=2}^{3} x_{i11} = x_{11} \tag{1}$$

Production conditions are described by production functions:

$$x_{11} = f^{11}(y^0{}_{11}, z_{11}) \tag{2}$$

$$x_{i1} = f^{i1}(y^0{}_{i1}, z_{i1}) \tag{3}$$

$$x_{i2} = f^{i2}(x^0{}_{i11}, z_{i2}, \theta) \qquad i = 2, 3 \tag{4}$$

Households consume goods and supply labour, and are assumed to conform to the von Neumann–Morgenstern axioms. Assume further that their utility functions take this form:

$$u^k = u^{k1}(x_{ki1}, z_{k1}) + \rho_k u^{k2}(x_{ki2}, z_{k2}, \theta) \tag{5}$$

$$i = 2, 3 \qquad k = 1, 2 \dots K \qquad t = 1, 2$$

where ρ_k is the kth household's 'felicity discount rate', and x_{kit} is consumption of the ith good at time t. Note that (5) does not exclude dependence of the time 2 preference ordering on the state of the world.

Households maximise:

$$\bar{u}^k = \int u^k h_k(\theta) \, \mathrm{d}\theta \tag{6}$$

where $h_k(\theta)$ is the kth household's probability density function (p.d.f.) on θ. Finally, I adopt as the planner's social welfare function:[1]

$$U = U(\bar{u}^k) \tag{7}$$

where:

$$U(\bar{u}^k) = \sum_k \alpha_{k1}\left(u^{k1} + \rho_k \int u^{k2} h_k(\theta) \, \mathrm{d}\theta\right) \tag{8}$$

The planner's problem is then to maximise U, subject to constraints represented by equations (1)–(4), and the additional constraints:

$$\sum_k x_{kit} = x_{it} \tag{9}$$

$$\sum_i z_{it} = \sum_k z_{kt} \qquad t = 1, 2 \qquad i = 1, 2, 3 \tag{10}$$

The solution procedure I adopt for this problem reflects the following view of the 'planning process'. Since production and exchange take place after the state of the world is known, the planner must determine at time 1:

---

[1] This s.w.f. is individualistic in the sense that it is based on the household utility functions and probability beliefs. Note that the planner is attempting to maximise households' expected utilities in the light of their own probability beliefs, rather than his own, if he has any. The weights, α_{k1}, are positive constants, and will be identified below with the reciprocals of the marginal utilities of households' time 1 incomes. This procedure of taking a weighted sum is, of course, equivalent to generating a Pareto-optimum by maximising the utility of one household subject to fixed levels of utility of all others. For applications of this in the certainty case, see Davis and Whinston [6], and R. Rees [17].

(a) state-contingent outputs, consumptions, and labour supplies for time 2, which are contingent also on capital stocks chosen at time 1;
(b) outputs, consumptions, and labour supplies at time 1, where the total output and allocation of capital goods must be chosen in the light of their effects on the state-contingent time 2 allocation.

The solution procedure is then the following: the optimal time 2 state-contingent allocation is found by maximising, for a *given* value of θ, the s.w.f.[1]

$$\sum_k \alpha_{k2}(u^{k1}+\rho_k \int u^{k2}h_k(\theta)\,d\theta)$$

subject to the time 2 production and market-clearing constraints, and taking capital stocks as predetermined. The necessary conditions for an optimal state-contingent resource allocation at time 2 are given by:

$$\left.\begin{array}{c} \rho_k\alpha_{k2}\dfrac{\partial u^{k2}}{\partial x_{ki2}}-\lambda_{i1}=\rho_k\alpha_{k2}\dfrac{\partial u^{k2}}{\partial z_{k2}}+\lambda_2=0 \\[2mm] \lambda_{i1}-\lambda_{i3}=\lambda_{i3}\dfrac{\partial f^{i2}}{\partial z_{i2}}-\lambda_2=0 \end{array}\right\}\quad(11)$$

together with the constraints. The Lagrange multipliers λ_{i1} and λ_2 are market-clearing prices, payable at time 2. Accordingly, given that these prices are measured in 'unit of account', or money (which plays no other role in the analysis), the state-contingent weights α_{k2} are in dimensions: money at time 2/utility at time 1. Denote the planned time 2 state-contingent values of $x_{ki2}z_{k2}$ by $x^*_{ki2}z^*_{k2}$. Regarding now each u^{k2} as a function of $x^*_{ki2}z^*_{k2}$, the planner's problem at time 1 is to maximise:

$$\sum_k \alpha_{k1}(u^{k1}+\rho_k \int u^{k2}(x^*_{ki2},z^*_{k2})\,h_k(\theta)\,d\theta)$$

subject to time 1 market-clearing and production constraints, and regarding both capital stocks and θ now as variable. The optimum conditions are:

$$\left.\begin{array}{c} \alpha_{k1}\dfrac{\partial u^{k1}}{\partial x_{ki1}}-\mu_{i1}=\alpha_{k1}\dfrac{\partial u^{k1}}{\partial z_{k1}}+\mu_2=0 \\[2mm] \mu_{i1}-\mu_{i3}=\mu_{i3}\dfrac{f^{i1}}{z_{i1}}-\mu_2=0 \\[2mm] \sum_k\int \rho_k\alpha_{k1}\left\{\dfrac{\partial u^{k2}}{\partial x_{ki2}}\dfrac{dx^*_{ki2}}{dx_{i11}}+\dfrac{\partial u^{k2}}{\partial z_{k2}}\dfrac{dz^*_{k2}}{dx_{i11}}\right\} \\[2mm] h_k(\theta)\,d\theta-\mu_{11}=0 \\[2mm] \mu_{11}\dfrac{\partial f^{11}}{\partial z_{11}}-\mu_2=0 \end{array}\right\}\quad(12)$$

together with the constraints.

[1] Note that the weights α_{k2} used in finding the state-contingent time 2 allocation differ from α_{k1}, those used in making a time 1 resource allocation. The α_{k2} are given the interpretation as the reciprocals of the state-contingent marginal utilities of time 2 incomes of households.

The interpretation of these conditions is quite straightforward. At each time period, for given capital stocks and θ, marginal rates of substitution between consumption goods are equal for all consumers, and equal also to the corresponding marginal rates of transformation. Likewise each household's marginal rate of substitution between consumption of the ith good and labour supply is equal to the marginal product of labour in production of that good. The condition relating to the allocation of capital to the ith consumption good is given in the third line of (12), and has the following interpretation: an increment of capital to the ith sector permits an increment of consumption at time 2 to each household in each state of the world, and requires an increment of labour from it, where increments of consumption and labour are chosen optimally. The expected net present values of utility gains to households are then weighted, summed, and equated to the present marginal opportunity cost of the capital good, to determine optimal investment. Note that this 'present expected social marginal utility' of investment must be equal in each sector. Furthermore if we substitute into this condition, from conditions (11), for the marginal utilities of consumption and labour, we obtain:

$$\sum_k \int \frac{\alpha_{k1}}{\alpha_{k2}} \left\{ \lambda_{i1} \frac{dx^*_{ki2}}{dx_{i11}} - \lambda_2 \frac{dz^*_{k2}}{dx_{i11}} \right\} h_k(\theta) \, d\theta - \mu_{11} = 0 \qquad (13)$$

i.e. the net expected present value of welfare gain to each household is found by valuing its incremental consumption and labour supply, which depend on θ, at the state-contingent prices of the consumption good and labour respectively, and then discounting at the household's *time preference rate*,[1] α_{k1}/α_{k2}.

To comment briefly on the planner's model and its solution: it is clearly the centralised counterpart of an economy with complete markets in state-contingent commodities and labour supplies, but where prices are actually paid at time 2 for state-contingent deliveries *contracted for* at time 1. From conditions 11 it is clear that if α_{k2} is identified with the reciprocal of the state-contingent marginal utility of time 2 income of household k, while α_{k1} is that for time 1, a perfectly competitive economy with the relevant markets would achieve the same allocation.

Turning to the market economy, in which markets in state-contingent commodities do not exist, a number of previous contributions, especially those of K. Borch [4], and P. A. Diamond [8], lead one to expect that the planner's optimum will not be achieved. However, the important problems for present purposes are, first, to understand fully why this is the case, in the context of the present model; and second, to consider how this particular kind of market failure determines formulation of the appropriate second-best model.

[1] Thus, given the dimensions of α_{k1} and α_{k2}, the dimension of their ratio is money at time 1/money at time 2. For a given value of θ, the interpretation of α_{k1} and α_{k2} as the reciprocals of the marginal utilities of income at times 1 and 2 respectively, imply that they show the *equilibrium* rate at which a *certain* amount of money at time 1 would be traded for one unit of money paid at time 2 in that state of the world.

The market economy

The economic agents in this economy are households and firms, where one of the latter, producing x_2, is state-owned. Since the object is to establish conditions under which the private sector will satisfy the conditions of the planner's model which relate to it, or exactly why it does not do so, I ignore for the time being the production and investment decisions of the state-owned firm.

Households supply labour and buy public and private sector consumption goods at times 1 and 2, but only at time 1 do they buy/sell bonds and ordinary shares in private sector firms. At time 1 they receive income from existing stock and bond holdings (which are the result of past decisions), from stock which they buy at time 1, and from their supply of labour. Thus, we have:

$$Y_{k1} = \sum_s (\beta^0_{sk1} + \beta_{sk1}) \pi_{s1} + w_1 z_{k1} + r^0 n^0_k \qquad (14)$$

where Y_{k1} is time 1 income, π_{s1} is profit of the sth firm, $s = 1, 2, \ldots S$, β^0_{sk1} and β_{sk1} are, respectively, the share in the sth firm already owned by household k, and the share in it which is bought or sold at time 1. Clearly,

$$-\beta^0_{sk1} \leqslant \beta_{sk1} \leqslant 1 - \beta^0_{sk1}$$

while

$$\sum_k \beta_{sk1} = 0$$

all s. The wage rate, w_1, is known with certainty, r^0 is the interest *factor*, with $r^0 - 1$ as the interest *rate* on bonds. It is assumed that bonds are issued for one period only, and then redeemed, at an interest rate which is determined at the time of issue. I assume that there is no risk of default on bond redemption by any issuer. The net bond holding of maturing bonds at time 1 is denoted by n^0_k, where $n^0_k > 0$ if the household is a net lender and $n^0_k < 0$ if a borrower. All variables with superscript 0 are predetermined at time 1 and play no real part in the analysis.

Household expenditure at time 1 is given by

$$E_{k1} = \sum_{i=2}^{3} p_{i1} x_{ki1} + n_{k1} + \sum_s \beta_{sk1} e_{s1} \qquad (15)$$

Here, p_{i1} is the known market price of good x_i at time 1, n_{k1} is the net bond acquisition of the household (positive for lending, negative for borrowing), and e_{s1} is the market value at time 1 of the equity of firm s. These two equations then give the time 1 budget constraint for consumer k:

$$\sum_i p_{i1} x_{ki1} + n_{k1} + \sum_s \beta_{sk1}(e_s - \pi_{s1}) - w_1 z_{k1} - \gamma^0 = 0 \qquad (16)$$

where γ^0 denotes the sum of predetermined values. Analogously, the time 2 budget constraint is given by:

$$\sum_i p_{i2} x_{ki2} - r_1 n_{k1} - \sum_s \beta_{sk2} \pi_{s2} - w_2 z_{k2} = 0 \qquad (17)$$

where $\beta_{sk2} = \beta^0{}_{sk1} + \beta_{sk1}$, and r_1 is the interest factor which is determined at time 1. There will be no incentive for the household to trade in shares at time 2, because at time 2 the market value of a firm will equal its known profits, and so the cost of a shareholding exactly equals the return from acquiring it. Thus, all trade in shares takes place at time 1 only.

Household k maximises:

$$\bar{u}^k = u^{k1}(x_{ki1}, z_{k1}) + \rho_k \int u^{k2}(x_{ki2}, z_{k2}, \theta) \, h_k(\theta) \, d\theta \qquad (18)$$

subject to the budget constraints in (16) and (17).

The household makes its optimal choices in the following way: at time 1, it *expects* state-contingent prices and wage rate $p_{i2}(\theta)$ and $w_2(\theta)$ to prevail, and it expects the state-contingent profits of the sth firm to be $\pi_{s2}(\theta)$. Its entire budget constraint in (17) is therefore state-contingent. For any given choice of β_{sk2} and n_{k1} at time 1, and for any given state of the world, the household will plan to choose $x_{ki2}z_{k2}$ which maximise (18) subject to its time 2 budget constraint. The optimal values, $x^*{}_{ki2}z^*{}_{k2}$ satisfy the conditions:

$$\rho_k \frac{\partial u^{k2}}{\partial x_{ki2}} - \delta_{k2}p_{i2} = 0 = \rho_k \frac{\partial u^{k2}}{\partial z_{k2}} + \delta_{k2}w_2 \qquad (19)$$

together with the budget constraint. δ_{k2} has the usual interpretation as the marginal utility of time 2 income, and has dimension: utility at time 1/ money at time 2. Its equilibrium value depends not only on θ but also on the particular set of price, wage and profit expectations.

At time 1, the household must choose values for consumption, labour supply and stock and bond transactions, in such a way as to maximise:

$$\bar{u}^k = u^{k1}(x_{ki1}, z_{k1}) + \rho_k \int u^{k2}(x^*{}_{ki2}, z^*{}_{k2}, \theta) \, h_k(\theta) \, d\theta \qquad (20)$$

subject to the time 1 budget constraint. The solution is given by the conditions:

$$\left.\begin{aligned}
&\frac{\partial u^{k1}}{\partial x_{ki1}} - \delta_{k1}p_{i1} = \frac{\partial u^{k1}}{\partial z_{k1}} + \delta_{k1}w_1 = 0 \\[6pt]
&\rho_k \int \left\{ \sum_i \frac{\partial u^{k2}}{\partial x_{ki2}} \frac{\partial x^*{}_{ki2}}{\partial n_{k1}} + \frac{\partial u^{k2}}{\partial z_{k2}} \frac{\partial z^*{}_{k2}}{\partial n_{k1}} \right\} \\[2pt]
&\qquad h_k(\theta) \, d\theta - \delta_{k1} = 0 \\[6pt]
&\rho_k \int \left\{ \sum_i \frac{\partial u^{k2}}{\partial x_{ki2}} \frac{\partial x^*{}_{ki2}}{\partial \beta_{sk1}} + \frac{\partial u^{k2}}{\partial z_{k2}} \frac{\partial z^*{}_{k2}}{\partial \beta_{sk1}} \right\} \\[2pt]
&\qquad h_k(\theta) \, d(\theta) - \delta_{k1}(e_{s1} - \pi_{s1}) = 0
\end{aligned}\right\} \qquad (21)$$

together with the budget constraint. Note that I have assumed that there are no corner solutions, and in particular that β_{sk1} satisfies its constraints as an inequality. δ_{k1} is time 1 marginal utility of income.

The last two conditions in (21) can be simplified as follows: in each of them, the terms in {} represent the effect of changes in the relevant decision variable on time 2 utility *via* its effect on time 2 income, and so they can be written, respectively, as:

$$\int \delta_{k2} r_1 h_k(\theta)\, \mathrm{d}\theta - \delta_{k1} = 0 \tag{22}$$

and:

$$\int \delta_{k2} \pi_{s2} h_k(\theta)\, \mathrm{d}\theta - \delta_{k1}(e_{s1} - \pi_{s1}) = 0 \tag{23}$$

Recalling that r_1 and δ_{k1} are non-stochastic, (22) can be written:

$$\frac{\bar{\delta}_{k2}}{\delta_{k1}} = \frac{1}{r_1} \tag{24}$$

where $\bar{\delta}_{k2}$ is the expected value of δ_{k2}, and where the left hand term is equal for all households regardless of probability beliefs. Rearranging (23) yields:

$$e_{s1} = \int \frac{\delta_{k2}}{\delta_{k1}} \pi_{s2} h_k(\theta)\, \mathrm{d}\theta + \pi_{s1} \tag{25}$$

Thus, given the prevailing market price of each firm, e_{s1}, known current profits, π_{s1}, and expectations of future profits, the household's demand for goods and supply of labour at time 1, and its net holdings of stock and bonds, will be determined in such a way as to satisfy the conditions in the first line of (21) and in (25).

Underlying this equilibrium will also be a set of planned, state-contingent demands for goods and supplies of labour at time 2, which, together with the repayments on bonds and the state-contingent dividends on shares, determine δ_{k2} as a function of θ.

To interpret further the conditions in 25: δ_{k2}/δ_{k1} is the household's rate of time preference, since, for given θ, it can be shown to be equal to the marginal rate of substitution between current and future income.[1] Thus, equation (24) implies that the expected values of time preference rates are equal in equilibrium for all households, though this does not imply in general that time preference rates are equal for any given θ. Equation (25) suggests an interpretation of the household's share-buying decision: it discounts its expectation of the firm's future profit in each state of the world by the corresponding discount rate δ_{k2}/δ_{k1}, and values the whole distribution of the future profits at the expected value of these present values. It then adjusts its share purchases—which causes δ_{k2}/δ_{k1} to vary inversely with the direction of adjustment, assuming diminishing marginal utility of income in each period —until its valuation of the total present worth of the firm's profit stream is equal to the prevailing market price of the firm. From this it follows that an increase in e_{s1} will, other things being equal, reduce a household's equilibrium demand for shares in firm s, while an increase in π_{s2} will, other things again equal, increase this equilibrium demand. Only if households' marginal utilities of time 2 income are proportional for each θ or independent of θ, will discount rates be equal. This latter case requires both that utility is

[1] The discussion is similar to that of the preceding footnote and so need not be repeated.

linear in income, and that θ enters additively into the utility function or not at all.

As we would expect, this implies that the household is risk-neutral, and so its discount rate becomes $1/r_1$. Let

$$\bar{\pi}_{s2}^k = \int \pi_{s2}h_k(\theta)\,d\theta$$

where the k superscript emphasises that profit expectations and probability beliefs may differ among households. Then, in equilibrium, it is always possible to find some number $\rho^k{}_s$ such that:

$$\rho^k{}_s\bar{\pi}_{s2}^k = e_{s1} - \pi_{s1} = \int \frac{\delta_{k2}}{\delta_{k1}}\,\pi_{s2}h_k(\theta)\,d\theta \qquad (26)$$

Thus, $\rho^k{}_s$ can be thought of as the kth household's equilibrium subjective discount rate, which it applies to the expected value of the profits of the firm. Clearly, the $\rho^k{}_s$ will be equal, for all k, only if the $\bar{\pi}_{s2}^k$ are equal. A sufficient, though not necessary, condition for the latter is that each household expects the same π_{s2} in each state of the world, and has the same p.d.f. over states. In general, however, we have to allow that the $\rho^k{}_s$ may differ for at least some k.

To consider now the decisions of firms: I assume that firms wish to maximise shareholders' wealth, implying maximisation of the market value of shares, e_{s1}. If firm s produces the capital good, then we have simply:

$$e_{s1} = \pi_{s1} = p_{11}x_{s1} - w_1 z_s - r_0 n_{s0} \qquad (27)$$

where p_{11} is the price of the capital good, x_{s1} and z_s are output and labour input respectively, and n_{s0} is the firm's net bond holding. Given the production function:

$$x_{s1} = f^s(y^0{}_{s1}, z_s) \qquad (28)$$

the equilibrium of the firm is given by the condition:

$$p_{11}\frac{\partial f^s}{\partial z_s} - w_1 = 0 \qquad (29)$$

i.e. price is equated to short-run marginal cost.

If firm s produces the consumption good, it has to decide on current output, the amount of new capital to install, and its sources of finance. In the present model, it has been assumed that households may borrow and lend at the same interest rate as firms, and that there is no default. Hence, it can be shown[1] that the Modigliani–Miller proposition, to the effect that market

---

[1] A brief proof can be given, along the lines of the approach in Mossin [14]. Let the value of the firm be denoted by $e_{s1} + b_s$, where e_{s1} is the equity and b_s the bond issue. If it can be shown that the budget constraint of any shareholder is unaffected by the composition of the value of the firm as between e_{s1} and b_s, it follows that his demand for shares in the firm, and therefore the value of the firm, are independent of the composition. To show that the budget constraint of the kth household is independent of the debt-equity mix, consider the budget constraints in equations (16), (17) and for

value of the firm is independent of its debt equity ratio, holds for this model. Accordingly, for simplicity I assume that firms issue no debt. In addition, new investment is assumed to be financed entirely out of current profits, shareholders being left to achieve individual time preference optima by buying or selling shares and bonds, as in the standard Fisher–Hirshleifer model under certainty. It then follows that the profit relations for firms are given by:

$$\pi_{s1} = p_{31}x_{s1} - w_1 z_{s1} - p_{11}x_{s11} \tag{30}$$

$$\pi_{s2} = p_{32}x_{s2} - w_2 z_{s2} \tag{31}$$

$$s = 1, 2, \ldots S$$

with production functions:

$$x_{s1} = f^{s1}(y^0{}_{s1}, z_{s1}) \tag{32}$$

$$x_{s2} = f^{s2}(x_{s11}, z_{s2}, \theta) \tag{33}$$

The managers of firms are assumed to have particular expectations concerning the values of p_{32} and w_2 for each value of θ, and also to have p.d.f. $h_s(\theta)$. There is no reason for identity of price expectations and probability beliefs, either among firms, or as between firms and households.

Clearly, the crucial determinant of the investment decision of the firm is the way in which it views the dependence of its market value on future profit. In the absence of complete markets in state-contingent commodities, with their corresponding equilibrium prices, the firm lacks the objective data on which to calculate the present values of future profits. Given its price expectations in each state of the world, the firm can calculate the relation:

$$\pi^*{}_{s2} = \pi^*{}_{s2}(x_{s11}, z^*{}_{s2}, \theta) \tag{34}$$

where $z^*{}_{s2}$ is the state-contingent optimal level of labour input, and, for each x_{s11} and given θ, satisfies the condition:

$$p_{32}\frac{\partial f^{s2}}{\partial z_{s2}} - w_2 = 0 \tag{35}$$

---

simplicity assume: $\beta^0{}_{sk1} = n^0{}_k = 0$. Solving for n_{k1} in (16) and substituting into (17) gives:

$$y_{k2} + r_1(y_{k1} - \sum_s \beta_{sk1}e_{s1}) + \sum_s \beta_{sk1}(\pi_{s2} - r_1 b_s) = 0 \tag{i}$$

where

$$y_{k1} = w_1 z_{k1} + \sum_s \beta_{sk1}\pi_{s1} - \sum_i p_{i1}x_{ki1}$$

and

$$y_{k2} = w_2 z_{k2} - \sum_i p_{i1}x_{ki1}$$

(i) can be rewritten as:

$$y_{k2} + r_1 y_{k1} + \sum_s \beta_{sk1}\pi_{s2} - \sum_s \beta_{sk1}r_1(e_{s1} + b_s) = 0$$

Thus, varying the asset composition of the firm as between e_{s1} and b_s, holding their total unchanged, leaves the budget constraint unaffected.

where p_{32} and w_2 are the firm's expected price and wage rate, given θ. More-over, from the well known envelope theorem,[1] we have that, for given θ,

$$\frac{\partial \pi^*_{s2}}{\partial x_{s11}} = \frac{\partial \pi_{s2}}{\partial x_{s11}} + \frac{\partial \pi_{s2}}{\partial z_{s2}} \frac{\partial z^*_{s2}}{\partial x_{s11}} = \frac{\partial \pi_{s2}}{\partial x_{s11}} \tag{36}$$

as a result of (35). Thus we may write $\pi^*_{s2}(x_{s11}, \theta)$ as the relevant time 2 profit function. Each profit distribution will be evaluated in the market accord-ing to shareholders' probability beliefs and discount rates, and the problem of the firm is to choose x_{s11} in such a way as to maximise its current market value.

A natural way to proceed would seem to be as follows. Conditions (21) yield for each household a set of demand functions for goods, bonds, and shares, and a supply function of labour. The arguments of these functions are prices, wages, the market values of firms, e_{s1}, current profits π_{s1}, and the distribution of expected future profits, π_{s2}. For a given set of values of these arguments, the *ex ante* demands of each household for a share in the sth firm, β_{sk2} can be aggregated to give a total market demand for shares,

$$\beta_s = \sum_k \beta_{sk2}$$

Of course, in equilibrium

$$\beta_s = \hat{\beta}_s = 1$$

where

$$\hat{\beta}_s = \sum_k \hat{\beta}_{sk2}$$

is the aggregate of shares actually held. It is obviously possible for e_{s1}, π_{s1}, π_{s2} to be such that

$$\sum_k \beta_{sk2} \gtrless 1$$

but, on the assumption that

$$\frac{\partial \beta_{sk}}{\partial e_{s1}} < 0$$

all, s, k, such a disequilibrium situation would be eliminated by movements in e_{s1}. Then the firm maximises the equilibrium value of e_{s1} by choosing, at any current actual value of e_{s1}, those values of z_{s1} and x_{s11} which maximise β_s. Hence, although it cannot be assumed that the firm knows individual shareholder discount rates and probability beliefs, it does seem reasonable to assume that the firm sees itself as confronting an aggregate demand function for its shares:

$$\beta_s = \phi^s(e_{s1}, \pi_{s1}, \pi_{s2}) \tag{37}$$

---

[1] See, for example, Samuelson [20].

where only π_{s1} and π_{s2} (up to a probability distribution) are under its control. For given choices of z_{s1} and x_{s11}, e_{s1} will be determined by the condition:

$$\phi^s(e_{s1}, \pi_{s1}, \pi_{s2}) = 1 \tag{38}$$

Suppose, for the moment, that the firm *successfully* maximises its share value. If β^*_{sk2} denotes the equilibrium holding of shares in the sth firm by the kth household, this implies that:

$$\sum_k \beta^*_{sk2} e_{s1} = \sum_k \beta^*_{sk2} \left\{ \pi_{s1} + \int \frac{\delta_{k2}}{\delta_{k1}} \pi_{s2} h_k(\theta) \, d\theta \right\} \tag{39}$$

is at a maximum with respect to z_{s1} and x_{s11}. That is, the firm has acted *as if* it has solved the problem:

$$\max \sum_k \beta^*_{sk2} \left\{ p_{31} f^{s1} - w_1 z_{s1} - p_{11} x_{s11} + \int \frac{\delta_{k2}}{\delta_{k1}} (p_{32} f^{s2} - \right.$$

$$\left. w_2 z^*_{s2}) h_k(\theta) \, d\theta \right\} \tag{40}$$

implying that it has chosen z^*_{s1} and x^*_{s11} which satisfy:

$$\sum_k \beta^*_{sk2} \left(p_{31} \frac{\partial f^{s1}}{\partial z_{s1}} - w_1 \right) = p_{31} \frac{\partial f^{s1}}{\partial z_{s1}} - w_1 = 0 \tag{41}$$

$$\sum_k \beta^*_{sk2} \int \frac{\delta_{k2}}{\delta_{k1}} p_{32} \frac{\partial f^{s2}}{\partial x_{s11}} h_k(\theta) \, d\theta - p_{11} = 0 \tag{42}$$

where note, the integrand in the second condition is the present value of the marginal product of capital, valued at the price expectations and discount rate of household k. Recalling equation (26) this second condition can also be written:

$$\sum_k \beta^*_{sk2} \rho^k_s \int p_{32} \frac{\partial f^{s2}}{\partial x_{s11}} h_k(\theta) \, d\theta - p_{11} = 0 \tag{43}$$

where ρ^k_s is the equilibrium discount rate of household k on the profits of firm s.

If the firm does not succeed in maximising its market value, because it wrongly perceives the market demand curve for its shares, then in general the resulting values of the β_{sk2} and ρ^k_s will be different, while if the distributions of marginal value products of capital which result from non-optimal choice of x_{s11} are substituted into (42) or (43), the equalities there will not hold. On the other hand, whatever the perceived demand function, a necessary condition for its maximisation is that the condition in (41) should be fulfilled, and this follows from the fact that time 1 prices and marginal products are certain.

The assumption that the firm correctly perceives the relation between its profit stream and the market demand for its shares, is clearly extreme. The individual discount rates ρ^k_s depend on household income, and the expectations they hold about future wages, prices and profit. The firm must announce its investment plans and/or profit forecasts *before* these discount rates are determined, therefore, previous market data may not help the firm since income and expectations may change over time. In fact, if ρ_s is the firm's own estimate of its equilibrium market discount rate, then it determines its investment to satisfy the condition:

$$\rho_s \int p_{32} \frac{\partial f^{s2}}{\partial x_{s11}} h_s(\theta)\, d\theta - p_{11} = 0 \tag{44}$$

where p_{32} is the *firm's* price expectation. Only in the special case in which the firm correctly guesses the market demand relation will (43) and (44) be equivalent. In any other case, its share value will not be maximised.

This completes the discussion of the conditions which characterise the time 1 equilibrium of the market economy. I now consider the comparison with the planned economy.

The optimality of the market economy

Unlike the Diamond model [8], where the implication of the absence of complete markets in state-contingent commodities was that linearity constraints were placed on household consumption over states of the world, the market economy fails to achieve a Pareto-optimum in the present case because of the absence of the price information which such markets would make available. To see this, suppose that in each state of the world, we have that:

$$p_{i2} = \lambda_{i1} \qquad w_2 = \lambda_2 \qquad \mu_{i1} = p_{i1} \qquad \mu_2 = w_1 \tag{45}$$

Given the definitions of α_{k1} and α_{k2}, it is immediately clear that the relevant conditions for the planner's resource allocation in (11) and (12) are identical to the corresponding conditions for household consumption and labour supply in (19) and (21). Similarly the conditions for choice of labour inputs are identical in the two models.[1] Thus, interest centres on the conditions determining investment in consumption goods in the two economies. Given the assumptions made in (45), and the additional assumptions that:

(*a*) the firm successfully maximises market value
(*b*) $p_{11} = \mu_{11}$

[1] As was pointed out by the discussant of this paper when it was given at the Conference, the planner's economy is set up in terms of industries, while the market economy is concerned with individual firms. For present purposes, it suffices to assume that the private sector consumption good is produced by only one firm, denoted s, which however acts as a price-taker. More rigorously, the production functions in the planner's model relating to the private sector good should be replaced by the functions f^{st}, $t=1, 2$, and the constraints by:

$$\sum_k x_{k3t} = \sum_s x_{s3t} \qquad t=1, 2$$

where the production functions f^{st} are identical to those of the corresponding private sector firms. It is not difficult to show that the following discussion does not change materially.

it is possible to show that in fact the market economy does achieve a Pareto-optimum. The condition determining investment in x_3 is:

$$\sum_k \beta^*{}_{sk2} \int_{\delta_{k1}}^{\delta_{k2}} p_{32} \frac{\partial f^{s2}}{\partial x_{s11}} h_k(\theta)\, \mathrm{d}\theta - p_{11} = 0 \qquad (46)$$

But, taking the time 2 budget constraint at the optimal solution for given θ, with n_{k1} and $\beta^*{}_{sk2}$ constant, and differentiating totally gives:

$$\sum_i p_{i2}\, \mathrm{d}x^*{}_{ki2} - w_2\, \mathrm{d}z^*{}_{k2} = \beta^*{}_{sk2}\, \mathrm{d}\pi_{s2} \qquad (47)$$

Dividing through by $\mathrm{d}\pi_{s2}$, substituting for $\beta^*{}_{sk2}$ in (46), and recalling (36) gives:

$$\sum_k \int_{\delta_{k1}}^{\delta_{k2}} \left\{ \sum_i p_{i2} \frac{\mathrm{d}x^*{}_{ki2}}{\mathrm{d}\pi_{s2}} - w_2 \frac{\mathrm{d}z^*{}_{k2}}{\mathrm{d}\pi_{s2}} \right\} \qquad (48)$$

$$\frac{\mathrm{d}\pi_{s2}}{\mathrm{d}x_{s11}} h^*{}_k(\theta)\, \mathrm{d}\theta - p_{11} = 0$$

i.e. that:

$$\sum_k \int_{\delta_{k1}}^{\delta_{k2}} \left\{ \sum_i p_{i2} \frac{\mathrm{d}x^*{}_{ki2}}{\mathrm{d}x_{s11}} - w_2 \frac{\mathrm{d}z^*{}_{k2}}{\mathrm{d}x_{s11}} \right\} h_k(\theta)\, \mathrm{d}\theta - p_{11} = 0 \qquad (49)$$

which is identical to the corresponding condition in the planner's model. Thus, if the price and wage expectations of all firms and households coincide with each other, and with the 'true' equilibrium prices and wage which would result if trading in time 2 state-contingent goods and labour actually took place, the market economy would achieve a full Pareto-optimum. Also required are that profit expectations are correct, and that the firm successfully maximises its market value.

The purpose of the above discussion was not to suggest that the market economy will in practice achieve a Pareto-optimum, but rather to emphasise that the reason for its failure to do this is the absence of the price-information function which state-contingent markets would fulfil. The reason for the difference between this and the analyses of Diamond [8], Borch [4], and Hirshleifer [11], is the assumption that production and exchange take place when the state of the world is known. This implies that households and firms can *plan* in terms of state-contingent commodities and labour supplies, but the absence of markets in these means that the equilibrium prices, which would be known to an omniscient planner, are not available in formulating these plans.

The second-best economy

The market economy discussed above can be called second-best on three grounds. First, it will not in general achieve the first-best optimum corresponding to the solution to the planner's model. Thus, absence of omniscience, or the markets which substitute for it, is one source of the second-best. The second ground is that in general, price and wage expectations may differ among households, and so intertemporal marginal rates of substitution will not be equal, since each household equates each particular intertemporal MRS to the ratio of expected price at time 2 to price at time 1. This is true regardless of whether firms successfully maximise market values. Finally, firms may not succeed in maximising their market values, implying that investment is non-optimal. In this section, I am concerned with the implications of all this for public sector resource allocation. The fiction of the omniscient planner is no longer useful for this purpose. If one really existed, then the problem would be solved by his communicating the relevant state-contingent prices to households and firms. Rather, we have to recognise that whether we adopt a general or piecemeal approach (cf. the introductory discussion) the public sector planner will himself have available only his own expectations about future prices, profits, etc., together with a set of probability beliefs.

There are two types of economy which may be envisaged. The first is an economy in which the expectations of all economic agents, including public sector planners, concerning all future variables are identical. The second is one where expectations differ. To take first the 'identical expectations economy', the important question is whether firms correctly perceive the market demand function for their shares, and so maximise their share values, or not. If they do so, then we have what may be called a 'quasi-first-best' situation, in the sense that the resource allocation satisfies the necessary conditions for a Pareto-optimum, relative to the *given set* of expectations. These expectations may not be correct, in the sense that they do not satisfy the equalities in (50), but, in the absence of omniscience, a planner who adopted the same set of expectations would at time 1, not be able to make a Pareto-optimal change[1] in the resource allocation.

On the other hand, the important difference between this case and the true first-best case is that at time 2, actual consumption and labour supply will differ for households, and output and labour input for firms, from the plans which they made at time 1.[2] It is then the case that *expost*, different time 1 decisions would have been preferred to those made *ex ante*, and so there is room for regret. Nevertheless, a non-omniscient planner with the same expectations as everyone else, cannot improve things at time 1.

In this situation, the output decision of the public enterprise at time 1,

---

[1] In the sense that he could not change the resource allocation in such a way as to put at least one household in a preferred position, and none in a less preferred position, in the light of the expectations and probability beliefs which they hold at time 1.

[2] Thus, if households and firms are correct in their expectations, they will at time 2 implement precisely those plans which they formulated at time 1, given that their utility functions remain unchanged. From conditions (19) we have:

$$\frac{\partial u^{k2}}{\partial x_{k22}} \Big/ \frac{\partial u^{k2}}{\partial x_{k32}} = \frac{p_{22}}{p_{32}} \qquad \frac{\partial u^{k2}}{\partial x_{ki2}} \Big/ \frac{\partial u^{k2}}{\partial z_{k2}} = \frac{p_{i2}}{w_2} \qquad (i=2,3)$$

which are precisely the conditions which will result from time 2 optimisation. Provided that price, wage and profit expectations turn out to be correct, the budget constraint which will prevail at time 2 will be that expected at time 1, for the value of θ which occurs. Hence, the actual solution values to the above conditions and the budget constraint will be the same both for plans at time 1 and actual choices at time 2.

and its planned state-contingent output decision at time 2, will satisfy the condition that short-run marginal cost equals price, and this also determines its labour demands. The main question of interest is therefore the determination of the optimal investment in the public enterprise.

Clearly, if the public enterprise were to issue shares, finance investment entirely out of retained earnings, and act so as successfully to maximise its market value, then its investment will satisfy the necessary condition for optimality,[1] relative to the given price expectations, just as does that of the private firm. In other words, we have the result which by now we would expect from a first-best model—the public enterprise optimises by acting as if it were a private firm.

Suppose, however, that the investment of the public enterprise is financed entirely by debt issue. Since I have earlier made the assumption of no default risk, to be consistent I have to assume in this case either that the government uses taxation to make up for any deficit the industry may incur in some state of the world, or that profits in all states of the world are at least sufficient to redeem debt and pay interest. It is not my intention in this paper to consider the important issues raised by the existence of taxation, and so I adopt the latter assumption. The consequence of complete debt finance is that the public enterprise does not have market information on the basis of which to attempt to maximise its market value. The optimal condition for its investment remains that given in (12), and the problem is to obtain information on the household discount rates.

A solution suggested by several earlier writers, and in particular Hirshleifer [10], is for the public enterprise to use the equilibrium market discount rate of a private sector firm with the same proportionate distribution of expected time 2 profits. In the present case, from equation (26) we have:

$$\rho^k{}_s = \int \frac{\delta_{k2}}{\delta_{k1}} \frac{\pi_{s2}}{\bar{\pi}^k{}_{s2}} h_k(\theta) \, d\theta \tag{50}$$

so that a household's equilibrium discount rate on a firm's expected value of profit depends on the proportionate profit distribution, and will clearly be the same for any two firms having proportional expected profit distributions. The valuation of time 2 profits of the two firms will therefore differ only by this proportionality factor. If the public enterprise uses the comparable private sector discount rate, it is acting *as if* it were maximising its share value, and in the identical expectations economy in which firms successfully maximise market values, this leads to optimal public sector investment.[2]

---

[1] The argument here follows exactly that used for private sector firms above, and so will not be repeated.

[2] Note that the preceding discussion implicitly assumed that each household held some amount of each share, i.e. $\beta_{sk2} > 0$ all k. If for at least one k we have $\beta_{sk2} = 0$, then the corresponding optimal condition for that household reads:

$$\int \frac{\delta_{k2}}{\delta_{k1}} \pi_{s2} h_k(\theta) \, d\theta \leqslant e_{s1} - \pi_{s1}$$

i.e. we have a corner solution, and the derived discount rate gives only an upper limit

However, this holds neither for an identical expectations economy in which firms do not succeed in maximising share values, nor for an economy with diverse expectations. In the former case, the total of private sector investment will not be optimal even relative to the given set of expectations, since we will have:

$$\sum_k \int \frac{\delta_{k2}}{\delta_{k1}} \left\{ \sum_i p_{i2} \frac{dx^*_{ki2}}{dx_{s11}} - w_2 \frac{dx^*_{k2}}{dx_{s11}} \right\} h_k(\theta) \, d\theta - p_{11} \neq 0 \quad (51)$$

Thus, although the public sector planner could impute, from the values of e_{s1}, π_{s1} and π_{s2} for the comparable private sector firm, a discount rate which would correspond to households' valuations of the future profit of the public enterprise, this discount rate has no normative significance if private sector investment is non-optimal. Essentially, we are in a second-best situation, and so the conditions determining optimal public sector investment will in general not correspond to those in the first-best situation. This is further discussed below.

If expectations are not identical, then there is a further reason for the existence of the second-best, namely the inequalities of intertemporal marginal rates of substitution and transformation, and so again the discount rates implied by stock market equilibrium do not have normative significance. In effect, it would be possible to make Pareto-optimal improvements by inducing, for example, households with differing intertemporal marginal rates of substitution to trade current consumption for planned state-contingent future consumption, something which the absence of the relevant markets does not make possible in the market economy. In other words, even if a central planner takes as given the diverse set of expectations in the economy, he would be able to bring about welfare improvements at time 1. Moreover, if he regards his own set of expectations as the only permissible ones, then he would see scope for improvement in bringing the time 1 resource allocation into conformity with them. Of course, any household with different expectations to the planner may well regard itself as worse off as a result of the planner's 'improvements', and so there is an element of paternalism here which is not fully consistent with the individualistic s.w.f. adopted in this paper.

I conclude this discussion by briefly considering the formulation of the second-best problem when it cannot be assumed that we have an identical expectations economy in which firms have maximised market values. The problem is taken to be the piecemeal one of optimising for the public sector only, taking conditions in the private sector as given.

The variables with respect to which the constrained maximisation would be carried out are consumptions and outputs of public sector goods, and

---

to the required household discount rate. This further weakens the normative significance of market discount rates from the point of view of social welfare maximisation— a substantial section of the community may have higher time preference rates and risk-aversion than those of the households which own shares, and no information on these higher rates can be gained from market data.

public sector output. In the identical expectations economy, the constraints would be the public sector production functions and market-clearing conditions, together with a constraint expressing the inequality of the marginal social expected present value of private sector investment and its current marginal cost. The conditions determining public sector investment will then contain terms involving the partial derivatives of these with respect to public sector investment, and in general these conditions could not be satisfied by discounting public sector investments at some private sector discount rate. In the economy in which expectations are not identical, constraints expressing the inequalities of intertemporal marginal rates of substitution and transformation would also have to be included, and again the corresponding partial derivatives would appear in the conditions determining optimal public sector outputs and investment. These would imply, in addition to the above conclusion on investment, that marginal cost pricing of public sector outputs at times 1 and 2 is not optimal. Finally, it would have to be assumed that the resulting optimal prices for public sector goods at time 2 would be communicated to households, who would then base their own plans on them.

4. Conclusions

In this paper I have tried to set out the problems which a theory of public sector resource allocation under risk should consider, to assess the extent to which the existing body of theory provides solutions to these problems, and to formulate a model which will permit further analysis of them. The main conclusions of the formal model are as follows: because of the assumption that production and exchange take place when the state of the world is known, households and firms can be assumed to *plan* in terms of state-contingent consumption, production, and labour supplies. However, the absence of markets in state-contingent commodities and labour supplies implies the absence of known equilibrium prices on which to base these plans, and they depend for their formulation on the expectations held by economic agents. These expectations may be neither identical as between different decision-takers, nor, *ex post*, fulfilled. Furthermore, there is nothing to suggest that firms will succeed in choosing investment plans which maximise their stock-market valuations. In an extreme case in which expectations are identical and firms succeed in maximising market valuations, the economy achieves what may be termed a 'quasi-Pareto optimum', in the sense that although the resource allocation may not correspond to that chosen by an omniscient central planner (or achieved by an economy with complete markets in state-contingent commodities and labour supplies), a non-omniscient planner could not make a reallocation which would be Pareto-optimal, in the light of individual preferences, probability beliefs and the common set of expectations. However, if we relax these assumptions, even this quasi-Pareto optimum will not be achieved, and the problem of optimal public sector resource allocation becomes one of the second-best. In particular, the implicit discount rates on future profits of private sector firms have no normative significance for the problem of optimising public sector investment.

An explicit formulation of the second-best problem has not been attempted here, largely for reasons of space, but also because it would take a form familiar from the theory of second-best under certainty. Of more interest would be the application of the model to the wider class of problems mentioned in the introduction. An important group of problems would be those concerned with taxation. These should be considered both from the point of view of determining principles of optimal taxation under risk, and of determining optimal public sector pricing and investment rules given the existence of non-optimal taxes in the economy. The consequences of imperfections in goods and factor markets should also be analysed. Finally, it would be useful to examine the relation between general equilibrium optimality criteria and the partial equilibrium rules in which they would have to be embodied.[1] Within the limitations of a static, two-period model, we would then have a reasonably well-developed body of theory on public sector resource allocation under risk.

References

1. ARROW, K. J. 'The role of securities in the optimal allocation of risk-bearing', *Review of Economic Studies*, April 1964.
2. ARROW, K. J. and LIND, R. C. 'Uncertainty and the evaluation of public investment decisions', *American Economic Review*, June 1970.
3. BAUMOL, W. J. and BRADFORD, D. F. 'Optimal departures from marginal cost pricing', *American Economic Review*, June 1970.
4. BORCH, K. The *Economics of Uncertainty*, Princeton Studies in Mathematical Economics no. 2. Princeton, 1968.
5. BROWN, GARDNER JR. and JOHNSON, M. B. 'Public utility pricing and output under risk', *American Economic Review*, March 1969.
6. DAVIS, O. A. and WHINSTON, A. B. 'Welfare economics and the theory of the second best', *Review of Economic Studies*, 1965.
7. DEBREU, G. *Theory of Value*, New York, 1959.
8. DIAMOND, P. A. 'The role of a stock market in a general equilibrium model with technological uncertainty', *American Economic Review*, Sept. 1967.
9. DIAMOND, P. A. and MIRRLEES, J. 'Optimal taxation and public production', I and II, *American Economic Review*, March 1971 and June 1971.
10. HIRSHLEIFER, J. 'Investment decision under uncertainty: applications of the state preference approach', *Quarterly Journal of Economics*, May 1966.
11. HIRSHLEIFER, J. *Investment, Interest and Capital*, Prentice-Hall, 1970.
12. LIPSEY, R. G. and LANCASTER, K. 'The general theory of second best', *Review of Economic Studies*, 1967.
13. MALINVAND, E. 'Risk-taking and resource allocation' in *Public Economics*, ed. J. Margolis and H. Guitton, Macmillan, 1969.
14. MOSSIN, J. 'Security pricing and investment criteria in competitive markets', *American Economic Review*, December 1969.

[1] In a recent paper [18], I have examined the question of the appropriateness of expected value of consumer surplus as a benefit measure, in assessing transport investments which change the probability distributions of journey times. I show that where a traveller can be assumed to conform to the Neumann–Morgenstern axioms, and the corresponding utility function is separable in income and journey time and linear in income, then he will act as if he maximised expected consumer surplus, and it is an appropriate welfare criterion. This result would seem to me to hold also in the case of a good, but I hope to examine this question further in another paper.

15. RADNER, R. 'Competitive equilibrium under uncertainty', *Econometrica*, January 1968.
16. REES, J. A. and REES, R. 'Demand forecasts and planning margins for water in south-east England', *Journal of Regional Studies*, April 1972.
17. REES, R. 'Second best rules for public enterprise pricing', *Economica*, August 1968.
18. REES, R. 'Evaluating the benefits of investment in transport reliability', mimeographed.
19. ROTHENBERG, T. J. and SMITH, K. R. 'The effect of uncertainty on resource allocation in a general equilibrium model', *Quarterly Journal of Economics*, August 1971.
20. SAMUELSON, P. A. *Foundations of Economic Analysis*, Harvard University Press, 1963.
21. WILLIAMSON, O. E. 'Peak-road pricing and plant indivisibilities', *American Economic Review*, Sept. 1966.

Public sector resource allocation under conditions of risk: Discussion*

H. A. John Green

My discussion of the main conclusion of the author's paper will be different from what I had expected it to be, since a preliminary version of the paper had led me to believe that his views on the Pareto-optimality of his market model were quite different from those he has now expressed.

I should like first, however, to make a few comments about the model itself. The assumption that individual utility functions are additive over the two time periods seems to me an innocuous simplifying device. Capital goods in effect last for only one time period in the model; at this stage in its development, it is legitimate to arrange the assumptions in such a way that one does not have to worry about depreciation or optimal terminal capital stocks.

A point of somewhat more substance is that, in any legitimate comparison of the results of allocation by an omniscient planner with the results of allocation by markets, the two models must make identical assumptions about those features of the economy which are independent of institutional arrangements. I have in mind in particular assumptions about technology. In the planner's economy there is a single production function for each industry; in the market model each industry is divided into firms, each with a production function. If these two technologies are to be consistent, it must make no difference whether an industry consists of one firm or a thousand, and as is well known this implies that all firms in a given industry have identical production functions with constant returns to scale. The only point in the analysis where firms in a given industry seem to differ is in the probability density functions over states of the world which they use to compute their expected profits, and in the discount rates they apply to expected profits to calculate their present values. But since all firms in a given industry are (as has just been shown) exactly alike and (as will be shown in a moment) known to be alike, their profit distributions over states of the world will be the same, so that the shares of all firms in a given industry will in equilibrium sell for the same price. Thus the model can be simplified considerably by recognising that each industry can be regarded as consisting of a single firm.

* This discussion was based on an earlier draft of the paper.

Coming now a little closer to the question of Pareto-optimality, we must recognise that in any intertemporal model, with or without uncertainty, a Pareto-optimum may fail to be achieved because prices at t_2 are not accurately predicted at t_1. In the absence of forward markets for all commodities, decisions taken at t_1, may lead to an allocation at t_2 which is different from that which an omniscient planner would have established, simply because prices at t_2 are wrongly predicted. The author does not mention this, and I think that he must be taken as implicitly assuming by default that all individuals and firms know exactly what all prices and profits will be at t_2 in every single state of the world. This makes what the author refers to as the 'elimination of short-term uncertainty' a very strong assumption indeed.

Finally, an earlier version of the author's paper led me to expect him to argue that his market equilibrium under uncertainty was in some sense a Pareto-optimum. In fact this is not what he has argued, and I am happy to concur in his conclusion that unless there is a complete set of markets for contingent claims, or all individuals and firms are as omniscient as the omniscient planner (which would eliminate the need for markets) no Pareto-optimum can be achieved in general. (It is, however, possible as Diamond has shown, to achieve a 'constrained Pareto-optimum by imposing restrictions on the consumption patterns, or utility functions, of individuals and on the way in which uncertainty affects production functions.)

After the author had reached this negative conclusion, he referred to ways in which the public sector might rectify the failure of private markets to attain a Pareto-optimum under uncertainty. I confess that I do not know what he has in mind here, and should very much like to see an elaboration of this point.

Micro-economic risk and the social rate of discount[1]

8

Neville Topham

1. Introduction

The notion of investment implies the exchange of a present sacrifice for a future benefit. The choice between two such options is not straightforward. It is true that in normal circumstances the evaluation of a present sacrifice is reasonably reliable; but given the enigmatic nature of the future and our inability to make perfect forecasts, estimates of future returns are not invariably accurate; so that investment is *necessarily* accompanied by uncertainty. This well-known point has lately become an issue that further complicates the debate which surrounds the selection of a social rate of discount.

The debate is primarily normative, and seeks to determine those projects that should be undertaken, on the basis of the criteria for a Pareto efficient outcome. The ramifications of the discussion, as Baumol [2, p. 796]* has pointed out, are wideranging; for not only is the choice between one project and another at issue, but also the split between the public and the private sector, and third, the overall level of investment in the economy. It is hardly surprising that the debate has focused on these two latter issues, since any verifiable conclusions would have important implications for policy. However, the inattention of writers to the difficulty of working policies based on their proposals raises the question of their relevance to the world of practical affairs; for it is evident that important allocational problems and crucial behavioural assumptions are involved. The far-reaching nature of such policies lessens the reliability of an appropriate reaction by decision-making units. For example, it may be argued along with Peacock and Wiseman [21] that there are customary levels of taxation, which are not easily displaced; so that prescriptions which imply swingeing increases in taxation to finance a large public sector may not readily be adopted.

[1] For their useful comments, I am indebted to Professor R. J. Nicholson and R. W. Houghton, University of Sheffield, Professor Alan Williams, University of York, K. Maunders and P. S. Milne, University of Hull, and to the Discussant and Editor. The usual disclaimer is in order. I am grateful to the SSRC for their financial support.

* Numbers in square brackets relate to references on p. 154.

It is well-known that the profession is divided over what ought to be the discounting factor for the public sector. The purpose of this paper is not to enter that debate, but to consider recommendations that emanate from it in the light of positive analysis.

Section 2 is designed to enquire whether microeconomic risk is a relevant cost from the point of view of private sector decision-makers, and consequently to consider whether it is a constituent of the social opportunity cost of capital (SOC). It appears that this is so. Even if financial markets provided owners of capital with a satisfactory hedge, human capital would still be exposed to risk. And given that they have an area for manoeuvre, management would invest less.

In section 3 the problem of risk pooling and the appropriateness of the pooling argument in the public sector is examined, and it is shown first that it is doubtful whether public sector assets are sufficiently independent of one another, both for macrogovernments and microgovernments. The public sector operates in a limited number of areas, and items which go to make up social overhead capital are often unlikely to display independent uncertainties. Second, where more than one level of government exists, it is not possible for citizens to hold a pooled portfolio of public sector assets. Thus again the pooling argument breaks down for microgovernments. Third, the risk of public sector investments is assumed by the taxpayers. In the case of microgovernments, because neither property rights nor real ventures are satisfactorily pooled, the risks associated with the variability of returns at the microeconomic level are assumed by local residents. Thus decision makers who are concerned to maximise a local social welfare function will take account of microeconomic risk. Fourth, while the influence of the technostructure will moderate the objective function, microeconomic risk remains incorporated in it. Supporting empirical evidence is provided. It is then demonstrated that of the two prescriptions of welfare economics, neither the SOC rate nor the social time preference (STP) rate is likely to result in the resource allocation required by normative arguments as a justification for its introduction.

Before proceeding, it needs to be indicated that although the paper is concerned with risk premiums in relation to the discount rate, this should not be taken to imply that this is the most appropriate way to handle risk in assessing the viability of individual investment projects. The analysis presented here is essentially positive. The paper is couched in terms of the discount rate as a basis of comparison with the marginal conditions of welfare economics.[1]

Some discussion of the role of various microeconomic units is appropriate.

[1] For example, it may be argued that the risk of a project varies over time. The response is twofold. First, the argument which follows is concerned not with a particular project, but with the marginal risk to the programme that the inclusion of that project entails. Second, even if discount rates vary over time, because of intertemporal variations in risk or STP, there must be some rate that will reduce the stream of net benefits (B') to the same present value that would ensue if varying rates were used as appropriate during the life of the project; i.e. a notional rate (h) can be found

They are the agency for decisions in both the private and the public sector, and it is likely that perception of risk at this level will raise problems. A discussion of the appositeness of the debate concerning the social rate of discount is therefore made from this standpoint.

2. Private sector pooling

At the outset, it is necessary to distinguish between microeconomic and macroeconomic risk. Hirschleifer [12] has termed the latter 'social variability', and it affects in the same direction the outcome of all investment; so that it may arise from the business cycle, and almost certainly will arise in the event of war and national disaster. Microeconomic risk[1] is comprehensively defined, and is concerned with the likelihood that the actual outcome of a programme may differ—for whatever reason, except any appropriate to macroeconomic risk—from its anticipated outcome.

One way to deal with the possibility of an unsatisfactory outcome is to insure against it, but in respect of investment, markets for such a course of action generally do not exist. A further possibility is to 'reinsure'—to engage in or hold a share in a number of undertakings, so that on insurance principles the overall outcome is virtually certain.[2] If risk can be pooled satisfactorily in this way, it may be argued that it should be ignored when investment decisions are made. It would appear that the relative ability of the public and the private sector to pool risks is of crucial importance in the search for the optimal discounting factor.

The *standard pooling argument* takes the following form. If by a pooling of independent risks a large firm is able to borrow at a lower rate than a small firm, it follows that the government, which by virtue of its size is a better pooler of microeconomic risks than even the largest firm, should use a still lower discounting factor.[3] Thus, although private risk-aversion brings about

---

[1] No distinction is made between risk and uncertainty in this paper. The distinction is becoming obsolete, but some writers retain the distinction in game-theoretic problems: see Quirin [22, pp. 199–200].

[2] This is an unusual use of the word 'reinsurance', but it is so used in this context; see Samuelson [23, p. 96].

[3] For an early expression of this view, see Samuelson [23] and Vickrey [26]. Since the issue arose in the discussion, it is worth emphasising that the statistical law of large numbers provides the basis for the standard pooling argument. However, pooling can take place also when the redistribution of an existing portfolio results in a new set of holdings with overall a lower variance than that associated with previous holdings. In the state-preference approach to risk, pooling takes place across different states of the world: the ice-cream manufacturer, fearing the possibility of a cold summer, diversifies into hot-dogs; so that no matter whether the state of the world is hot or cold, he is assured of a return. I use in the text a notion of pooling embodying whichever of these two approaches is appropriate to the particular context.

---

which when substituted for the varying rates (p) will bring about the following result:

$$\sum_{i=1}^{n} \frac{B'_i}{(1+h)^i} = \sum_{i=1}^{n} \frac{B'_i}{\prod_{j=1}^{i} (1+p_j)}$$

a situation in which the marginal return on private investments is higher than it otherwise would be, risk (it is argued) is a socially irrelevant cost. The corollary is that a discounting factor is chosen for the public sector that reflects STP rather than SOC.

Some examination of the possibility of pooling in the private sector is required. From society's standpoint, it is as equally true of the private as it is of the public sector that so large is the body of projects undertaken the overall result is not in doubt. Suppose the multifarious decision-making units in the private sector on average require, because of *inter alia* microeconomic risk, 20 per cent on marginal investments and act accordingly, it is virtually certain that on average this is the rate which will be returned. The return required by a firm depends upon the degree of exposure to risk and its entrepreneurial attitude to it. What then determines entrepreneurial reaction to risk? In part, the reaction finds its origin in subjectively determined risk aversion and traditionally in the degree to which owners of capital can hedge against risk. Economists who advocate (Arrow [1]) and sympathise with (Hirschleifer and Shapiro [12]) the pooling argument point to market imperfection and market segmentation as factors which limit pooling. Support for market segmentation is based on theoretical grounds and on empirical observation. Hirshleifer and Shapiro point out that trading in an incalculable number of future contingent claims is required if consumers are to be enabled to acquire a basket of titles to future consumption that matches their preferences and is certain regardless of eventualities. Similarly, Arrow states that markets for reinsurance do not exist; if they did, pooling could take place, and firms could ignore risk in their investment decisions: they could reinsure the risks with the whole of the private sector, and thus be on a par with the public sector.

Likewise, in a somewhat restricted model in which firms invariably maximise stock-market valuation and wealth-owners diversify their holdings, Diamond [7] has demonstrated that the stock market plays an important role in the pursuit of optimal resource allocation. And Pauly [20], taking up this lead, has suggested that the financial markets can be effective poolers of risk through the agency of diversified portfolios, sales of securities of large firms, and for small wealth holders unit trusts and insurance annuities. While it is true that many markets perform the function of risk markets, their performance is imperfect; adequate and perfect risk markets would eliminate all risks to the firm, and as Arrow [1, p. 30] reminds us, 'we know that this elimination has not occurred'.

If it had occurred, the differential between the marginal return on private investment and the bond rate could, on the basis of these arguments, be wholly accounted for by macroeconomic risk. This however is the position that Pauly has taken up. In consideration of bond-financed government investment, he distinguished between the riskiness of public sector investments to the lender and to the taxpayer. He argued that the unique rate at which risk-avoiding individuals are prepared to loan money on government bonds (*henceforth designated as r*), is not appropriate for use as a social rate of discount because it fails to take account of the risk to society associated with public investments, which is assumed by the taxpayer. Macroeconomic risk also affects the public sector, and consequently r understates the required return to society, since it ignores the assumption of the social cost of this type of risk by taxpayers. Therefore, he concluded that the return to corporate stockholders when macroeconomic risk is included and microeconomic risk ignored (*henceforth r'*) was the correct discount rate for both the public and the private sector, and—ignoring tax-induced distortions—there was no justification for subsidising private industry in order to equate the marginal return on private investment with r, as Baumol [2] had suggested.

However, as Arrow concludes, it is clear that individual firms face situations which are different in their exposure to risk. The markets therefore tend to a situation where *risk-compensated* rates of return are equal among alternative investments, but where actual rates differ. In other words, premiums exist which compensate for exposure to risk. Empirical evidence supports this contention, and moreover the results that Fisher and Hall [10, p. 91] report indicate that with 'some reasonable assumptions, significant and instructive measurements of the relationship between risk and the rate of return can be obtained. . . . Firms with large standard deviations have higher mean profit rates, while firms with positively skewed distributions have lower profit rates'.[1] Notwithstanding these remarks, it may be objected that existing institutions afford a sufficiently good proxy to a perfect market situation to provide equity holders with an adequate hedge against risk. In these circumstances, it may be conceded that what the Pauly model described is a real life possibility, which forces us to enquire further why different rates of return exist and why statistically they are associated with the variability of profits accruing to particular firms.

A problem arises with the Pauly model because implicitly it is based upon traditional rather than managerial capitalism. In the former, the decision-taker has private property rights over his investments, and the undertaking of risks, the receiving of rewards, and the making of decisions are all combined in the one individual. No longer is this universally true.[2] Ever since Berle and Means [3], the profession has recognised the separation of ownership and control in the firm. So far as this debate is concerned, the crucial point about traditional capitalism is that the entrepreneur who carried the risk also made most of the decisions which determined its extent. But diversification of ownership reduces the constraint on management to act with the owners' welfare in mind, and thus whose welfare is to be maximised—the owners' or the management's—becomes a moot point in managerial capitalism.

---

[1] Some interesting remarks on this and similar work may be found in Seagraves [25, p. 443]. More recently Caves and Yamey [5] have drawn a distinction between exogenous or 'true' risk and endogenous risk, which arises because of various risk-augmenting activities by oligopolistic firms. Fisher and Hall (11) have acknowledged the distinction and suggested further modifications to their analysis. All this is limited in extent and serves only to reduce the risk premiums estimated by Fisher and Hall in their earlier paper and does not affect the qualitative argument presented here.

[2] When it was universally true, there were no share markets.

Ironically, when the Pauly model and other associated work is projected into this situation, it pushes managerial capitalism to the limit, and owners lose virtually all control over management. Ownership is stratified as never before. But this approach anticipates management ignoring microeconomic risk—being now irrelevant to the ownership, because of its resort to reinsurance facilities—and undertaking therefore a larger investment programme.

But physical capital is not the only factor of production to be affected by risk. The social problems associated with redundant and unemployed skills highlight the way in which microeconomic risk affects human capital. Because of the complex way in which their rewards (present and anticipated) are made up, those engaged in management are employed in a particularly 'risky business'. Among top managers as a whole, 'current bonuses (excluding stock-option profits) account for 30 per cent of the total remuneration', whilst 'mobility . . . is very low indeed' (Marris [15, p. 67]). Clearly, the success of the individual firm and the fortunes of the men who control it are intimately bound up.

Recently, Lewellen and Huntsman [13] have argued that on *a priori* grounds the economic self-interest of owners and managers cannot be neatly separated out because, as indicated, an amount of management compensation is derived from stock options and stock-related pay arrangements. They go on to report that in a number of single equation regressions, with executive rewards (comprehensively defined) as the dependent variable, and with reported company profits and sales as the two explanatory variables, the former is nearly always statistically significant whereas the latter never is. They conclude that this is suggestive of there being sufficient incentive for management to act in accord with shareholder interests. However, whilst it is true that certain large firms appear to encourage *inter alia* stockholding by management, it is doubtful whether the explicit motivation is mainly a desire to conflate the interests of stockholders and management. As Marris points out, the men at the top 'are not owner-managers, because their holdings represent small proportions of their total wealth, and the associated dividends small proportions of their total incomes' [15, p. 18]. And bonus schemes, which are to be found at all levels in the firm, are usually designed to increase internal efficiency. Nevertheless, the conclusion that managerial capitalism 'can in large measure still be analysed by models which are based on the assumption of profit seeking behaviour' [13, p. 79] is justified. It is consistent with existing theory of the firm. However, some may argue that the nub of the issue is the distribution of profits, and to the degree to which this is generally agreed Lewellen and Huntsman were guilty of erecting a straw man in contrasting sales with profits variables. The profits distribution issue gives important theoretical justification for the contention that microeconomic risk is important to both owners and managers.

There are two factors which limit the freedom of action of the manager-controlled firm. First, markets for homogeneous managers do not exist. That is one reason perhaps why mobility is low. Managers endeavour to differentiate their services, being mindful of the importance of transfer earnings, and at the highest levels of management an important determinant of the evaluation of these is no doubt the record of the firm with which a person has been associated. Second, and as is well known, the stockmarket valuation of the firm's shares imposes a discipline because of the possibility of involuntary takeover; in such an event, the upper echelon of the management structure is liable to be dismissed from office, forfeiting the rewards and status that go with it. It is this ultimate constraint that binds management and alerts it to the financial implications of its investment programmes and other activities.

The conclusion to be drawn from this section is that microeconomic risk is a relevant cost so far as decision takers in managerial capitalism are concerned, just as it was in traditional capitalism. Those models where it is not represent a curious hybrid in which firms virtually lose their identity. A pooling of private sector property rights therefore is unlikely to eliminate microeconomic risk from remaining an important consideration in the investment decision process. The viability of the firm, its record and its prospects, are as important and as vital to today's managers as they were to yesterday's entrepreneurs. This is a factor with which Pauly's model cannot cope. Similarly, what legitimacy the pooling argument has for the public sector depends on whether there are imperfections and segmentation of risk markets for human capital rather than for physical capital.[1]

3. Public sector pooling

The pooling argument, it may be reiterated, rests on the ability of the public sector and the inability of the private sector to pool risks; so that microeconomic risks may be ignored in public sector investment decisions, whereas they may not in the private sector, as we have seen. The validity of public sector pooling is now examined.

First, it is questionable whether a pooling of real ventures can readily be accomplished in the public sector. A 'pooling of risk is actually more easily accomplished on the financial side', as Schwartz [24, p. 138] remarks. To be successful it is necessary that projects are relatively independent of one another, i.e. that their covariance is low.[2] But the government produces many times fewer varieties of goods and services than does the private sector. Moreover, almost 50 per cent of gross fixed domestic capital formation in the United Kingdom is accomplished by the public sector, of which about 40 per cent is attributable to education, highways, and housing. In the case of the local authorities in England and Wales, 60 per cent of their capital budget was devoted to education and housing in the year ended March 1969, and a further 10 per cent was devoted to highways. Items which constitute social overhead capital are often of a piece, and are then unlikely to display inde-

---

[1] Income risks for labour services are not pooled; partly this is because of the indivisibility of labour service provision and partly because generally facilities do not exist that would allow individuals to reinsure salary streams one with another.

[2] Pooling can reduce the variance of aggregate returns even though the projects pooled are not entirely independent, provided they are not perfectly correlated.

pendent uncertainties. In these circumstances, it is doubtful whether pooling has any significant effect.

Second, and connected with this point, there are problems associated with public sector property rights. The property rights of assets in the public sector are vested in the individual residents of the appropriate community.[1] De Alessi [6] has discussed the relative difficulties of exchanging property rights in public and private sector assets; because of high transaction costs and indivisibilities, such difficulties are greatest in respect of public sector assets.[2] Generally it is not possible to acquire a balanced portfolio of community assets when the individual is subject to more than one level of government. Economics aggregate the public sector in order to arrive at the certain-outcome solution. But in most countries there are a large number of state and/or local governments (microgovernments), most of which are answerable to a state or local electorate. They are not agents of the federal or central government, and belong to the set of microeconomic units in the same way that firms do. The opportunities for 'reinsurance' within a microgovernment are not much different to those in a large firm. As we shall see, therefore, microeconomic risk affects local governments, and thus the appropriate discounting factor for them is $r'' > r'$ in order to provide a premium for microeconomic risk. Premiums for both microeconomic and macroeconomic risks are incorporated in r'', but a premium in respect of the latter only for r'; the bond (riskless) rate is taken to be r.

The third point requires some preliminary explanation. Microgovernments may account for a substantial part of the public sector. In Britain, for example, local authorities are the major providers of social overhead capital, and in 1968 accounted for 45 per cent of public sector and 22 per cent of gross fixed domestic capital formation. For the most part, they borrow to finance their capital expenditure, requiring central government approval to do so. But the crucial point about this system is that whereas negatively the government is in a position to prevent key capital expenditures, its powers on the positive side amount only to the ability to exhort local authorities to undertake work which the government thinks is desirable.[3]

---

[1] Buchanan and Wagner [4, p. 149] take a somewhat more restrictive line, and argue that the 'establishment of a set of property rights would permit states (microgovernments) to set prices upon and require the purchase of the right to migrate to that state'. This may be so. But if governments enforce a zero-price situation, it is optimal to leave the institutional organisation of property rights on an informal basis, as is currently the practice.

[2] As De Alessi points out, the 'only way an individual can change his portfolio of ownership in government organisations is to move from one jurisdiction to another or to change the structure of the organisations. This procedure is far more expensive than changing one's portfolio of ownership in private organisations' (p. 17).

[3] Financial assistance is also given. Capital grants are important only in respect of certain expenditure on highways and police. A complex system of current financial assistance exists in the form of specific and (mostly) block grants. The most important current grants in respect of capital expenditure are housing subsidies. While these may be regarded in part as investment allowances, a problem arises if they are too-often revised. A recent White Paper sets out the government's proposals to recast the existing housing-subsidy system, notwithstanding the fact that this goes back

Consider now some similarities between microeconomic units in the public and in the private sector. Pauly's illustration of risk assumption by the holders of public sector property rights (taxpayers) extends immediately to the private sector in consideration of bond finance, which is responsible for three-quarters of all external financing by US firms. Purchasers of private sector bonds require them to yield the return r plus a risk premium to cover the contingency of earnings being insufficient to service corporate debt. However, the risks associated with bond-financed investments at the microeconomic level extend also to stockholders, who acquire the property rights of the assets. Clearly, the higher the debt/asset ratio, the more likely it is that after-tax profits will provide reduced dividend cover. Or worse, it is possible that a sharp fall off in profits may force a firm to default on debt payments and go into liquidation, in circumstances in which this would not have occurred but for the leverage in question. Such imputed risk is assumed by stockholders in precisely the same way that taxpayers shoulder it in the public sector. No originality is claimed for this argument, which is of course no more than the basis of Kalecki's principle of increasing risk and Duesenberry's [8] marginal-cost-of-funds (MCF) schedule. The problem of investment determinants has been thoroughly researched by econometricians, much of whose work is summarised by Evans [9]. There is some evidence to suggest that firms take such imputed costs into account when determining their investment programmes.

In some work by the author and R. J. Nicholson [18], it was assumed that microgovernments were welfare maximisers, and thus in their investment programmes attempted to maximise the present social value of particular projects, i.e. the properly discounted flow of net social benefits. Thus, public sector projects may be ranked according to the value of the discount rate necessary to equate the benefit cost ratio with unity, from which information it is possible to derive a social marginal efficiency of investment (SMEI) schedule. Analogously, it is possible to consider a social marginal cost of funds (SMCF) schedule, which reflects, *ceteris paribus*, the financial structure of the microgovernment.

These schedules are shown in Fig. 8.1, where the real rate of interest is shown on the ordinate and investment on the abscissa. For the moment, r is taken to be the bond rate, $r'-r$ the premium in respect of macroeconomic risk, and $r''-r'$ that in respect of microeconomic risk. For expositional purposes, the diagram is drawn so that the MCF schedule is identical for all firms. Clearly, this is not generally the case. The schedules of individual firms will all start out at the same point on the ordinate: the initial part of the schedule comprises internal funds, which can be used either to finance investment or be loaned out at the market rate of interest. However, the slopes of the schedules will differ, reflecting differing variability of profits. For example, low-risk industries such as public utilities will have relatively flat MCF schedules, whilst firms in high-risk sectors such as prospecting will

---

on previous promises that were given to encourage housing authorities to undertake capital works, see Department of the Environment [27].

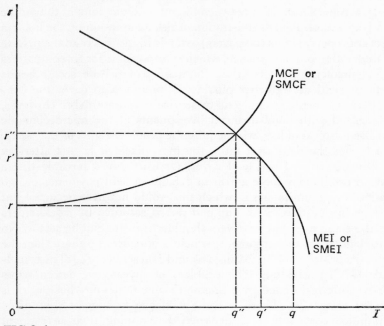

FIG 8.1

have somewhat steep curves. The differing slopes will give rise to differing risk premiums, as was observed by Fisher and Hall [10]. It needs to be pointed out, however, that profit variability is a condition of the schedule, whereas changes in the financial structure of the firm are reflected in movements along it, which is a factor that was not examined by them. The principle that Kalecki introduced is one of increasing *existing* risk. The greater the leverage the greater the risk that arises from variability in profits. Both constitute microeconomic risk.

Of course, microgovernments are in little danger of liquidation because of their powers of coercing the holders of property-rights (taxpayers) to accept negative dividends (taxes). However, the financial implications of their investment programmes carry with them the risk of unforeseen or unrequited tax payments to balance their current accounts, and these are as much an imputed cost of microeconomic risk as dividends foregone. Clearly, the higher is local bond finance to the value of local assets, the greater will be the possibility of such a contingency.

Whilst it was not possible in the econometric work to estimate the SMEI and SMCF schedules separately,[1] it was possible to draw tentative conclusions about their forms. The results paralleled those derived from US

---

[1] The problem is that the endogenous *real* rate of interest is not observable, and an acceptable surrogate could not be devised. Of the two endogenous variables in the system, the real rate of interest and investment in housing, only the latter was measured, and estimation was confined therefore to the unrestricted reduced form.

private sector studies: financial constraints played only a minor role in explaining the investment behaviour of the microgovernments studied. Nevertheless, the data were consistent with some positive curvature for the SMCF schedule. Later work [19][1] reinforces this finding. This may be seen from the following regression equation, which refers to a cross-section analysis of the largest forty-one country boroughs in England and Wales (t statistics in parentheses):

$$y = -4356 \cdot 0 + 539 \cdot 9x_1 + 60 \cdot 5x_2 + 275 \cdot 1x_3 + 1223 \cdot 2x_4$$
$$(2 \cdot 32) \quad (1 \cdot 50) \quad (2 \cdot 45) \quad (0 \cdot 49)$$

$$+ 216 \cdot 2x_5 - 15752 \cdot 1x_6 - 1 \cdot 4x_7 \quad R^2 = 0 \cdot 4638$$
$$(2 \cdot 33) \quad (0 \cdot 92) \quad (2 \cdot 19)$$

where $y =$ capital payments on housing, 1962–68[2]
$\quad x_1 =$ percentage of houses overcrowded, 1961
$\quad x_2 =$ cost index, 1961
$\quad x_3 =$ debt interest as proportion of rateable value, 1961
$\quad x_4 =$ ratio of rent income to gross valuation, 1961
$\quad x_5 =$ recent local-authority building, prior 1962
$\quad x_6 =$ ratio of dwellings 1961 to anticipated households, 1971
$\quad x_7 =$ quadratic form of x_3.

What is important from the point of view of this analysis is the behaviour of x_3 and x_7. It may be expected that x_3 will have a positive sign. The actual level of the variable may be high because capital expenditure, which is mainly loan-financed and of which housing is a large part, has been high in the past, implying positive correlation with the dependent variable if a high level of capital expenditure is maintained. But it is reasonable to assume that the higher the level of debt charges, the more reluctant authorities will be to take on further debt because of microeconomic risk. The introduction of variable x_7 tests this possibility; it was assumed that this would be negative after x_3 had been taken into account. Despite the problem of multicollinearity that was raised when the quadratic form of the existing variable x_3 was also included in the equation (the zero order correlation between x_3 and x_7 was 0·975), not only are the two variables signed as anticipated, but more importantly both are significant at the 5 per cent level. Given these findings, it is not unreasonable to assume for the purpose of this section that the schedules have the form suggested in Fig. 8.1.

Consider now a microgovernment that provides only one commodity. Its investment programme is bond-financed and it competes for funds in the capital market. I have already argued that the appropriate local social rate of discount from the point of view of the decision taker is $r'' > r' > r$. Clearly in the absence of constraints emanating from the financial structure and reflected in the SMCF schedule, microgovernments would in Fig. 8.1 proceed with Oq projects. But if the central government attempted to enforce

[1] In which further details may be found.
[2] Adjusted for price changes, expressed per 1000 of the population, and averaged over the years stated.

r' as the discount rate for use with investment criteria, the schedules indicate that where financial constraints are recognised local authorities would invest less than Oq'. A microgovernment that is aware and takes account of the microeconomic and macroeconomic risks assumed by its taxpayers will undertake Oq'', where $SMEI = SMCF$, because these matters are precisely those which determine the curvature of the SMCF schedule.

As is implied in the foregoing, the investment analyst is concerned not with the risk premium on a project, but with the way in which the variability of that project affects the diversification (and yield) of the whole programme. When local authorities, for example, construct houses to rent—an activity that in the recent past has accounted for about a half of their capital budget— the projects which go to make up the programme are by no means independent. We may summarise that because of the inability of owners to pool public sector assets adequately, the lack of statistical independence in, and the financial implications of their capital programmes, the standard pooling argument cannot be sustained for microgovernments.

By analogy with the previous section, some analysis is required of the role of management in the public sector—the public bureaucracy or techno-structure. The problem of whose welfare is to be maximised—the owner's, the management's, or that of some other group—arises again. It may be argued that in the private sector the possibilities of detecting non-optimal behaviour on the part of management are more favourable. For example, a consistent policy of selecting less-remunerative projects would no doubt be reflected in the state of the company's accounts. On the other hand, the more that public projects incorporate services which are not traded, the less it would seem are the possibilities of detecting non-optimal decision making. Even where, ostensibly, r'' is a policy criterion, project running costs may be watered so as to dilute the risk premium on the discount rate. Moreover, where insolvency is not a possibility, the technostructure may be more inclined to resolutely pursue its own goals. In this kind of situation, the true discount rate will be less than r''.

It may be objected that the decision maker does not enjoy the freedom of action implied by this kind of argument. As McKean [16, p. 12] contends,

spending choices result from individual decisions—those of voters, legislators, the heads of departments or ministries, departmental employees, and so on. Each individual involved in this process has somewhat different views and values from the others—that is, he has to take his own, or what might be called a parochial, viewpoint. At the same time he must reckon with the viewpoints of the others. In taking his stand and deciding what action (if any) he will take, he considers the wishes of others, expressed or sensed, and the rewards offered and penalties threatened by others. The Secretary of Agriculture cannot act without any regard for the views of his subordinates, the White House, and Congress; and congressmen and the President cannot form their positions com-pletely without regard for the attitudes of voters, other congressmen, and depart-mental officials. Consequently, spending decisions are the result of a network of conflicting views and considerations. Individuals not mysterious group entities, make decisions, yet those choices are by no means independent of other persons' views.

This situation introduces bargaining into the decision-making processes. McKean [16, p. 20] adds:

> If a public official's action will use up someone's property or damage certain interests, he will probably find a cost associated with that action. He will feel the complaints of those damaged or the inconvenience of trying to mollify them. Or the cost may be embarrassing or expensive enmities among his colleagues or retaliation by other officials. He has to bargain with many people that are affected and, in one way or another, encounter costs if he makes decisions that impose sacrifices on others. From those who are benefited, on the other hand, he can bargain for compensation.

The implication is that these bargaining processes constrain the public bureaucracy and push it toward the achievement of optimal solutions. A further point is that governments may be mindful of the risk of particular projects. Successful projects may not achieve the weight of publicity that those which are unsuccessful achieve. This limits the political practicability of pooling, in which case decision makers would take account of microeconomic risk. The argument is more forceful when the leading officials of the public bureaucracy may be voted out of office. But if the political consequences of the failure of certain public investments are serious, the activities of the public bureaucracy will be constrained by the elected representatives' awareness of this fact.

Some writers maintain, by contrast, that because of, among other things, the interactions of various levels of management and the higher detection costs involved, there exists a situation in the public sector which allows the decision maker to pay considerable regard to his own preferences. The opportunity cost of using resources in which a decision maker has shared property rights are very much lower than those in which he has exclusive private property rights. This encourages the use of devices equivalent to a lower discount rate in order to ensure that the capital budget is as high as possible (cf. De Alessi, [6]). This state of affairs is not in conflict with the assertion that, as in the private sector, the management has a vested interest in the growth of the 'public firm'. In our paper [18], Nicholson and I made provision for the activities of the technostructure; we reasoned that high activity in the recent past would be a positive influence on capital expenditure, even after other factors had been taken into account. The variables associated with 'impetus' have been a consistently important feature of our work. Variable x_5 represents the impetus argument in the regression equation on p. 144 and it will be seen that it is important and established at the 5 per cent significance level.[1]

---

[1] It needs to be borne in mind, however, that if suitable tests could be devised private sector studies might reveal similar findings. One important study by Monsen, Chiu and Cooley [17] indicates that owner-influenced firms perform better than management-influenced firms: the mean ratio of net income to net worth being for the former 12·8 per cent and for the latter 7·3 per cent.

We now enter an important part of the argument. Suppose an acceptable surrogate was available for the real rate of interest, which is expressed on the ordinate in Fig 8.1. This would permit estimation of the two schedules using an estimating technique appropriate for sets of simultaneous equations. Variable x_5 cannot be classified exclusively as an SMEI or SMCF determinant, since it relates not to the welfare of the community but to the utility of the town hall technostructure. There are arguments to support its inclusion in both schedules. It could be regarded as a shift parameter in, or one affecting the slope of, the SMEI schedule. Economic reasoning would support the former (i.e. a shift parameter), since presumably prospective benefits would be viewed optimistically and costs treated conservatively on all projects incorporated in the investment programme.

Now consider the incorporation of x_5 in the SMCF schedule, in order to examine the hypothesis that management will be less concerned than the ownership by variability risk when some benefits are of a non-monetary nature. As was indicated on p. 142, in a cross-section analysis the MCF schedule is for all observations secured to the position on the ordinate denoting the market rate of interest. What is the position with regard to the local authorities under examination? Certain internal funds are available; these may be loaned out or substituted for loan finance, and in either case the market rate of interest appears to be the appropriate point on the ordinate from which the SMCF schedule should start out. This, however, is not what occurs in practice. Such funds are loaned to spending committees within the authority at the average rate of interest at which all local debt is held (Nicholson and Topham [18, p. 277]). Whilst it follows that the various SMCF schedules will not necessarily emanate from the same point on the ordinate, it is unlikely that their distribution along it will be widely dispersed. The average rate of interest for the observations in the regression equation on p. 144 was 4·37 with a standard deviation of 0·19; so that for the purposes of the analysis it is reasonable to assume that the schedules do issue from a single point. This hypothesis justifies the inclusion of variable x_5 in the SMCF schedule, and its role would be that of a slope parameter for the reasons outlined above.

Now in dear-money periods the average rate of interest on local debt will stand below the bond rate, and conversely in cheap-money periods. Local debt management from a financial viewpoint is analogous to national debt management. Provided the SMCF schedule has positive curvature, it follows that in cheap-money periods, a recommendation to local authorities to use r (STP) as the hurdle rate will not necessarily cause the authority to undertake all projects in which the benefit cost ratio exceeds or equals unity using that rate of discount.

It may be, however, that more than Oq investment in Fig 8.1 would be undertaken; for the outcome will depend on the force of the combined effect of x_5 as a shift parameter on the SMEI schedule (moving it to the right) and as a slope parameter on the SMCF schedule (reducing its slope). Likewise in cheap-money periods we cannot demonstrate on an *a priori* basis whether the level of investment that would ensue from an STP rate recommendation would fall short of or exceed Oq. It will depend on the divergence between r and the local average rate of interest, on the slope of the SMCF schedule, and on the effects of technostructure parameters on the two schedules.

The previous section of this paper showed that firms take account of micro-economic risk. The SOC rate is therefore r'' in Fig. 8.1. If this rate were recommended, would an optimal balance of investment between the public and the private sector occur? Again, we cannot be sure. We do not know whether the private or the public sector is the more risk averse. Even if SOC rates were recommended appropriate to the risk classification of the particular public investment programme, we cannot be certain that managers in the public and the private sector are equally risk-averse, nor that technostructure parameters will be of equal importance in corresponding analyses. The outcome is again indeterminate. A Pareto efficient outcome is only one of many that is possible.

4. Conclusion

Local authorities in England and Wales account for about 45 per cent of public investment. Further work will determine whether the empirical findings given here and elsewhere [18, 19] extend to other tiers of authority and other categories of public expenditure. Current research does not reveal contrary indications. More importantly, the arguments presented in the paper apply to local authorities *de jure* and *de facto*. It would seem that although important parts of the arguments do not apply *de jure* to the nationalised industries, they do so *de facto*. There is no reason to believe that the managers of nationalised industries feel other than responsible for the state of their organisation's accounts, and thus are mindful of the possibility of an unanticipated outcome. Moreover, it would appear that the size of their capital programmes are partly determined by animal spirits or the desire for a quiet life (negative animal spirits), so that the impetus argument is applicable. The nationalised industries and the local authorities together account for about 90 per cent of the public sector investment programme in Great Britain. But before any strong statements may be made, further research is required, particularly in respect of the nationalised industries, and for other countries. For this analysis is suggestive that microeconomic units in both the public and the private sector regard microeconomic risk as a relevant cost; the unsolved problem is the degree to which it affects the managerial firm on the one hand and the public firm on the other. Clearly, the consequences of recommending the optimal social rate of discount merit attention at least to the same extent as the time spent searching for it.

Finally, it is as well that microeconomic risk is relevant. It is by no means certain that where this is not the case there exists a more desirable world than the one in which we live. When microeconomic risks have been eliminated, and when there exist perfect markets for entrepreneurs and other members of the technostructure, management is no longer as dependent on the success of the firm and is not therefore motivated to strive as keenly for it. In these circumstances, the determinants of motivation have been dealt a heavy blow. This is an important point, because as Harvey Liebenstein has stressed, motivational or X-efficiency may be more important than allocative efficiency.

References

1. ARROW K. J. 'Discounting and public investment criteria', in *Water Research*, ed. A. V. Kneese and S. C. Smith, Johns Hopkins Press, 1966.
2. BAUMOL, W. J. 'On the social rate of discount', *American Economic Review*, **58**, no. 4 (1968), 799–802.
3. BERLE, A. A. and MEANS, G. C. *The Modern Corporation and Private Property*, Macmillan, 1932.
4. BUCHANAN, JAMES, M. and WAGNER, RICHARD E. 'An efficiency basis for federal fiscal equalisation', *The Analysis of Public Output*, ed. Julius Margolis, Columbia, 1970, pp. 139–58.
5. CAVES, R. E. and YAMEY, B. S. 'Risk and corporate rates of return: comment', *Quarterly Journal of Economics*, **85**, no. 3 (August 1971), 513–17.
6. DE ALESSI, LOUIS. 'Implications of property rights for government investment choices', *American Economic Review*, **59**, no. 1 (1969), 13–24.
7. DIAMOND, P. A. 'A stock market in a general equilibrium model', *American Economic Review*, **57**, no. 4 (1967), 759–76.
8. DUESENBERRY, J. S. *Business Cycles and Economic Growth*, McGraw-Hill, 1958.
9. EVANS, M. K. *Macroeconomic Activity*, Harper & Row, 1969.
10. FISHER, I. N. and HALL, G. R. 'Risk and corporate rates of return', *Quarterly Journal of Economics*, **83**, no. 1 (1969), 79–92.
11. FISHER, I. N. and HALL, G. R. 'Risk and corporate rates of return: reply', *Quarterly Journal of Economics*, **85**, no. 3 (1971), 518–22.
12. HIRSCHLEIFER, J. and SHAPIRO, D. L. 'The treatment of risk and uncertainty', in *Public Expenditure and Policy Analysis*, ed. R. H. Haveman and J. Margolis, Markham, 1970.
13. LEWELLEN, WILBURG and HUNTSMAN, BLANE. 'Managerial pay and corporate performance', *American Economic Review*, **60**, no. 4 (1970), 710–20.
14. LEIBENSTEIN, H. 'Allocative efficiency vs. "X-efficiency",' *American Economic Review*, **56**, no. 3 (1966), 392–415.
15. MARRIS, ROBIN. *The Economic Theory of 'Managerial' Capitalism*, Macmillan, 1964.
16. MCKEAN, RONALD N. *Public Spending*, McGraw-Hill, 1968.
17. MONSEN, R. JOSEPH, CHIU, JOHN, and COOLEY, DAVID E. 'The effect of separation of ownership and control on the performance of the large firm', *Quarterly Journal of Economics*, **83**, no. 3 (1968), 535–51.
18. NICHOLSON, R. J. and TOPHAM, N. 'The determinants of investment in housing by local authorities: an econometric approach (with discussion)', *Journal of the Royal Statistical Society*, A**134**, no. 3 (1971), 273–320.
19. NICHOLSON, R. J. and TOPHAM, N. 'Investment decisions and the size of local authorities', *Policy and Politics*, No. 1, pp. 23–44.
20. PAULY, MARK V. 'Risk and the social rate of discount', *American Economic Review*, **60**, no. 1 (1970), 195–8.
21. PEACOCK, A. T. and WISEMAN, J. *The Growth of Public Expenditure in the United Kingdom*, Allen & Unwin, 1967.
22. QUIRIN, G. D. *The Capital Expenditure Decision*, Irwin, 1967.
23. SAMUELSON, P. A. 'Principles of efficiency—discussion', *American Economic Review*, **54**, no. 2 (1964), (papers and proceedings), 93–6.
24. SCHWARTZ, E. 'The cost of capital and investment criteria in the public sector', *Journal of Finance*, **25**, no. 1 (1970), 135–42.
25. SEAGRAVES, J. A. 'More on the social rate of discount', *Quarterly Journal of Economics*, **54**, no. 3 (1970), 430–50.

26. VICKREY, W. 'Principles of efficiency—discussion', *American Economic Review,* **54**, no. 2 (1964), (papers and proceedings), 88–92.
27. DEPARTMENT OF THE ENVIRONMENT, *Fair Deal for Housing,* Cmnd 4728, HMSO, 1971.

The integration of project and sector analysis[1]

9

P. G. Sadler

It is, of course, general in the developing world for individual countries to undertake national planning. This usually takes the form of nominating the sectors into which development effort, in the form of capital, the allocation of foreign loans, the assistance of expatriate advisers, and so on, will be channelled. Also, the proportion by which each sector is intended to expand is usually stated in the plan, and to a great extent a national plan can be seen as a statement of aims which the planning body considers are both feasible and consistent with each other, as well as being the most desirable attainable mix. At the same time, it is also general for such countries, faced with the need to ration scarce resources during the period of the implementation of the plan, to use some method of project appraisal which, using given criteria, will measure the anticipated contribution which will be made by each project to a stated maximand. It is obvious that where national planning is being undertaken, then the criteria used in project selection must be consistent with those used in plan formulation. That is, the attainment of a maximand in the former will imply a maximum contribution to the aims of the latter. Consequently, where a method aims to maximise the present value of government-held reinvestable surplus (as in the Little and Mirrlees, or OECD method) or the present value of future consumption (as in the Sen, Marglin or UNIDO method), then these aims should be consistent with the overall, wider aims of the national plan. Methods of plan construction have, of course, been developed over many years and, while often outside agencies such as expatriate consultants are employed to assist in this process, the right to formulate a national plan unhindered by outside interference is properly regarded as an integral part of national sovereignty. Any attempt by outside bodies to interfere with this would be an infringement of the rights of nations.

[1] The author is indebted to Mr Maurice Scott of Nuffield College for many helpful comments on an earlier draft of this paper and to many friends at the Conference on Small Regions organised by the Economics Department of the University College of North Wales and the Centre for Environmental Studies, where an early version was presented. Also to Mr Colin Bruce, of the International Bank for Reconstruction and Development, with whom initial thoughts on this problem were exchanged. Errors and omissions are, of course, the exclusive property of the author.

However, more and more interference of another form is taking place in the sphere of project selection, a sphere in which the techniques have been developed largely independent of macroplanning methods. Aid-giving bodies either require a cost-benefit analysis of projects to be submitted as support for applications for project assistance, or perform their own investigations and draw up their own social cost-benefit report. Where there is more than one method available, it is tempting for countries to adopt methods which show up their own projects in the most favourable light, and aid-giving agencies often have to recast reports according to a method they have adopted as standard in order to make valid comparisons between applications.

It may well be that the criteria of such methods are not consistent with those of the method of plan formulation adopted by the country concerned. The present paper is the result of work undertaken by the author in Africa at the UNECA headquarters at Addis Ababa on behalf of Nuffield College, and arose from the difficulty of attempting to reconcile a series of projects which had been analysed according to one of the accepted methods of project analysis [1]* with an analysis of a national plan, also undertaken according to one of the recognised methods [2]. While much of what follows will refer to these two methods, it is hoped that the underlying generality of the problem will not be lost to the reader.

Much discussion has been generated recently concerning the applicability of the criteria, and the validity of the assumptions, in many forms of project analysis. For example A. K. Sen [3] and P. Das Gupta [4] criticise the OECD method, *inter alia*, on the grounds that it assumes that the planning authority have power to affect the policy of the country on such matters as tariffs and export taxes. These are, of course, instruments in the macro-planning sphere, and many of the problems of choice of project selection method would be solved if the criteria for both macro- and micro-planning were reconciled beforehand.

The theoretical basis of economics relies heavily on simplifying assumptions. Many of these assumptions concern human motivation, others concern the environment in which the theoretical construct, or model, is being operated. In the positive approach to economics we are able to test these assumptions via the quality of the predictions made, in the sense that they may not be true, but are consistently useful. However, in the normative sphere such as national planning, it is of vital importance that the assumptions we make in the theoretical constructions which guide our planning activities are valid. Stating the obvious, it would be foolish to use a model applicable to a closed economy when the one for which we were planning was an open one. Less obvious is the danger, for example, of using average consumption propensities to mean marginal, or assume that production can be maximised, while consumption demand can be minimised by taxation, whereas the two may be interdependent, in that the incentive to output may be the anticipation of consumption through higher income. The semi-input-output method of

* Numbers in square brackets relate to references on p. 165.

Tinbergen [2], used for convenience in this paper, makes the assumption that consumption is held constant, and is now illustrated. Suppose the following system:

$$V_1 = a_{11}V_1 + a_{12}V_2 + a_{13}V_3 + a_{14}V_4 + a_{15}V_5 + X_1 - P_1 + c_1Y + J_1$$

$$V_2 = a_{21}V_1 + a_{22}V_2 + a_{23}V_3 + a_{24}V_4 + a_{25}V_5 + X_2 - P_2 + c_2Y + J_2$$

$$V_3 = a_{31}V_1 + a_{32}V_2 + a_{33}V_3 + a_{34}V_4 + a_{35}V_5 + X_3 - P_3 + c_3Y + J_3$$

$$V_4 = a_{41}V_1 + a_{42}V_2 + a_{43}V_3 + a_{44}V_4 + a_{45}V_5 + c_4Y + J_4$$

$$V_5 = a_{41}V_1 + a_{52}V_2 + a_{53}V_3 + a_{54}V_4 + a_{55}V_5 + c_5Y + J_5$$

V_i = change in production in sector i

X_i = change in exports of sector i

P_i = change in imports of sector i

a_{ij} = marginal input–output coefficients from sector i into sector j.

c_i = marginal propensity to consume the product of sector i

Y = change in gross national product = $\sum\limits_{n=1}^{i} Y_1, Y_2 \ldots Y_n$

where Y_i is change in value added in sector i

J_i = change in investment demand for output of sector i

Sectors 1, 2 and 3 are international sectors, in that their output is, or could be, part of the import or export activity of the country. Sectors 4 and 5 are national sectors, whose output cannot enter into international trade, such as internal transport, building and construction, and so on. Increases in sectoral value added would then be as follows:

$$Y_1 = V_1(1 - a_{11} - a_{21} - a_{31} - a_{41} - a_{51}) = a_{01}V_1$$

$$Y_2 = V_2(1 - a_{12} - a_{22} - a_{32} - a_{42} - a_{52}) = a_{02}V_2$$

$$Y_3 = V_3(1 - a_{13} - a_{23} - a_{33} - a_{43} - a_{53}) = a_{03}V_3$$

$$Y_4 = V_4(1 - a_{14} - a_{24} - a_{34} - a_{44} - a_{54}) = a_{04}V_4$$

$$Y_5 = V_5(1 - a_{15} - a_{25} - a_{35} - a_{45} - a_{55}) = a_{05}V_5$$

Finally, assume that the marginal capital output ratios for each of the i sectors is K_i.

The maximand for the system is the value added per unit of capital investment. Thus, the benefit to cost ratio for, say, sector 1 would be the increase in value added in that sector plus the increases in sectors 4 and 5 rendered necessary by the increases in sector 1, divided by the value of the capital required to facilitate each of these increases. This would be

$$\frac{a_{01}V_1 + a_{04}V_4 + a_{05}V_5}{K_1V_1 + K_4V_4 + K_5V_5}$$

If this is computed for each of the three international sectors, then a ranking of each is automatically achieved according to the value added divided by outlay of capital for an increase in each sector's output of one unit. It must be noted here that although input/output linkages are assumed between the international sectors, these need not be considered in the calculations, as for example if sector 1 used some of the output of sectors 2 and 3, we would presume that any increase in demand on sectors 2 and 3 occasioned by an increase in output of sector 1 will be met from a reduction in exports or an increase in imports. This is quite reasonable, for in choosing the best sectors according to this criterion, the planning authority is saying 'it is best to concentrate on the sectors giving us the best returns on capital and to import the products of those industries where the return is lower'. In practice, of course, as well as shortage of capital, restraints on the availability of resources, and the ability to import and export will need to be considered, and this will require a programming solution producing a vector of changes in outputs for many sectors, but the essential first step is the calculation of the benefit/cost ratios shown.

Given a change in value added in sector 1 (or 2, or 3) then we can compute the changes in sectors 4 and 5, as we have two equations in two unknowns.

$$V_4 = a_{41}V_1 + a_{44}V_4 + a_{45}V_5$$

$$V_5 = a_{51}V_1 + a_{54}V_4 + a_{55}V_5$$

The method requires, however, either that consumption remains constant, i.e. the increase in value added is taxed away, or that the increase in consumption in each sector will be independent of the manner in which the increase in value added is achieved, i.e. the marginal propensity to consume will be the same for each sector irrespective of how the increase in national product (the sum of increases in value added), is distributed. Under either assumption, a maximisation of value added per unit of extra investment leads to a maximisation of savings and the least adverse effect on the balance of payments, for if

$$\Delta \text{ savings} + \Delta \text{ imports} = \Delta \text{ investment} + \Delta \text{ exports}$$

then given that exports are exogenous, a unit change in investment will lead to a total change on the LHS of one unit. Under the first assumption (all increase in income is taxed away so that consumption, and therefore imports, remain constant), then Δ savings will be 1, *ceteris paribus*. Under the second assumption, with constant and universal savings and consumption propensities, the maintenance of a maximum proportion of the increase generated within the country is synonymous with maximising value added, and therefore savings from a given investment is maximised. So, for a given increase in investment, the increase in imports would be minimised.

At first sight, the method would appear to be suitable for project selection also. Simply apply the same criterion, maximisation of value added per unit of investment. In fact, this is a very common method in frequent use. Two main criticisms apply. One is that the length of life of the capital is not taken into account. (It should technically be possible to do so, but where this method is used, most analysts seem to prefer to use the payback period in conjunction with the value added method, rather than introduce a time discount factor and maximise some form of present value of value added.) This objection is not considered here, however,[1] and attention is focused on the second, which is the assumption that consumption effects are either nil or can be disregarded. Projects with a high value added in developing countries may well achieve this by using large quantities of unskilled labour. This is precisely the area in which consumption can be expected to increase most when income increases. Also, depending both on the type of project and its location, the spectrum of consumption of the unskilled labour will change. The increase in the income of a labourer in the country may result in extra consumption of marketed goods obtained from the local economy, but where the employment of the unskilled labour also entails moving the labourer from a rural into an urban area, then the transformation of consumption patterns may be very marked indeed. Further, increases in income of the unskilled labourer may be the most difficult from political and administrative points of view to tax, whereas an increase in income of a profit earner, or rent taker, may be quite easily taxed. This type of income, too, may be coupled with a low marginal propensity to consume. In this case, it may be more advantageous from the savings and balance of payments point of view to have a slightly lower value added but a greater increase in savings. Once we allow for changes in consumption in this way, we cannot use the savings-plus-imports and investment-plus-exports identity, for different consumption patterns can reduce exports or increase imports, can affect the level of savings, and might even affect the level of investment, so that the initial injection for the project being analysed can cause a change in the given level of investment. We can no longer adopt a single maximand, value added, and regard the other two problems as being automatically allowed for. There must now be a form of compromise, in which the desirability of various factors must be weighted. How much weight should be given to current consumption, which is what much of development is all about, and how much to saving, which allows for increases in future consumption and increases the rate of growth. Solutions will always contain some compromise on this.

By contrast, the new methods of benefit/cost analysis pay particular attention to the problems created by increased consumption, and also to the need to take a view of the costs and benefits over time. Usually the latter is accomplished by using a present value technique, but the treatment of the former depends upon the nature of the maximand adopted. For example, where the maximand is the present value of the reinvestable surplus created, using the investable funds in the hands of the government as numeraire, as in the Little and Mirrlees approach, then any extra consumption generated will be treated as a cost. How much of a cost will depend upon the relative value of present consumption versus the future consumption anticipated by an equivalent amount of investment. More important, it will depend on whose

---

[1] Professor E. T. Nevin, University College, Swansea has made a suggestion on how this could usefully be achieved, for which I am much indebted, and I hope to use it in a later paper.

consumption we are considering. The deprivation of consumption to a low income peasant is valued differently from that of a high income rentier. A simple explanation may serve to illustrate some basic points in the method.

Consider a hypothetical project in a developing country. It requires imported machinery. This will be a direct charge on foreign exchange, and can be priced at world prices.[1] It will use raw materials or semi-finished goods which will either be imported or if manufactured at home could be exported. These will be valued at their price on the world market, as this illustrates the cost of obtaining them, or the opportunity cost of using them. (Adjustment will be made for internal transport costs also if this is a significant part of total costs.)

Goods and services which do not, and cannot, enter into world trade will be used, e.g. electricity, transport, gas, cement. These, of course, are manufactured or provided at home and use labour, goods which are obtained or could be sold on the world market (i.e. tradable goods), and again some non-tradables, which in turn can be analysed into labour, traded, non-traded, etc. This is a problem in matrix algebra, and by inversion methods, the proportion of each non-tradable good which can be allocated to each category can be found.

It will use labour directly, and this will be of various forms: expatriate labour, which will repatriate some of its income and which will be a direct charge on foreign exchange (this labour will also consume goods while in the country, which will be valued at world prices and included as a cost), also skilled labour, which is scarce, and can be included at a very high figure because of this (usually at a price close to its full wage, as this would be its opportunity cost in a perfect market, and the market for this type of labour would probably be competitive, at least on the demand side). Each type of labour has its own shadow price. But so far we have shown little departure from the value added method. The Little and Mirrlees method does not use value added as a criterion, however, but attempts to maximise the level of investable surplus created, consistent with a pre-agreed allocation between present and future consumption. This is exemplified in its treatment of the shadow wage of unskilled labour. This labour is deemed to come largely from agriculture and even though this may be via the large army of unemployed, one may assume that this is replenished from the countryside, and that there is in fact a marginal product in agriculture foregone when an individual takes up employment in industry. Call this marginal product M. The unskilled labourer is deemed to consume all his income, so that his increased consumption is also a cost in the relative sense, in that it will reduce the amount available for reinvestment. Call his wages in industry C. If he is not taxed, then he will consume C. If we were only interested in reinvestment, and gave no weight to present consumption by the low income groups, then the shadow cost of his labour would be its marginal product in agriculture plus the extra

---

[1] Whether to use world prices, as in the Little and Mirrlees method, or actual prices, as in for example the Sen and Marglin method, has been a matter of separate debate but does not affect subsequent arguments in the paper.

consumption generated (in total, $C-M$). The shadow wage would be $M+(C-M)$ or, of course, C. But development must mean something for the peasant of today, and an allowance is made for this by permitting a portion of the difference between the wage in industry and in agriculture to be given equal weight with investment. If we call this proportion $1/S$, then the shadow wage of unskilled labour would be as follows: $SW=C-(1/S)(C-M)$.

$1/S$ can be anything from 0 to 1 depending on the size of S, which should always be equal to or greater than 1. Thus, if we were completely indifferent between present and future consumption, S would be equal to 1, and we would not penalise consumption at all. SW would equal M. If, however, we regarded the future as all important, and all present consumption were to be treated as cost, then S would equal infinity, and the shadow wage would equal C (for further detail, see [1]). It is the $1/S$ factor which reflects the planner's view of present and future requirements.

The need to make an adjustment equivalent to the money wage to establish social costs is not difficult to see. If there is imperfection in the market for labour, or for goods, or anything else, which necessitates cost benefit analysis, then it is likely that there will be an imperfection in the capital market also, and *inter alia*, the rate of interest will not adequately reflect the true social rate of discount, even if we abstract from all the other philosophical arguments concerning the relationship between them. The value of S in the above equation is arrived at as follows. Suppose a marginal project on which there is a rate of reinvestment r (i.e. the proportion not committed to consumption) and which employs n men per unit of investment cost. Given a flow of such projects, the growth of future consumption could also equal r. Suppose too that, having regard to the present level of income and consumption, the level of anticipated investment, and the rate of population growth, it is estimated that by the time t the country will have reached the point at which present versus future consumption will have been brought into balance. We can regard t as our time horizon. Thus, the value of capital accumulation at a reinvestment rate of r over a period t from an initial unit of investment, would be $(1+r)t$. In present value terms, this would be $(1+r/1+i)^t$ where i is the social rate of discount. (i can be expected to be lower than r, as there is likely to be an expanding population and a low level of income, as well as lower degrees of uncertainty attaching to public as opposed to private investment. All these will increase the gap between r and i.)

There will also be extra consumption generated by this extra investment, and given that this consumption grows at an annual rate of r also, this will have a present value of

$$(C-M)\,n\left[1+\left(\frac{1+r}{1+i}\right)^2\ldots+\left(\frac{1+r}{1+i}\right)^{t-1}\right]$$

(If n is the number of units of labour employed per unit of investment, and $C-M$ is the increase in consumption caused by the transfer of each unit of labour from the subsistence sector to the industrial sector, then $(C-M)n$ is the increase in the first year, but this grows at the rate of n per annum.

To find the present value equivalent, it must be discounted at the rate of i_1.)
The formula yields

$$\frac{(C-M)n}{r-i} \left[\left(\frac{1+r}{1+i}\right)^{t-1} \right] (1+i)$$

Adding the value of capital accumulation generated and the value of future consumption, we get

$$\left(\frac{1+r}{1+i}\right)^t \left[\left(\frac{c-m}{r-i}\right) n(1+i)+1 \right] - \left(\frac{c-m}{r-i}\right) n(1+i)$$

This is the cost, in present value terms, of *not* devoting resources to one unit of investment, and therefore the cost, in a relative sense, of a unit of present consumption. So, if one unit of consumption foregone and subsequently invested has a present value of S, then for every S units of extra investment achieved, we should allow 1 unit of extra consumption.

Similarly in the calculations we will include as a cost the extra consumption which is generated by the increased income to nationals from rent and profits. This is arrived at after allowing taxation and saving. Thus, presented with a set of financial costings for a project, conversion factors can be calculated for each of these headings and applied to the costs to arrive at the social costs in accordance with the method outlined. Calculated for each year over the life of the project, and also including the benefits in the form of present value and of output, we can calculate the net present value of the reinvestable surplus anticipated from the proposal. The method is, of course, adaptable to variation, in that if there are income differentials in regions, this will be shown up in S if a project is tested in different hypothetical locations. Similarly, weighting may be given to S on a political rather than an economic basis to favour backward regions or to achieve regional equality within a certain period. There are many variations which can be played on this theme, but essentially we will have the net benefit, as defined according to our pre-agreed criteria, and if it is positive, it is automatically taken that the project is worth undertaking.

The problem now arises that if a national plan is formulated choosing sectors according to the Tinbergen method, but project selection is carried out according to the Little–Mirrlees method, then unless the simplifying assumptions made in the macro planning sphere do, in fact hold, the plan will be suboptimal and the project selection method will not ensure that the projects selected will make the maximum contribution to the fulfilment of the national plan. This could be overcome by adopting consistent criteria for both project selection and national planning, and if the Tinbergen approach could be made sensitive to the changes in consumption which would be generated by increased value added, then it would eliminate a substantial part of the inconsistency which would otherwise arise.

The following suggestion to accomplish the elimination mentioned is a proposed adaptation of a regional model at present in operational use at Bangor [5], which is, in turn, derived from a model by R. Artle [6]. Briefly, most regional input–output models which include changes in demand as an endogenous part of the model treat these changes as functions of the total value added, but in a small region the manner in which the value added is distributed among the sectors is crucial. For example, suppose a small village of twenty families. One family owns the local farm, ten families are supported by a worker in trade A in a nearby town, nine families by a worker in trade B in the same town. Each of the families spends 10 per cent of its income on the produce of the farmer. Suppose now that the workers in A have a 5 per cent increase in income which changes their consumption pattern and they no longer demand local goods. Their increase will be more than offset by the fall in the income of the farmer, and the total effect is negative. On the other hand, an increase in the incomes of workers in B could have an exactly opposite effect if the produce of the local farm was a superior good to them. The same type of change can arise in developing countries. As individuals move from the subsistence to the monetary sector, and especially if this move entails urbanisation, a radical change in their consumption patterns can result, so that the effect of the increased income is not fed back to the countryside in the form of increased demand for foodstuffs but may be switched abroad for imported goods, or at least increase home demand for goods which were hitherto exported. The model we are using has been developed to predict this type of change; and using Artle's notation, is reproduced below.

Suppose a system as follows:

$$\text{Vector } X = [X_1 X_2 \ldots X_n]$$

$$\text{Vector } Y = [Y_1 Y_2 \ldots Y_n]$$

$$\begin{bmatrix} a_{11} \, a_{12} \ldots a_{1n} \\ a_{21} \, a_{22} \ldots a_{2n} \\ \\ a_{n1} \, a_{n2} \ldots a_{nn} \end{bmatrix} = A = \text{Matrix of input/output coefficients}$$

$$\begin{bmatrix} b_{1h} & 0 \ldots 0 \\ 0 & b_{2h} \\ \\ 0 & 0 \ldots b_{nh} \end{bmatrix} = B_h = \text{Income creation coefficients for each of the } h \text{ receiving sectors } (h = n+1, \ldots p)$$

$$\begin{bmatrix} C_{1h} \, C_{1h} \ldots C_{1h} \\ C_{2h} \, C_{2h} \ldots C_{2h} \\ \\ C_{nh} \, C_{nh} \ldots C_{nh} \end{bmatrix} = C_h = \text{Propensities to consume of each of the } h \text{ sectors}$$

which yields:

$$X - AX - C_{n+1}(1-A)\,B_{n+1}X \ldots C_p(1-A)\,B_p X = Y$$

Factorising:

$$X = (1-A)^{-1}\left[1 - \sum_{n+1}^{p} C_h(1-A)\,B_h(1-A)^{-1}\right]^{-1} Y$$

Vector X shows changes in the level of activity in each of the n sectors. Some of these sectors will be national, as in the Tinbergen model. Matrix A is the usual matrix of input–output coefficients. Bh is a series of h diagonal matrices, each element in the diagonal showing the income created in income group h by a unit change in output of the corresponding producing sector. C_h is a series of h square matrices, each column vector of which shows the marginal propensity to consume of each of the income sectors from each of the appropriate output sectors. The vector Y is now the total of the changes in X which have not been devoted to intermediate production or consumption. When placed upon the computer, the model can be manipulated to test for the capital inputs necessary in the national and international sectors for a given change in output of each international sector in turn. This will yield changes in output in the appropriate international sector and the appropriate national sectors, which multiplied by the respective capital output ratios will give the net cost in terms of capital required. The benefits are a little more complicated to find, but the total of the created consumption in each category can be printed out by the computer as well as the vector Y. The vector Y would be the total surplus over and above consumption for the increase postulated in each international X, but some of this would be taxation, some savings, etc. The income and consumption information obtained, together with information on the tax structure of the country, would enable Y to be apportioned and appropriately weighted. If it were deemed that private saving was worth two-thirds of public saving (i.e. taxation) then the components of Y would be adjusted accordingly to yield, say, $\bar{Y}$. But, in the section on project analysis above, it was pointed out that an increase in consumption now may be allowed as part of the benefits if it accrues to the peasant or low income sectors. This proportion, call it λ, will be computed by reference to the S factor and the marginal product in agriculture. $1/S(C-M)$ is the amount of consumption we allowed against the unskilled worker's wage C, so that

$$\lambda = \frac{1/S(C-M)}{C}$$

and the total benefits for each increase in an international sector would be $\Sigma \bar{Y} + \lambda \Sigma C_u$ where Cu is consumption of the unskilled worker in industry, and the benefit/cost ratio appropriate to each sector is now $(\Sigma \bar{Y} + \lambda \Sigma C_u)/\Sigma X_i k_i$.

References

1. *Manual of Industrial Project Analysis in Developing Countries*, vol. ii, Paris, OECD.
2. TINBERGEN, J. *Development Planning*, WUL, 1967.
3. SEN, A. K. 'Control areas and accounting prices', *Economic Journal*, March 1972, Supplement p. 486.

166   P. G. Sadler

4. *Industrialisation and Productivity*, 1970.
5. SADLER, P. G. *Input–output and Small Regions*, Centre for Environmental Studies Conference Papers no. 2.
6. SADLER, P. G. *Regional Multipliers*, Regional Research Paper no. 4, Economics Research Unit, Department of Economics, UCNW, Bangor.
7. *Papers and Proceedings of the Regional Science Association*, 1961.

The integration of project and sector analysis: Discussion

J. A. Mirrlees

Apart from the rather abstract literature on decentralisation of plans, there is little discussion by economists of the relationship between planning methods and procedures for project appraisal. Mr Sadler has pointed out one important conflict between such methods. It is not the only conflict, but it is remarkable that the treatment of labour in planning models is so different from that suggested by writers on the choice of techniques and investment projects generally. Mr Sadler argues that the conflict should be put right by changing the planning models. I agree with him. Labour has been neglected in planning methods for reasons of analytical convenience. It need not be: there is room for more economics in planning models than has been customary, and a move in that direction is welcome.

Tinbergen's semi-input–output method is an important and elegant application of input–output data, which has the advantage of emphasising trading opportunities. Its chief imperfections are the neglect of labour and the oversimplified treatment of capital. I like to think of it in the following 'dual' formulation, which brings out these imperfections clearly. Each commodity has a shadow price p_i, which is equal to its border (or world) price, m_i, if it is a traded good. Capital has a shadow price, which we may as well denote r. Then, for each commodity i,

$$p_i = \min \left(m_i, \sum_j p_j a_{ji} + r k_i \right) \qquad (1)$$

m_i is infinite (or very high) for the nontraded goods. If there is to be any domestic production of traded goods, which will be necessary unless foreign borrowing is very high, we must have

$$p_{i_1} = \sum_j p_j a_{ji_1} + r k_{i_1} \; (= m_{i_1}) \qquad (2)$$

for at least one of the traded goods. $p_{i_1} = m_{i_1}$, since otherwise it would 'pay' to export an infinite amount of the commodity. The requirement (2) then determines r, which is, to put it differently, the maximum benefit/cost ratio. Notice that only *one* tradable sector should produce, unless the export price falls with increased sales. Then two become equally profitable: but this changes all the shadow prices and the next sector that is worth bringing into production may *not* be the one second in 'order of priority' (an unfortunate phrase) in the Tinbergen calculation.

In passing, one should note and question the assumption that all capital goods are imported, but this morning we must pass on to labour. If production of commodity i has labour coefficient n_i, we should introduce a shadow wage w, and rewrite (1) as

$$p_i = \min \left(m_i, \sum_j p_j a_{ji} + rk_i + wn_i\right) \tag{3}$$

How determine w? The requirement that at least one sector produces is not enough. If fixed production coefficients adequately describe all sectors, we can go on to claim that, in general, at least two sectors must produce, but *which* two depends on the factor supplies available. We can draw the usual isoquant for the production of one unit of foreign exchange. The corners show what can be done with one tradable sector alone, accompanied by the necessary production in the non-tradable sectors. For example, one might have:

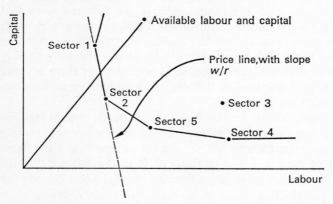

The Tinbergen method can be used to compute this frontier.

But there are circumstances when it may not be too inaccurate to estimate w exogenously, particularly those discussed by Mr Sadler. It is supposed that we are restricting discussion to the 'industrial', or at least nonagricultural sectors of the economy. Labour can come from agriculture or go back there. If we know the marginal productivity of labour in agriculture, that can give us w in (3), and the semi-input calculations are possible. This will not be a very good method if, for example, the marginal productivity varies substantially with employment in industry, or if it is importantly affected by r. But for many developing countries, these possibilities are unlikely.

Indeed we can go further, and this is the point emphasised by Sadler. If the commitment to allow consumption out of wages is costly, that cost can be represented by a requirement to provide goods, entirely analogous to the needs for material inputs into the sector. In effect, the coefficients a_{ij} are increased to allow for these consumption costs.

The proportion of consumption that is to be regarded as cost has to be estimated exogenously. In principle it depends on r, and also, I suppose, on the accounting prices of commodities. At present, we know so little about shadow wages, that it is perhaps best to guess on the basis of general observations of the economy and its government or to use simple aggregative models, which can tell us more about the future possibilties so relevant to assessing the cost of labour than input–output models, with their fixed coefficient assumptions and need for disaggregated demand data.

At present, then, I see the whole decision-taking procedure as having three levels. A long-term aggregated model or argument can be used to estimate the shadow wage rate. With this estimate, we can go on to use input–output in deriving sectoral accounting prices, and an estimate of the capital cost— the accounting rate of interest as the OECD Manual calls it. These accounting prices can be used in detailed project appraisals (and in other discussions of microeconomic policy). Mr Sadler brings out very clearly the first two steps in this procedure. I hope he would agree it is important to go on to the third stage for the actual decisions. It seems to me worth presenting the procedure so starkly because economists have to consider it against others, and they must see it clearly if they are to find its faults. But perhaps it would not be so bad an outcome if some country adopted it.

University efficiency and university finance[1]

10

Richard Layard and Richard Jackman

Universities are often inefficient. In section 1 we quote some examples of this, especially their failure to exploit the new media of communications. But the question is why the inefficiency occurs and how it can be reduced. It seems mainly caused by the difficulty of measuring the output of individual teachers and of institutions, and thus of paying them appropriately. We therefore explore the efficiency effects of different ways of paying teachers (section 2) and of financing institutions (in section 3). The analysis assumes that universities are labour-managed enterprises, and leads to some piecemeal policy conclusions.

1. University efficiency

When people complain of university inefficiency, they may mean that the choice of techniques is inappropriate (e.g. too high a staff/capital ratio) or they may mean that the wrong outputs are being produced (e.g. too much research). Though these issues are interrelated it is important to distinguish between them. If we knew the university production function, efficient allocation would of course generally require us to secure three sets of equalities: the marginal rates of substitution between factors should equal their relative marginal social costs; the marginal rates of transformation between products should equal their relative marginal social benefits; and the social value of the marginal product of each factor should equal its marginal social cost. Unfortunately, little is known so far about the university production function, though a good deal is known about the school production function [13, 28]* and work is afoot on universities.[2] Equally, not much is known about

[1] We are grateful to L. P. Foldes, H. G. Johnson, A. K. Sen, B. A. Weisbrod and G. L. Williams for useful comments and suggestions. Richard Layard is grateful to the Nuffield Foundation for a Small Grant which financed a visit to the USA in 1971 during which he began thinking about this subject.
[2] The Higher Education Research Unit, LSE, is currently estimating cross-sectional production functions in five subject-groups in the UK.

* Numbers in square brackets relate to references on p. 187.

the shadow prices of many of the main outputs, particularly research [5], so that remarks such as 'we need not double research by 1980 but we must double teaching output' are little more than assertions of value judgment. However, rather more is known about the prices of the main inputs such as student time, staff time, and non-staff inputs, and this makes it easier to think about questions of the choice of techniques provided one is willing to guess at marginal rates of factor substitution.

Before coming to the new media, we shall give a few examples of apparent inefficiency in the use of the old. One class of these concerns the use of student time, which teachers tend to treat as a free good although it accounts for about half the total real cost of universities. A small example illustrates this point. Suppose one is teaching a course where a book on the reading list will be read in the library by, on average, n students. One can either put the catalogue numbers on the reading list or leave each student to look them up individually. Efficiency requires the former, unless n is less than the ratio between the price of one's own (or one's secretary's) time and the price of students' time.[1] Yet how often do we do it? Moreover, the provision of books and articles often seems inadequate relative to the provision of teachers. If, as undergraduates in some institutions allege, they spend two hours a week looking for books and articles, the cost of this search will normally exceed the cost of all the materials which their library provides for them.[2]

Turning to the use of staff time, one is struck by the passion for small teaching groups and the proliferation of optional courses.[3] Yet all the evidence suggests that students' gains in cognitive understanding are independent of class size over a wide range of class sizes [11, 15]. The psychic benefits to students may of course be higher in smaller classes, since the possibility of personal contact between teachers and students is higher. However there is no reason to suppose that these contacts, which are clearly an important means whereby students discover their talents, are best produced jointly with cognitive learning, rather than by separate arrangements in which teachers participate, but with personal guidance rather than exposition as the goal. So there must be many cases where classes are inefficiently divided into

[1] Once a student is enrolled in a college the price of his time in the Catalogue Room is of course equal to the present value of the returns to time used in its next best use. Normally this is some alternative type of study. If it is efficient for him to be studying, then the present value of returns to study must at least equal the value of the earnings he could (given no indivisibilities) command with the same time. The reader should note that we are not attributing inefficiency to the fact that the university does not pay for its students: we are saying that it misuses the time of students having enrolled them.

[2] These remarks assume that students' time is worth £0.50 per hour, so the cost per student per year is £30. The average number of bound volumes per student in university libraries in the UK in 1968–69 was about 115, but less than half of these were probably used by undergraduates, say 50. If these books cost on average just over £2 and depreciate over two years at a 10 per cent interest rate, the annual cost of these 50 books is £20.

[3] For a good discussion of the economies to be had from controlling these phenomena, see [2].

sections, and there is an excessive input of teaching time and an inadequate input of guidance.

Against this point of view it may be argued that, although the inputs of teaching time are unnecessary for producing teaching output, they are important for research; they train researchers and keep them abreast of current knowledge. This argument is particularly strong when applied to the proliferation of options, which, though it reduces class sizes, enables people to teach the subject areas of their research. If this is true, the joint-product nature of the university justifies what seems inefficient from the teaching point of view; and the choice of techniques may be efficient, in the sense that the university is producing on its research/teaching production possibility frontier.

However, when the new media are introduced into the production set, this argument becomes implausible. The issue here is complex and we shall only sketch a basic argument: a fuller treatment appears elsewhere [14]. Television, film, programmed texts, and computer-assisted learning are clearly most suited to teaching well-structured bodies of knowledge. Here they offer clear scope for reducing costs per student-hour without loss of quality, if used on a large enough scale. In fact many of the advocates of the new media believe that quality would be improved—by individualising the process of instruction (students pacing themselves, and so on); by disseminating more widely the influence of the few outstanding teachers; and by making economic the allocation of more preparation time to any particular hour's worth of teaching materials. Against this, others argue that quality per student-hour is bound to fall, owing to the absence of direct human contact, lack of personal feedback and external pacing, and the like. In fact, however, the finding of the available surveys of empirical evidence [10, 7, 27, 24] is that student achievement is fairly similar whatever teaching medium is used— neither better nor worse. Moreover, the new media seem to be as successful in teaching problem-solving ability as in teaching concepts and facts. Attiyeh, Bach and Lumsden [1] found that students who spent twelve hours reading one of their programmed introductory economics texts without any live teaching did as well on questions testing the application of economic theory to real problems as students who had taken twenty-one hours coursework and read the associated textbook.

As regards student attitudes to the new media, these are sometimes favourable and sometimes unfavourable, depending on the exact circumstances of the change. Moreover a new medium is almost always liked more by those who have experienced it than by those who have not [10]. Just as there are televised and computer-based courses which have failed to attract students to whom live instruction was also available for the course, there are others where, even in competition with a popular instructor, the new medium has swept the field [26]. At the State University of New York at Oneonta, the introductory economics course is now taught to all students, except one undersubscribed live section, by two hours a week of prerecorded television and one hour of informal discussion sections with faculty members; the new system is preferred to the old, and is cheaper [21, 12]. The general conclusion must be, as before, that students want and need contact with staff, but it is unlikely that this is produced most efficiently as a complementary output with the learning of formally structured material, and it may not be produced at all by large lecture courses.

On the cost side the basic argument for the new media derives from the large overhead costs involved in the preparation of any teaching material. Effective teaching requires not only the preparation of exposition and of exercises, but also an evaluation of each component part. If these overhead costs are incurred in each teaching institution, there is a degree of duplication that has become quite unnecessary now that the new media are available. Of course, if there were only one university teaching introductory economics, it would almost certainly be cheaper to teach the subject by live instruction only—probably even without a printed textbook. But there are in this country, say, a hundred introductory economics courses, each taught by a different live instructor who works out his own course. In general university teachers are conscientious and devote much time to devising what they consider makes the best course. And yet, in the event, most of the courses will be very similar, most could be improved if more time were devoted to the preparation of better problems and expositional sequence, and many of them are taught by people who lack a talent for teaching. Such a situation seems highly irrational when we now have the means to devise a few competing packages which could do much of the job a great deal better and more cheaply.

Space precludes giving detailed statistics of cost. But the following comparison of videotape with live lectures may give some impression of the issues. Whereas the cost of lectures is roughly proportional to the number of presentations, videotape involves substantial fixed costs of two kinds. First, there is the cost of producing the master tape, which depends on the complexity of the production. The cost of this per presentation falls directly with the number of institutions using the material. Second, there is the cost of the equipment needed to present the material (videotape recorders and TV sets). The cost of this per presentation again falls directly with the number of presentations for which it is used. However, provided the production is of the simplest kind, it will be cheaper than live lecturing, even if used in only two institutions, provided those institutions are using their equipment for at least sixty-five presentations a year. The more complex the production the larger the number of participating institutions (or of presentations per institution) needed to make it economic.[1]

So it seems that there are well-established possibilities of reducing costs per unit of output by the selective use of new media, provided these are adopted on a sufficiently large scale. In the immediate future the best bet appears to be the use of programmed texts and videotape to replace much live exposition. The materials currently available are often of poor quality; but even those that are good are rarely used outside the institution where they were prepared, even though they are sometimes made available free of charge.

---

[1] For a fuller discussion see [14].

Thus the potential scale economies of the media are wasted and their use fails to expand. The question is: Why are institutions unwilling to use materials they have not themselves produced, when these could be used to reduce their own teaching commitments, liberating time for research or other teaching? It cannot be due to an objection in principle to other people's materials, for on that principle each university should provide its own textbooks. Can it be due to the infant industries, chicken and egg, problem? Until there is a reasonable market the incentive to produce is small and quality may be poor; but equally until the quality is good, the market remains small. All one can say is that this problem has not prevented the spread of a whole host of new commercially produced items, especially in the communications industry. Of course, the universities are not in business to make a profit and may therefore lack the incentives affecting commercial manufacturers. But textbooks are not produced by universities, but by publishers and authors, and neither publishers nor computer firms have ventured far into the new media. The reason is that they do not trust the market; they doubt the demand.

So can there be some feature of universities (either intrinsic or due to their methods of financing) which makes them likely to reject efficient techniques of producing the teaching and research that society wants? A casual glance at the main users of bought-in materials suggests that there may be. The main users are private firms and the armed services. There are now in the USA many schemes whereby local firms buy televised Master's courses in engineering for their employees and pay at least the full incremental media costs.[1] But there are very few cases of one university buying such facilities from another. Similarly the new media are widely used for training, both by firms and the Army. Though the material here may be more clearcut than much of what is taught in universities, it is idle to pretend that there are no routine manipulations which university students must master.

So we need to look closely at the non-profit nature of the university and its objective function to see whether these provide any explanation of university inefficiency. But we also need to look at the internal processes of universities and examine whether it is within their power to be efficient even in achieving their own objectives.[2]

2. Problems of internal pricing

Universities as labour-managed enterprises

First, we have to identify the university's process of decision-making. Most universities in this country are formally governed by mainly lay councils, but most of the effective decisions are probably taken by academics, some of them *ex officio* and others elected by other academics. So the most relevant

[1] The most celebrated examples are at Stanford, Florida State University, University of Colorado and Southern Methodist University.
[2] For interesting discussions of utility-maximising non-profit institutions see [20] and [9].

simple model seems to be that of the labour-managed enterprise, the relevant labourers being in this case only the academic staff. The objective of the enterprise is then to maximise the welfare of its members subject to the production functions, the budget constraint and any other externally imposed constraints.

Why are universities run in this way unlike most other enterprises? The answer seems to lie in the difficulty of measuring their output. If teaching and research could be readily measured, students or governments would be willing to pay for defined quantities and the form of organisation would probably be autonomous hierarchically organised units, whether privately or publicly owned. But given the problem of output measurement there are two obvious possible methods of providing for quality control: internal democratic self-government or external bureaucratic management (e.g. as in France). Each has obvious dangers, as Adam Smith pointed out [25].

> If the authority to which the teacher is subject resides in the body corporate, the college, or university, of which he himself is a member, and in which the greater part of the other members are, like himself, persons who either are, or ought to be teachers; they are likely to make a common cause, to be all very indulgent to one another, and every man to consent that his neighbour may neglect his duty, provided he himself is allowed to neglect his own. In the University of Oxford, the greater part of the public professors have, for these many years, given up altogether even the pretence of teaching.
>
> If the authority to which he is subject resides, not so much in the body corporate of which he is a member, as in some other extraneous persons, in the bishop of the diocese for example; in the governor of the province; or, perhaps, in some minister of state; it is not indeed in this case very likely that he will be suffered to neglect his duty altogether. All that such superiors, however, can force him to do, is to attend upon his pupils a certain number of hours, that is, to give a certain number of lectures in the week or in the year. . . . From the insolence of office too they are frequently indifferent how they exercise it, and are very apt to censure or deprive him of his office wantonly, and without any just cause. The person subject to such jurisdiction is necessarily degraded by it, and, instead of being one of the most respectable, is rendered one of the meanest and most contemptible persons in the society.

There are it seems some who think this latter model describes our present situation. But we shall assume that our universities do have at least sufficient discretion to be regarded as labour-managed.

But because they are not paid for their outputs, there is no automatic mechanism such as that which ensures that classical labour-managed enterprises in perfectly competitive industries free of external effects will in long-run equilibrium be allocatively efficient [16]. Instead universities may receive their incomes in a block grant, or in the form of a per student fee or in many other ways. This inevitably makes possible a divergence between the university choice of inputs and outputs and what the rest of society would like, since in a labour-managed enterprise the preferences of the teachers will play a preponderant role. We shall discuss this problem in section 3 and ask how different forms of external finance are likely to affect university behaviour. But first we consider the internal problem that arises because universities are unable to measure the output of their own staff. This makes it difficult for universities to achieve even their own objectives.

The objective function and the ideal pricing of output

We can best think about this by imagining what the university would do if it could pay teachers for their output. Suppose that all teachers have the same utility function and that the university aims to maximise the average level of utility of its members. The key question is: What affects individual utility? Clearly, the teacher values his wage, the way he spends his time, the products of his labour and also the quality of the university where he works. While he values the use of his time for its own intrinsic satisfaction, he may value his outputs for other reasons also—for example a good research reputation may raise his future earnings from outside work. The reputation of the university is valued for similar reasons and also because it attracts good students and colleagues. This reputation depends on the teaching and research outputs of the institution, which teachers may also value as goods in themselves. They differ from the other sources of individual satisfaction in that they are collective goods which affect the welfare of all. For this reason each teacher cannot be left to do what he likes; for, unless motivated to do so, he will not take into account the effect of his decision on the welfare of his colleagues. Instead he should be paid for each unit of output an amount equal to the sum of its marginal value to all individuals.[1] In this way, the university could achieve its objective of maximising average welfare if individual outputs were measurable.

The actual payment of teachers and the problem of information

But unfortunately, measurement is difficult. One alternative now open is to pay for inputs, just as Oxford and Cambridge pay for tutorial supervision and many universities for examining. The scope for this approach seems wider than is currently practised. In principle, if production functions were fully known, it could achieve exactly the same results as paying for output. The same is true of the policy most commonly followed, namely regulation, by which certain dimensions of the teacher's inputs are laid down, in return for which the teacher gets his wage in the form of a block grant.

The difficulty with regulation is that not many dimensions of work can in fact be effectively policed: one can require so many hours of teaching of such and such type, residence in the UK, and the like, but control over quality is inevitably poor. Moreover, regulation makes it difficult to take advantage of the different teaching and research talents of different individuals, and all tend to be given the same teaching load whether or not their comparative advantage is in that line.

Pricing problems also seem to explain many of the problems referred to in

[1] For a more formal exposition see Note I (p. 185 below).

section 1 of this paper. First, there is the alleged lack of concern about the quantity and quality of teaching output as opposed to research. A possible explanation is as follows. The university will wish to pay its members on the basis of their expected productivity. But how is this to be assessed? It is widely believed that teaching capacity is more difficult to evaluate than research capacity and that an academic's accumulated research is often used as a proxy measure of the potential value of his current teaching and research output. This may be particularly the case when he moves from one university to another. If this is so, it introduces an extraneous element into the individual teacher's utility function, for he now values his current research output more highly relative to his teaching output, purely because of the higher command over future income which it gives him. This in turn will affect the level of teaching load for which he is willing to vote.[1]

Given this it might well be asked why even the current amount of teaching is done. Three possible explanations can be offered. The first, and most charitable, is that teachers obtain direct utility from their own and their colleagues' teaching output. A second is that they enjoy the teaching input (holding forth), even if they are not especially concerned with whether anything is learnt. A third, and perhaps important, explanation is that certain forms of teaching activity are an important input into research, which in this sense is produced jointly with the teaching output. Most people believe that, at any rate in theoretical subjects, there is a high degree of complementarity between research and teaching (especially lecturing or other forms of systematic exposition), and this must certainly be one important source of resistance to replacing live instruction by effective teaching.

Thus, pricing problems affect the university's ability to achieve its own true objectives. However, these need only be accepted if the cost of improved information on the teaching performance of individual teachers exceeds its benefit. The most obvious source of better information is the use of systematic student questionnaires, which could provide direct information to the teacher himself as well as relevant data to those who set his pay [18]. There would be costs—of administration and lost ease—but the potential benefits seem in the context of this paper to be great.

Similar arguments apply to the problem of organising desirable innovations in teaching methods. Teachers when they leave a university carry as a claim to future income only their past research, and someone who is likely to move in the near future has little incentive to devote time to innovations which will benefit others but not himself. A similar problem arises in the determination of the rate of reinvestment in the classic labour-managed enterprise where workers have no property rights in the assets of the enterprise [19]. It is therefore not surprising that innovations in teaching methods are as often made by the

---

[1] Owing to the public goods characteristics of university outputs, teachers would always be willing to vote for higher required outputs than they would themselves voluntarily deliver. But this is particularly so of teaching, owing to its low private monetary reward. For evidence that teachers would on average prefer to do less teaching relative to research see [29].

older as the younger staff—a situation not paralleled in manufacturing enterprises, where a reputation for profitable investment decisions provides an excellent claim to future income. The Prices and Incomes Board's proposal to formalise payments for innovation in teaching therefore deserves strong support [18].

Pricing problems also arise over the teachers' use of students' time. This is clearly an input into the production function of each university teacher but he does not pay for it. This would create no problem if the teacher were paid for his net output, but he is not. He therefore has little incentive to economise in the use of his students' time. This is one of the main reasons why syllabuses become overloaded, the other reason being that teachers are using their students as stimuli to their own research. There are of course limits to this process given that students are free agents. They can often opt out of excessively overloaded courses or refuse to do the full volume of reading and writing expected. But the problem of effectively coordinating the institution's use of students' time remains a severe one.

The teacher as entrepreneur

At this stage someone might point out that these kinds of incentive problem arise in any organisation. This is true. But the difficulty is probably more acute in universities, because the problem of policing the individual worker is greater due to the individualistic and non-cooperative nature of the basic production process, which at present depends critically on the face-to-face interaction between the lone teacher and his students.

However, this suggests one obvious general solution for our problems, which is for universities to be 'deschooled' and teachers to be self-employed. In this scheme we replace the university as the entrepreneur hiring services from the teacher, by the teacher as the entrepreneur hiring services, where necessary, from the university. All payments for teaching services would be made directly by the consumers to the teachers, who would rent their rooms from the university. The function of the university would be to provide capital facilities, to certify the teachers and to provide the necessary informational and administrative services to establish effective contacts between students and teachers. If a coordinated teaching programme were felt to be necessary, teachers could bid for the right to give particular courses but they would collect their fee at the door. Such a Smithian scheme has many attractions. It brings the cutomers' evaluation of teaching output directly on the teacher, and so overcomes the problem of teachers being paid on the basis of past research rather than current teaching.[1] It also makes it more likely that student time will be economically used. But its main defects are the classic ones adduced by Coase in his explanation of the existence of the firm [8]. These are the transaction costs involved in using the market to organise a process in which there is a degree of interdependence between the outputs of

---

[1] According to [6] there is no prospect of progress unless teachers are paid directly for their output.

many different agents.[1] The higher the ratio of non-teacher inputs to teachers, the more important the coordinating role of the university organisation becomes; and if the arguments about new media and innovation are accepted, more non-teacher inputs may be what are needed at the moment. There is also the obvious danger of teachers exploiting their monopoly of their own differentiated product.

A final and less radical proposal for expanding the role of prices in achieving university efficiency is to give a greater entrepreneurial role to departments, who would receive a general budget out of which they would pay for the factors they employ. This type of limited internal pricing is now becoming more prevalent and could further encourage efficiency if departmental incomes were in some degree related to the department's output [3, 4]. But the more important internal reform involves the deliberate and costly gathering of more information about teaching performance.

3. Problems of external finance

This brings us to the question of the optimum method of financing institutions, as opposed to individuals. There are a number of ways in which governments can alter the conditions in which universities make their decisions and we shall try to discover how some of these affect the staff/student ratio and the output mix. Specifically we shall examine the effects of salary regulation and grant levels, the question of block versus *per capita* finance, and the wisdom of separate finance for research and innovation. We shall start by assuming bureaucratic financing (viz. fixed income and student numbers for each university).

The regulation of salaries and the size of grant

In the classic labour-managed enterprise the workers determine their own average level of pay, but in universities the government may, as in Britain, restrict this freedom by imposing salary scales and maximum senior/junior staff ratios.[2] The purpose of this is presumably to prevent university teachers feathering their own nests and paying themselves more than their supply price out of public money. In a full-blooded socialist market economy with free entry this problem does not of course arise; for, if one enterprise is paying more than the going wage, others are set up in that industry until the product price has fallen sufficiently to eliminate the wage differential. But in a state-financed system free entry may not be possible. So a system of unregulated wages may involve inequitable transfers of income. It may also be allocatively inefficient.

[1] The same considerations may explain why teachers are not paid in relation to their teaching hours.
[2] There are obvious difficulties in enforcing any particular level of salaries, given that institutions can decide where to place individual teachers on the scale, and when to promote them [17]. Likewise, they can always vary non-wage benefits and the quality of recruits. The actual system must therefore lie somewhere between the regulated and unregulated extremes.

The allocative problem arises because, when deciding on the number of colleagues to hire, university teachers realise that each additional teacher reduces their own income. This cost they balance against the value to them of the extra teacher's output, be it his research performance, his contribution to reduced teaching loads or whatever. The resulting equilibrium could well be inefficient. Suppose for example that teachers were only interested in the level of output per teacher and in their own wage. Equilibrium would then require that the average product per teacher be increasing with the number of teachers, so as to offset the monetary loss to existing teachers involved in hiring a new one.[1]

A more general problem is that, whereas under regulated wages the government can always bring about any desired staff–student ratio by varying the grant paid to the university, this may not be possible under unregulated wages. For the higher the level of grant the greater the cost of an extra teacher to those already employed. This is analogous to the problem in labour-managed factories that a remission of rent may reduce output and employment in the firm [16]. On the other hand, higher incomes may raise the marginal value which teachers place on their colleagues' output so that an increase in the grant leads to an increase in employment. But there may still be some maximum number of teachers beyond which no variation of grant can induce the university to go.[2]

If, however, wages are fixed, the existing teachers experience no monetary cost from an expansion in their number, and employment expands till the subjective value of the output of the additional teacher falls to zero, or, as is more likely, until the budget is exhausted. If the wage is fixed at the supply price, the number of teachers employed for a given grant will be larger than if the wage is either unregulated or regulated above its supply price. By varying the grant it should always be possible to achieve the desired staff–student ratio, and at minimum cost to the taxpayer.[3]

The staff–student ratio and the output mix

The staff–student ratio will of course be simultaneously determined with the balance between teaching and research, and if an increase in grant raises the staff–student ratio, it can be expected to alter the output mix. The direction of the change will depend on the precise form of the teachers' utility function. Suppose that teachers value research output per teacher (R) and teaching output per teacher (T) and that the marginal rate of substitution between these is independent of their wage. Suppose too, that the production function of R depends only on the way each teacher uses his time, while the production function of T depends on this and on the staff–student ratio. An increase in

---

[1] An illustrative example is given in Note II, which is however mainly concerned with points coming later in the text.

[2] The government, by varying the grant, could always reduce the number of teachers to any desired number.

[3] A further argument in favour of payment at the supply price is that any other price would distort the choice between teachers and other factors of production.

the staff–student ratio reduces the maximum teaching output per teacher (T), as each teacher has fewer students with whom to work; but it leaves his maximum research output unchanged.[1] It therefore shifts the production possibility curve in from PP' to PP'' in Fig 10.1. Given homotheticity in the utility function this increases R/T, and hence the share of research in university output. Conversely a cut in grant would be expected to cut research output relative to teaching, as common belief suggests.

However, it is equally possible that teachers, while valuing research output per teacher (R), value teaching output per *student* (I). With this new variable measured on the horizontal axis, a rise in the staff–student ratio (n/s) shifts the production possibility curve out from PP'' to PP' and decreases R/I. However, the change in the university's balance of output (R/T) is indeterminate, since $R/T = (R/I).(n/s)$ and the fall in R/I may be proportionately less than the rise in n/s.

Thus neither of two widely different utility functions suggests that increasing the staff–student ratio will definitely raise the share of teaching in output, while one of them leads to the view that this share will be reduced.

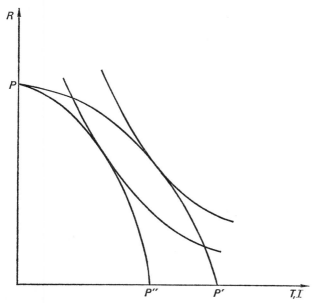

FIG 10.1

Per capita versus block grant finance

We turn now to the effects of replacing a block grant conditional on fixed student numbers by a system of *per capita* finance with the university free to take as many students as it wants. This has been widely advocated as a

---

[1] More realistically, of course, we should allow for the influence of other inputs. Both maximum R and T would change, but their rate of transformation would probably change as shown in the diagram.

7

remedy for university inefficiency and in particular as a method of increasing the emphasis on teaching relative to research [22, 23].

However, a first look at the question suggests that this conclusion is by no means obvious. For instance suppose the outputs which teachers value depend only on the ratios between the various inputs, as we assumed in our recent example. Then if a block grant is replaced by a *per capita* grant of equal size, as has been suggested [22], the university's choice of staff–student ratio and output mix would be unaffected.[1] The only difference is that the scale of university becomes indeterminate. This is true whether or not wages are regulated.

If there are not constant returns to scale, a university receiving a *per capita* grant can choose its own size, whilst under bureaucratic finance this choice is constrained. It can be shown that under *per capita* finance if the university values its outputs in the same way as society it will choose to operate at the socially most efficient scale. But nothing can be said *a priori* about the balance of outputs at this scale as opposed to any other.[2]

We have however so far ignored one of the main arguments put forward in support of the view that *per capita* financing would tilt the output mix towards teaching. The argument is this. Under *per capita* finance universities can no longer count on having any students unless they can attract them, whereas under the bureaucratic system they are sure of receiving their quota. The number of students wanting to go to a university depends on its teaching and research, but primarily on its teaching. Therefore, teaching output will rise relative to research if a block grant system is replaced by a *per capita* system.

There are severe problems in finding a convincing formulation of this argument. Let us begin with a world of perfect competition between identical universities. It then follows that, if under bureaucratic finance there is no excess demand for places from students, universities are already under pressure to maintain the standard of their teaching—any relaxation would lead to a loss of students from the system. If on the other hand there is excess demand universities can, under *per capita* finance, expand, if they wish, without improving teaching standards. In this case, the final situation depends on whether the total number of students is allowed to grow. The government could presumably limit this by selecting those students for whom it was willing to provide *per capita* finance. But if it did not and instead accepted an open-ended commitment, the movement to equilibrium would be likely to involve an increased pressure towards higher standards of teaching.

Should total student numbers remain constant, there will only be an increase in teaching if universities wish to expand because they have been constrained at less than their perceived optimum scale, and if there are intrinsic *differences* in production arrangements between universities or they face a rising supply curve of students. If there were intrinsic differences in efficiency or if some universities had a greater taste for teaching, they would

---

[1] The same would be true of its wage if this was unregulated.
[2] The points made in this section are formally illustrated in Note II.

attract all the students from the other universities, which would be forced to close unless they retaliated by improving their teaching. Equally if the supply curve of students facing a particular university were rising, in the sense that more teaching per student was needed to attract more students, some universities might find it worth their while to pinch from others by raising their offering. In the British case one might question whether universities offer such a differentiated product that they are in this situation. Moreover, to the extent that they are, this already applies to each category of student quality and may influence university behaviour even under the block grant.

Finally, students may in fact have great difficulty in assessing teaching and, like universities in paying staff, may make their assessment on the basis of research reputations. For all these reasons the line of argument expressed at the beginning of this section seems fraught with question marks.

Paying separately for research and innovation

One other suggestion is sometimes made for effecting a shift to teaching [18]. This is to offer universities a separate payment for research, in the hope that the reduced block grant would be used for teaching. But it seems unlikely that this would in fact happen. If the university receives a given income in the form of a block grant plus a payment related to its research output, this seems bound to lead to a higher research output (and less teaching) than if the same sum were given as a single unconditional grant. For while this system provides an additional motivation for research, it does not remove any of the incentives that were there before. Administrative controls to ensure that the research grant is spent only on research could not help. Likewise administrative controls to ensure that the block grant was spent on teaching would be difficult to enforce, but if enforceable could be used equally with undifferentiated grants.

However, if paying for things the universities will do anyway is ill-advised, it may be well worth while to pay them for things they would not do but which are socially desirable. As we have seen, innovation falls into this category. The University Grants Committee has followed just such a policy, giving earmarked money to individual universities for use on new media. However, this has typically had little or no effect on the teaching methods of the universities because good teachers have not believed that the materials they developed would ever reach a wider market, such as that reached by their textbooks. The answer seems to be for media development to be sponsored by the central government either on its own or through consortia of universities or professional associations. These methods should ensure a sufficient market for the materials. A consortia of northern universities have successfully developed a packaged course in computer science that is used in each university. But this type of development is still more important in the bread and butter subjects, such as economics, where the real costs arise. If the natural sponsor for such an enterprise is the professional association, we would urge that the Association of University Teachers in Economics take this role upon itself.

4. Summary

In sum, the universities seem to be inefficient in their choice of techniques and may be inefficient in their choice of outputs. The main reason for these problems is the difficulty of measuring the outputs of individuals and of institutions.

Mainly because of this difficulty, universities in Anglo-Saxon countries are constituted as labour-managed enterprises, and the utility functions of individual teachers thus affect the universities' input and output mix. It may or may not be true that teachers value the research output of their university relatively more highly than society does. But in any case the difficulty of measuring individual teaching output leads to teachers being paid largely for their past research. This greatly raises the value to them of their own current research output, and in turn reduces the incentive to introduce new teaching methods and materials, since the institution gains more from these than the individual teacher. Teachers will also value highly those kinds of teaching activity, like lecturing, which are most complementary to research but can be most efficiently replaced by packaged materials.

One proposed solution is to transfer the entrepreneurial role to the individual teacher who would be paid directly by students or research councils, according to their judgment of his output. But in fact the degree of interdependence between different university activities seems to make it worth while to preserve the university as a 'firm'. However, there may be more scope for pricing in the relation between universities and their constituent departments and for more piecework payment of individual teachers. A more fundamental need, however, is to improve information about teaching output, and this provides a strong case for the use of student questionnaires on individual courses.

Another approach is to alter the external stimuli to which universities are exposed. Here we have examined a number of proposals that have been put forward for raising the output of teaching relative to research. The first, a cut in university income for a given number of students, seems likely to have this effect. The second would replace the existing block grant to universities (with student numbers fixed) by an equivalent grant per student, with the university free to determine its own size. However, it is not clear that this would have the desired result. If the outputs that teachers value are produced by processes subject to constant returns to scale, there might be no change, and, if they are not, the direction of change is unpredictable. However, this argument assumes that an individual university faces an infinitely elastic 'supply curve' of students. But if institutions can only attract more students by raising their teaching output per student and they wish to expand, then a move to *per capita* finance may indeed raise the output of teaching relative to research. Better information on the teaching outputs of individual institutions might also have this effect. A third suggestion has been that universities should receive separate earmarked payments for research and teaching. But as it is not administratively easy to earmark money for teaching, earmarking might well raise relative research output rather than lowering it. However, separate payments for development work on teaching materials would have the desired effect, and are best organised on an interuniversity basis, perhaps through professional associations.

Note I

Assume

$$U_i = U\left(W_i, L_i, X_i, Q\left[\sum_{j=1}^{n} X_j\right]\right)$$

where U_i, W_i, L_i and X_i are respectively the utility, wage, labour input vector and output vector of the representative ith teacher, n is the number of teachers, and Q is some function of the university output vector. Assume too a separate and identical production function relating the inputs and output of each teacher and having a unique inverse function $L(X_i)$. The university now has to select a wage function which, when presented to individual teachers, will lead them to maximise collective welfare. Suppose this linear. Then

$$W_i = a + p_x X_i$$

where p_x is a price vector. If the university has fixed income (Y^0) and staff (n) and no other inputs, the budget constraint may be written

$$a = (Y^0 - p_x \sum X_i)/n$$

To maximise average welfare we require

$$\frac{\partial\left(\sum_{i=1}^{n} U_i\right)}{\partial X_j} = \frac{\partial U_j}{\partial X_j} + \sum_{i \neq j} \frac{\partial U_i}{\partial X_j} = 0$$

However, the maximising individual will set $\partial U_j/\partial X_j = 0$, so we require

$$\sum_{i \neq j} \frac{\partial U_i}{\partial X_j} = \sum_{i \neq j}\left(U_{W_i}\left[-\frac{p_x}{n}\right] + U_Q Q_{X_j}\right) = 0$$

$$\therefore \qquad p_x = n \frac{U_Q}{U_{W_i}} \cdot Q_{X_j}$$

where U_Q, Q_{X_j} and U_{W_i} indicate partial derivatives. Since all individuals have the same utility functions and production functions, U_W and Q_X will be the same for all individuals.

Note II

In what follows we confirm that

(a) the output mix is the same under block and *per capita* finance, given constant returns and unregulated wages,

(b) the same is true, given regulated wages,

(c) the size of university under *per capita* finance is optimal if teachers value outputs as society does.

We shall assume throughout that labour is the only input (it can be shown that introducing other inputs makes no difference). We shall also assume a utility function involving wages (W), research per teacher (R) and teaching per teacher (T). The results would not be affected if teaching per student (I) were used instead, provided both T and I depend only on ratios such as the proportion of time (r) which teachers spend on research and the staff–student ratio (n/s).

Unregulated wages

$$U = U(W, R, T)$$
$$R = R(r)$$
$$T = T\left(r, \frac{n}{s}\right)$$

(a) Block grant finance: $Y^0 = nW$; $s = s^0$

1st order conditions are

$$\frac{\partial U}{\partial n} = -U_W \frac{Y^0}{n^2} + U_T T_{n/s} \frac{1}{s^0} = 0$$

$$\frac{\partial U}{\partial r} = U_R R_r + U_T T_r = 0$$

(b) *Per capita* finance: $g^0 s = nW$

1st order conditions are

$$\frac{\partial U}{\partial n} = -U_W \frac{g^0 s}{n^2} + U_T T_{n/s} \frac{1}{s} = 0$$

$$\frac{\partial U}{\partial s} = U_W \frac{g^0}{n} - U_T T_{n/s} \frac{n}{s^2} = 0$$

$$\frac{\partial U}{\partial r} = U_R R_r + U_T T_r = 0$$

The first two equations are identical to each other, and, with the third, are identical to those in (a) if $g^0 = Y^0/s^0$.

Regulated wages

(a) Block grant finance: $Y^0 = nW^0$; $s = s^0$

1st order conditions are

$$n = \frac{Y^0}{W^0}$$

$$\frac{\partial U}{\partial r} = U_R R_r + U_T T_r = 0$$

(b) *Per capita* finance: $g^0s = nW^0$

   1st order conditions are

$$\frac{n}{s} = \frac{g^0}{W^0}$$

$$\frac{\partial U}{\partial r} = U_R R_r + U_T T_r = 0$$

As before, these equations are identical to those in (a) if $g^0 = Y^0/s^0$.

Optimum scale under *per capita* finance

(The result is the same under regulated and unregulated wages; regulated wages are assumed. Thus $g^0s = W^0n$.) With non constant returns assume

$$U = U(W, R, T)$$

$$R = R(r)\,h(n)$$

$$T = T\left(r, \frac{n}{s}\right).f(s)$$

   1st order conditions are

$$\frac{\partial U}{\partial n} = U_R R(r)\,h'(n) + U_T T_{n/s} f(s)\,\frac{1}{s} = 0$$

$$\frac{\partial U}{\partial r} = U_R R_r h(n) + U_T T_r f(s) = 0$$

$$\frac{\partial U}{\partial s} = -\,T_{n/s}.\frac{n}{s^2}\,f(s) + T\left(r, \frac{n}{s}\right) f'(s) = 0$$

Combining the first and third equations to eliminate $T_{n/s}$

$$U_R R(r)\,h'(n) + U_T T\left(r, \frac{n}{s}\right) f'(s)\,\frac{s}{n} = 0$$

As n is increased by 1 unit, its effect on utility via research plus its effect on utility via teaching (s/n being instantaneously constant) is zero. Under normal assumptions about the utility function, it is sufficient for such a maximum that $h(n)$ and $f(s)$ are convex upwards.

References

1. ATTIYEH, R. E., BACH, G. L. and LUMSDEN, K. G., 'The efficiency of programmed learning in teaching economics: the results of a nationwide experiment', *American Economic Review*, May 1969.
2. BOWEN, H. R. and DOUGLASS, G. K. *Efficiency in Liberal Education*, McGraw-Hill, 1971.
3. BRENEMAN, D. W. (Ed.), *Internal Pricing Within the University—a Conference Report*, Office of the Vice-President (Planning), University of California, December 1971.

4. BRENEMAN, D. W. 'The Ph.D. Production Process', paper presented to National Bureau for Economic Research Conference on Education as an Industry, 1971.
5. BYATT, I. C. R. and COHEN, A. V., *An Attempt to Quantify the Economic Benefits of Scientific Research*, Department of Education and Science, HMSO, 1969.
6. CALVIN, A. D., in K. G. Lumsden (Ed.), *Recent Research in Economics Education*, Prentice-Hall, 1970.
7. CHU, G. C. and SCHRAMM, W. *Learning from Television: What the Research Says*, Institute for Communications Research, Stanford University, 1967.
8. COASE, R. H. 'The nature of the firm', *Economica*, 1937.
9. CULYER, A. J. 'A utility-maximising view of universities', *Scottish Journal Political Economy*, November 1970.
10. DUBIN, R. and HEDLEY, R. A. *The Medium may be Related to the Message. College Instruction by T.V.*, University of Oregon Press, 1969.
11. DUBIN, R. and TAVEGGIA, T. C. *The Teaching–Learning Paradox*, University of Oregon Press, 1968.
12. GORDON, S. D. 'Optimising the use of televised instruction', *Journal of Economic Education*, Autumn 1969.
13. HANUSHEK, E. 'Teacher characteristics and gains in student achievement: estimation using micro data', *American Economic Review*, May 1971.
14. LAYARD, P. R. G. 'The cost-effectiveness of new media in higher education' in K. G. Lumsden (Ed.), *Efficiency in Universities*, The La Paz Papers, 1973.
15. MCKEACHIE, W. J. 'Research on teaching at the college and university level', in *Handbook on Research and Training*, ed. N. L. Gage, 1963.
16. MEADE, J. E. 'The theory of labour-managed firms and of profit-sharing', *Economic Journal*, March 1972 (Supplement).
17. METCALF, D. 'Some Aspects of the UK University Teachers Labour Market', paper presented at the AUTE Conference, Aberystwyth, March 1972: Chapter 11 of this book.
18. NATIONAL BOARD FOR PRICES AND INCOMES, Report no. 98, *Standing Reference on the Pay of University Teachers in Great Britain*—First Report, Cmnd 3866, HMSO, December 1968.
19. NEUBERGER, E. and JAMES, E. *The Yugoslav Self-Managed Enterprise. A Systemic Approach*, Working Paper no. 26, Economic Research Bureau, State University of New York, Stony Brook.
20. NEWHOUSE, J. P. 'Towards a theory of non-profit institutions: an economic model of a hospital', *American Economic Review*, March 1970.
21. OFFICE OF EDUCATIONAL COMMUNICATIONS, State University of New York, *Assembling the Revolution*, mimeographed, 1970.
22. PEACOCK, A. T. and WISEMAN, J. *Education for Democrats*, Institute of Economic Affairs, Hobart Paper 25, 1964.
23. PREST, A. R. *Financing University Education*, Institute of Economic Affairs, 1966.
24. SCHRAMM, W. *The Research on Programmed Instruction: An Annotated Bibliography*, US Government Printing Office, 1964.
25. SMITH, A. *Wealth of Nations*, Book V, ch. 1, part iii, Art. ii.
26. SUPPES, R. and MORNINGSTAR, M. 'Computer-assisted instruction', *Science*, 17 October 1969.
27. TICKTON, S., ed. *To Improve Learning. An Evluation of Educational Technology*, vols. i and ii. R. R. Bowker and Co., 1970.
28. US DEPARTMENT OF HEALTH, EDUCATION AND WELFARE, *Do Teachers Make a Difference?*, US Government Printing Office, 1970.
29. WILLIAMS, G. L., BLACKSTONE, T. and METCALF, D. *The Academic Labour Market*, Elsevier Publishing Co. (forthcoming).

University efficiency and university finance: Discussion

M. Blaug

I welcome this paper as one of the first, in this country at any rate, to explore the implications of university finance on teaching methods and the mix of teaching and research. That is not to say, however, that I am altogether happy with the way the paper is formulated. Moreover, I personally found the excursions into the empty formalism of utility maximisation less than helpful, and somewhat pretentious.

My substantial disagreements with the paper begin on the first page; 'Universities are often inefficient'; 'If we knew the university production function, efficient allocation would of course generally require us to secure three sets of equalities. . . . Unfortunately, little is known so far about the university production function', etc. All this suggests that the problem of efficiency would be solved if only we knew certain technical facts, such as the mix of inputs that would maximise the learning of students, or the mix of inputs that would maximise the research activities of members of staff. But, surely, the problem of university efficiency is the lack of consensus about the variables that are to enter into the objective function, namely, those outputs which are to be maximised subject to the budget constraint and certain technical relations summed up in the phrase 'production function'. In particular, whose objective function are we talking about? That of the paymaster or that of university academics?

That brings me to the Layard–Jackman model of the university as a labour-managed enterprise, or, in Culyer's language, as a club of utility maximisers. I agree that this is the relevant model for British universities but I doubt the Layard–Jackman thesis that universities are in effect organised as labour-managed enterprises because of the objective difficulties of measuring the outputs of teaching and research. The problem of quantifying the benefits of research has not inhibited industry and research councils from paying for research in much the same way that tangible goods and services are paid for in the market place. Similarly, teaching is not really as difficult to assess as academics like to pretend. Indeed, a useful model of universities ought to predict the well observed tendency of academics to resist any and all attempts to measure the effectiveness of teaching.

Most of us will recall the universal jeers that greeted the PIB proposal in 1968 to introduce student assessment of teaching as one and only one element in the decision to promote particular members of staff. The participants in the debate, all of whom rejected the notion of relating salaries in any way to student opinion, divided neatly into a minority who simply denied the possibility of objectively assessing the quality of teaching, and a majority who asserted that it was already being assessed informally by heads of departments. Now, it must be conceded that there is very little hard evidence that 'publish or perish' is the basic principle of promotion policies in universities. On the other hand, causal empiricism certainly confirms the idea of a research bias in determining salaries. In any case, as soon as it is argued that the quality of teaching is, in fact, taken into account in making promotions, it remains only to decide how to assess that quality as objectively as possible, in which case encouraging students to express their views can only aid assessment.

By the way, it is interesting to ask oneself how university teaching is now assessed, given the absence of student assessments and the prevailing taboo against attending a colleague's lectures: obviously, it is done, if it is done at all, by talking to students on a casual basis or by inference from a man's performance in a staff seminar. Is it conceivable that anyone could oppose the use of any and all supplements to such crude devices? Apparently, yes. When Mr Culyer presented his 'Utility-maximising view of universities' at the AUTE conference three years ago,[1] he generated a surprising number of realistic predictions about British universities. He denied, however, that a research bias in promotion policies was one of them and elsewhere he has suggested that the quality of teaching is, in fact, taken into account in rewarding British academics.[2] Now, Layard and Jackman stress the actual difficulty of evaluating teaching capacity and use it to account for the bias towards research. They pose the interesting question why, in such circumstances, there is even as much teaching as there is. They find some reasons in the utility functions of teachers, although it would be much more plausible to argue that a minimum amount of teaching of a tolerable quality is one of the constraints imposed by UGC on universities; in other words, teaching gets a high value in the objective function of the UGC but a low value in the objective function of academics.

All this is to say that it is far from clear whose utility we are maximising and which are variables and which are parameters in the objective function of universities. The problem is made more difficult in that our observation of university behaviour, from which we infer the arguments in the objective function, are distorted by the peculiar methods of financing institutions rather than students, in the form of block grants rather than *per capita* grants, with operating costs financed quite separately from capital costs. We need to be cautious, therefore, in interpreting models of universities as labour-managed enterprises.

[1] Since published in the *Scottish Journal of Political Economy*, November 1970.
[2] D. C. Corner, A. J. Culyer, 'University teachers and the P.I.B.', *Social and Economic Administration*, April 1969.

Two hundred years ago, Adam Smith took a profound interest in the problem of rewarding workers in non-profit institutions so as to harness self-interests to the interests of society as a whole. This topic soon dropped out of economics and it has only come back in recent years. The present paper is to be congratulated, not only for reviving this theme, but also for applying it so boldly to our own sector of activities.

Some aspects of university teachers' labour market in the UK[1]

11

David Metcalf

This paper is divided into two sections. The first section discusses some interesting features of the university teachers' labour market. It is emphasised that the market consists of non-competing groups but its operation is subject to a number of constraints such as uniform salary scales. In addition, the effects of certain institutional features of the market, for example the trade union and the tenure system, are analysed. The second section sets up a more formal model to explain how different faculties respond to differences in labour market pressure.[2]

1. The labour market

Background

In October 1969 there were approximately 30,000 university teachers, 28,000 of these were distributed as follows: professors 12 per cent, senior lecturers 19 per cent, lecturers 69 per cent. The remaining 2000 were so-called other (mainly research) staff, many of whom had salaries less than the bottom of the lecturer scale but who had academic status. The percentage distribution of the 28,000 university teachers (i.e. excluding other grade) by university type was: Oxbridge 9·4, London 16·6, Scotland 12·9, Wales 3·0, Old Civic 25·1, Young Civic 10·2, New 7·5 and ex-CAT 13·1. The percentage distribution by faculty was: humanities 18·4, social science 19·7, pure science 30·5, applied science 15·1, and medicine 16·3.

The 30,000 university teachers are employed by forty-four universities.

[1] I am most grateful to a number of colleagues at LSE and elsewhere for discussion of some of the points contained in this paper, particularly Mark Blaug, Keith Cowling, Harry Johnson, Richard Layard and Gareth Williams. This paper is drawn from a more comprehensive economic analysis of the university teachers labour market, which is itself part of a still broader economic/sociological/statistical analysis, financed by the (now defunct) National Board for Prices and Incomes and undertaken in the Higher Education Research Unit at LSE. The main findings will be reported in Williams, Blackstone and Metcalf (1972).
[2] Unless otherwise stated, the evidence in this paper is from the November 1969 Survey, a 1-in-10 sample survey of the university teaching profession.

Some 86 per cent of the finance of these institutions comes via the UGC from the government [10]*. University institutions are established by the state through a Charter of Incorporation.

The individuals in the university teaching profession are extremely well qualified academically: 40 per cent have a UK first class honours degree, and a further 21 per cent have a UK upper or undivided second class honours degree. The highest degree of 52 per cent of the individuals is a PhD and of 14 per cent is a Master's. Only one-quarter have no higher degree.

The profession has expanded rapidly over the last decade. Staff numbers more than doubled between 1960 and 1970. This is a cross-section study and as such is not concerned with the growth of the profession. However, this growth has a specific implication for the analysis of pay. Social science and applied science grew substantially faster than the other faculties. Given the constraints on the free operation of this labour market, this growth has some important predictions for interfaculty differentials in pay and staff quality. These predictions are analysed below.

Non-competing groups

The foundations of classical wage theory are summarised in two famous principles: first, Adam Smith's principle of net advantage, or compensatory principle; second, the concept of non-competing groups developed by John Stuart Mill and Cairnes. These two principles are central to an analysis of university teachers' pay. The university teachers' labour market consists at any one time of a series of non-competing groups. That is, although university teaching is normally considered a single unified occupation, in fact the persons comprising this 'occupation' consist of a series of groups with entirely different training. The human capital embodied in an historian is different to that embodied in an engineer. Clearly the alternative employment of an engineer is (say) in the civil service or in industry—as an engineer. He will not be competing for a university teaching post in history. Thus we have an 'internal' labour market, for university teachers as a whole, and a series of 'external' labour markets by discipline.

Under such circumstances the theory predicts that (a) *within* each non-competing group there will be a tendency to equalise net advantages, (b) *between* each group there will be very little mobility, thus maintaining for a substantial time the uneven distribution of the total advantages and disadvantages of the different groups (occupations). Thus a relative scarcity of engineers will result, *ceteris paribus*, in their pay being greater than that of historians. However, three constraints exist which inhibit such a pay differential developing within the university profession. The constraints are national uniform salary scales, a maximum permissible proportion of teachers in the senior grades and the policy of the teachers' trade union, the Association of University Teachers.

* Numbers in square brackets relate to References on p. 210.

Salary scales

One inhibition on the free operation of the labour market is the existence of national uniform salary scales. These scales apply to all universities except Oxford and Cambridge and all subjects except clinical medicine. The scales consist of an incremental scale with minimum and maximum points for lecturers and senior lecturer/readers; and for professors a minimum salary and maximum average salary.

Why do salary scales exist in this profession?[1] They are desired by and/or affect both the demand and supply side. From the supply side there are two reasons for salary scales. First, they provide cohesiveness (or 'equity') to a profession comprising a series of non-competing groups. Cartter [6, p. 482] has suggested that in the USA, where pay is individually negotiated, 'too much information (on salaries) can fan rivalries and petty jealousies'. Possibly salary scales circumvent such jealousies whilst simultaneously providing adequate information on pay. Second, salary scales provide security additional to that provided by the tenure system: they provide an individual with knowledge of his probable pay for a number of years in advance.

Four further suggestions as to why national uniform salary scales exist evolve from a consideration of the demand side. First it is possible that uniform salary scales forestall, within any subject, the concentration of talent in relatively few institutions. That is, without the constraint imposed by uniform salary scales across all universities certain institutions might acquire a disproportionately large share of the high quality individuals within a discipline.[2] Such a concentration may be particularly serious for a large number of institutions if we accept Stigler's Law which maintains that there are at any one time, no more than fourteen 'super'-scholars in any discipline. This argument for salary scales may be countered on two grounds. (a) If a university could afford high quality individuals it may circumvent the salary scale constraint by offering other advantages such as free housing, superior research facilities and generous travel expenses. (b) The argument itself may be reversed. It is possible that the existence of uniform salary scales inhibits an equal distribution of talent: less prestigious universities, or those suffering from locational disadvantages are, because of national scales, unable to compensate for these disadvantages and are therefore unable to attract or retain high quality individuals. Removing the scales would, so the argument runs, enable such institutions to compete effectively in this labour market.

---

[1] The arguments developed here with respect to salary scales apply *pari passu* to the maximum permissible senior staff ratio; no more than 35 per cent of the academic staff of any university may be in the grades above lecturer.

[2] This argument is analogous to that advanced up to 1960 by the Football League in favour of the retention of a maximum wage for professional footballers. 'The basis of the Football League's defence of the system was the principle of equality among clubs. The maximum wage clause gave clubs more equal chances of attracting the best players' [17, p. 185]. A rule with similar intention (the 'reserve rule') exists in baseball, see Rottenberg [16]. Note, however, that the budget constraint imposed by the method of financing universities, via the UGC, will itself inhibit such a concentration of talent.

This counter argument is probably false. There is no *a priori* reason why removal of the salary scales would result in the prestigious or locationally advantaged universities paying (after taking into account the relative non-monetary advantages) less than the less prestigious institutions for the service of a given individual. Indeed, casual observation of the US university labour market, where there are no national uniform scales, suggests a much more unequal distribution of talent than in the UK (cf. [6, pp. 486–93]).

Second, with a given amount of finance, existing university teachers have an incentive to reduce recruitment and raise their own salaries. With the expansion of the universities after World War II the University Grants Committee therefore laid down national uniform salary scales to ensure that taxpayers got 'value for money', i.e. to ensure that the increase in Exchequer payments to finance the expansion did not lead to substantially higher pay for existing university teachers with little increase in employment. Third, it is possible that the existence of salary scales facilitates collusion among the universities, specifically among university administrators (employers) acting as agents for the government, and that this monopsony situation results in lower salaries than would occur in a labour market without such scales. This possibility is, however, unlikely. Most university teachers have alternative employment opportunities in the private sector of the economy. Those few teachers who have no such opportunities, mainly humanities teachers, are possibly receiving, because of the existence of uniform salary scales, substantial economic rent from their university employment. Thus monopsony elements will manifest themselves via a restriction on employment rather than earnings. Fourth, employers may desire salary scales because it is costly to evaluate constantly the performance of each individual. It is therefore assumed that productivity rises with age (experience), for example because of learning-by-doing, and the individual receives a quasi-automatic progression along the salary scale.

The existence of national uniform salary scales, together with the relatively small number of employing institutions and freedom of movement with the university system, yields the intuitive prediction that, for homogeneous labour, wage dispersion will be relatively small in this market after allowing for relative locational advantages. The first two factors lower the cost of obtaining information on pay, whilst the third inhibits the persistence of interuniversity wage differentials.

Trade union

The third factor which inhibits the development of intersubject or interfaculty pay differentials is the Association of University Teachers. The AUT is an industrial trade union. It represents, with one major exception, all the occupations (defined by subject—i.e. training) in the university sector. It has persistently and successfully insisted, during pay negotiations, that there should be no formal non-medical pay differentials by faculty.

It is perhaps natural that in an industrial union equity should override economic efficiency as a principle of pay determination. Nevertheless, it is important to ask why those groups who are (temporarily at least) in relatively short supply do not secede from the AUT. The answer, historically at least, is probably that for any small group (subject) the disadvantages of facing a potentially powerful monopsony with a relatively weak monopoly have outweighted the advantages of belonging to a large comprehensive trade union.

The only group strong enough to negotiate individually are medical staff, who are represented by the British Medical Association. The medical faculty, in fact, is the only group (subject) which has a craft trade union which negotiates pay outside the university system. That is, economists, historians and engineers, for example, whilst frequently belonging to professional institutes, cannot belong to their own craft trade union because no such union exists. The AUT certainly recognises the power of the craft oriented BMA. Perkin [12, p. 26] states that 'Medical teachers are still difficult to recruit to the AUT because they feel, rightly or wrongly, that the BMA is a more adequate defender of their interests'.

The equity arguments of the AUT are all-pervasive. One strand of its arguments in pay negotiations is normally (and, of course, correctly) a comparison of university pay with pay in similar occupations. However, the AUT frequently considers the university teaching profession harshly treated when efficiency considerations impinge on its equity arguments. For example, Perkin, the AUT's historian, bemoaning the relatively low pay of university teachers in the early 1950s goes on to say 'unfortunately . . . the conditions of work (in university teaching) were so attractive that there never was in this period a problem of recruitment' [12, p. 141].

Whilst the AUT is against formal pay differentials by faculty it does not inhibit the free operation of the labour market in other ways. For example, it does not deliberately restrict entry into the profession, nor does it lay down hiring standards. That is, once the government has decided on the number of universities and the universities on the number of staff they desire, the AUT does not attempt to shift the labour supply schedule to the left. Whilst the AUT does not operate directly on the supply side of this market, one of its goals has an important affect on the demand side. The AUT is reluctant to condone a worsening of the staff/student ratio. Although this policy is ostensibly held for educational reasons, it has the important effect, in a period of expansion, of shifting the demand schedule for staff rightwards. University heads (e.g. vice-chancellors) are in general agreement with this policy and combine with the AUT to form a united front against the ultimate employer, the government.

The effects of salary scales, maximum senior staff ratios and the equity policy of the AUT are fully discussed below.

Tenure

Seventy-four per cent of university teachers have permanent tenure; that is, they cannot be dismissed except for infringements of contractual obligations

of a fairly specific nature. Permanent tenure is normally granted after satisfactory completion of a probationary period, usually around five years.

The economic rationale underlying the tenure system has been developed
by Alchian [1], Alchian and Kessel [2] and Culyer [7]. These writers develop
a model in which universities are utility maximisers (rather than profit
maximisers). Alchian and Kessel argue that:

> Job security, whether in the form of seniority or tenure, is a form of increased
> wealth for employees. Since it makes for more pleasant employer–employee
> relations, it is a source of utility for employers. The incentive or willingness of
> owners to grant this type of wealth to employees and thereby increase their own
> utility is relatively strong because profits are not the opportunity costs of this
> choice (p. 168).

Culyer, using the same underlying objective function provides the link with
academic freedom. He sees a potential conflict situation between administrators and academics. This conflict situation develops because administrators
maximise utility via the achievement of factors such as a 'quiet life' and a
'good image in local society'. As administrators and managers have wide
discretion in the use of their authority this poses a threat to the security of
employment of teachers, especially

> if teachers wish to propound unpopular ideas, or ideas which the administrators
> and lay members of governing bodies such as the Council in many universities
> find uncongenial . . . (therefore security of tenure) is precisely the sort of
> institution which would be predicted to develop, and where universities are
> owned by the state, security of tenure emerges as a defence against the additional
> possible threat of political interference (p. 354).

This underpinning of the institution of tenure,[1] which evolves from economic
theory, is consistent with the description of the historical growth of the
institution of tenure in the interwar period given by Perkin [12, pp. 81–5].
This analysis is, however, not the whole story. Tenure is desired from the
supply side by existing staff and from the demand side by some departmental
heads and administrators. At times when there is a substantial excess supply
of potential university teachers both departmental heads and the frustrated
(excluded) potential teachers may wish that the institution of tenure did not
exist. The demanders of labour (departmental heads, etc.) could, under such
circumstances, raise the quality of their departments by terminating the
contracts of some individual and rehiring from the pool of currently excluded
teachers. This would simultaneously raise the net advantages of the newly
hired individuals who were previously excluded.

The institution of tenure has, potentially at least, three important labour

---

[1] Note that Culyer's reasoning produces a narrower rationale for tenure than that
of Alchian and Kessel. Tenure in Culyer's model is a device to protect *Lehrfreiheit*
and to protect teachers from the arbitrary hiring and dismissal policies of university
administrators. The reasoning of Alchian and Kessel allows that the institution of
tenure exists for additional reasons, for example, to provide a satisfactory environment
to undertake research—no anxiety about the ultimate productivity of the research
being present.

market effects. First, it may effect the height of the age–earnings profile in university teaching compared with that profile in other occupations. University teachers may be trading income for security and therefore, *ceteris paribus*, lifetime earnings may be less than in other occupations.

Second, James [8] suggests that tenure may effect the *shape* of the age–earnings profile. Specifically it may be steeper than it would be if perfect competition prevailed in this labour market. Under perfect competition the individual and the university would enter a short term contract, say one year, the individual receiving a wage equal to his net marginal product. Under the tenure system the university is wedded to the individual for life after permanent tenure is granted around age thirty. The reverse is not true: the individual will quit his university when the present discounted value of expected future returns is greater at an alternative institution. It is possible that, after the granting of permanent tenure, the rate of increase of an individual's productivity may decline or become negative, whilst he nevertheless continues his quasi-automatic progression up the salary scale. Given the finite probability that wages may exceed marginal product in the period after tenure has been granted (i.e. in the middle and old age ranges) the university has an incentive to pay less than marginal product in the younger age ranges to ensure that it never becomes a 'net lender' to the individual.[1] The age–earnings profile may therefore rise more steeply than the marginal productivity schedule, the point of intersection being around the year of conferment of permanent tenure.[2]

This reasoning is appealing but contains a weakness. It is suggested that universities pay less than marginal product in the younger ages. Such a result is possible if restrictions on labour mobility exist, but less likely in the more competitive circumstances of this market where no such restrictions hold and where, in general, an individual would move to another university if he was being paid less than his marginal product. However, such mobility may be inhibited by a number of factors:

(*a*) All universities may pay less than marginal product prior to tenure.
(*b*) Labour mobility may impose monetary and psychic costs. The individual may consider that the benefits are insufficient to compensate for these costs. The benefits will extend for a few years only (i.e. up to the year of conferment of permanent tenure) because once the individual has tenure he can adjust the time and intensity of his input irrespective of the university of employment.
(*c*) If an individual derives psychic benefits from teaching at his particular

[1] Perkin [12, 84] provides some interesting anecdotal evidence of just such behaviour in the interwar period.
[2] This reasoning also provides an explanation of why supplementary earnings are positively related to basic salary. In the early years of his career the individual concentrates on his university occupation, ensuring that his research and teaching productivity are adequate to gain his permanent tenure. He therefore has low supplementary earnings during this period. When he receives tenure he is able to substitute paid non-university work for some part of his university work.

institution he will not move. Presumably this factor will be stronger the more prestigious the institution.

(*d*) It is unlikely that an individual knows clearly the value of his services to his university. He may be able to determine his annual value only by applying for and being offered a job at another institution and he may be reluctant to make such an application for fear of not being offered such a post.

If these factors do inhibit mobility at young ages the original argument is restored: it is quite possible that the age-earnings profiles are steeper than the age-marginal productivity profiles.

Third, the tenure system protects the individual from the effects of obsolete training. It is probable that the frontiers of knowledge advance in many subjects sufficiently rapidly that some individuals are unable to keep abreast of developments in their field. Further, even if an individual is able to keep up-to-date by hard work the incentive to do so lessens as he ages because the time period available to capture the stream of benefits from such investment is shortened. Nevertheless, we observe (evidence not presented here) that the pay of the lowest decile of teachers progresses monotonically up to almost £3000 per year by age sixty. If the assertion that the training of some individuals becomes obsolete is accepted, this finding hints that the penalty for such obsolescence is not large.[1]

Training

A consideration of some aspects of training further complicates the relationship between wages and marginal product. It is particularly interesting to consider whether circumstances exist such that universities will finance the on-the-job training of their junior staff. The large proportion of such training is general, that is, it raises the productivity of the trainee by the same amount in other universities (and possibly outside the university system) as in the university where the training is received. The theoretical underpinnings of the economics of training [3] produce the result that such general training will be financed by the employee. If the employer financed the training he would have to pay less than marginal product when the training was completed in order to capture the return on the investment. However, the employee could leave at the end of the training period and collect his full marginal product

---

[1] It will be noted that implicit in these remarks about the tenure system is the notion that earnings of tenured faculty will continue to rise with age. We observe this to be true. Yet some of the deleterious labour market effects of the institution of tenure, from the employers and excluded employee viewpoint, could be eliminated by no longer granting quasi-automatic wage increases to tenured individuals. Annual wage increases and job security (tenure) are conceptually different. If a departmental chairman announced that all tenured individuals would never receive another wage increase (and may even experience a wage cut) whilst they remained at that university this may encourage substantial (voluntary?) labour mobility, and enable the chairman to change the quality mix of his department. This is precisely what happened at the Economics Department of the University of Rochester in the early 1960s.

elsewhere thus causing a loss to the original employer. Therefore the employer will not finance the general training.

The above result may be qualified in (at least) two instances. First, the university may supply the training in order to attract trainees and inspect and evaluate them. Such an evaluation is not worthless to the university for it allows the university to select sufficiently competent employees and to reject those who do not reach an adequate standard. Thus the university might be willing to incur some of the training costs in an effort to attract a larger stream of trainees so as to acquire otherwise more costly information.[1]

Second, if universities are considered prestige maximisers they may be prepared to finance the training. This may be particularly true of 'centres of excellence'. Even though such institutions may pay a wage greater than marginal product during training, the employers (e.g. dean, vice-chancellor, top administrators) may not attempt to stop an individual moving to another institution after training because they derive utility from the fact that their newly trained individual is upholding the reputation of the original institution in his new university.

It will be noted that the payment of a wage greater than marginal product during training (i.e. at young ages) is the opposite to the relationship between these variables suggested in the discussion of the institution of tenure. Clearly, the actual relationship between wages and marginal product is the result of a number of factors pulling in opposite directions.

2. Faculty differentials

Theory[2]

Uniformity of salary scales has not been matched by uniformity of labour market pressure in various faculties. The implications of the existence of uniform salary scales and unequal labour market pressure may be seen with the help of a very simple analytical model (Fig 11.1). Assume:

1. Two faculties A and B.
2. The existence of the uniform salary scale and maximum permissible senior staff ratio imposes a maximum wage (W_m) on this labour market.
3. Actual and potential staff have two quality levels, represented by degree

---

[1] This paragraph is based on one of Richardson's [15] qualifications to Becker's theory of general training. Note the analogy between experiencing employees and Nelson's [11] idea of gaining information on goods by experience (as a substitute or complement to search).

[2] This is a cross section study, but it is interesting to speculate on the bare bones of a possible time pattern of adjustment. The desired stock of teachers (K^*) could be a function of the number of students (S) and their aspirations (A). ΔK^* would then be a function of ΔS and ΔA plus making good any depreciation in the existing stock, itself primarily a function of the vintage of the stock. Earnings in this model would be some function of the gap between K^* and K. Supply would be a lagged function of earnings. This model is analogous to the classic hog cycle: the lagged adjustment in supply is superimposed on an accelerator determined demand. The instability in the adjustment process may be compounded by government policy with respect to subsidies to post-graduate training.

class I and II. Individuals with degree class I are higher quality than those with degree class II. (Degree class represents in this simple model all other quality indicators such as age, experience and higher degree.)

4. Total desired employment (N^*_t) is identical in both faculties.
5. Each faculty hires, subject to the maximum wage constraint individuals with degree class I in preference to those with degree class II.
6. No posts are left vacant.

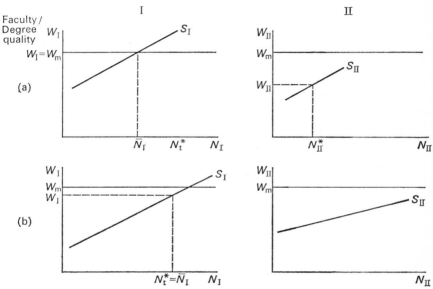

FIG 11.1.   **Model to explain faculty differentials**

We define a relatively tight faculty as the one where a given quality individual receives the highest pay.

Let $\bar{N}$ denote actual employment and N^* denote desired employment. The model may be stated formally as follows:

If

$$\bar{N}_\mathrm{I} < \bar{N}^*_t \tag{1}$$
$$N^*_t - \bar{N}_\mathrm{I} = N^*_\mathrm{II} \tag{2}$$

and

$$W_\mathrm{I} = W_m \tag{3}$$
$$W_\mathrm{II} \leq W_m \tag{4}$$

If

$$\bar{N}_\mathrm{I} = N^*_t \tag{5}$$
$$N^*_\mathrm{II} = 0 \tag{6}$$

and

$$W_\mathrm{I} \leq W_m \tag{7}$$

At the particular point in time we are considering, faculty A is unable, because of the maximum wage (W_m) in university and the abundant alternative employment opportunities for individuals with A-type training to fill its desired total employment (N^*_t) by hiring solely degree class I individuals. It hires $\bar{N}_I$ such persons at wage W_m. Thus A's labour market is in disequilibrium. To ensure that no posts are left vacant it must still hire $N^*_t - \bar{N}_I$ individuals. The A market is cleared by lowering the quality-mix.[1] The excess demand $N^*_t - \bar{N}_I$ spills over on to the class II quality portion of the market. N^*_{II} such individuals are hired at wage W_{II}. Faculty B hires N^*_t individuals entirely from the class I quality market at wage W_I. The supply schedule to university teaching of class I persons with B-type training is more elastic than the similar schedules for those with A-type training, reflecting the fewer employment opportunities for the B-type trained individuals at given wages.

Despite its simplicity this model is powerful. It predicts first, that the pay of an individual of given quality will be higher in faculty A than in faculty B. (Note, however, that the pay differential will be smaller than it would have been had there been no maximum wage.) Second, the quality-mix of staff in faculty A will be inferior to that in faculty B. Third, that wages and quality by faculty will tend to be inversely related. The disequilibrium situation in faculty A will be observed primarily from the quality-mix. The institutional constraints inhibit the development of a substantial wage differential. Faculty A is a tight faculty because a given quality individual receives a higher wage in that faculty B; alternatively for a given wage staff quality will be superior in faculty B than in faculty A.

This simple model is adequate to demonstrate that universities have two broad categories of response to the problems caused by unequal labour market pressure by faculty coupled with uniform salary scales [5].

They are:

1. Net advantages may be adjusted to enable universities to recruit and retain staff as effectively in tight faculties as in those where staff are relatively abundant. For example:

(a) the establishment of a higher proportion of senior posts in faculties where recruitment is most difficult, after allowance for interfaculty differences in age distribution;

(b) placing individuals in tight faculties higher up the uniform incremental scale, i.e. paying these people higher salaries within a grade;

(c) allowing differential access to supplementary earnings (which will be the result of having no formal rules on access to outside earnings);

(d) provision of other facilities, e.g. research assistance and light teaching loads.

2. Alternatively, universities may not adjust net advantages, but instead accept the recruitment consequences:

---

[1] Discussion of the quality dimensions of labour markets is much neglected. For some noticeable exceptions see McCormick [9], Reder [13, p. 275 and 14].

(a) new posts may not be created in certain faculties because of anticipated recruitment difficulties;

(b) vacancies in established posts may persist for relatively long periods of time;

(c) interfaculty differences in quit rates (wastage) will occur;

(d) hiring standards may have to be relaxed in the tight faculties. The standards may be defined in terms of: age; experience; degree quality; field of specialisation; personality, etc.

In the next section we present the evidence on the relative weight universities have attached to some of these avenues of adjustment, and infer which faculties are relatively tight and which are relatively loose.

Evidence

The following faculty breakdown is used: humanities; social science; pure science; applied science; and medicine.[1] We examine first the extent to which universities have attempted to equalise net advantages between any given faculty and the employment and pay opportunities available to the members of that faculty outside university. We then examine the other ways universities have adjusted to interfaculty differences in labour market pressure. The examination of university pay, supplementary earnings and other methods to equalise net advantages plus certain quality and wastage indicators allows inferences to be drawn as to which are the relatively tight faculties.

Methods to equalise net advantages

1. *Basic salary.* The first avenue of adjustment to allow for interfaculty differences in labour market pressure confers, *ceteris paribus*, a higher average and (cross-section) lifetime basic salary on the members of the tight faculty as compared to the salary received by those in other faculties. The result may be achieved by placing a lecturer or senior lecturer or reader of a given age in the tight faculty at a higher point on the uniform salary scale than a teacher of the same age in another faculty, or by promoting a given individual at a younger age. Also, whilst the professional salary bill is constrained by a university average, professors' salaries may vary across faculties. Age–earnings profiles are particularly useful here as they overcome the problem, present when simple average salaries by faculty are considered, of apparent interfaculty differences in salary which are in fact attributable to interfaculty differences in age distributions. The age earnings statistics are presented in Table 11.1. Note that our problem is not one of occupational choice but of

---

[1] It is recognised that the true non-competing groups are narrower than faculty level (e.g. the labour market for economic historians is very different from that of econometricians) but presentation of evidence at a lower level of aggregation is unwieldy. Bald evidence on interfaculty pay differences is available from regression analysis alone. However, we desire to see how the labour market is operating. Regression analysis indicates that *ceteris paribus*, an individual in faculty A is paid more than an individual in faculty B. But it does not indicate *why* this result occurs.

interfaculty differences in labour market pressure. It is therefore not correct
to discount earnings. The differences in labour market pressure may occur at
all age groups. Reference to the table shows that the earnings for all non-
medical faculties are very similar: the profiles rise (at a decreasing rate) until
age 44 to 49 and then flatten out or fall. The similarity of the profiles is
probably the result of the existence of formal salary scales: it is intuitively
surprising that the (undiscounted) lifetime earnings over ages 24 to 65 differ
(excluding medicine) by only 7 per cent.

TABLE 11.1. *Mean basic salary (£) by age and faculty, 1969*

Age range	Humanities	Social science	Pure science	Applied science	Medicine	All
Under 25	1169	1295	1134	1238	1338	1221
25–29	1540	1703	1570	1793	1724	1636
30–34	2083	2248	2157	2351	2408	2219
35–39	3632	2836	2858	2963	3031	2863
40–44	3172	3262	3330	3231	4098	3361
45–49	3477	3600	3842	3546	4574	3772
50–54	3627	3490	3861	3455	4817	3803
55–59	4271	3262	3681	4187	6008	4092
60+	3632	3684	3749	4255	5736	3949
Total: Age 24–65	126,971	125,404	130,123	134,398	169,054	133,645

2. *Supplementary earnings.* The second method to equalise net advantages for
each faculty with those in alternative employments is to allow differential
access to supplementary earnings (Table 11.2). It is not necessary to have
formal rules allowing members of tight faculties more access to these earnings.
Rather, this result will occur in the absence of any rule governing supplementary earnings: the very reason faculties differ in tightness is the fact that
variation exists in the alternative opportunities and rewards for the members
of the different faculties.

The monetary returns to university teaching include supplementary
earnings and basic salary, which together comprises total income. Lifetime
income figures calculated from pre-tax age incomes streams for those aged
24 to 65, again suggest that applied science is a tight faculty and humanities
is a loose faculty. The inclusion of supplementary earnings in the lifetime
income calculations boosts the earnings of all university teachers (as compared
with lifetime earnings calculated solely from basic salary figures) by slightly
over £17,000. However, the allowance for supplementary earnings still does
not produce wide variation lifetime income by faculty. Excluding medicine,

TABLE 11.2. *Mean total income (£) by age and faculty, 1969*

Age range	Humanities	Social science	Pure science	Applied science	Medicine	All
Under 25	1736	1447	1129	1279	1440	1337
25–29	1682	1901	1694	1955	1835	1781
30–34	2337	2558	2331	2487	2560	2422
35–39	3072	3374	3949	3164	3285	3471
40–44	3602	3951	3550	3552	4267	3712
45–49	3808	4139	4175	3979	4916	4177
50–54	3989	4135	4268	3899	5129	4259
55–59	4687	3565	4134	5537	6337	4629
60+	4018	4320	4259	4766	7031	4556
Total: Age 24–65	141,729	145,662	147,188	152,740	185,261	150,928

the highest lifetime income (applied science £152,740) is only 7 per cent greater than the lowest (humanities £141,729).

The consequences of not adjusting net advantages[1]

As an alternative to adjusting net advantages, universities may decide instead to accept the consequences of not doing so. This may involve, for example, a relaxation of hiring standards or the persistence of vacancies. We have evidence on a number of indicators of interfaculty differences in quality. It is appreciated that variables such as age, experience, class of first degree and highest degree are not perfect proxies for quality but they are probably tolerably accurate. Hiring standards may be relaxed by recruiting younger, less experienced poorer qualified persons in tight than in loose faculties. We examine interfaculty differences in these variables for the total stock. This provides evidence on the cumulative effects of the differential quality by faculty of those recruited and retained. In addition we present evidence on the hiring standards applied to recent recruits.

1. *Age.* It is expected that the tight faculties will have lower mean ages and a higher proportion of their numbers aged under 25 or under 30 than the loose faculties. This expectation is based on the assumption that, *ceteris paribus*, universities would prefer to appoint an older rather than a younger individual. However, a young mean age may also result not from the fact

[1] The model developed earlier suggested that universities may relax hiring or retention standards in certain faculties relative to others. This suggests that the flow of recruits to one faculty may be of poorer quality than the flow to an alternative faculty. The evidence presented in Table 11.3 and the text relates (separately) to both the quality of the stock of university teachers by faculty and of recent recruits by faculty. For additional information on the quality of recruits see Bibby [4].

TABLE 11.3. *Interfaculty quality and wastage differences, 1969*

Evidence		Humanities	Social science	Pure science	Applied science	Medicine	All
Age							
Proportion aged under 25	(1)	3·8	6·2	3·5	5·7	1·8	4·3
Mean age	(2)	38·6	37·0	36·2	37·9	38·4	37·4
Experience							
Mean years of experience	(3)	9·7	7·2	7·9	7·2	8·6	8·1
Proportion who received their first degree 1962 or later	(4)	29·4	37·7	29·9	25·6	29·1	30·6
First degree							
Proportion who have first or upper second class honours degree	(5)	64·1	62·2	68·3	55·4	21·5	61·2
Highest degree							
Proportion whose highest degree obtained is:							
None	(6)	33·3	30·5	14·3	32·3	26·8	25·4
Diploma	(7)	11·2	14·1	3·7	3·2	19·2	9·0
Master	(8)	15·5	27·5	7·0	14·5	4·9	13·6
PhD	(9)	39·9	27·9	75·1	49·9	49·1	50·0

Wastage

Per cent of stock quitting (10)	1·5	3·0	2·7	2·1	5·0	2·7
Per cent quitting who hold firsts/Per cent of stock who held firsts (11)	0·67	0·59	0·60	0·74	0·75	0·60
Per cent quitting who hold doctorates/Per cent of stock who hold doctorates (12)	0·53	0·75	0·67	0·88	0·67	0·71

Source: Wastage evidence from UGC *Recruits and Quits Survey*, 1967–68. All other evidence from November 1969 Survey as follows: Rows (1) and (2) Table 8B (129); Row (3) Table 6A (29); Row (4) Table 18B (176); Row (5) Table 13B (139); Rows (6)–(8) Table 14B.

that a faculty is tight, but simply because there are no older persons around capable of teaching the subject. This is a real possibility if a faculty has expanded rapidly and the content of the normal course has changed substantially (for example few relatively old persons have had the training required to teach econometrics). It is not possible to disentangle these two effects.

Some evidence on interfaculty differences in age distributions is presented in Table 11.3, rows (1) and (2). Row (2) shows that the difference in the highest and lowest mean age by faculty is only 1·4 years. The evidence suggests that humanities is a loose faculty: that faculty has, excluding medicine, the highest mean age (row 2) and the second lowest proportion of its stock aged under 25.

2. *Experience*. Evidence on interfaculty differences in experience is presented in rows (3) to (4) of Table 11.3. We apply similar reasoning to that for age above, i.e. it is expected that the tight faculties will have relatively less experienced staff than the loose faculties. This is, because, *ceteris paribus*, it is assumed that universities prefer more experienced individuals to less experienced ones. Row (3) shows that only 29·4 per cent of humanities teachers received their first degree in 1962 or later, whilst 37·7 per cent of those in social science received their first degree in 1962 or later. The evidence on experience strongly confirms that of age—humanities is a loose faculty, whilst social science is tight.

3. *Quality of first degree*. The quality of first degree is probably a tolerable proxy for ability and motivation. One consequence of not adjusting the net advantages by faculty to those prevailing in alternative employments is that the tight faculties will tend only to be able to recruit and retain persons whose first degree quality is inferior to those in the loose faculties.

The results again suggest that social science and applied science are tight faculties (row 5). The results for the first degree quality of recent recruits (namely, those who entered the profession in 1967–69) are very similar to those for the whole stock. Humanities has the highest proportion both with firsts and with firsts plus upper seconds. Social science is, excluding medicine, the faculty with the lowest proportion of firsts and firsts plus upper seconds.

4. *Higher degree*. It is expected that, *ceteris paribus*, universities would prefer to recruit or retain a person with a higher degree rather than a person without one. A further consequence of not adjusting net advantages is that the tight faculties may be forced to hire and retain a smaller proportion of persons with higher degrees than the loose faculties. The underlying theory is as follows. Pursuit of a higher degree entails costs. Given UK students tend not to pay the tuition costs themselves, the main private costs is foregone earnings. Typically, to undertake a diploma course results in a cost of one year's foregone earnings; a master's course one to two years' foregone earnings, and a doctorate three years' foregone earnings.

The evidence on higher degree possessed by faculty is in rows (6) to (9). It suggests that pure science is a loose faculty and social science is a tight faculty. Only 14·3 per cent of those in pure science have no higher degree, whilst 75·1 per cent have doctorates. In social science 30·5 per cent have no higher degree and only 27·9 per cent have doctorates. Clearly for many social scientists the masters is the terminal degree: a third of this faculty hold masters degrees.[1]

5. *Wastage.* Evidence on interfaculty differences in wastage is presented in rows (10) to (12) of Table 11.3. It is expected that, *ceteris paribus*, proportionately more and/or better qualified persons will quit in the tight faculties than in the loose faculties.

The evidence is taken from the UGC *Recruits and Quits Survey.* The wastage figures are corrected for death and retirement; also they do not include inter-UK university transfers. They refer therefore solely to quits which result in employment other than in UK universities. The figures refer to session 1967–68, the latest year available when this work was undertaken.

Row (10) shows the proportion of those in a post at 31 December 1967 who left university during session 1967–68. This is the simplest wastage indicator. The evidence supports the hypothesis that humanities is a loose faculty. Also it indicates that medicine, despite having substantially higher lifetime earnings than the other faculties experienced significant wastage problems.[2]

Rows (11) and (12) give evidence on the qualifications of those quitting. Because there exist important interfaculty differences in the proportion of the stock holding first class honours degrees and doctorates it is necessary to correct raw wastage data to allow for interfaculty differences in the qualifications of the stock in each faculty. As all the figures are less than unity this shows that the qualifications of those quitting in each faculty are inferior to the qualifications of the total stock in that faculty. The evidence tends to support the findings this far concerning the tight and loose faculties: the ratio of the proportion of those quitting who hold firsts to the proportion of the stock with firsts (row 11) is, excluding medicine, highest in applied science. The ratio of the proportion of those quitting who hold doctorates to the proportion of the stock with doctorates is highest in applied science and social science (row 12).

Summary and conclusions

This section has attempted to demonstrate how the different faculties have adjusted to differences in labour market pressure given the constraints of uniform salary scales and maximum permissible proportion of senior staff. These constraints do not apply to medicine. It was shown that universities

[1] This pattern is repeated for the qualifications of new recruits (those who entered the profession in 1967–69). Only 13·7 per cent of social scientists hold a doctorate whilst 52·8 per cent of those in pure science do. Pure science also has the lowest proportion of persons (27·7 per cent) who have no higher degree. See November 1969 Survey, Table 149 (471).

[2] Additional evidence, not presented here, shows that for each faculty except applied science the proportion of the stock quitting declines monotonically as we move up the academic hierarchy from assistant lecturer (still in existence in 1967–68) through professor. This supports the hypothesis that interoccupational mobility is greater at young ages.

have two broad methods of adjustment to interfaculty differences in labour market pressure. To get similarly qualified people in all faculties they must pay persons in the tight faculty more than those in the loose faculty. Or, they may accept the consequences of not adjusting net advantages and lower hiring standards in the tight faculties. The evidence suggests that in 1969:

1. Humanities was, on all counts but one, a loose faculty. That is, it had the lowest income position and is the best quality faculty (except in the case where quality is defined as proportion with doctorates). Also a very low proportion of those with doctorates quit the faculty.
2. Social science appeared to be a tight faculty. It did not adjust by paying particularly high basic salaries but allowed its members access to larger outside earnings than those obtained in other faculties. It also lowered its hiring and retention standards.
3. Pure science paid a relatively high basic salary. It is the faculty with the highest qualifications. Such evidence suggests that it adjusted to outside labour market pressure to enable it to compete effectively with the alternatives open to its members.
4. Applied science paid the highest basic lifetime salary and income after medicine. It had the least experienced members. A relatively low proportion of its number have first or upper seconds. A relatively high proportion of its doctorates quit. All this is evidence that it was a tight faculty.
5. Medicine, because it is on a higher formal salary scale from the other faculties, received the highest lifetime salary and income. This enabled that faculty to recruit and retain relatively old and experienced individuals, and generally to compete with the National Health Service.

References

1. ALCHIAN, A. 'Private property and the relative costs of tenure', in *The Public Stake in Union Power*, ed. P. Bradley, Virginia, 1958.
2. ALCHIAN, A. and KESSEL, R. 'Competition, monopoly and the pursuit of pecuniary gain', in NBER, *Aspects of Labour Economics*, New York, 1962.
3. BECKER, G. *Human Capital*, NBER, 1964.
4. BIBBY, J. 'University expansion and the academic labour market', *Higher Education Review*, 1971.
5. BOWEN, W. 'University salaries: faculty differentials', *Economica*, 30, no. 120 (1963).
6. CARTTER, A. 'Economics of the university', *American Economic Review*, 55, no. 2 (1965).
7. CULYER, A. 'A utility-maximizing view of universities', *Scottish Journal of Political Economy*, 17, no. 3 (1970).
8. JAMES, E. 'Some notes on the faculty resources at a university', USA, Stoneybrook University (mimeo), 1970.
9. MCCORMICK, B. 'Monopsonistic competition in the labour market', *Quarterly Journal of Economics*, 1960.
10. NATIONAL BOARD FOR PRICES AND INCOMES. *Standing Reference on the Pay of University Teachers in Great Britain. First Report*, Cmnd 3866, HMSO, 1968.
11. NELSON, P. 'Information and consumer behaviour', *Journal of Political Economy*, 78, no. 2 (1970).
12. PERKIN, H. *Key Profession*, Routledge & Kegan Paul, 1969.

13. REDER, M. 'Wage differentials: theory and measurement', in NBER, *Aspects of Labor Economics*, Princeton University Press, 1962.
14. REDER, M. 'Wage structure and structural unemployment', *Review of Economic Studies*, **31** (4), no. 88 (1964).
15. RICHARDSON, R. 'Notes on general training', LSE (mimeo), 1970.
16. ROTTENBERG, S. 'The baseball players' labour market', *Journal of Political Economy* (1956).
17. SLOANE, P. 'The labour market in professional football', *British Journal of Industrial Relations*, **7**, no. 2 (1969).
18. STIGLER, G. *The Intellectual and the Market Place*, Free Press of Glencoe, 1963.
19. WILLIAMS, G., BLACKSTONE, T. and METCALF, D. *The Structure of the Academic Labour Market*, North Holland, forthcoming (1973).

Some aspects of university teachers' labour market in the UK: Discussion

B. A. Corry

May I preface my remarks by reminding those present that Dr Metcalf's analysis is meant to apply not to 'them' but to 'us'. That is to say that, as with the Layard–Jackman paper (chapter 10 above), we seek to apply labour market theory to our own industry—Academia. And as we may perhaps expect, a great deal of scepticism is, and will be expressed, about the applicability of the 'them' analysis to 'us'. The relevance of the theoretical apparatus will be questioned and, even where the facts seem to support the model, alternative explanations based on 'personal knowledge' will be proffered.

Dr Metcalf has ranged over a good many points and I only have time to pick out one or two for further consideration. My basic stand is to support him in his general approach to this subject. For far too long labour market investigations have tended to assume, almost *a priori*, that where they are confronted with institutional constraints, such as fixed salary scales, the usual market force analysis is inapplicable Dr Metcalf has argued (with some supporting evidence) that if we hold steadfast to the homely (Adam Smith) concept of net advantage rather than the 'official' wage rate, we will be able to trace out the operation of changing demand/supply conditions and the reallocation of labour process in the market place.

Of course even if the system succeeded in bolting down net advantage so that increased demand could not be met by accelerated promotion, greater research facilities, quality variation and the like, the change demand/supply relationships for different faculties would show up in differential degrees of job vacancy and this phenomenon, on its own, could work as the reallocation mechanism (as indeed has been argued in other connections by e.g. W. B. Reddaway). Government may oil the job vacancy mechanism by encouraging differential rates of supply of different types of labour. Indeed in my view this is usually how the education system has worked in the UK. To take but one example from our own field of economics; the SSRC sponsored 'taught' MSc programmes have rapidly increased the supply of economists for academic, government and research as anyone trying to place graduate students currently will know only too well.

In fact as we know and as Metcalf has so rightly emphasised, universities have responded to differential rates of excess demand by altering net advantage and by varying quality (although I would place the latter in the former type of strategy). The options listed by Metcalf are:

(a) use of the range of salary scales (upping the increments as we call it);
(b) permissive attitude towards moonlighting;
(c) greater research/secretarial expenditure to key workers;
(d) varying the normal skill/age requirement for a particular post.

The interesting strategy is (d). If I may rephrase it in a semidynamic form it seems to hypothesise:

$$M^k{}_{\text{Norm}} = F(D^k - S^k) \qquad F^1 < 0$$

where $M^k{}_{\text{Norm}}$ is the normal skill requirement for the Kth type of labour. The evidence seems to point to (b) and (d) as the actual adjustment process used by universities. This surely is not surprising—they are the (apparently) cheapest strategies (I must emphasise here the operative word *apparently*). It is an interesting question to ask under what conditions it is possible for producers to vary the quality of its basic inputs. The answer must surely be when the final demand is inelastic with respect to output quality. Or, to put that point slightly differently, where it is difficult conceptually to measure output. Both these points obviously apply to academia.

Let me turn now to Dr Metcalf's evidence. It is primarily cross-section and seeks to illustrate via statistics of age, moonlighting and qualifications how the university system has responded to market forces. As I understand the model its predictions are essentially time-series ones. It predicts for example that if we have two faculties with different rates of excess demand, the average age of appointment for a particular post in the faculty with the higher excess demand will be falling *relative* to the other faculty. The cross-section results give us absolutes not relatives. Under what circumstances can we make absolute (actual age) predictions? We require that the system (a) be in full equilibrium and (b) that with zero excess demand in all faculties the age/quality profiles will be the same for all faculties. Is point (b) likely to hold? Quite frankly I don't know, but there are good reasons for some doubts. Let me sketch in some major problems. Assume (conceptually) that the total lifetime marginal product curve of an academic is compounded of three such curves: the research curve, the teaching curve and the administrative curve. Presumably these curves will not necessarily peak at the same time for any particular individual or faculty nor is there any reason why interfaculty curves should coincide. Thus it seems plausible that the research curve for a mediae-val economic historian will peak much later than that for a pure mathematician. Moreover for certain subjects the curves may be shifting 'backwards' (towards the origin)—with earlier maximum points. This may occur in particular when innovation is rapid and new areas of a discipline are being opened up (econometrics is an obvious example from our field). Thus in certain cases to be young is not merely to be beautiful but also to be better.

Finally a few random points in certain other features on Dr Metcalf's paper. The speaker asked how the present tenure and salary structure system affected labour mobility. It seems to me that the greatest incentive to movement in the current system is the (semi) fixed ratio of senior to junior posts. Higher salaries require promotion and promotion (usually) means movement. It is therefore not clear to me that abolition would increase mobility.

Second, does the present system work in the employers' interest? The employees' interest? or both? (I set on one side the public interest!) I have already suggested why the employers would prefer the moonlighting cum quality variation strategy, but should the workers prefer this? They may prefer incomes to be raised this way rather than by actual increases in the 'official wage'. It is a sort of limit pricing and a possible barrier to entry. Moreover moonlighting is a voluntary activity and each individual can choose his optimum dose. A formal pay increase with extra work commitment may not find universal support among the workers.

III

On Keynes

The collected writings of John Maynard Keynes: some visceral reactions

12

Elizabeth Johnson

When your programme committee first asked me to give this talk today, they suggested the title, 'The collected writings of John Maynard Keynes: some reflections'. They were interested, as I understood it, in the reactions of a non-economist—as I am—exposed to the mass of papers accumulated by this great man, to the opportunity to scrutinise not just the formal manuscripts, the correspondence with other economists and the great names of his day, but also the casual notes and jottings, the day-to-day scribblings on the backs of envelopes of the man who changed the economic thought of our world. I quickly discovered, on reflection, that my reflections might far better be described as 'gut reactions'—hence my somewhat euphemistic title.

These are very personal reactions, reflecting my own background and up-bringing in another country, my family, my education and my precise generation—the very biased reactions of one non-economic, non-English, non-establishment individual. I will attempt to present them in such a way, that by inference and imagination, you will be able to fill in for yourselves what your own reactions might be to this charming, irritating, but unmistakably great man.

I never met Keynes. When my husband and I arrived in Cambridge in January 1949, he had already been dead for over two years. And yet his memory was very present and alive in the place—a sense of a sort of aura still hovering over everything he had touched. People spoke affectionately of 'Maynard' as if he had just been gone away for a little while, in that manner in which one speaks the dead friend's name in an attempt to conjure him back to life again, if only for an instant. People still wondered aloud, 'What would Maynard think?'—which was the habitual reaction of his circle to any new idea they had or any proposal. These people, most of them twenty years or so younger than Keynes, mourned him as a contemporary.

I tell you this to give you some idea of my excitement when I first saw Keynes's papers and held some of them in my hands. After his death they had been sorted out into two lots in the top of the house at 46 Gordon Square.

Those having to do with economics and public life were bequeathed to Richard Kahn, and those that were purely personal were to be deposited in the library at King's College, Cambridge, with the stipulation that they were not to be available until all the protagonists were dead. Before the papers left Gordon Square they were used by Roy Harrod in writing his *Life of John Maynard Keynes* (Macmillan, 1951). They were then divided into the two categories, public and private, put into tea chests and taken by van to Cambridge. The economics papers were literally jampacked, one stack on top of another, into a big cupboard without any shelves, in the old Marshall Library in Downing Street. That was the way I first saw them, heaped together in bundles and boxes and old-fashioned wicker files that crumbled to the touch. Many of them were coated with that greasy library grime that comes away on your hands and is so hard to wash off; some of the typed outside copies seemed to be vanishing faintly before your eyes, with yellowed fraying edges, ridged with the rust of decaying paper clips. On the other hand, the inside papers, protected, were fresh and white and authoritative-looking with the high quality embossed writing paper of those palmier days; the signatures of the famous stood out boldly inked as if newly inscribed.

Let me give an impression of what there was to be found. Bundle after bundle turned up from the various periods of his life. There were schoolboy essays from Eton, papers written for the Cambridge Apostles, a sheaf of encouraging letters from Alfred Marshall to his most promising student, the first memoranda of a fledgling civil servant, the lecture notes of the aspiring young don—these last complete with pasted-in paragraphs from the current newspaper columns, to be used as bad examples of the conventional wisdom of City men and bankers who should know better. To continue, there were the scissored and cannibalised drafts and redrafts for the Report of the Commission on Indian Finance and Currency, a bewildering load of miscellaneous Treasury memoranda from World War I, notes for political speeches and talks to groups at the House of Commons, cheque-stubs and pocket diaries elastic-banded together, jotted figures that look like records of winnings at bridge, passages copied out of books for remembering. Last but not least were the 34-odd bulky scrapbooks into which his mother pasted the literally thousands of newspaper cuttings mentioning his name—in varying tones of admiration and vituperation—from English, American and European newspapers and magazines. A lifetime on paper.

I suppose the fun of editing papers is the pleasure of legitimate eavesdropping—voyeurism made respectable. But a lot depends on the subject. Keynes's father kept a diary but it was very dull—he would say 'Florence was very upset', but he would not say what she was upset about. As an adult, Keynes did not keep a diary or any kind of daily journal, but his letters and memoranda, though businesslike, could also be chatty and deliciously or maliciously catty. He lived such a busy and varied life, he was into so many things and knew so many people, that the papers are full of encounters with famous names—General Smuts, Shaw, the Webbs, Wittgenstein, T. E. Lawrence, Frank Harris, Stanley Baldwin, to reel off an assorted few.

At a first glance, certain things leapt out—Keynes's suggestion as junior clerk of two years' service that the Indian Government's conception of the requirements for a Director of Statistics were hopelessly outdated; the small green notebook in which he recorded his first earnings from his writings (in September 1908 the sum of 7s 6d from the *Economic Journal* for a note on 'Rents, prices and wages'); his declaration of conscientious objection to conscription; a list of invitations and sampling of acceptances to a party at 46 Gordon Square studded with the now well-known names of Bloomsbury; his farewell letters on leaving the Paris Peace Conference; a bet with Winston Churchill on the outcome of the 1929 election; a few of the amusingly libellous memoranda that flowed from his desk during the years of World War II. There were intriguing bits like scraps of paper with notes exchanged with—whom?—passing comments during boring meetings, and the odd phrase or paragraph noted down for future literary use. Most provoking to the curiosity are the echoes of something he had written in an earlier letter turning up in a correspondent's reply. 'Your description of chairman's brain makes me shriek with laughter', wrote Sir Ernest Cable when they were both grappling over the Indian Finance and Currency Report with Austen Chamberlain—and how one longs to have seen that description! In the days before typists and carbons there are precious few of Keynes's own letters to go by, except when he considered something important enough to make a copy or a draft in his own writing.

Then there were the few fascinating bits that got into the economics papers by mistake—an erotic sketch of Leda and the swan, deftly pencilled by a gifted Bloomsbury hand; the letter from a friend recounting the delights of a homosexual pick-up in a pub. These had got into the wrong box—but generally speaking things had been well sorted.

The papers had already been sorted according to time and subject as a result of Harrod's work. This must have been an easy and natural division because of Keynes's own habit of sticking anything he was doing at a particular time onto a spike; and as he tended to be intensively involved in one subject at a time the material on the spikes was automatically sorted. When a spike became full he dumped its contents into a wooden box or chest; in fact he liked to visit country sales in search of old chests for his papers, and had quite a few of them.

What is it that makes a man consciously save his papers, including the inconsequential scraps of scribbled conversation exchanged at committee meetings? What are the intimations of immortality? Part of the process, I am sure, lies in simple inertia, coupled with the habit of keeping things that people had in those more spacious days, with their rambling houses and capacious attics and the absence of all the consumer durables we now have to fill up our rooms. But there assuredly was a great deal more to it than the accident of time and space. Keynes *knew* that he was a great man. Nurtured from the start as the brilliant boy, the eldest pride and joy of a cultivated, intellectual Cambridge family (philosopher father and civic-minded mother), he knew from the beginning that *Keynes* rhymed with *brains*. And very early on, first among his Cambridge and Bloomsbury friends and then, by the time he was thirty, out in the wide world he must have learned that with his witty, charming talent of reason he could persuade others to go along with him—if not all the way in his direction, at least considerably far along the path. So he saved the record, because he was proud of it, because he had a sense of family and a sense of history, and because he knew it was a valuable one.

There is so much—lists of books read, lists of books bought, a list of 'Papers to be Written', followed 'Monographs', 'Treatises', and 'Textbooks', the whole scheme dated 30 January 1909. There are plans with chapter headings for whole books, including 'An Introduction to Economic Principles', which was to run to three volumes with the note that these might be sold as Penguins at sixpence each, with a de luxe edition at three guineas. For a book to be called 'An Examination of Capitalism' he had already started the first chapter on 'The Babylonian economy'.

But it is not all there—there are big gaps. The files he had removed from the Treasury turned out to be only a few drops from a vast ocean of memoranda contained within the bounds of the Public Record Office. Here and there are questions left hanging. Did he ever write that anonymous article that so-and-so asked him for? Why did he treat a certain person in such-and-such a way? And for such a busy man, many of the pages of his diaries, expectantly scanned for clues, turned out to be disappointingly blank.

Nevertheless a strong sense of personality emerges—delightfully impetuous when young, charming with its wit, admirable in its quick intelligence and generous sympathy, impressive in its capacity for intense hard work—and insulting in its arrogance born of absolute self-assurance. One gets echoes from the letters of his correspondents; some people pitch their letters to the tone of the person whom they are addressing, or at least the tone as they conceive it, and this can vividly conjure up a sense of personality, or of the part of that person which the writer is attempting to appeal to. In addition, Keynes seems to have been the kind of person that some people address their mental conversations to. Between 1911 and 1945—thirty-four years—a French financial journalist named Marcel Labordère wrote him a long series of letters on the money market and his own ideas of economics. Margot Asquith, as a widowed old woman unable to sleep at night, poured out her diatribes against her husband's former adversary Lloyd George to him (regardless of the fact that Keynes had re-espoused Lloyd George's cause in the meantime).

One thing that the papers demonstrate very clearly, with no ambiguity, is how Keynes worked. He seems to have been a non-stop worker in that he always had something on the go, even on holidays. He claimed himself to write 1000 words a day, a good professional average, but the volume of paper shows that on many days he exceeded this, even assuming that he was not counting dictated letters. Through the 1920s and 30s he must have averaged close to an article a week for the press—and this on top of lectures, journal articles, books, memoranda for various bodies, editing the *Economic Journal* and other projects. While he was in the Treasury during both world wars the volume was certainly as great, if not even greater.

He started his working day with breakfast in bed. (When Duncan Grant and Vanessa Bell decorated some cupboard doors for him by depicting the contrasting breakfasts eaten in London and Rome, the doors were the doors of a *bedroom* cupboard.) He accomplished a great deal of routine work in the mornings while still in bed, much of it financial. He kept track of all his dealings very methodically, preserving cheque-stubs and brokers' statements in the manner, one imagines, of his thrifty and orderly parents and ancestors. When he was young he of course wrote his own letters out by hand, as did, at that time, practically all of his famous correspondents. After World War I he used a typist and kept carbon copies, so that the volume of what was preserved became automatically swollen after 1919. He seems to have dictated a lot of his letters—some of his last secretary's shorthand notes still exist—but lecture notes, articles, memoranda and still many other letters were written out by hand.

One form of communication that Keynes did not like was the telephone. He admitted that it was useful for calling up intimate friends and must have used it for keeping in touch with his brokers, but in 1922 he was complaining in a letter to the *New Statesman* of the nuisance of having to leave his study on the third floor and to be interrupted by

> any unconcentrated person who finds it easier to ring up than to write a postcard, any hostess making up her party, any American tourist to these shores who thinks he would like a few words with me, is entitled by the existing conventions, *and is able*, suddenly and at any hour to interrupt my business and make me attend to theirs . . .

This overdemocratic habit of intrusion so exasperated him when he was negotiating in Washington that he concluded that the only way to get an uninterrupted interview with an important person was to shelve the appointment and achieve the conversation by calling the person up on the phone himself.

Let me say a little about how he worked as an economist.

He started off his career in the military department of the India Office, not very enthusiastically, whiling away his time between memoranda on the dating of lieutenants' commissions and the despatch of pedigree Ayrshire bulls to Bombay, by working on his own dissertation on probability with which he hoped to gain a King's College fellowship. But the situation changed when he was moved to the Department of Revenue, Statistics and Commerce, where in the brief two years he spent there he began to lay down a sound knowledge of the special peculiarities of the Indian financial and currency situation. This interest persisted when he went back to join the faculty at Cambridge, and although his lectures there were on money and the stock exchange, he kept up his contacts at the India Office, in 1911 producing a long paper on 'Recent developments of the Indian currency question' for the Royal Economic Society, which became the nucleus of his book on *Indian Currency and Finance*.

The Indian currency system was an extremely complicated one, grown up over the years, and one is impressed by Keynes's seemingly effortless mastery of detail—every tree in the wood is there and standing in its right place. The research for the book resulted in his appointment to the Royal Commission on Indian Finance and Currency of 1913–14. When one reads through the evidence and the various drafts of the Commission's Report, it almost seems that Keynes, the youngest member (he was thirty) amongst all those bankers and businessmen and titled individuals who had spent their working lives in India, was the only person involved in the hearings who really understood the system. (The one exception was Lionel Abrahams, the India Office civil servant who had invented much of it and from whom Keynes had learned.) Nor had Keynes ever set foot in India.

This mastery of detail enabled him to complete a 60-page plan for a state bank for India in a little over a month. Marshall, who had had his own experience with the Indian system said that he was 'entranced by it as a prodigy of constructive work. Verily we old men will have to hang ourselves', he wrote, 'if young people can cut their way so straight and with such apparent ease through such great difficulties.' Finally, Keynes became deeply involved in the redrafting of the main report. Here his complete grasp of the whole field enabled him to rescue his confused colleagues from perpetrating a logical mistake and to win their consent to a major change in principle by a small change of wording in two crucial phrases.

This command over detail, never losing sight of the whole, stood him in good stead when he entered the Treasury in 1915. By this time it is clear that he wrote quickly, usually with very little changing or crossing out. The Treasury was a small body in those days and often it was necessary for him to master the facts and write the needed memoranda on some totally new subject within twenty-four hours. During two weeks in September 1916, he reported to his father, he had 'written three major memoranda, one of which has been circulated to the Cabinet, and about a dozen minor ones on all kinds of subjects, as well as helping . . . with the Vote of Credit and the Budget, and keeping going with routine, and the *Economic Journal* in the evenings'.

My fellow-editors who had worked for the Treasury during World War II, where they were accustomed to the redrafting of their thoughts by many hands, were surprised to find the department so small in World War I that Keynes's minutes and memoranda went via the Joint Permanent Secretary straight to the Chancellor of the Exchequer, with usually only the slightest of verbal changes on the way. More often than not, if the Americans were concerned, the change would be designed to make the memorandum more cautious and tactful. Keynes's memoranda thus became official documents; his handwriting exists beside the printed Cabinet Papers in the Public Record Office. He was in charge of all foreign lending and borrowing, an astonishing position of influence for a man hardly turned thirty-five.

Keynes's resignation from the Paris Peace Conference—where he was the chief Treasury representative—changed the manner of his work again and took him from being a member of the establishment to being its informed outside critic, a sort of official-unofficial position he was to occupy for many years. He wrote *The Economic Consequences of the Peace* during August and September 1919; the book was published 12 December 1919, and became a runaway bestseller. It is a book written in great passion and yet with much solid information in it. The reason Keynes was able to turn it out so quickly was not only because of the vehemence of his feelings, but also that he had so much material at his finger tips. He not only incorporated his plan for the cancellation of inter-allied debts and the financing of the reconstruction of Europe into his chapter on 'Remedies' (this plan had been adopted as official policy by Lloyd George, but was rejected by President Wilson), but he simply lifted informative sections on Germany's capacity to pay reparations from the Treasury memorandum that he had produced on the subject. And, to the fury of the Poles, who discovered it, he made use of large chunks of information from the German representatives' replies to the allies when they were pleading their case. Nevertheless, he gave away no official secrets and sent out seventy-three free copies of his book to former colleagues, friends and acquaintances in a list that reads like a top-stratum sample of *Who's Who*.

The Economic Consequences of the Peace was a turning point in Keynes's life, and although he never once stopped being an economist, for the next twenty years he was also conspicuously and devotedly a journalist and propagandist, trying to persuade the world to follow a path of reasonableness in article after article. He himself saw to the syndication of these articles over the world press—with a very clear idea of just how much money each kind of article in each particular paper should bring in. The success of *Economic Consequences* gave him a wide and partisan audience—he was venerated in Germany and vilified in France. There is plenty of evidence from the clippings in the scrapbooks and his exchange of correspondence with former Treasury colleagues that these writings exerted a strong influence on the side of moderation in the long and rather tedious series of international meetings and confrontations that attempted to accomplish all the mopping-up needed after the Treaty of Versailles.

Because of the speed and apparent ease with which Keynes worked, one is tempted to imagine him as dashing into print. 'Fling pamphlets to the winds', he said. But I would like to describe to you in a little more detail one of the projects he undertook at this time because it illustrates so well, not only his seriousness, but his great capacity for taking pains with things in order to get them right, and his resourcefulness when confronted with obstacles over a long haul. This was his editorship in 1922 of the series of twelve *Manchester Guardian Commercial* supplements on 'Reconstruction in Europe'. The idea was to present the problems and their possible solutions in articles by the foremost authentic experts of the time; the result was a 782 page volume of bound issues. It was published in French, German, Italian and Spanish, as well as being distributed in England and the United States.

Keynes was anxious to get the very best and not only those whom he described as the 'flash' contributors. He enlisted the aid of Carl Melchior in gathering articles in Germany; Melchior was only one of many acquaintances from his wartime and Paris experience, whom he was able to call upon for help. For example, he was able to ask for assistance from the Premier of Belgium, and in England he could go to Asquith and Lord David Cecil among many others. He was persistent in tracking down contributors—when he could not get Lenin, he settled for Gorky; when Bergson declined, he went for Croce. He was particular to get a balance of shades of opinion, and careful, particularly with Russia and the new countries, to get material from the inside, to balance what was put out by the embassies.

He took an enthusiastic interest in every detail—from the quality of the paper to the design of a special decorative heading, from the printing of facsimiles of the bank notes of the new European countries to the assembling of dignified photographs of the bearded captains of the world mercantile marine, and the collection of a wonderful series of cartoons on the high cost of living, taking in Victorian England and nineteenth century France, as well as the England, United States and Germany of the early 1920s. He kept up to a 21-day production schedule over twelve issues. He wrote fourteen articles himself, four of which reappeared as part of *A Tract on Monetary Reform*. He interested himself in arrangements for distribution and took fifty copies with him to the international meeting at Genoa to give to key people—he was attending the conference as the special correspondent of the *Manchester Guardian*. The British financial delegation, headed by the Chancellor of the Exchequer, held a special meeting to hear him discuss his article on a plan for the stabilisation of the European exchanges. They thought this too radical to endorse officially, but they held a second meeting to discuss his article on 'The forward market in foreign exchanges' and brought these suggestions into the British draft proposals.

But while Keynes produced weekly articles and investment columns for the *Nation* and letters to the newspapers and pamphlets a-plenty to persuade, he was also working away at the basic economics that finally emerged as *A Treatise on Money* and *The General Theory of Employment, Interest and Money*. Here one finds him working in a different way, not rushing his words into print, hot off the griddle, but teaching his material over a period of years, discussing it with and testing it on colleagues. *A Treatise on Money* had a long gestation period, from 1924 to 1930. Keynes was not completely satisfied with it, but got it out quickly in the end. Then Piero Sraffa, Richard Kahn, James Meade, Joan Robinson and Austin Robinson (who nicknamed themselves 'the Circus') devoted a whole term to discussing it with Keynes. Their discussions had an important influence on the transition to the ideas of the *General Theory*, on which Keynes had begun to work. By 1934 he was lecturing from early proof sheets and in January 1935 he sent the first proofs to Dennis Robertson for comment. But Robertson was not in sympathy with what Keynes had written, and the second proofs were read and commented on and adapted from discussions with Richard Kahn, Joan Robinson,

Roy Harrod and Ralph Hawtrey. Some extensive revision took place in the light of these discussions—but this fascinating story is the subject of *Towards the General Theory*, edited by D. E. Moggridge, volumes XIII and XIV of *The Collected Writings* of John Maynard Keynes.

Working, relaxing, endlessly devising, the personality that emerges from Keynes's papers is very strong. Often as I have been reading them, I have asked myself, 'If I had actually met him, would I have liked him?' In spite of some doubts, the answer would almost certainly have been 'yes'—I would have been charmed.

On first looking through the papers it seems impossible to respond in any other way then very positively, with an enthusiastic 'yes'. From the earliest times, with a great deal of youthful impulsiveness, there is the great generosity of spirit. Keynes was always for the underdog—lashing out against a proposal to fix a quota system for Indian students at Cambridge, a vigorous champion of the rights of women in the university and in the outside world. He courageously stood up for his conscientious objector friends in their struggles with their local tribunals and courted trouble by putting himself on record, even though his position was protected by his important work at the Treasury, as a conscientious objector, as he phrased it 'to surrendering my liberty of judgment on so vital a question as undertaking military service'.

He never surrendered his liberty of judgment. It was not cold judgment. His dramatic and idealistic resignation from the Paris Peace Conference came at the end of five months of attempt after attempt to achieve a just settlement. While the statesmen of Europe haggled over the milliards of will-o'-the-wisp reparations with which they confidently hoped to solve all their financial problems, he tried to fight against the lack of imagination that insisted on the delivery of milch cows as a partial payment from a starving Austria. (According to the British Director of Relief in Austria, it was only through Keynes's initiative in the Supreme Economic Council that famine was averted there in 1919.)

During the long months in Paris Keynes arranged to have the German financial representatives brought to stay near by so that some real discussion could take place; some of the story is told in 'Dr Melchior: a defeated enemy'. At these meetings Keynes gave the Germans the impression of trying very hard to understand their difficulties and to arrive at the truth. He was such a proper Britisher, very alert for the main chance whenever the interests of the Treasury or his country were at stake—yet he treated the ex-enemy as human beings and they divined his sympathy.

Quick and generous sympathy, the free giving of his time and himself—this is the impression one receives from the letters and replies to letters, from the clippings and contemporary reports. The periodical *Time and Tide*, in a character sketch of Keynes written in 1921, described him as 'endowed in a high degree with the power of making half an hour's conversation an event that lives in the memory and feeds the mind'.

With so much goodness, gaiety and charm evident, what is there in the papers to dislike about him? Well, with deeper reading certain doubts set in. As a Canadian-half-American with a sort of delayed-action time fuse from my own background of colonial distrust and prejudice concerning the English ruling classes, I found myself very often feeling extremely sympathetic for some of the people who came into collision with him.

In the beginning he seems to have been rather a social snob, regaling his parents with the names of the great and near-great with whom he had been hobnobbing. At the same time he was very quick to make use of any of these acquaintances, even while sometimes seeming contemptuous of them—in their political need to compromise—in spite of the respectful care with which he wrote to them. One of these was Austen Chamberlain, another was Asquith (here Keynes defended the relationship by saying 'My real friend is Margot'); both these men were considered by some to have been under Keynes's thumb, although this is not borne out by the papers. His influence was not of the *éminence grise* kind; his advice was sought at certain specific points. In turn he could ask for help, and did, when he needed it. His real influence was more general and cumulative—he influenced public opinion and that influenced the politicians.

But to return to my theme: he was an opportunist, ready to step into action the first chance he got, purposefully inserting himself into the Treasury by reminders of his presence in the shape of helpful memos. He was pushing, at first for his own advancement, but later to get things done as he saw right; he was absolutely confident in his own ability to solve his own country's— and other countries'—problems.

This self-confidence—and his early success—made him very arrogant. He was quick, he was resourceful, he was proud of his power to see straight through to what he thought was the heart of the matter. He was impatient and intolerant of slower human beings, and this is the way he generally regarded Americans. When he first went to the United States on a special financial mission with Lord Reading in 1917, he earned Reading's admiration and gratitude for his quick grasp of all the complex details of negotiation— but also, among the Americans, he earned a reputation for intolerable rudeness. Later he mellowed and managed to work amicably and profitably with those individual Americans whom he found sympathetic. He had the habit of some Englishmen of thinking of ordinary Americans as uncultured and naive—and crass, to boot, in wanting to be paid back their war debts. While he also did not like most of the French and had many tiresome controversies with them, it seems to me that he took more trouble to butter them up, as representatives of an older, polished civilisation, than he took with the unsophisticated Americans. But he did make exceptions for kindred spirits.

Part and parcel with this intellectual arrogance was his insularity. This took a number of different forms. His Cambridge–London–Sussex axis was his universe. As a youngster in the India Office he refused the small advancement of a resident clerkship because it would have meant disrupting this rhythm. While he was prepared to be abroad for long periods on Treasury business and near the end of his life spent many months in the United States, travel did not seem to be something that he appreciated as a learning experience. Although like any privileged Englishman of his class he took holidays on the continent and even ventured to Morocco and Egypt, these were holidays; and it did not seem important to him, as an expert on Indian finance, to go to India to acquire information at first hand. He was appointed to a Royal Commission on tariff policy that was supposed to travel and take evidence there in 1921–22, but when he had to choose between taking the time to travel to India and fulfilling his responsibilities in England, he resigned from the Commission. I think he automatically assumed that as an Englishman he had nothing particularly valuable to learn by travel.

Another aspect of his insularity was the insularity of his class. He had no sort of imagination about what life might be like for the working class, although he was very concerned to make their life richer and safer, and to extend to them the delights of leisure and culture enjoyed by his own kind of people. His sympathies were with the underdogs, but his experience gave him no idea of their problems. He only knew them as servants. His advice was middle-class advice. 'Now is the time to stock up on sheets', he told housewives during a textile slump—assuming that there was money to be spent on sheets. When prices were rising he suggested that housewives should transfer their purchases from articles that had increased more in price to those that had increased less—not very useful advice to the working-class woman who had no money to juggle around with anyway. In 1939 his plan for compulsory savings held little attraction for people who had never been accustomed to the idea of having anything to save. The unescapable fact is that Keynes was not the common man—and this not only because of his intellectual and personal gifts but because of the advantages of his time and place and especially of his individual upbringing.

Let me tell you about his parents' house in Harvey Road, Cambridge. My husband and I were invited to tea there by Keynes's parents in the spring of 1949. To two young Canadians this was a revelation of another world. One received the impression of a highly ordered and highly organised life, tea at a certain time, dinner at a certain time, a day blocked out to accommodate the duties of the servants. Then there was the rather daunting conversation: one felt that these cultivated elderly people, established over the years in their comfortable, well ordered Cambridge home, were confident to express an opinion on any subject in the world whatsoever, absolutely certain in the rightness of their views and of their right of authority to assert them. To take a trivial example, one which I may be inventing after so long an interval, let us say that we were told that the North American habit of central heating was enervating—it was the kind of remark that Cambridge people were always making in those chilly days.

There is a passage in chapter 2 of *The Economic Consequences of the Peace* in which Keynes describes the expectations of the pre-1914 world, which is interesting for what it takes for granted:

The greater part of the population, it is true, worked hard and lived at a low standard of comfort, yet were, to all appearances, reasonably content with this lot. But escape was possible, for any man of capacity or character at all exceeding the average, into the middle and upper classes, for whom life offered, at a low cost and with the least trouble, conveniences, comforts, and amenities beyond the compass of the richest and most powerful monarchs of other ages. The inhabitant of London could order by telephone, sipping his morning tea in bed, the various products of the whole earth, in such quantity as he might see fit, and reasonably expect their early delivery upon his doorstep; he could at the same moment and by the same means adventure his wealth in the natural resources and new enterprises of any quarter of the world. . . . He could secure forthwith, if he wished it, cheap and comfortable means of transit to any country or climate without passport or other formality, could despatch his servant to the neighbouring office of a bank for such supply of the precious metals as might seem convenient, and could then proceed abroad to foreign quarters, without knowledge of their religion, language, or customs, bearing coined wealth upon his person, and would consider himself greatly aggrieved and much surprised at the least interference. But, most important of all, he regarded this state of affairs as normal, certain, and permanent.

Here Keynes is describing his own experience. Let us notice what he takes for granted: that success was possible *for any man of capacity or character at all exceeding the average.* In the passage as it continues, it is clear that he is thinking of his own circumstances. What he leaves out is the fact of his extraordinary background—the inestimable advantages of Harvey Road, of Eton and King's and Bloomsbury—advantages not shared by every man of capacity and character, be he English working man or American tourist. Keynes was very proud of his family background, but seemed to be a little myopic about what a head start it had given him in the world.

Harvey Road may have given him what to my eyes were weaknesses, but it gave him his tremendous strength—his faith in his own good sense and his ability to bring about the ultimate triumph of human reason. 'I still suffer incurably from attributing an unreal rationality to other people's feelings and behaviour (and doubtless to my own, too)', he wrote in 1938 in 'My early beliefs', and he spoke of 'the impulse to protest'. He protested against suffering, poverty and ignorance and he had a vision of better times when the main economic problems of the world would be solved and economists would be like dentists. He never stopped trying for better solutions. 'I do not hope to be right. I hope to make progress', he jotted down on a piece of paper which somehow managed to be kept.

I met Keynes through his papers and I was both charmed and exasperated. The things which charmed me belonged to his own personality and the things which exasperated me belonged to his time and place and upbringing. That is hardly something to resent about a man who strove to go so far ahead of his time. I am very grateful to have had the opportunity to have read his papers.

IV

Macro and Monetary Economics

On the foundations of monetary theory[1]

13

F. H. Hahn

I am interested in an economy where money is of no intrinsic worth and is universally accepted in exchange. An agent who holds money now contemplates its exchange for money in the future. If not, then a mild non-satiation postulate ensures that no money would now be held. It follows that a minimum requirement of a representation of a monetary economy is that there should be transactions at varying dates. An economy which has transactions at every date I shall call a *sequence economy*.

A good of given physical characteristics available at a given place at a given date may be the subject of transactions at all dates not later than its date of availability. Let us say that transaction dates are *inessential* if the set of equilibria attainable by an economy is independent of these dates. If transaction dates are inessential then the description of the economy is not altered by concentrating all transactions at the first date. Accordingly in such an economy money is *inessential* in the sense that no monetary variable need enter into the description, or determination, of that economy's equilibrium. It is important to distinguish the property, 'money is inessential', from the quite different property, 'money is *neutral*'. By the latter, as usual, I want to characterise the claim that the set of equilibria of an economy is independent of the quantity of money (provided that the latter is always positive).

To fix ideas let us consider an Arrow–Debreu economy with all transactions concentrated at the first date. Since it does not matter in what follows I suppose there to be a unique equilibrium with price vector p^*. Let us see whether there is an equivalent sequence economy which can be derived from this one.

First, let us allow transactions at every date in every good with availability date not preceding the transaction date. There is a full vector of Arrow–Debreu prices at every date and I call it q^t. If in this enlarged economy equilibrium is attained when each q^t is proportional to p^* as viewed from t, then nothing will have been altered by allowing transactions at every date.

[1] This paper is, in part, based on a more technical one. An attempt has been made to report on the latter and on other work in a manner which it is hoped makes it comprehensible to those not working in abstract general equilibrium analysis.

A condition for this to be the case is that the sequence of markets and the extra prices should not make possible more information on the environment than was available when transactions were concentrated in the first period. This point has been splendidly discussed by Radner [13]* and we may refer to this requirement as the *absence of sequential learning*.

But let us go further and permit only spot transactions at every date. Intertemporal transfers would now require the storage of some good or goods which may be costly and there are difficulties with the replacement of contingent markets. Let us therefore introduce money (which can be costlessly stored). At the initial date give money the accounting price of one. Its subsequent account prices depend on the state. In particular the accounting price at date t in state s is such as to preserve proportionality between the spot prices in terms of money at date t and states and the Arrow–Debreu prices p^* in terms of money for state s viewed from t. Then there would be an initial distribution of money between agents and a terminal obligation to hold money such that the economy's equilibrium would be the same as it was when all transactions were concentrated at the first date. (The terminal conditions arise from the artificiality of considering a finite economy.)

If the derivation of this equivalent sequence economy is possible then money is inessential as are the transaction dates. To obtain such an inessential economy (a) there must be absence of sequential learning and (b) the prices at all dates must be known to all agents at any date. In addition, as I shall later argue, certain assumptions are required about transaction costs. I find it difficult to persuade myself that an economy satisfying these requirements is a promising foundation for the study of money.

If one looks back at the steps just taken one sees that money was introduced to sustain the intertemporal connectedness of an equivalent sequence economy of spot markets. It will be clear that the same result could have been achieved by creating a contingent futures market, one for each state, in unit of account and for each pair of adjacent dates. This leads one to the following formulation.

Under classical conditions every Pareto-efficient allocation of an inessential economy must be independent of transaction dates. The manner of its decentralisation however does not have this independence. But every decentralisation must leave agents with the identical opportunities as they have in the decentralisation associated with transactions which are all concentrated at the first date. In particular, if money is part of the decentralisation then money yields a return, contingent on states. Since every equilibrium is Pareto-efficient this conclusion applies to all equilibria.

The main content of the monetary theory of an inessential economy is implicit in its construction: there is nothing we can say about the equilibrium of an economy with money which we cannot also say about the equilibrium of a non-monetary economy. But the money of this construction is only a contingent store of value and has no other role. Moreover its existence is fortuitous since there is nothing which demands the sequential structure which

* Numbers in square brackets relate to References on p. 241.

will necessitate the introduction of such a store. Lastly the assumptions which I have already discussed and which seem required for an inessential economy are rather unacceptable.

It may help the understanding of these ideas if I relate what I have just said to a recent and very interesting paper by Grandmont and Younes [5], a paper which is itself related to the ancient dichotomy controversy.

Grandmont and Younes start with a sequential structure which is unexplained. Indeed in their economy the only means of transferring wealth from one date to another is by means of storing money. There is no uncertainty. Money is also given the role of a medium of exchange by the following device: all purchases require the exchange of money and only a part of the money receipts from sales can be used for purchases of the same date as the sales. (A similar rather arbitrary scheme is to be found in the work of Ross Starr [18] and in a recent paper by Kurz [10, 11].) The model, and in particular the role of money is a good deal different than it was in the economy I discussed earlier.

But let us see whether in certain circumstances the construction is isomorphic to an inessential economy. Consider an inessential economy with all transactions concentrated in the first date so that it has no money. Suppose it has an equilibrium of the kind that in its equivalent sequence form no household would be transferring wealth between dates and that there is no pure time preference. So one might just as well call this a stationary equilibrium. But the stationary equilibrium of this fictional economy must also be an equilibrium of the Grandmont–Younes economy. For all we need to do is to fix the accounting price of money and give each agent a money stock which the Grandmont–Younes rule requires for the transactions indicated by the equivalent fictional sequence economy. All agents now have the same best choices as before since the money stocks simply take care of the extra constraint. One concludes that certainly money is inessential in all stationary equilibria of the Grandmont–Younes economy. This conclusion is of course related to the account of these matters by Archibald and Lipsey [1].

Indeed one can verify that the isomorphism to an inessential economy need not be confined to stationary states. Certainly if money is the only means of storage the isomorphism must in general fail to hold. But money is not the only means of storage nor the only costless means (recall Keynes's remarks on land). If then some non-money costless storage is possible then one can adjoin to any inessential economy a stream of money going to each agent and a sequence of accounting prices of money, such that every inessential equilibrium is also a monetary equilibrium.

To sum up. One may introduce money into a model of the economy by introducing an *ad hoc* constraint of the Grandmont–Younes variety which ensures that agents hold money. Since this constraint can always be exactly met in a stationary equilibrium of the inessential economy by an appropriate distribution of money stocks and in general by an appropriate sequence of money stocks and prices of money, one can ensure that money is inessential. If there are equilibria of the inessential economy not realisable in the monetarily constrained economy it is because monetary management has not neutralised the transaction constraint, or because money is the only means of storage. Moreover it is easy to show that Pareto-efficiency in this construction requires money to be inessential.

Lastly, in this connection, consider Patinkin's theory. I showed some ten years ago [7] that every equilibrium of the inessential economy is realisable in the Patinkin economy. This is because money is held only when it has a positive exchange value and Patinkin gives no reason why a zero-accounting price of money should be inadmissible. Put slightly differently, Patinkin gives no reason why he can insist on an always positive accounting price of money in an economy which otherwise is inessential.

After all this I can state with some precision what it is that I have in mind when I claim, as I now want to claim, that the foundations of monetary theory have not yet been laid. The position of formal theory on this matter can be summed up as follows: the representations of the monetary economy used, are either isomorphic to an inessential economy, or if not (as in the case of Patinkin) give no account of either the role of money or the sequential character of their construction. But the inessential economy does not need money and one must give reasons for grafting on to it monetary constraints. These reasons have not been given. In particular until recently no study has been undertaken to see whether the commonsense advantages claimed for money can be shown to hold in the inessential economy. Until recently no rigorous studies have been made to discover (a) whether the postulated sequential structure is inherent in the process of exchange, the economies of information and the computational demands on agents, (b) whether if so the resulting intrinsic uncertainty concerning the terms at which future transactions can be undertaken allows one to formulate an interesting and coherent notion of short-run equilibrium, and (c) whether there is a sequence of short-run equilibria which it is useful to designate as an equilibrium. A good many people have now realised that it is questions such as these which require answers and that the real problems of monetary theory are connected with the task of obtaining representations of an economy in which money is essential. Much remains to be done. The literature on the optimum quantity of money suggests that it is not widely realised that the task needs doing.

Of course I have been speaking only of works of formal theory and not of macro-economics in general or Keynesian economics in particular. Certainly no one working in the framework of the *General Theory* would be tempted to enunciate Pareto-efficient theorems for money. Let me quote from Professor Joan Robinson [15, p. 90]: 'The General Theory is a "monetary theory" only in the sense that relationships and institutions concerned with money, credit, and finance are necessary elements in the "real" economy with which it is concerned.' Precisely. But while there is not here any one to one relation to an inessential economy it is the case that the *General Theory* is notoriously deficient in its treatment of relative prices and sufficiently informal and evocative as to allow continuous controversy as to its content for almost forty years. But that Keynes was the first economist to notice the tension—I do not claim contradiction—between the paradigm of the inessential economy and monetary phenomena seems hard to dispute. His insistence on the fundamental importance of the intrinsic sequential structure of a monetary economy which allows the future to play a dangerous game with the present, is enough to support the claim I have made.

I now turn to some of the work that has been going on to lay the foundations. This work is in its infancy and it is likely that in retrospect it will be seen that some false steps have been taken. The intellectual debt everyone in this field owes to Roy Radner is very great.

The natural place to start is by taking the claim that money has something to do with activity of exchange, seriously. There are a number of ways of setting about this. Ostroy [12], Starr [16, 17, 18] and others have studied exchange activities in an economy without money and production. Their aim is to show that the introduction of money allows Pareto-superior outcomes. These are achieved partly because it permits an economy in exchange effort and partly by the avoidance of the coincidence of wants. The last point bears expansion. It is of course not true that such double coincidence is required by a proper barter economy for there is no reason why one should not accept in exchange a good in one transaction which one proposes to exchange again in another. But this introduces both a speculative and a costly element into non-monetary transactions, some of which are avoidable when money is present. For it is one of the rather noteable features of a monetary economy that it permits agents to unbalance their books in goods at any moment of time. This is a point to which I shall return.

But while this work makes precise some of the claims on behalf of money it has not led to a rigorous formulation of sequence economies using money. It also, so it seems to me, is open to a methodological objection.

When we consider a pure exchange economy we do so only in a contingent and preparatory way. Plainly we must build sufficiently robustly not to have to start all over again when production is allowed. But there is an important feature of a monetary economy, certainly familiar since Adam Smith, which makes the extension to production difficult. This is of course that a monetary economy allows specialisation and that specialisation will indeed be a feature of such an economy because, at least to the individual agent, there are increasing returns to specialisation. None of us are jacks of all trades. Accordingly the comparison of a given barter economy with a monetary one when the endowments of agents are the same in both misses an important feature of a monetary economy which one may loosely call the division of labour. No doubt a historical account of a transition between the two economies with due attention to this point is possible, but an analytical one is hard. It also seems to me unnecessary to take so historical a stance. My preference is to start with a fully fledged monetary economy and to study those features of it which make money essential in the sense in which I have been using that term.

Taking this position one is naturally led to a study of markets and in particular to an examination of those features of the situation which cause there to be markets at every date and hence to ensure the sequential structure which is required. It is not unimportant to stress that one is really looking for something stronger, viz. an explanation of why the transaction date may be essential.

Foley [3] and I [8], independently decided to study these questions by adjoining a transaction technology to the traditional pure exchange economy. Foley did not formulate an explicit intertemporal structure and so our results differ a great deal. Recently David Starrett [19] has achieved an elegant simplification of what I had to say and has extended the story. I do not wish to go over the ground again in any detail, but after a bare summary start where Starrett left off.

The market technology is not independent of the available institutions and in particular it is not independent of the institution of money. If one considers the set of dated purchases and sales which is feasible, I simply assume that the set without money is wholly contained in the monetary set. Here I short cut the detailed comparison between barter and monetary exchange. In my first attempt at all this I had, however, to leave unresolved an explicit formalisation of the demand for money and I shall take this opportunity to report on some progress with this. In the terminology I then adopted I regarded money at t traded at t as both anonymous and named, that is such trade incurred no transaction costs, but the distinction between named and anonymous continued to apply to money at traded before t. This is a point of some importance, to which I return.

A good deal of the initial effort was simply directed to the unexpectedly difficult task of showing that an equilibrium relatively to the transaction technology exists. I leave this to one side except to note (a) that the equilibrium is described by two price vectors, one for sales and one for purchases; and (b) that it is a feature of the equilibrium that many feasible transactions are not profitable, that is potential markets are inactive. I took the market technology to be convex while noting this was a bad assumption. Presently I shall consider how one might proceed when this assumption is relaxed. There was no uncertainty.

The interesting features which emerged were these:

(a) Agents were constrained by a sequence of budget constraints. In general no 'present value' calculations could be made which were independent of the agent or of his plans.

(b) The efficiency of the economy has to be defined not only relatively to the transaction technology but also relatively to the endowment matrix.

(c) In general the equilibrium of the economy attained when all prices are announced is not efficient in the sense in which I have just defined it. (Starrett has produced some very nice examples of this inefficiency.)

(d) Only quite peculiar transaction technologies allowed the economy to be inessential.

(e) I noted the difficulty of dealing with producer decisions when no present values were defined.

F. H. Hahn

(*f*) I concluded that it was premature, to say the least, to formulate theorems of the optimum quantity of money.

Now Starrett has shown rigorously that the inefficiency results can be avoided, if the sequential budget constraints can be avoided. He avoids them in just the way in which I earlier constructed an equivalent sequence economy, that is he introduces a costless set of markets in unit of account. Kurz [11], just recently, has used the same device and rather more incautiously seems to believe it to be a route by which money can be shown to be efficiency enhancing. The Starrett result is beautifully proved, but I believe that it proves too much. For it seems to me implausible to require an intertemporal transaction in apples to use resources without making the same demands on all intertemporal transactions including that in money or unit of account. Indeed one of the popular theories of the transactions demand for money relies rather heavily on the transactions costs in forward money. If this is admitted then the Starrett route out of the difficulty is not possible.

I should now add that I am also rather less impressed than I was at first inclined to be, with my own inefficiency theorem. For while it is mildly surprising at first sight it also supererogatory. For one is after all concerned with an economy which is sequential and yet has announced prices and no uncertainty. When these stringent restrictions are dropped it will not be clear, as I argued earlier, how to characterise the equilibrium of an economy. To demand that all expectations be fulfilled at each date now strikes me as leading to uninteresting conceptualisations. All the real work remains to be done here, and the most promising route probably lies with Radner's idea [14] of a statistical equilibrium. How to characterise efficiency in that context is still quite obscure.

But let me return more explicitly to money. The difficulty which is found is that one must not just show that a transaction equilibrium is possible but that in each such equilibrium money will be held. This is of course familiar but, if precision is required, not easy to accomplish. There is another difficulty. If the existence of this or that market is to be treated as an economic unknown of the problem then so must be the periodisation of the construction. That is reasons, if they are available, must be given why one should not deal in continuous time and so for instance perhaps lose the comforting 'non-coincidence of payments and receipts'. If one considers the problem it soon becomes apparent that one will want to do without the convexity of the transaction technology.

I now come to work which is not yet completed and can therefore only deal with such results as are now available.

There are a number of routes which one can take when non-convexities are present. One of these is to deal with a continuum of agents. Another is to study a fictional convex hull economy and to show that every equilibrium of the fictional economy will be 'close' to that of an actual economy if the number of agents is large enough. Roger Whitcomb is pursuing the first of these lines of attack for the present problem and Walter Heller [9] has pursued the latter. I have taken a different route largely because I do not seek those answers which can be obtained when the non-convexities have been suitably sterilised. I want them to be very much present in the final description. As it turns out this can be, at least partially, achieved.

Let us consider the case of pure set-up costs. Here every market at t requires an input vector of goods dated t, if it is to operate at a positive activity level. The set of net markets vectors obtained by subtracting the vector of fixed input vectors is strictly convex. The periodisation of the economy is, for the moment, taken as given.

There is no theorem which states that competitive equilibrium is impossible in the presence of non-convexities. What is the case is that one can construct examples satisfying the axioms of agents' behaviour which do not permit a competitive equilibrium. One can ask whether the reverse procedure is possible. That is, can one for the present problem characterise a class of cases for which equilibrium does exist in spite of set-up costs? If so will this class be interesting? With a reservation to be mentioned shortly I want to answer both questions in the affirmative.

The economy which I consider has money and is of finite duration. We can calculate the maximum number of markets this economy could have. To each such market assign the number one if it is active and the number zero if it is not. This procedure gives rise to some difficulty because I shall want zero to designate the state when no exchanges in the good which this market represents are possible rather than a state of affairs when at the going prices no agent wishes to be active in this market. This causes a complication with the definition of equilibrium to which I return later.

One can now consider the set of economies which can be constructed by assigning zero or one to the various markets. For instance, one such economy arises when zeros are assigned to all markets and we call this the *trivial* economy. Another special case will be the economy in which zeros are given to all futures markets and I call this the *spot* economy. In general one can associate a number with every combination of zeros and ones which is technically possible.[1] If that number is k, the resulting economy is called the *k-economy*. It is important to remember that in many of these economies the optimising actions of agents are conditional on the impossibility of exchange in some markets.

The kind of result one is looking for is the demonstration that for some k-economy with set-up costs an equilibrium exists when k is not the trivial economy. Of course this may be possible for many k's. But every equilibrium is relative to k and that of course is bound to leave a loose end.

The next step is to particularise. A household in the economy is described by its preferences, its endowments and its entitlement to the profits of marketeers. Debreu has provided a measure of 'distance' between households

[1] For example, if the technology of a given market requires as inputs the 'output' of some other market, then both will have to be permitted if the first one is.

which I will not now use. But, intuitively, one is looking for cases where these distances are sufficiently large (given the market technology) as to be associated with gains from trade which are sufficient to 'overcome' the set-up costs in at least some markets. It is not very easy to make this precise but it can be done.

The most interesting route is to suppose households to have identical preferences but very different endowments. There are a number of measures of this difference which one can use but what one is looking for is really a measure of 'specialisation'. For as I have argued earlier, the pure exchange theory is only a preparatory construction for the production economy. It is one of the features of the monetary economy that it leads to some specialisation of agents. The underlying, and yet to be formally articulated, story of specialised endowments is that they are the outcome of specialised production activities. We are not endowed with potatoes because we have specialised in teaching economics.

The technicalities of the appropriate measure and subsequent procedures are somewhat involved and I reserve them for another occasion. Here I will only give an intuitive sketch.[1]

To fix ideas consider the simple case of no transaction costs first. The equilibrium of this economy will be Pareto-efficient. Let x_h^* be a Pareto-efficient allocation to h. Consider the set of x_h which is no smaller (in the vector sense) than either the endowment of h or some vector on the indifference surface through h. This set is non-convex if the endowment does not lie on the indifference surface. A measure of its non-convexity is the inner radius.[2] Under certain regularity assumptions or preferences this radius is related to the gains from trade for this household. We can calculate the radius for each household and taking every Pareto-efficient allocation in turn find the smallest of the largest of the radii amongst households, say r^*. If all households have the same endowment, since they have the same preferences, r^* is zero. In general, given the preferences r^* depends on the endowment matrix. Moreover the length of the trade vector depends on r^*. Thus one can say that for a certain set of endowment matrices, the inner radius r^* is at least r^{**} and the length of the trade vector at least t^* in equilibrium (since every equilibrium is Pareto-efficient).

When transaction costs are considered the argument is a good deal more complicated.

If for any k one takes the convex hull of the transaction technology, the resulting fictional economy has a k-equilibrium. Every such equilibrium can be shown to have the property that there exist no transactions different from the equilibrium ones in any one period *given* each household's transactions in all other periods, which are both feasible in the convex hull and Pareto-superior. I call this property *quasi-efficiency*.

[1] I have here made some changes from the presented version, mainly to improve the exposition.
[2] For a definition and discussion see [2]. Since this was written a technically simpler method not using this route has turned out to be available. But it is not very easily verbalised and I thought it best to stick rather closely to the paper as presented,

Essentially one can now use quasi-efficient allocations as one used Pareto-efficient allocations, to calculate the appropriate inner radius. It is now rather more complicated to relate the latter to the endowment matrix since the transaction technology enters into the construction. But one can characterise, given the transaction technology, a set of endowment matrices such that every quasi-efficient allocation in some k-economy has a trade vector of length greater than some number. Moreover if the actual endowment is in that set then the trade vector belongs to the transaction technology (and not just to its convex hull). Since every k-equilibrium is quasi-efficient, one has then shown that there is a k-equilibrium in the actual transaction technology.

But these are really all technicalities designed to formalise the idea that if agents are sufficiently 'specialised' and the economy's endowment of each good is large enough relatively to set-up costs, the gains from trade will overcome the latter in at least some markets. I now want to note some problems and conclusions which are of economic interest.

The first point I have alluded to already several times, viz. that the equilibrium of a k-economy is in one respect peculiar. This is so because it gives no conditions under which markets which have been excluded, essentially by prohibition, would in fact be excluded on economic grounds. This is specially serious when an equilibrium exists for different k's. In fact we cannot leave matters there. For I must be able to show that at least one k-equilibrium is a proper sequence equilibrium with spot markets at every date. If not, then it will be hard to maintain the basic postulate that the exchange technology is defined for a monetary economy. In fact it would be highly desirable to be able to exclude all k's which are not sequence k's. This, if achievable, would of course not exclude futures markets.

Consider the set of k for which an equilibrium exists. Under mild assumptions this includes at least one sequence k. Suppose that it also includes some k' with the characteristics that it has no markets after some date t which precedes the terminal date. The ideal resolution of our difficulties would be to show that every such k'-equilibrium is Pareto-inferior to some proper sequence equilibrium. One would then have grounds for considering only sequence equilibria, although I still would not know why one rather than another should hold.

Although I believe on general economic grounds that this route should be possible I have run into rather formidable difficulties in pursuing it. At the moment I have only a rather weaker result.

Let us say that a given k-equilibrium is *complete* if there is no k'-equilibrium in which all the markets in k have been assigned the number one. It is important to remember here that if a market has the number one trade is permitted on that market but need not take place. That is one distinguishes between markets which simply do not exist and markets which are not active. With some extra assumptions one can show that only sequence equilibria are complete. The idea is that when a theory of the setting up of markets comes to be developed complete equilibria will be of special interest. For instance in considering whether an excluded market can profitably be set-up one expects the calculating potential marketeer to suppose all presently existing markets to continue in existence. This is far from satisfactory but it is as far as I have got and I suppose that a full theory will in fact be only interested in complete equilibria.

If we agree to this resolution the next problem is to show that every sequence equilibrium will in fact use money. In thinking about this I shall not worry about the terminal date problem and simply patch it up by brute force. Even so reflection will show that the problem is not straightforward. Thus it is perfectly possible that the sequence equilibrium we are interested in is a stationary one for every household, and why should it then store money? It almost looks as if in spite of all the effort one will have to introduce some *ad hoc* and fortuitous constraint like that of Grandmont–Younes.

It is now that what I have called periodisation becomes of central importance. Sticking to discrete time we can yet make our fundamental intervals as short as we like. Since each market has a set-up cost it is then not too hard to show that there will be some intra-period storage and that one can exclude full stationarity, fundamental interval by fundamental interval. Of course one must now specify a storage technology. One then takes advantage of the costlessness of money storage and the 'specialisation' of endowments which we needed in the first place, to arrive at the desired results.

This can probably be greatly improved upon by the following further modifications.

(*a*) One allows composite markets which have their activities specified by a flow of outputs and inputs, the set-up costs being incurred at the date of contract. For instance the forward sale of labour for five days is such an example if payment were made at the contract date *or* if given other markets, the payment date were of no significance. In any case set-up costs will of course encourage such markets. The modification required in the technical procedure I have so far used is small.

(*b*) One allows for transactions costs incurred by households themselves. This of course requires more convexification etc. but I do not pursue this.

I now want to emphasise not only that the construction I have just given is in some ways incomplete—there are a good many properties still to be studied—but also that even if it were complete it would be quite inadequate. Certainly the economy and money are essential but it is all a pale shadow of the real thing. I have not allowed for uncertainty and my prices are announced. Rather worse I have nothing to say about non-equilibrium situations. All these are serious defects and they will not be easily cured.

One is tempted, at least for the present, to try something rather less ambitious and in particular to study the short period only. Grandmont [4] and Green [6] have recently done this, as did Arrow and I [2] in a somewhat simpler context. Surprisingly it turns out to be rather difficult to establish even some of the minimal results one would like. But Green has elegantly shown what is required for a short period equilibrium to exist when he allows in principle a full set of markets, spot and future, at the present and the next date. The expectations of agents of the prices in the next period are given by probability distributions. He paid no explicit attention to the question of money.

The next step is to rectify this and I also believe to introduce much simpler expectations and more rule of thumb behaviour by agents. There is also a further difficulty noted by Arrow and myself. Short period equilibrium runs into formidable difficulties if one allows agents to have had a prior history. That is if they start the period with commitments from the past, specially commitments specified in terms of money. This will have to be explored much more thoroughly and it is likely that this is where the abstract formulations make important contact with Keynesian economics.

After all this it will not come as a surprise that I believe that we are only at the beginning of a theory of the economy in which money is essential. In particular I think that we have for a good long time been on a quite unimportant and uninteresting track. The challenge of monetary theory is not the neutrality theorem or related results; it is the required reconstruction of our paradigm if we are to make sense of money.

I should like to conclude on a defensive note. To many who would call themselves monetary economists the problems which I have been discussing must seem excessively abstract and unnecessary. They are accustomed to recognising the importance of expectations and uncertainty and liquidity and they are also predominantly macro-economists. Will this preoccupation with foundations, they may argue, help one iota in formulating monetary policy or in predicting the consequences of parameter changes? Are not IS and LM sufficient unto the day? Or put in Friedman's recent terms, is it not more fruitful to be Marshallian and to put the Walrasian search for generality and rigour behind us?

I am surprisingly sympathetic to some of these hypothetical objections but I wish to maintain that they can be valid without casting doubt on what I regard to be one of the central reasons for the studies on which I have reported. This is to do away with a dichotomy which has nothing to do with Patinkin and the classicals. This dichotomy is best seen when the same economist's writings on IS and LM are compared with his writings on welfare economics. Or when a 'long-run' is involved which has great difficulty in living with any 'short-run'. In short, the dichotomy which arises when we do monetary theory when money is essential and all other theory when money is inessential. It may well be that the approaches here utilised will not in the event improve our advice to the Bank of England; I am rather convinced that it will make a fundamental difference to the way in which we view a decentralised economy.

References

1. ARCHIBALD, G. C. and LIPSEY, R. G. 'Monetary and value theory: a critique Lange and Patinkin', *Review of Economic Studies*, **26**, no. 1 (1958), 69.
2. ARROW, K. J. and HAHN, F. H. *General Competitive Analysis*, Holden–Day, 1971.

3. FOLEY, D. K. 'Economic equilibrium with costly marketing', *Journal of Economic Theory*, **2** (1970).

4. GRANDMONT, J. M. 'On the short-run equilibrium in a monetary economy', CEPREMAP Discussion Paper, February 1971, Paris.

5. GRANDMONT, J. M. and YOUNES, Y. 'On the role of money and the existence of a monetary equilibrium', *Review of Economic Studies* (forthcoming).

6. GREEN, J. R. 'Temporary general equilibrium in a sequential trading model with spot and futures transactions' (1971), unpublished.

7. HAHN, F. H. 'On some problems of proving the existence of an equilibrium in a monetary economy', in *The Theory of Interest Rates*, ed. F. H. Hahn and F. P. R. Brechling, Macmillan, 1965.

8. HAHN, F. H. 'Equilibrium with transaction costs', *Econometrica* **39**, no. 3 (1971).

9. HELLER, W. P. 'Money and transactions with set-up costs', discussion paper, University of Pennsylvania (Dept. of Economics), June 1971.

10. KURZ, M. *Equilibrium with Transaction Costs and Money in a Single Market Exchange Economy*, Institute for Mathematical Studies in the Social Sciences, Technical Report no. 51, Jan. 1972.

11. KURZ, M. *Equilibrium in a Finite Sequence of Markets with Transaction Costs*, Institute for Mathematical Studies in the Social Sciences, Technical Report no. 52, Feb. 1972.

12. OSTROY, J. M. 'Exchange as an economic activity', PhD dissertation, Northwestern University, 1970.

13. RADNER, R. 'Competitive equilibrium under uncertainty', *Econometrica* **38**, no. 1 (Jan. 1968).

14. RADNER, R. *Existence of Equilibrium Plans, Prices and Price Expectation in a Sequence of Markets*, I and II; Technical Report no. 5, Centre for Research in Management Science, University of California, Berkeley, June 1970.

15. ROBINSON, J. *Economic Heresies*, Macmillan, 1971.

16. STARR, R. M. 'Structure of exchange in barter and monetary economics', Cowles Foundation Discussion Paper no. 295, June 1970.

17. STARR, R. M. 'Equilibrium and demand for media of exchange in a pure exchange economy with transaction costs', Cowles Foundation Discussion Paper no. 300, October 1970.

18. STARR, R. M. 'The price of money in a pure exchange economy with taxation', Cowles Foundation Discussion Paper no. 310, June 1971.

19. STARRETT, D. 'Inefficiency and the demand for "money" in a sequence economy' (1972), unpublished.

Analysis of the determination of the stock of money[1]

14

Charles Goodhart

1. Introduction

It is generally the case that macro-economic models are constructed around a framework of accounting identities. For example, Keynesian models are based on the national income accounts. In monetary theory the identity $MV = Py$ plays a central role. There is nothing reprehensible about constructing a model around a solid framework of identities. Indeed the process of distinguishing key identities, whose existence or importance had not been previously recognised, has played a major role in the development of theory; for example a relatively minor extension of the Keynesian identities led to the formulation of Kaldor's theory of distribution [15]*.

It is, therefore, not in the least pejorative to state that modern analysis of the determination of the money stock, at least as commonly taught in most universities, is firmly based on an identity. In this analysis the money stock (M) is defined as comprising two main components, being respectively currency (C) and bank deposits (D) held by the general public.[2] It is, therefore, possible to set down the following identity,

$$M = D + C \qquad (1)$$

which must hold exactly by definition. Similarly it is possible to define the sum of currency held by the general public (C) and the cash reserves of the banking sector (R) as 'high powered money' (H). If the currency in the hands of the public was transferred by them to the banks in exchange for bank deposits, the banks' cash reserves would rise equivalently. High-powered money can, therefore, be regarded as the total of existing assets which either

[1] I am very grateful to my colleagues in the Economic Section of the Bank, especially Miss Margaret Mayne, for their help, criticism and support in the preparation of this paper. More generally, the development of my views on this subject has been much influenced by my reading of the works of Professor Tobin. I remain, however, personally responsible for all the opinions and errors exhibited in this paper.

[2] For a detailed note on various possible alternative definitions of the stock of money in the UK, see [2].

* Numbers in square brackets relate to References on p. 260.

are, or potentially could be, used as cash reserves by the banking sector. The term 'high-powered' reflects the fact that bank deposits are some multiple of the banks' cash reserves, so that—assuming that the banks maintain fairly stable reserve ratios—one would see a multiple increase in bank deposits accompanying an increase in the banks' cash reserves. The additional identity,

$$H = R + C \tag{2}$$

(where H is high-powered money, R banks' cash reserves), can thus also be set down, which again must hold by definition.

By algebraic manipulation of these two identities it is possible to arrive at a third identity,

$$M = H \frac{(1 + C/D)}{(R/D + C/D)} \tag{3}$$

describing the money stock in terms of the level of high powered money and two ratios, R/D the banks' reserve/deposit ratio, and C/D the general public's currency/deposit ratio.[1] Since this relationship is also an identity it always holds true by definition; changes in the money stock can, therefore, be expressed in terms of these three variables alone.

To be able to express changes in the money stock in terms of only three variables has considerable advantages of brevity and simplicity, though even these advantages may be lost in those circumstances where there is a plethora of differing kinds of banks and deposits, each involving separate reserve ratios. Nevertheless the use of such an identity does not in any sense provide a behavioural theory of the determination of the stock of money,[2] although it is not entirely unknown in the literature for economists to regress changes in the money supply on changes in H, R/D and C/D and claim that the resulting excellent fit provides support for the money multiplier theory (see for example [7, 8]).

To provide a behavioural theory from the underlying structure of identities requires further steps. First it is necessary to examine the behavioural relationships which determine the desired levels of the variables in the system. The next stage is to explore the dynamic process which ensues when some shock causes the desired value of one, or more, of the variables in the identity to diverge from its actual value.

2. Deficiencies of the usual approach

The main theme of this paper will be that these subsequent steps, necessary to move on from a *description* of the movements in the money stock in terms

[1] An array of slightly differing identities can be obtained from algebraic manipulation of the two basic identities. The differences between them have no analytical significance. See [11, esp. App. B], and [4, esp. Chs 1 and 2].

[2] 'Money supply multipliers' can, however, also be derived as a reduced form solution of a somewhat larger system containing parameters determining aspects of the portfolio allocation of the public and of the banks, cf. the excellent paper by Jaffee, [13, pp. 6–8]. If the parameters in this system are taken as constant, however, then this alternative approach also contains virtually no behavioural content.

of accounting identities[1] to a *theory* of its determination, have not, broadly speaking, been taken far enough. A common disadvantage of using identities, which show the definitional or accounting relationship that must hold between assets, as the basis for analysis is that they tend to obscure the key role played by relative price (yield) movements in the adjustment process; indeed the adjustment process is often described, in the case for example of both the consumption and the money multipliers, as a purely mechanical process in which relative price (yield) movements do not enter at all. This potential defect in this approach to the analysis of the determination of the stock of money is made far more serious by a general failure to probe the behavioural factors determining the level of, and changes in, the high powered money base. Whereas most studies (e.g. [3, esp. pp. 242–56]) in this field in recent years have taken into consideration the effect of relative price (yield) movements on the desired values of R/D and C/D, there still seems little or no awareness that taking the level of H as exogenously given pushes out of sight the most important parts of the adjustment process.[2] All too often in the literature this total is taken as given, as exogenous, as fixed by the authorities, and no further steps are taken to examine the factors determining its level. A number of arguments may be deployed against this common practice.

As a start, ask the question why should the authorities seek to set the level of high-powered money at any particular value? The answer which is usually supplied is that they do so in order to achieve some desired level of the money stock, not out of concern for the level of H *per se*. But if the authorities are trying to fix the level of the money stock, then they presumably attempt to alter H in a way which would offset variations in the two other elements in the basic multiplier identity. To the extent that they can do so, it is misleading to ascribe causal significance to a description of changes in the money stock in terms of variations in the three separate elements of the identity. It is the money stock that should in this case be treated as the exogenous element in the system, while H is not independent, but instead is endogenous. Only if variations in the other two elements in the identity cannot be predicted by the authorities would it be proper to regard H as exogenous.

---

[1] Indeed we have several of these descriptive accounting identities, since it is perfectly possible to describe the change in the money stock in terms of alternative identities, relying, for example, on banking balance sheet identities to work from bank assets to bank liabilities. This is, in broad terms, the approach used in the description of domestic credit expansion and movements in the money stock in official statistical publications in this country (see [1a] and [5]).

[2] Even in Jaffee's paper [13], which compares, and to some extent reconciles, the 'old' [money multiplier] and the new [Tobin] view of the determination of the stock of money, his simplified model takes high powered money as given. In this respect his analysis also precludes a proper examination of major parts of the complete portfolio adjustment process of the banks and the public.

In a number of models, the ability of the banks to borrow from the Central Bank, as lender of last resort, is explicitly treated by taking borrowed reserves as endogenous, a behavioural function of relative interest rates and other factors. It makes, however, no significant difference to the arguments in this paper whether it is the level of H, of unborrowed reserves, of free reserves, or some other variant of the monetary base, which is treated as exogenous.

9

Of course, it may be argued that the authorities are not in a position to observe and to offset variations in the banks' reserve ratio or the public's currency/deposit ratio perfectly. It is even possible to undertake statistical tests to see how far the authorities have undertaken such offsetting action.[1] To that extent there may be some useful behavioural information to be obtained by examining the variations in the three elements of the basic identity separately. But if that is the case presented, one can ask why it is not taken further. Several of the monetary flows which bring about changes in the total of high powered money are no more under the direct control of the Central Bank than are the changes in the banks' reserve ratios, for example foreign exchange inflows under a regime of fixed exchange rates,[2] encashment of national savings, etc. If it is recognised that the authorities may find it difficult to offset completely all variations in, say, the banks' reserve ratios, then will they not have just as much, or even more, difficulty in offsetting monetary flows, not under their direct control, causing variations in H?

The only distinction which may be prayed in aid of the practice of taking the level of high-powered money, but not the level of the money stock, as exogenously given is that data on the total outstanding volume of high-powered money are, in principle at least, continuously available to the authorities, while banking statistics are gathered only at intervals. The information, potentially available, might therefore enable the authorities to control H with a greater precision than M. This argument has some, but not much, validity. Banking data are generally collected sufficiently frequently to prevent unforeseen systematic variations in reserve or currency/deposit ratios developing far enough to distort the authorities' aim. The main complications for the authorities do not come in *observing* the fluctuations in those elements in H or M not under their direct control but rather lie in the technical task of *offsetting* them. In this respect fluctuations in certain elements, which affect the level of H, for example foreign exchange inflows, government budget deficits, have in the UK during recent years at least posed a far more difficult problem for the monetary authorities in trying to achieve their objectives than have the variations in the reserve ratios or the currency/deposit ratios.

It would, therefore, seem difficult to sustain the argument that the degree of control which the authorities can maintain over H is qualitatively different from their ability to control M. If so, this implies that it is wrong to take the level of H as exogenously given. Either the authorities can and do want to offset autonomous variations in all these other monetary flows, so that on these two strong assumptions the money stock itself is the proper variable to take as exogenous, rather than H. Or alternatively if one wishes to probe further into the *process* of the determination of the money stock, it is necessary

[1] For example, Courchene and Kelly [6] examine how far the Bank of Canada offsets changes in currency holdings outside banks.
[2] Economists working at the IMF under the guidance of J. J. Polak and V. Argy, have taken the lead in the analysis of the interrelationship between domestic credit expansion, external currency flows and changes in the domestic money stock. Recent issues of IMF Staff Papers include several articles on this subject.

to examine more closely the determinants of changes in the level of high-powered money itself rather than treat these as given.

The second reason why it is wrong to take H, or M for that matter, as given exogenously, is that these variables would be policy targets, not exogenous variables, in those circumstances when the authorities are trying to fix their level. There is an important methodological difference between these two. Exogenous variables are those whose values are determined outside the system under consideration. Policy targets are control variables whose value the authorities at the very centre of the system attempt to set. To treat policy targets as exogenous variables implies that the authorities do not alter their control variables in response to the developments of the system.

It is perhaps true that the response of the authorities to economic developments is more fitful, wayward and unpredictable than the response of the mass of consumers. Apart from abrupt changes in direction caused by political events, the authorities are, possibly, more liable to be influenced by the changing fashions of economic theory. Even so, the presumption that the reactions of the authorities are less predictable than those of consumers, or trade union leaders for that matter, is doubtful. The authorities do react, and often in a highly predictable fashion,[1] to changes in past, current and predicted developments in the economy. For example in the UK it has usually been possible to predict a good deal about changes in certain policy instruments by looking at only two variables, the level of unemployment and the level of foreign exchange reserves.[2]

It is, therefore, mistaken to take a policy target as given independently of the previous history of the development of the economy. If an economist wants to study the past, to understand what happened, he has to regard such policy targets as more akin to endogenous variables than to exogenous variables. Rather than taking H or M as exogenous, the economist should construct a reaction function. Of course, it remains true that the change of policy will continue to have an independent effect, whether or not the change is some predictable function of other economic developments, in just the same way as a fluctuation in consumption has an independent effect on the economy, whether or not it is a predictable function of other economic developments. But it does mean that the statistical techniques required to evaluate the effect of past changes in policy need to be considerably more subtle and complex than would be the case if policy was indeed arbitrarily selected.

Taking H, or M, as given, whether treated as a policy target or exogenous variable, would appear to require the prior assumption, even if not made explicitly, that the authorities' intentions—whether or not they are entirely successful—are to control these monetary aggregates. If the authorities have other targets, for example to control the level of interest rates, then they may not also be able—as in the case of the above example—to control the

---

[1] One of the best papers on this subject is by Wood [24]. One of the few empirical studies on the authorities' reactions in the UK is provided by Fisher [9].

[2] Fisher [9, pp. 821–31], also see Goodhart [12].

level of H or M independently. To take another example, in a relatively small, open country in circumstances conducive to a large interest elasticity of international capital flows, the authorities may choose to maintain fixed exchange rates. If so, they can act to control domestic credit and foreign exchange flows, but their power to alter either H, M, or the level of domestic interest rates is strictly limited.

To treat H, or M, as an exogenous variable, or a policy target, therefore involves a strong, positive, assumption about the authorities' behaviour. It may be possible to decide on logical grounds how the authorities ought to behave, but the treatment of H, or M, as exogenous or a policy target in any exercise to explain past events implies a positive claim about how they have behaved. This is an empirical matter. Those who have seriously studied the behaviour of the monetary authorities in those countries, with whose monetary history I am familiar, have usually come to the conclusion that with the exception, to a greater or lesser extent, of the most recent years the monetary authorities have not treated the rate of change of monetary aggregates as target variables. Instead they have usually sought to control interest rates.[1]

The third reason, therefore, why it is wrong to treat H, or M, as exogenously given, or as a policy target, is that it is based on an implicit positive assumption about the behaviour of the authorities, which has in the past been generally invalid. It is curious that certain economists who are most vocal in their criticisms of Central Banks for failing to adopt control of the monetary aggregates as their target nevertheless base their policy prescriptions on the behaviour of a model which incorporates the assumption that the monetary aggregates have in fact been exogenously determined.

This approach to the determination of the money stock, relating M to an exogenously determined level of H via the basic identity, has been criticised thus far on the grounds that it involves implicit assumptions about the actions of the authorities, which are invalid. The final and more serious argument for abandoning this analytical approach, or rather for developing and extending it along different lines, is that it leads to an erroneous appreciation of the underlying dynamic process whereby a change over time in the stock of money occurs, and in particular frequently causes a complete failure to comprehend the proper role of the banks and the public in the process.

At the most simplified level, this approach often leads pedagogues to explain changes in the quantity of money in terms of a mechanical multiplier, in which high-powered money gets passed from hand to hand like a hot potato. The portfolio adjustments of the banks in this description apparently

---

[1] 'Whereas everyone agrees that the monetary authority is capable of determining the money stock, we must nevertheless recognise that we live in the real world where there are lags and where the monetary authority apparently has never sought to control the absolute level of the nominal stock of money, opting instead to affect "credit conditions" ': Klein [16].

'However, concern over market interest rate movements has been a major factor influencing Federal Reserve acquisition of Government debt over the last two decades': Stewart [22].

See also [21] esp. ch. 5 by N. Thygesen.

play no role in the process, except in so far as they may seek to alter their reserve ratios. The public's asset preferences are seemingly irrelevant to the determination of the stock of money except in so far as they seek to alter their cash/deposit ratios. Such teaching, and I can alas find quotations from a number of textbooks along these lines,[1] is such an incomplete way of describing the process of the determination of the stock of money that it amounts to misinstruction.

At a more advanced level, however, the 'money multiplier' can be regarded as a quasi reduced form of a larger system of structural equations describing aspects of the portfolio allocation of the banks and the public in response to changes in some relative prices (cf. [13]). But even in such expositions the level of H, high-powered money, is taken as given. The effect of this assumption is to abstract from many of the more important facets of the process of portfolio adjustment. As one probes deeper to examine the determinants of H itself, so the process whereby the stock of money changes as a result of an interplay of portfolio adjustments by banks and the general public in response to relative price (interest rate) changes will come more clearly and more completely into view.

3. The determination of the monetary base

The first step in arriving at a more satisfactory theory of the determination of the money stock is to abandon the assumption of a given stock of high-powered money, and to proceed to an examination of the factors which determine this total. This can be done without prejudice to the subsequent empirical issue of what the authorities may be seeking to achieve. In order to do this it is possible to turn to yet another accounting identity, taken from the accounts of the flow of funds (see e.g. [1]), which describes how the financial deficit (or surplus) of each sector is financed by flows of funds through the various financial markets. In order that this accounting identity may be satisfied, it is necessary that a public sector deficit, after taking account of certain financial transfers, e.g. import deposits, local authority loans for housebuilding etc., must be financed by borrowing from other sectors, by issuing additional debt to them or by running down claims upon them, e.g. foreign exchange reserves which represent claims on the overseas sector.

The provision of finance to the public sector occurs in a variety of ways [1b]. For the purpose of this analysis such borrowing may be grouped into three components, finance which directly brings about an increase in high-powered money, ΔH; finance raised by other domestic borrowing; finance raised by receiving the sterling counterpart of accommodating a currency outflow. It may be useful to subdivide this second item, the finance obtained by other domestic borrowing, into three separate components, the use of

[1] For examples of the kind of analysis being attacked, see Fisher [10, chs. 4 and 5], and Jordan [14]. It is, however, unfair to single out particular individuals in this fashion, since this approach is so commonly utilised.

funds to repay maturing debt, transactions (borrowing or repaying) in non-marketable debt, e.g. premium savings bonds, national saving certificates etc., and operations in marketable debt. This accounting identity can then be expressed algebraically as follows:

$$PSD = OMO + NMD - MAT + ECF + \Delta H \qquad (4)$$

where *PSD* is the public sector deficit after taking account of various financial transfers such as import deposits, *OMO* represents the outcome of the authorities' operations in marketable debt, *NMD* represents the outcome of transactions in non-marketable debt, *MAT* shows the required use of funds to pay off maturing debt, *ECF* gives the total finance obtained from, or required for, accommodating external currency flows and ΔH represents the increase in the public sector's monetary liabilities, high-powered money.[1]

This accounting identity can equally well be reversed, to show the various financial flows accompanying any change in high powered money, as follows:

$$\Delta H = PSD - OMO - NMD + MAT - ECF \qquad (5)$$

This identity at least points the analysis towards explicit consideration of those elements in the financial system which have traditionally been the main concern of the authorities, the size of the public sector deficit, operations in public sector marketable debt, the relative attractions of public sector non-marketable debt, the weight of maturities to be financed, the impact on the foreign exchange market—and on the reserve position—of a balance of payments deficit (or surplus).

Certain of these financial flows in equation (5) are, largely or entirely, outside the control of the monetary authorities. For example, the volume of maturities to be refinanced in any one year is ineluctably determined by prior contractual arrangements. The problem of refinancing maturities can be exaggerated, however, since holders, such as financial institutions, who are attempting to maintain a balanced portfolio, can usually be tempted to switch regularly towards slightly longer dated debt to maintain the desired balance of their portfolios. Even so, the occasion of a maturity reduces the transaction cost to holders of moving out of public sector debt, and causes such holders, of necessity, to reconsider their investment plans. For such reasons maturities of debt issues of a kind bought previously in large quantities by less active portfolio managers, especially in the personal sector, can be expected to cause more serious refinancing problems to the authorities.

Although the monetary implications of any proposed fiscal change may be given considerable weight in the determination of fiscal policy, many other considerations of very different kinds, however, also enter, and may well sway the judgment about the proper balance between expenditures and revenue of the public sector. To this extent short-term variations in the size

---

[1] Including for this purpose the increase in bankers' balances with the Bank of England Banking Department (counterbalanced by holdings of public sector debt by the Department).

of the deficit must also be regarded as outside the control of the monetary authorities. Indeed variations in the size of the public sector deficit may on occasions even hinder the intended thrust of monetary policy.[1]

Moreover, it is difficult to devise fiscal measures that can be frequently altered without involving considerable disturbance of one kind or another. It is therefore usual to alter tax rates and forward expenditure plans only once a year in the annual Budget. Even then, lags intervene between the policy change and the resulting effect on monetary flows, so that the public sector deficit in any given year may be conditioned as much by the previous Budget as by current fiscal changes. For all these reasons the monetary authorities cannot hope to vary the size of the public sector deficit in the short run as a flexible instrument for the purpose of achieving some desired rate of growth in the monetary aggregates. This problem is seen in even more extreme forms in other countries where the executive face difficulties on occasions in obtaining legislative agreement to their fiscal proposals.

In principle it would be possible to envisage the authorities frequently varying the rates of interest offered on non-marketable debt for the purpose of inducing some desired level of flows into these instruments. In practice, however, for reasons that are not germane to this paper, rates on some of these instruments have been notable rather for their constancy.[2] Thus in periods of monetary squeeze rates offered on non-marketable securities have generally tended to become less competitive. The result has been that flows of funds into national savings have tended to move inversely with fluctuations in market interest rates. Evidence of this can be obtained from some simple regressions, as shown below:

$$NMD_t = 18 \cdot 98 - 47 \cdot 98 \ dC_{t-1} - 31 \cdot 54 \ dC_{t-3} + 0 \cdot 594 \ NMD_{t-1}$$
$$(18 \cdot 70) \qquad (22 \cdot 54) \qquad (0 \cdot 14)$$

$$\bar{R}^2 = 0 \cdot 56$$

$$NMD_t = 18 \cdot 58 - 65 \cdot 09 \ dBS_t - 34 \cdot 63 \ dBS_{t-1} + 0 \cdot 594 \ NMD_{t-1}$$
$$(22 \cdot 19) \qquad (23 \cdot 74) \qquad (0 \cdot 12)$$

$$\bar{R}^2 = 0 \cdot 61$$

where NMD represents inflow into non-marketable debt in £ million (seasonally adjusted), dC is the change in consol rates and dBS the change in building society deposit rates, observed quarterly over the period 1963 Q3 to 1970 Q4.

It therefore appears that three of the monetary flows (maturities, public sector deficit, non-marketable debt) out of the set of flows, which must by accounting identity equal the change in the monetary liabilities of the public

---

[1] Professor Tew [23] has termed the financing requirement which arises from the public sector deficit and debt maturities, 'the flood'. In order to check the growth of the monetary aggregates, the authorities have to undertake the often extremely difficult task of damming this flood.

[2] For example the rate of interest on Post Office Savings Bank ordinary accounts, retitled National Savings Bank ordinary accounts in 1969, remained constant at $2\frac{1}{2}$ per cent from the foundation of POSB in 1861 by Gladstone until 1970 when Jenkins took steps to raise the rate offered.

sector (ΔH), are not generally subject to the immediate or precise control of the monetary authorities. If these three flows should require a very large amount of financing, then any attempt to restrict the rate of growth of the monetary aggregates would impose a considerable pressure upon a central bank's operations in marketable debt.

The likelihood of capital inflows from abroad as domestic interest rates rise, thus altering the external currency flow to be financed (ECF), forms an apparent obstacle to the successful achievement of market operations intended to squeeze domestic liquidity. If such capital flows respond very sensitively, and in relatively large volume, to variations in financial conditions in any country, then under a regime of fixed exchange rates the autonomy of that country to undertake an independent financial policy is limited.[1] On the other hand in such conditions it becomes easier to achieve a desired level of international reserves by inducing large-scale capital movements. It is important to ascertain how far domestic monetary policy is, both in theory and in practice, constrained by international financial conditions.

Thus two of the monetary flows affecting the level of H (PSD and MAT) are to some considerable extent outside the control of the authorities, while another two (NMD and ECF) tend to respond perversely to interest rate changes, in that an increase in domestic interest rates will tend to lead to flows from these sources causing increases in the high-powered money base. In addition in some circumstances there could be expected to be some decline in the banks' desired reserve ratios as interest rates on earning assets rise relative to rates on reserves.

In order to achieve a desired level of H, or more usefully of M, the authorities have to try to offset movements, which may on occasions be very large, in all these other flows by inducing people to purchase, or if needs be to sell, marketable government debt.[2] These operations of the authorities are done in the open market, and the implication of this is that the authorities must accept a price at which the other party to the transaction will deal voluntarily, in order to induce a flow into, or out of, marketable securities.

The question whether it is preferable to view the authorities as operating

---

[1] It is occasionally argued that, if the interest elasticity of international capital movements is relatively large, it would be possible to lower the stock of money by lowering interest rates, an apparently perverse response. In reality, so long as the money stock is defined to include only resident monetary balances, i.e. to exclude non-resident balances, and so long as the banking system is not directly constrained by direct controls or interest rate ceilings etc., such perverse reactions will not take place. The apparent plausibility of such perverse responses comes from the use of misleading partial equilibrium analysis rather than a complete general equilibrium model.

[2] There is, however, some tendency towards negative covariation in these flows, i.e. they seem to interact in a way that produces some partial compensation, which alleviates certain of the difficulties facing the authorities. A large foreign exchange inflow usually encourages sales of gilts and also reduces company demand for bank credit. A big public sector borrowing requirement implies a large private sector surplus, which may induce large private sector purchases of public sector debt and, perhaps, lead to some reduction in the demand for advances. Moreover a large public sector borrowing requirement is more likely to coincide with an exchange outflow than with an inflow.

primarily on quantities or on prices in this market, or set of markets, is entirely without prejudice to the separate empirical issue of which variables form the targets for policy (e.g. monetary aggregates or interest rates). The authorities may operate on quantities in debt markets in such a way as to influence interest rates, or on rates in an attempt to obtain certain quantitative effects. Indeed the form of these operations may vary from market to market.

Nevertheless there is a distinction of some importance, relating to the practical characteristics of markets, between market interventions which take the form of quantitative offers and those which are expressed in price terms. Owing largely to the existence of costs of adjustment, it is not the case that markets are always able to clear instantaneously after some new development. If conditions change very markedly, so that the previous state of information on which market operators were basing their investment policies becomes clearly in need of major revision, a common reaction is to cease trading altogether, until a new considered basis for trading can be re-established. If the possibility of no trading, or even of no complete clearing, can exist, there will be circumstances in which the authorities cannot operate on quantities, but it will remain possible for them to operate on posted prices, even if no trades take place at such prices.

A related practical issue is that in those markets where the authorities might wish to operate primarily through quantities, they would not do so generally in a simple take-it-or-leave-it fashion. Instead the markets would usually be carefully prepared in advance for the quantitative offer. Tenders would be underwritten, prices discussed with key people in the market, repurchase clauses arranged, 'even-keeling' undertaken etc. It is not proper to disregard the circumscribed nature of the authorities' quantitative operations. It is, at any rate in this country, probably generally preferable to view the authorities as operating through prices rather than quantities in debt markets. Otherwise, far more attention would need to be given to the constraints on the authorities in their quantitative operations.

It may be helpful to recapitulate and to summarise the propositions made. The authorities do not fix the level of high powered money; instead their main policy instruments involve the fiscal arm of altering the public sector deficit and the debt management arm of intervening in debt markets. The latter intervention may take the form of changing quantities or prices, but it is, probably, somewhat more in accord with market realities, at least in this country, to envisage this as occurring through price changes. These interventions whether initially in quantitative or price form, alter relative prices and so induce portfolio readjustments. These readjustments then bring about changes in H, as well as in M.

Simplifying considerably (by setting NMD, MAT and the current account balance all equal to zero), these definitional relationships may be set out algebraically, as follows:

$$M_t = D_t + C_t \qquad (1)$$

$$H_t = C_t + R_t \qquad (2)$$

$$H_t - H_{t-1} = PSD_t - OMO_t - ECF_t \tag{5}$$

$$OMO_t = \frac{1}{r_{Bt}} B_t - \frac{1}{r_{Bt}} B_{t-1} \tag{6}^1$$

$$\therefore r_{Bt} OMO_t = B_t - B_{t-1}$$

$$ECF_t = F_t - F_{t-1} \tag{7}$$

where B_t = the number of nominal bonds outstanding (taken as Consols with a coupon of £1 per annum).

r_{Bt} = the yield on Consols.

F_t = the net stock of foreign assets held by the UK public, the rate of interest on which is taken as exogenous.[2]

4. The response of the private sector

In order to explore the ensuing process of the determination of the money stock, it is necessary to examine the response of the private sector to market interventions undertaken by the authorities. For this purpose it may be helpful to sketch out a greatly simplified, heuristic model of portfolio adjustment in the private sector, distinguishing between the banking sector and the non-bank general public. The general public is at any moment of time confronted with a set of market prices and has some overall stock of wealth, which it distributes between the varying available assets, and liabilities, in proportions that depend, *inter alia*, on the relative yields on these assets. Subject to the important qualification that observable yields on variable price assets may not be good proxies for expected holding period yields, one can express the posited behaviour of the non-bank public in terms of a set of behavioural equations, expressing the desired distribution of assets as a function of the existing vector of interest rates, subject to its balance sheet constraint.

In this simplified model the public is taken to hold four assets, bank deposits (D),[3] currency (C), foreign assets (F), and bonds (B_p), and one liability, advances (A). Currency has a zero yield. Interest is paid on the other assets, and charged on advances. The foreign asset has a fixed capital value. We ignore the public's holdings of equity in the banking system. The current account of the balance of payments is taken to be zero. The balance sheet constraint (W represents wealth) can therefore be treated either as

$$W_t = PSD_t + D_{t-1} + C_{t-1} + F_{t-1} - A_{t-1} + \frac{1}{r_{Bt}} B_{pt-1} \tag{8}$$

---

[1] Readers will, of course, recognise that this is a discrete approximation to the real world condition of continuously changing interest rates.

[2] This ignores also purchases of UK assets by non-residents.

[3] For simplicity we have not distinguished current and deposit accounts separately. In any extension of the model this could, of course, be done, though it would be rather hard to provide any operational index of the yield on current accounts.

or

$$W_t = D_t + C_t + F_t - A_t + \frac{1}{r_{Bt}} B_{pt} \tag{8a}$$

The behavioural equations, showing the proportions in which the assets will be held, can all be written in the general form:

$$\frac{Xi}{W} = f(r_B, r_F, r_D, r_A, W, Z) \tag{9}$$

where Xi is the ith asset, r_B, r_F, r_D, r_A the yields on the respective assets, and Z is a vector of other independent variables.

The behaviour of the banks is somewhat more complex, even in this greatly simplified model. (For a more detailed analysis, see [18].) The general public, for the purpose of this exposition, could be treated as distributing a given wealth between assets in response to changes in interest rates, which rates they have to accept as price takers. The banks, however, in several important instances do not act as price takers. The provision of advances by banks is not undertaken in an open market, unlike for example government bonds, which are traded on an open market. Instead advances are usually arranged on an individual basis between client and banker. In such circumstances banks set the rates on advances, adjusted for risk and any other special considerations, and accommodate the demand for loans forthcoming at these selected rates, even in circumstances where there is considerable competition between banks.[1] Similarly banks set the rates which they offer on deposits and accept all money placed with them at these rates. There are, therefore, two sets of behavioural equations for the banks, one determining these desired rates, and the other desired quantities in those instances where they do act as price takers, in addition to the familiar balance sheet identity that liabilities must equal assets, as set out below:

$$D_t + K_t = R_t + \frac{1}{r_B} B_{Bt} + A_t \tag{10}$$

where D represents deposits, K non-deposit liabilities (largely capital and reserve),[2] R cash reserve items, B_b bonds held by the banks[3] and A advances.

The rate offered by banks on deposits is likely to be a function of the rates available on earning assets[4] and the liquidity of the banks' portfolio, as

[1] Indeed it is rather when banks are constrained, say by rate ceilings or cartel agreements, from varying advances' rates freely, that they tend to revert to the attempt to offer a larger or smaller quantity of advances to borrowers—for example by varying risk categories—at the constrained rate. The new system of credit control, introduced in the UK in September 1971, has relaxed the constraints on the banks' ability to vary advances' rates autonomously, and so gives greater verisimilitude to the simplified model outlined above. See also [25].

[2] A further definitional equation gives

$$K_t = K_{t-1} + \frac{1}{r_{bt}} B_{bt-1} - \frac{1}{r_{bt-1}} B_{bt-1}$$

[3] There is, of course, another identity that $B = B_p + B_b$

[4] As Jaffee points out [13 pp. 12 and 19–20], the extent of competition will influence the spread between the rates charged on loans and offered on deposits.

represented by the reserve ration (R/D) and, perhaps, also by the investment ratio (B_b/D). The rate to be charged on advances will reflect the rate available on alternative assets, and the liquidity of the portfolio,[1]

$$r_D = f\left(r_A, r_B, \frac{R}{D}, \frac{B_b}{D}\right) \tag{11}$$

and

$$r_A = f\left(r_B, \frac{R}{D}, \frac{B_b}{D}\right) \tag{12}$$

The banks, however, act as price takers in deciding on their desired holdings of reserve assets and bonds. Since r_D and r_A are given by the above equations, the volume of liquid assets (including both bonds and reserves) available to the banks at any time is determined and their only remaining choice is the distribution in which these are held. The relative yield on reserve assets, as compared with bonds, depends on the yield on bonds, r_B, since the yield on reserve assets is assumed to be fixed at zero, and on the level of deposits, which is taken as a proxy for the requirement for reserves to meet possible cash drains. Thus the demand for reserve assets becomes:

$$R = f(r_B, D, D - A) \tag{13}$$

where the first two arguments in the function represent factors determining the relative yield of bonds and reserves, and the final term represents the available liquid asset constraint. In practice, however, once D enters as an argument in this equation, it is far from clear how, if at all, the division of the counterpart bank assets between bonds and advances affects the demand for reserves.[2] Given the total of liquid assets, and the demand for reserves, the demand by banks for bonds emerges as a residual.

The authorities may also intervene to affect the demand for reserves by

[1] Monti points out [18, p. 179], that 'Under all the objective functions considered, the optimal asset selection rule is to equate the marginal revenues from loans and from bonds (and also from reserves). Given the assumption of a perfectly competitive bond market, this means that the marginal revenue from loans must be made equal to the rate of return on bonds.... Neither the deposit interest rate, nor the parameters of the deposit demand function have any influence on it'. Unlike Monti, however, we allow for uncertainty, approximately, by including ratios reflecting the liquidity of the portfolio as arguments in the equation determining advances' rates. This provides an indirect link between deposit and advances' rates. Consider the case in which deposit rates are so low relative to advances' rates, that banks' portfolios are tending to become less liquid. This will push up actual rates on advances (and the implicit certainty equivalent yields on reserves and bonds), and thus encourage upwards pressure on deposit rates. The upwards movements in both advances and deposit rates will reduce advances and increase deposits, thus leading to a restoration of desired liquidity.

[2] Indeed it may even be more likely that, for a given level of D, a larger holding of advances, fewer bonds, would raise the demand for reserves. This is assumed to be so, to a very slight extent, in the Appendix to this paper. I am not aware of studies examining the response of desired reserves to shifts in banks' asset composition.

requiring adherence to some minimum reserve ratio,[1] X, in which case the equation would become, after dropping the term $D-A$,

$$R = f(r_B, X, D) \qquad\qquad (13a)$$

Setting such a required ratio tends to reduce the amplitude of variation in the desired ratio, and thus tends to increase the predictability and, perhaps, also the speed of the adjustment of the system to changes in the authorities' policy instruments.

General equilibrium systems of this kind can be estimated empirically, if the necessary data are available. A number of general equilibrium models of the UK financial system have been constructed and estimated in recent years, for example by Norton [19, 20], Wymer [26] and Miller [17]. Of these the model constructed by Miller is closest in sympathy to the simplified model outlined here. Although such estimation can be done, and will, I believe, be done in the Bank in due course, it is beyond the scope of this paper.[2]

For one thing the necessary time series data giving the market value of assets held by the various sectors are only now beginning to become available in the UK. The technical econometric problems of estimating portfolio stock adjustment processes are complex. The size of any model, that would represent a sufficiently close approximation to the real world to avoid the need for patently unrealistic assumptions, would probably be so large that it would be difficult to manage.

Nevertheless in the Economic Section of the Bank we do believe that this is the right approach to take.[3] We are keen to foster the provision of better balance sheet data. We are putting a good deal of our research effort into econometric investigations of portfolio adjustment processes.

Because we think this approach is better than any other, a model of this kind often lies in our minds, even if we do not yet have accurate empirical estimates of the coefficients involved. For this reason it is worth while trying to explore the workings of such a system, even if this has to be done in somewhat qualitative terms.

For example, consider the effect of a change in the price of government debt brought about by the authorities. It is, perhaps, worth repeating that treating the authorities' intervention in this market in price rather than quantitative terms is without prejudice to the choice of intermediate targets and accords more closely with institutional realities. The first issue of importance is how this change in price will affect the expected holding period yield on government debt. If the authorities' actions can trigger off unforeseen

[1] Since the imposition of a required reserve ratio affects the liquidity of the balance sheet, X will also enter as an argument in equations (11) and (12).

[2] When this paper was presented at the AUTE Conference, it was accompanied by an Appendix setting out the model in greater detail, and providing a simulated solution to the system. This was largely the work of Miss M. Mayne. Considerations of length prevented the publication of the Appendix here, but copies can be obtained on request from the author, or Miss Mayne, at the Bank.

[3] I am prepared to hazard a prediction that I, or one of my successors, will be coming before you within the next few years to describe the Bank's general equilibrium stock adjustment model.

changes in expectations, then the effect of their intervention on the desired holdings of government debt will be to that extent unpredictable.

The second main issue is how far a shift into public sector bonds, induced by raising the holding period yield on such assets, will be financed by reducing net holdings of foreign assets[1] or by running down domestic monetary assets. To the extent that there was a much larger elasticity of substitution between UK public sector bonds and foreign assets than between UK public sector bonds and domestic monetary assets, the impact of open market operations would fall mainly on international capital flows and fluctuations in foreign exchange reserves rather than upon the domestic money stock.

Nevertheless an improvement in the relative attraction of bond yields should cause the public to wish to transfer some of its assets from deposits to bonds, thus putting pressure on the banks' reserves, since the transfer reduces bank cash reserves and deposits equally. In part this pressure may be absorbed by a reduction in the desired reserve ratio as the yield on bonds rises, but in a system in which limits are set by the imposition of a required reserve ratio this source of flexibility is likely to be limited. Instead the main response of banks is likely to be—given the behavioural equations (11)–(13)—to seek to regain equilibrium either by bidding for funds (raising r_d) and/or by selling bonds. Both these reactions in turn will lead to upwards pressure on advances rates (r_A).

Assuming for the purpose of this exposition that the authorities were content to allow the effect of the banks' sales of debt to be fully reflected in further price changes in bonds, then relative yields—abstracting from expectational complications—would move further in favour of bonds. The public would continue to move out of deposits into bonds. The banks' reserve position would only be assuaged through such sales by the reduction in deposits or as a result of rising capital inflows from abroad.

The banks will, however, to an extent depending on the relative cost of the alternatives as they appear to each individual bank, also respond to pressure by bidding more for deposits. This reaction is likely to have a stronger restorative impact on the banking system's reserve ratio, since it will shift relative yields in favour of deposits and against both public sector bonds and foreign assets.

So any attempt by the authorities to squeeze the banking system and to reduce deposits may be countered by the banks raising the stakes by bidding more for deposits. The question then is what determines how far the banks will and can go in matching the upwards pressure on rates.[2] Assuming that

---

[1] For this purpose a purchase of UK public sector debt by non-residents, either directly or via bank intermediation, may be treated as a reduction of UK net holdings of foreign assets.

[2] This might be taken as a rationale for the imposition of a Regulation Q. I would not accept this, however, on the grounds that movements in the money stock may, when unconstrained, represent a reasonably good indicator of the effects of policy, but do not have a direct causal impact on expenditures. Thus distortion of the monetary aggregates by direct controls prevents their use as a reliable indicator, without, very likely, having much effect upon total expenditures.

there are no direct constraints on rate movements, this largely depends on the interest elasticity of the public's demand for advances. If the demand for advances is interest inelastic, the banks will be able to match upwards pressure on rates, lifting both deposit and advances' rates, so that the authorities will have to press market intervention that much further to achieve a given reduction in deposits and advances.

To recapitulate the main argument up to this point, in the light of the somewhat sketchy general equilibrium model outlined, there would seem to be four main critical issues influencing the determination of the stock of money. These are (a) the size of the public sector deficit, (b) market reactions to the authorities' open market operations, (c) the elasticity of substitution between foreign and domestic assets and (d) the interest elasticity of demand for advances.

Consequently, the most useful statistical approach to the presentation of monetary data, for purposes of interpretation and analysis, is that which highlights these critical factors. Accordingly official monetary statistics, in the Bank of England *Quarterly Bulletin* and the CSO's *Financial Statistics*, contain tables (e.g. [1a, 5]) of that accounting identity in which changes in the money stock are expressed in terms of the following components: the public sector deficit, sales of public sector debt to the non-bank public, bank advances to the private sector and external financing of the public sector. As is obvious, this accounting identity does not of itself provide any theoretical explanation of the process of the determination of the money stock. But it should lead the user of the statistics to go further to enquire the reasons for the fluctuations in debt sales, in international capital flows, etc. One cannot display the complete working of the monetary system in a single table, but one can, at least, encourage users to ask the right kind of question about the more important behavioural relationships by one's choice of accounting identities.

5. Conclusion

None of these four critical issues, which affect the determination of the stock of money, appear in the money multiplier analysis. This is simply because virtually all the critical behavioural responses, and the great bulk of the basic process of portfolio stock adjustment in response to relative price changes, is subsumed—simply pushed out of sight—by the simple expedient of treating the high powered money base as given. The use of the money multiplier identity obscures, rather than illuminates, the fundamental nature of the process of the determination of the money stock.

The theory of the determination of the money stock ought to be treated as one branch of the more general theory of portfolio adjustment in response to relative price changes. Instead the use of the money multiplier identity short-circuits this approach—basically by taking H as given. And at its absolute worst, which is what is often taught to first year undergraduates, the money multiplier analysis does not explicitly involve or appear to require any interest rate changes at all. The process appears to be mechanical. There seems to be no need for the public or the banks to desire to hold voluntarily the volume of deposits established by the process. Instead they apparently cannot avoid treading the circular multiplier around and around (e.g. in period 1 the banks obtain ten in extra reserves and lend out nine, in order to restore their desired reserve ratio, then in period 2 they get back seven in cash from the public who have a currency/deposit ratio of 2/9, and of this the banks lend out . . . etc.). The only facets of their portfolio distribution choices which seem to affect the results at all are the public's desired cash/deposit ratio and the bank's desired reserve ratio.

All that is, to be blunt, absolute baloney. The determination of the money stock involves a process of general portfolio adjustment in response to relative interest rate changes. The time path of the process depends on the various speeds of adjustment of the various sectors to relative price changes. It is simply not true that the only way in which the banks and the public affect the process of the determination of the money stock is when they alter their reserve ratio and their cash/deposit ratio respectively. The process is not mechanical, and does not proceed in those awful circular series summing in the limit to the value of the multiplier.

The reason why this error of interpretation can continue to be perpetuated is that the assumption that H is fixed implies that the authorities can, and do, perfectly and instantaneously offset all the other behavioural responses of the banks and public, in order to maintain H at its desired level. As was pointed out earlier, in section 2, if you are prepared to swallow this, why not engorge the whole hog and assume that the authorities can also offset all variations in R/D and C/D in order to keep M at its desired level. Indeed it may be, in some circumstances, a fair approximation to the truth to argue that the monetary authorities are controlling the level of M. Nevertheless, taking H, or M, as given obscures the underlying process of monetary determination, and entirely abstracts from the problems that a Central Bank may face in trying to achieve such control.

References

1. BANK OF ENGLAND, *Quarterly Bulletin*. 'Analysis of Financial Statistics' published in each issue. (a) in **11**, no. 4 (Dec. 1971), Table J, pp. 468–9; (b) in *ibid*, Table L, cols 1–3, p. 472, and Table D, p. 460.
2. BANK OF ENGLAND, *Quarterly Bulletin*, **10**, no. 3 (1970), 320–6.
3. BRUNNER, K. and MELTZER, A. H. 'Some further investigations of demand and supply functions for money', *Journal of Finance*, **19**, no. 2, pt 1 (1964), 240–83.
4. CAGAN, P. *Determinants and Effects of Changes in the Stock of Money*, 1875–1960, Columbia University Press for NBER, 1965.
5. CENTRAL STATISTICAL OFFICE. *Financial Statistics*, no. 115 (Nov. 1971), 68–70, Tables 56–8.
6. COURCHENE, T. J. and KELLY, A. K. 'Money supply and money demand, An econometric analysis for Canada', *Journal of Money, Credit and Banking*, **111**, no. 2, pt 1 (1971), 230–1.
7. CROUCH, R. L. 'A model of the UK's monetary sector', *Econometrica* (July–Oct. 1967) pp. 392–418.
8. CROUCH, R. L. 'The genesis of bank deposits; New English version', *Bulletin of Oxford University Institute of Statistics, and Economics*, **27**, no. 3 (1965), 185–99.

9. FISHER, D. 'The objectives of British monetary policy, 1951–1964', *Journal of Finance*, Dec. 1968, pp. 821–31.
10. FISHER, D. *Money and Banking*, Irwin 1971.
11. FRIEDMAN, M. and SCHWARTZ, A. J. *A Monetary History of the United States, 1867–1960*, Princeton University Press for NBER, 1963.
12. GOODHART, C. 'British monetary policy, 1957–67', in *Monetary Policy in the Atlantic Community*, ed. K. Holbik, Federal Reserve Bank of Boston (forthcoming).
13. JAFFEE, D. M. 'The structure of models of financial intermediation', University of Essex, Discussion Paper no. 36, Oct. 1971 (mimeograph).
14. JORDAN, J. L. 'Elements of money stock determination', *Federal Reserve Bank of St Louis Review*, **51**, no. 10 (1969), 10–19.
15. KALDOR, N. 'Alternative theories of distribution', *Review of Economic Studies* (1955), pp. 83–100; reprinted in *Essays on Value and Distribution*, pp. 228–36.
16. KELIN, J. J. Discussion on D. Fand, 'A monetarist model of the monetary process', *Journal of Finance* (May 1970), p. 322.
17. MILLER, M. H. 'An empirical analysis of monetary policy in the United Kingdom from 1954–1965', unpublished PhD thesis, Yale University, 1971.
18. MONTI, M. 'A theoretical model of bank behaviour and its implications for monetary policy', *L'Industria Revista di Economia Politica*, no. 2 (1971), pp. 165–91.
19. NORTON, W. E. 'An econometric study of the United Kingdom monetary sector, 1955–1966', unpublished PhD thesis, University of Manchester, 1967.
20. NORTON, W. E. 'Debt management and monetary policy in the United Kingdom', *Economic Journal*, **79** (Sept. 1969), 475–94.
21. THYGESEN, N. *The Sources and the Impact of Monetary Changes: an empirical study of Danish experiences*, 1951–68, Copenhagen University Economic Institute, Study no. 17, 1971.
22. STEWART, K. 'Government debt, money and economic activity', *Federal Reserve Bank of St Louis Review*, **54**, no. 1 (1972).
23. TEW, B. 'The implications of Milton Friedman for Britain', *The Banker*, **119**, no. 522 (1969), 757–71.
24. WOOD, J. H. 'A model of Federal Reserve behaviour' in *Monetary Process and Policy*, ed. G. Horwich, Irwin, 1967.
25. WOOD, J. H. 'A model of commercial bank loan and investment behaviour', paper presented at the Money Study Group Conference, Bournemouth, Feb. 1972.
26. WYMER, C. Mimeographed papers, London School of Economics, 1970.

Analysis of the determination of the stock of money: Discussion

M. J. Artis

Charles Goodhart's paper has two main approaches. The first is a demolition job and the second begins the task of reconstruction.

The object of demolition is the high-powered money model of money creation. This is based on two behavioural assumptions, one concerning the banks' reserve-holding behaviour, the other concerning the non-bank public's desired holdings of the reserve asset; in addition, the supply of reserve assets is assumed to be exogenously given, generally as a result of the Central Bank's autonomous decision. In its simplest form, where reserve assets are synonymous with cash (that is, currency or deposits with the Central Bank), the model may be expressed as:

$$C = cD \qquad \text{(public demand for cash)} \qquad (1)$$

$$R = rD \qquad \text{(banks' demand for cash)} \qquad (2)$$

$$H = C + R \qquad \text{(exogenously determined supply of cash)} \quad (3)$$

$$M = C + D \qquad \text{(money supply definitional identity)} \qquad (4)$$

where C is currency in circulation, R is bank holdings of currency or demand deposits at the Central Bank, D is the level of bank deposits, M the supply of money, and H the exogenously determined level of high-powered money.

From this it follows that the money supply and the level of high-powered money are related as follows:

$$M = H\left(\frac{1+c}{r+c}\right) \qquad (5)$$

As Charles Goodhart's criticism of this way of looking at the money supply creation process is accomplished with considerable fervour, it is relevant to note three points about this model from the outset:

(*a*) the model, as expressed in (5) and the preceding equations appears in its simplest form. The behavioural equations (1) and (2) express a simple proportionality of the demand for cash to deposits; but it is quite possible to allow for more complicated (and presumably more realistic) behaviour without losing the flavour of the model. In a similar way, a level of greater generality may be attained by constructing a reaction function which would explain the Central Bank's determination of $\bar{H}$. Some, at least, of the criticism directed at the model may be regarded as criticism of its oversimplicity and to this extent it is worth pointing out that the model does permit of further elaboration.

(*b*) The general flavour of Charles Goodhart's criticism of this model is not new, but stems from the 'new view' school, the general thrust of whose ideas is to advance the substitution of more general equilibrium descriptions of financial processes for the truncated partial equilibrium processes represented by simple models such as this. Whilst this general endeavour clearly has great merit, it necessarily raises the question at what point the generalisation stops. This is closely linked with the next point.

(*c*) Models have their uses. The high-powered money model, in various degrees of elaboration, features in the pedagogy of monetary economics in a number of ways. For example, at its most basic level, the model underlines the distinction of 'cloakroom banking' from 'fountain pen money', and illustrates the need to control banks (in the sense of requiring some positive reserve-holding propensity); it can also be used to comment on the relative superiority of alternative definitions of reserve assets,[1] and on the nature of competition between banks and non-bank intermediaries. Any model abstracts from the confusion of 'reality' and it is probably not part of the purpose of Charles Goodhart's paper to state that the degree of abstraction implicit in the high-powered money model is in all its uses unforgiveably too great. On the other hand, he is concerned to argue that it provides not merely an inadequate but a positively misleading account of the process of money supply creation as it should be viewed in the UK today; this is surely true of the simple model, and although it seems to this commentator at least quite possible to teach the model with due emphasis on the need for elaboration and hence without seriously misinforming students (and this seems to be broadly the approach undertaken by Bain [2]), an attempt at a completely new approach is to be welcomed.

The obvious weakness of the model under attack is that interest rates are not explicitly included in it, and the strongest attack would be to show that the interest rate plays a key role both in determining H, and in entering into the 'true' functional relationships (1) and (2). As the paper stands, however, it criticises most strongly the assumption (3) that $\bar{H}$ is exogenously determined, asserting instead that Central Banks typically should be viewed as setting an interest rate. Little is said about the role of the interest rate in the behavioural equations (although this emerges in the new model proposed). This onesided emphasis is perhaps unfortunate since the proponent of the

---

[1] In this case, it should be noted, the analysis turns precisely upon the elaboration of more sophisticated demand functions for reserve assets, since one appealing way of deciding upon the superiority of one class of asset against another for purposes of formal designation as eligible reserve assets is that relative stability and simplicity of the demand functions be preferred to complicated and ill-understood relationships. (See J. M. Parkin's discussion of Wadsworth's paper in [3, pp. 222–7].)

high-powered money model could well argue that he was aware all along that changes in H were associated with changes in interest rates, indeed that he envisaged such changes as being brought about by open market operations. This is, surely, the normal background assumption. On the other hand, it is fair to say that economists have for some time recognised the need to incorporate interest rates in the demand functions for reserve assets, so that the next step forward is that taken by Charles Goodhart in proposing a more general model in which the assumption that H is exogenously given is relaxed.

The proposed model

Whatever the verdict on the first part of the paper, the alternative model proposed by Charles Goodhart needs to be assessed on its own merits. It is fair to say, though, that in one respect at least such an assessment cannot yet be made. As set out in detail in the Appendix, the model's parameters represent a stylised view of the true values, and for various reasons it will be some time before the full system can be empirically estimated. To take only one example, the model provides for the flexible setting of rates of interest on bank deposits and advances (its main novelty), but this is an empirical possibility only provided for us by the 'banking revolution' of September 1971; and we shall not be able to estimate the characteristics of this system until its operation has been evaluated over a reasonable period of time.

A feature of the model is that it combines together elements of the 'New View' of financial processes, where relative interest rates play a key role, with the old-style Bank of England/Central Statistical Office view of the factors determining money supply. (One thing that is clear is that the extreme form of this old view certainly represented a distortion of the process of money supply creation: see [1].) Thus, in the model presented the key exogenous policy variables are the public sector deficit, the bond rate and special deposits. Given the approach adopted, the manipulation of the model is very clearly set out and requires no further elucidation, though one point that might perhaps be noted is that the values of the reduced form multipliers listed in table 8 do involve substantial variation in the 'high-powered money multiplier' (as calculated from the ratio of $Dt + Ct/Rt + Ct$), according to the policy instrument change under consideration. This result is reassuring for the argument of the main paper, and it will be interesting to see how far it is sustained by the results of empirical estimation of the model especially when account is taken of the typical coordination of instruments in policy practice.

The constructive part of this paper amounts to a significant earnest of intent to explore the nature of a structural system in which the process of money supply creation can be seen as part of larger model in which the Bank's policy instruments and relative interest rates play a prominent role. But the proof of the pudding is in the eating, and the attainment of empirical results following this line of endeavour will be eagerly awaited.

References

1. ARTIS, M. J. and NOBAY, A. R. 'Two aspects of the monetary debate', *National Institute Economic Review*, **49** (Aug. 1969), 42–5.
2. BAIN, A. D. *The Control of the Money Supply*, Penguin, 1970.
3. CLAYTON, G., GILBERT, J. C. and SEDGWICK, R. eds. *Monetary Theory and Monetary Policy in the* 1970s, Oxford University Press, 1971.

15

A continuous disequilibrium econometric model of the domestic and international portfolio behaviour of the UK banking system[1]

Malcolm Knight

1. Introduction

This paper considers the behaviour of commercial banks in the United Kingdom in both domestic financial markets and the international market for Eurocurrency deposits.[2] The model which is specified and estimated attempts to answer such questions as the following: if the conditions of international supply and demand in the Eurocurrencies market are altered, what changes will take place in the UK banks' holdings of Eurocurrency deposits and advances *vis-à-vis* foreigners; what adjustments will occur in spot and forward exchange rates; and what (if any) effects will be felt on the level and structure of interest rates in the domestic financial markets of the UK?

Two links which may exist between the UK financial system and the rest of the world are considered in the theoretical model. The first is a direct link between the Eurocurrencies market and short-term domestic financial markets such as the market for local authority temporary debt. A second link arises from the possibility that the UK authorities may adjust their policy stance through changes in Bank rate and operations in the gilt-edged market in response to international factors such as changes in interest rates in foreign countries, or changes in (spot and forward) exchange rates, Eurocurrency yields etc. The direct link resulting from the transactions of the banks in domestic and international financial markets is the central theme of both the theoretical model and the econometric model which is derived from it and estimated. The link resulting from international influences on the policy responses of the authorities is considered in the discussion of the policy

---

[1] This study covers part of the research for a PhD thesis in the University of London. I am grateful to Professor Harry G. Johnson and Dr Clifford R. Wymer for their comments and suggestions. Any errors which remain are my own.

[2] The model discussed in this paper is part of a larger study which is concerned with the extent to which the financial sectors of the US and UK economies are linked to each other and to the rest of the world through the participation of banks in the two countries in the international markets for Eurocurrency deposits and loans. See M. D. Knight [16]*.

---

* Numbers in square brackets relate to References on p. 290.

subsystem of the theoretical model, but is not actually tested econometrically. In its Eurocurrency transactions, the UK banking sector (defined to include the overseas and foreign banks resident in the UK as well as the domestic banks) is assumed in the model to act mainly as an international financial intermediary, accepting Eurocurrency deposits from the rest of the world and holding a roughly similar quantity of claims on overseas residents. However, to the extent that the gross Eurocurrency liabilities of the UK banks are greater than gross foreign currency assets, some Eurocurrency borrowings may be transferred into sterling and invested in domestic securities. In this way changes in the yield in the Eurocurrencies market may affect certain markets within the UK financial system.

In view of the large number of behaviour units involved in international financial markets, and the lags in adjustment which may exist, it does not seem appropriate to maintain the usual simplifying assumption that there is full adjustment to equilibrium in all markets during each period. Thus, the model in this paper employs a recently developed technique for constructing and estimating continuous time dynamic models of financial markets in which disequilibrium portfolio adjustment processes determine actual holdings of securities by various sectors, and market adjustment processes determine interest rates in financial markets. Unlike most financial models, this approach does not require the system to be in equilibrium at the end of each discrete time period. Instead, continuous time non-attonnement processes are specified in which the adjustment functions depend on the excess supply or demand for securities by each sector, or on the excess of desired over actual interest rates. A discrete time approximation which maintains the structural form of the continuous model is then used to obtain full information maximum likelihood estimates of the parameters of the system.[1]

The theoretical model is designed to illustrate the possible relations between the banks' behaviour in two international markets (the markets for Eurocurrency deposits and advances), and the transactions of banks and other UK sectors in the foreign exchange market and several domestic financial markets (those for cash and money at call, Treasury and commercial bills, domestic deposits and advances, local authority temporary debt, and gilt-edged stock). The economy is divided into a banking sector, a private sector (composed of non-bank financial intermediaries, corporations and persons), a public sector (consisting of the central government and the monetary authorities), and an external sector.

Despite the high level of aggregation, however, the data currently available and the resulting limitations on the size of the estimated structural model imposed by the necessity of maintaining a reasonable number of degrees of freedom, render the theoretical model too large to be estimated by simultaneous techniques. Thus a smaller model designed to investigate the most interesting aspects of the full model is estimated. However, it seems best to describe the

[1] The specification of continuous disequilibrium financial models is discussed in detail in Wymer [21]. Wymer [22] derives the discrete approximation to the continuous system which is used in estimating the present model.

complete system first, so that the assumptions necessary to reduce the model to a size capable of estimation are apparent.

The theoretical model described below makes use of several assumptions which are also employed later in the estimated model. The first is that in all cases the adjustment follows the exponentially distributed lag form. Second, each adjustment equation is assumed to be a function of only one excess demand (or excess of desired over actual interest rate). On these assumptions, the adjustment functions will be second-order linear stochastic differential equations of the form:[1]

$$D^2 y(t) = \alpha\beta[\hat{x}(t) - x(t)] - \alpha D y(t) + u(t)$$

where $\hat{x}$, the (unobservable) desired level of x at time t, is assumed to be some linear function of variables exogenous to the decision-making unit specified by the function; D is the differential operator d/dt; and u is a stochastic disturbance term.

All of the adjustment functions in the theoretical model set out below and in the model derived from it and estimated in the last section are of this form. The model is thus a system of desired demand functions, adjustment functions, market identities, and portfolio identities.

2. The model

The sectors of the model (and their numbers) are:

1. Authorities
2. UK non-bank private sector
3. UK banks
4. Overseas residents

The notation of the model is:

(a) For security holdings, the letter denotes the type of security, while the subscript gives the sector which has issued or is holding the security. No subscript denotes a total holding.
(b) For interest rates, the letter subscript denotes the security to which the rate corresponds.
(c) A circumflex (^) over a variable denotes a desired value.
(d) When a security is held by only two sectors, an 's' superscript denotes the issuing sector's desired supply, while a 'd' superscript gives the other sector's desired demand.

---

[1] The assumption that each adjustment process responds with an exponentially distributed lag to a single excess demand implies that each adjustment equation in the model is of the form:

$$Dy(t) = \int_0^\infty \alpha e^{-\alpha\theta} \beta[\hat{x}(t - \theta) - x(t - \theta)] \, d\theta$$

Eliminating the integral and adding the disturbance term gives the second-order stochastic differential equation specified in the text. See Wymer [21].

All securities (*including* the Eurocurrency liabilities and claims of the UK banks) are valued in sterling. The term D in the adjustment functions is the differential operator d/dt. In the model set out below the disturbance terms are omitted for convenience.

Symbols of the model

The market for Eurocurrency deposits and advances

F_3 Eurocurrency deposit liabilities to foreigners of the UK banking sector (valued in sterling)

G_3 Eurocurrency advances to foreigners held by the UK banking sector (in sterling)

E_3 Net Eurocurrency liabilities to foreigners of the UK banking sector ($=F_3-G_3$)

r_F Acceptance rate on Eurodollar deposits by banks in London

r_G Yield on Eurodollar advances made by UK banks to overseas residents

Holdings of UK domestic securities

M_3 Cash in hand, balances with the Bank of England, and money at call and short notice (net) held by the banks

T Bills issued by the authorities and held by other sectors

T_2 Bills held by the private sector

T_3 Bills discounted by banks

L_3 'Liquid assets' (defined as cash and balances with the Bank of England, Treasury and commercial bills, and money at call) held by the aggregate banking sector

D_3 Sterling deposits of the banks (current and deposit accounts net of collections, inter-bank balances and 'other accounts')

B Total stock of UK government securities, excluding official holdings

B_2 UK government securities held by the non-bank private sector

B_3 UK government securities held by the banks

B_4 UK government securities held by overseas residents

A_3 Advances of the UK banks to the domestic private sector

N Total local authority temporary debt (excluding inter-authority holdings)

N_2 Local authority temporary debt held by the UK private sector

N_3 Local authority temporary debt held by the banks

UK interest rates and real variables

r_0 UK Bank rate

r_T UK Treasury Bill re-discount rate (market yield)

r_M Interest rate on call money (max)

r_B Gross redemption yield on long-term UK government securities

r_N Interest rate on local authority temporary debt (three months)

P Gross domestic product implicit price deflator

C_g, I_g, T_g UK government current spending on goods and services; investment; tax receipts

I Investment of the private sector

U UK unemployment rate (per cent)

EX Exports of goods and services

EI Imports of goods and services

ER UK official reserves of gold and foreign currency

Y Gross domestic product of the private sector

Exchange rates

x_0 Spot exchange rate: US dollars per pound sterling

x_T T-day forward exchange rate.

f Forward premium or discount on three-month forward US dollars against the pound (converted to an annual percentage)

The banking sector

The key adjustment functions around which the formal model is constructed are those for the behaviour of the banking sector[1] in domestic and international financial markets. The banks are assumed to have a portfolio of domestic assets and liabilities given by equation (1), and an international portfolio consisting of Eurocurrency liabilities and claims *vis-à-vis* overseas residents (equation (2)). These domestic and international portfolios are connected by the fact that, since the banks are able to transfer funds from the Eurocurrencies market into sterling assets, their net Eurocurrency deposit liabilities to foreigners, E_3, provide a source of funds which the banks invest in sterling securities. The aggregate (domestic and international) portfolio of the banking sector is given by:

$$L_3(t) = D_3(t) + E_3(t) - B_3(t) - N_3(t) - A_3(t) \tag{1}$$

[1] Since it is the relation between domestic and international financial markets rather than a complete description of the UK financial system which is of interest here, the definition of the UK banks is broader than that which is used in other studies. It includes, in addition to the domestic banks (the London and Scottish clearing banks), the accepting houses, overseas and foreign banks (the banks most active in the Eurocurrencies market) and the discount houses. Although this aggregation is unavoidable, it is unfortunate from several points of view. The fact that the aggregate sector contains at least three distinct classes of financial intermediaries implies that the behaviour of the sector will be less homogenous than would be the case at a lower level of aggregation. Some of the interesting behavioural relations which are lost in the process of aggregation are the transactions between the domestic banks and the discount houses in the markets for government securities, and in the components of 'liquid assets'; and changes in balances held between the clearing banks and the overseas and foreign banks. If sufficient data were available it would be preferable to disaggregate the banking sector into at least two subsectors—the domestic banks on the one hand and the overseas and foreign banks resident in the UK on the other. Such a disaggregation would be desirable because during the sample period of the model the domestic banks were bound by convention to maintain a different structure of liquid assets than the other banks, and because the overseas and foreign banks are more important participants in the Eurocurrencies market.

where

$$E_3(t) = F_3(t) - G_3(t) \tag{2}$$

First consider the domestic portfolio as a whole. During the sample period of the model, current accounts gained no interest, while the return on deposit accounts was tied, by agreement among the clearing banks, to the level of Bank rate which was determined by the authorities. Hence the banks could not attract domestic deposits by independently increasing the rates they paid.[1] The model assumes that total domestic deposits are determined exogenously to the banks by the UK private sector. The banks' problem of portfolio choice thus concerns their decision as to how to distribute their funds among 'liquid assets', government securities, and other investments. Liquid assets may be subdivided into cash (plus money at call) and bills discounted,

$$M_3(t) = L_3(t) - T_3(t) \tag{3}$$

The banks' behaviour towards the components of their liquid asset portfolio is described in equation (4). Since most of the call money is netted out of the aggregate banking sector because it is held between the banks and the discount houses, the small remaining amount of money at call is lumped into 'cash' and this total cash is assumed to be the residual security in the banks' liquid asset portfolio. Since the discount houses are included in the banking sector, and since they cover the tender of new Treasury Bills through a syndicated bid in addition to being the most active participants in the secondary market for bills, it is assumed that the strongest influence on the market yield on Treasury Bills will be the excess demand of the aggregate banking sector.

$$D^2 r_T(t) = \alpha_1 \beta_1 [\hat{T}_3(t) - T_3(t)] - \alpha_1 D r_T(t) \tag{4}$$

$$\hat{T}_3(t) = \gamma_{11} r_T(t) + \gamma_{12} r_M(t) + \gamma_{13} r_B(t) + \gamma_{14} D_3(t)$$

where

$$\alpha_1 \beta_1 < 0, \ \alpha_1 > 0; \ \gamma_{11} > 0, \ \gamma_{12} < 0, \ \gamma_{13} < 0, \ \gamma_{14} > 0$$

As indicated in equation (1), total liquid assets are viewed as the residual of the banks' longer-term domestic portfolio. Although the banking system as a whole will want to maintain a certain level of liquid assets, its individual subsectors have different motives for doing so. During the sample period of the model, the clearing banks were required by convention to maintain a specified ratio (28 per cent) of liquid assets to deposits. For the overseas

[1] It should be noted that the specification of bank portfolio behaviour in the model is based on the agreements and regulations which were in force during the period from 1962 to 1969. The announcement concerning 'competition and credit control', which was made by the Bank of England in May 1971, proposed that the clearing banks should abandon their agreement on the interest rate offered for domestic deposits. The announcement also proposed that the banks should adhere to a new minimum ratio of 'specified reserve assets' to domestic deposits. The inclusion of these recent institutional changes in the model would alter the specification of certain equations for the portfolio behaviour of the banks.

and foreign banks, no such liquid asset requirement existed,[1] but these banks presumably sought to maintain some minimum amount of liquid assets which was related to their domestic deposit liabilities, and perhaps also to their net Eurocurrency liabilities. In both cases, however, there exist alternative assets, such as short-term UK government securities, having similar liquidity and higher yield, which are not included in conventional 'liquid assets'. Thus, there is an opportunity cost in holding liquid assets in excess of the minimum prescribed either by convention or by some precept of 'prudent banking'. Equation (5) assumes, therefore, that the banks attempt to maintain their liquid assets at the desired level by adjusting their holdings of UK government securities.

$$D^2B_3(t) = \alpha_2\beta_2[\hat{L}_3(t) - L_3(t)] - \alpha_2DB_3(t) \tag{5}$$

$$\hat{L}_3(t) = \gamma_{21}r_T(t) + \gamma_{22}r_G(t) + \gamma_{23}r_B(t) + \gamma_{24}E_3(t) + \gamma_{25}D_3(t)$$

where

$$\alpha_2\beta_2 < 0, \ \alpha_2 > 0; \ \gamma_{21} > 0, \ \gamma_{22} < 0, \ \gamma_{23} < 0, \ \gamma_{24} > 0, \ \gamma_{25} > 0$$

Among the other securities which the banks hold, one which is of special interest to this study is local authority debt. In terms of the traditional analysis of the UK financial system, concentration on this market may appear somewhat novel, but as Sayers [18] has noted, the market in short loans to local government authorities 'developed rapidly from 1956 onwards and since the early sixties has become, in terms of sums traded, probably the largest of the money markets' (pp. 322–3). The growth of the market for local authority temporary debt has taken place at a time when the activities of the overseas and foreign banks in the market for Eurocurrency deposits and loans were also increasing rapidly, and it is often implied that the transactions in the two markets may be related.[2] The market for local authority temporary debt is included in the present model in order to determine whether it has significant links with the Eurocurrencies market. Since the local authorities' supply of temporary debt is unlikely to be responsive to the interest rate on it (at least in the short run), the total stock of debt is assumed to be set exogenously by the local authorities. Both the clearing banks and the overseas and foreign banks are substantial holders of local authority debt, so that the market rate of interest on these securities is assumed to adjust primarily to their excess demand.

$$D^2r_N(t) = \alpha_3\beta_3[\hat{N}_3(t) - N_3(t)] - \alpha_3Dr_N(t) \tag{6}$$

$$\hat{N}_3(t) = \gamma_{31}r_T(t) + \gamma_{32}r_F(t) + \gamma_{33}r_N(t) + \gamma_{34}f(t)$$

$$+ \gamma_{35}r_G(t) + \gamma_{36}D_3(t)$$

[1] The non-clearing banks had no obligation to maintain specified cash or liquid asset ratios during the period 1962 to 1969. In February 1968, however, the Bank of England announced a 'Cash deposits scheme' under which these banks could be called upon to hold a minimum proportion of their sterling and net foreign currency liabilities as cash deposits with the Bank of England. The competition and credit control announcement of May 1971 implies further changes in the institutional arrangements under which the non-clearing banks operate.

[2] See for example, Sayers [18], pp. 319–24, and R. N. Cooper [11], p. 122.

where

$$\alpha_3\beta_3 < 0,\ \alpha_3 > 0;$$

$$\gamma_{31} < 0,\ \gamma_{32} < 0,\ \gamma_{33} > 0,\ \gamma_{34} < 0,\ \gamma_{35} < 0,\ \gamma_{36} > 0$$

If the banks' holdings are related to their Eurocurrency liabilities and claims, Eurodollar interest rates and the forward discount on sterling should be significant explanatory variables in their desired demand function for local authority debt; and changes in Eurodollar rates and exchange rates will influence the local authorities' rate through the banks' adjustment function.

International Eurocurrency portfolio of the UK banks

We now turn from the UK banks' domestic behaviour to examine their transactions in the international market for Eurocurrency deposits.[1] The UK banks (especially the overseas and foreign banks located in London) are assumed to be leading international financial intermediaries in the market for Eurocurrency deposits and advances. The Eurocurrency portfolio of the banks is given by equation (2).

The total stock of Eurocurrency deposits lent to the UK banks is assumed to be determined exogenously to the model by Euro-deposit holders outside the UK. The banks must take this level as given, but they can alter the acceptance rate, r_F, which they are willing to pay on their Eurocurrency deposits according to their excess supply of these liabilities.[2]

---

[1] Although these deposits may be denominated in a number of currencies (Deutschmarks, Swiss francs, Guilders, etc.), by far the largest proportion are denominated in US dollars. Discussions with merchant bankers in the City indicated that there is substantial arbitrage between the markets for different Eurocurrencies. Thus, if the interest rate on three-month Eurodollars were to increase, the yield on (for example) Eurodeutschmarks of the same maturity discounted for the cost of forward cover would come to equal the new Eurodollar yield 'in a matter of hours'. Since the arbitrage processes are rapid, the model assumes that all Eurocurrency deposits, whatever their currency of denomination, can be viewed as a single security denominated in US dollars and bearing a yield equal to the Eurodollar rate.

[2] Since Eurocurrency deposits are assumed to be denominated in US dollars, the sterling value of the banks' Eurocurrency deposits and advances will change in proportion to changes in the spot sterling–dollar exchange rate. Although the UK banks may be interested in the sterling value of their net Eurocurrency liabilities, their behaviour towards their gross Eurocurrency liabilities and claims will be related to the dollar value of these quantities. In principle, the difficulties created by this difference in valuation are trivial, since the desired demand and adjustment functions for Eurocurrencies can simply be specified in terms of dollars and then converted into sterling for the purposes of satisfying the Eurocurrency portfolio identity (which is valued in sterling) by defining any dollar quantity B_i^* to equal the sterling quantity B_i times the spot exchange rate,

$$B_i^* \equiv B_i . x_0$$

Unfortunately for econometric work, if the spot exchange rate is allowed to fluctuate, the above equation is non-linear in variables, and cannot be introduced as an identity in the full information maximum likelihood estimation procedure. The solution adopted here is to value Eurocurrency liabilities and claims in sterling, but to include the spot exchange rate as a valuation dummy in the desired demand functions for F_3 and G_3.

$$D^2 r_F(t) = \alpha_4 \beta_4 [\hat{F}_3(t) - F_3(t)] - \alpha_4 D r_F(t) \tag{7}$$

$$\hat{F}_3(t) = \gamma_{41} r_F(t) + \gamma_{42} r_N(t) + \gamma_{43} f(t) + \gamma_{44} r_T(t)$$

$$+ \gamma_{45} r_G(t) + \gamma_{46} x_0(t)$$

where

$$\alpha_4 \beta_4 > 0, \ \alpha_4 > 0;$$

$$\gamma_{41} < 0, \ \gamma_{42} > 0, \ \gamma_{43} < 0, \ \gamma_{44} > 0, \ \gamma_{45} > 0, \ \gamma_{46} < 0$$

The banks may then determine the level of their Eurocurrency loans to overseas residents on the basis of the amount of deposits which they receive and relative yields (discounted for forward cover) in financial markets both within the UK and abroad. Thus the other adjustment function for the UK banks' participation in the Eurocurrencies market can take one of several possible forms. It is considered that the most likely possibility is that the banks are concerned primarily with their transactions as international financial intermediaries in the markets for Eurocurrency liabilities and claims, rather than on the amount of Eurocurrency net switching which they will do to augment their domestic portfolio. In this case, they will probably adjust their actual Eurocurrency advances to overseas residents in response to their excess demand for these assets:

$$D^2 G_3(t) = \alpha_5 \beta_5 [\hat{G}_3(t) - G_3(t)] - \alpha_5 D G_3(t) \tag{8}$$

$$\hat{G}_3(t) = \gamma_{51} r_N(t) + \gamma_{52} r_F(t) + \gamma_{53} f(t) + \gamma_{54} r_G(t) + \gamma_{55} F_3(t)$$

where

$$\alpha_5 \beta_5 > 0, \ \alpha_5 > 0; \ \gamma_{51} < 0, \ \gamma_{52} < 0, \ \gamma_{53} > 0, \ \gamma_{54} > 0, \ \gamma_{55} > 0$$

Since any Eurocurrency liabilities to foreigners which are non 'on-lent' to overseas residents in this way must, by definition, be 'switched' into sterling, E_3 (Eurocurrency net liabilities) is the residual of the banks' international Eurocurrencies portfolio and provides a stock of sterling funds which enters into their sterling balance sheet, augmenting their holdings of UK domestic securities. In the structure postulated above, however, the amount of 'Eurocurrency net switching' does not arise from the fact that the banks have some desired amount of *net* Eurocurrency liabilities which they wish to invest in sterling securities. Rather, it is the resultant of the banks' overall behaviour towards their international Eurocurrency portfolio.[1]

[1] It is also possible that the banks are primarily concerned with their Eurocurrency net-switched position. This alternative implies that equation (8) would be replaced by one in which the banks adjust their *net* Eurocurrency liabilities, E_3, in response to their excess demand for the amount of funds from the Eurocurrencies market which they wish to invest in UK domestic securities. In this case G_3, rather than E_3, would be determined by equation (2).

The distinction between these alternative specifications can be seen clearly if it is described in the terminology of the literature on international short-term capital flows. Since E_3 represents the stock of net Eurocurrency liabilities, DE_3 is the (instantaneous) change in net Eurocurrency liabilities, or in other words, the short-term capital flow between the UK financial system and the Eurocurrencies market. The question is whether these capital flows are the result of the banks' generalised portfolio

The foreign exchange market

Since changes in the net Eurocurrency liabilities to foreigners of the UK banks involve transfers of funds from foreign currency into sterling (or vice versa), they imply transactions in the market for foreign exchange. To the extent that their gross dollar liabilities do not equal their claims, therefore, the UK banks bear an exchange risk if they do not cover their net foreign currency position by transactions in the relevant forward market. Virtually all such transfers by the UK banks are covered against exchange risk by spot-forward 'swaps'. Thus, for example, if the banks transfer funds from the Euro-dollar market to invest in local authority three-month loans, they will have to sell dollars for sterling in the spot market. At the same time they will engage in a forward contract to sell a quantity of sterling (equal to the amount switched into local authority loans plus accrued interest) in exchange for dollars. In this way, the dollar value of the banks' net Eurocurrency liabilities is unaffected by any changes in the exchange rate during the three-month period in which they have these funds invested in sterling assets.

There will be a yield or cost on this hedging, depending on the relation between the spot exchange rate x_0 (defined as dollars per pound sterling) and the T-day forward rate: x_T. Thus, at any point in time, the profitability of such 'covered interest arbitrage' transactions between the Eurodollar market and domestic UK securities markets will depend not only on the interest rates prevailing in the two markets, but also on the yield or cost on forward cover as determined by the difference between the prevailing spot and three-month forward exchange rates. This is introduced into the model by assuming that, in determining the cost or yield on their covered net foreign currency position, the UK banks take account of the 'implicit interest rate' $f(t)$, which expresses the forward premium on foreign currency as an annual yield:[1]

(a)
$$f(t) = \left[\frac{x_0(t) - x_T(t)}{x_0(t)}\right] \frac{360}{T} \cdot 100$$

If the UK banks can switch their portfolios between sterling and Euro-currency assets on a covered basis, then the forward premium on foreign exchange—as well as interest rates—will enter their desired demand and supply functions for certain domestic and international securities. It is for this reason that f, the three-month forward premium on the dollar, is assumed to enter

[1] For example, if the current spot exchange rate (defined as dollars per pound) is 0·25 per cent above the current three-month forward exchange rate, then the forward premium on dollars is 0·25 per cent in three months or 1 per cent per year. This implies that to earn a covered rate of return on a sterling asset which is equal to the yield on its Eurocurrency advances, a bank must find a sterling security whose nominal yield is 1 per cent more than that on the Eurocurrency asset.

behaviour as in (8), or whether the banks operate specifically to stimulate capital flows. In this study the former specification is considered more plausible. However, the latter specification, in which short-term capital movements are the result of a single adjustment function, is more closely related to existing empirical studies of international capital flows. See Stein [19].

as an explanatory variable in the banks' demands and supplies of those securities most closely related to their international transactions, so that changes in, f, give rise to changes in the banks' holdings of local authority debt and Eurocurrency liabilities and claims.

At the same time, if the banks are significant transactors on their own account in the foreign exchange market, the short-term capital movements which their portfolio adjustments stimulate between UK financial markets and the Eurocurrencies market will also have some effect on the forward premium on foreign exchange. This simultaneous interdependence between Eurocurrency net-switching and changes in the forward premium on foreign currency implies that if net Eurocurrency liabilities are assumed endogenous to the structural model, 'f' should be regarded as endogenous also. Ideally, therefore, one would like to specify desired demand and supply functions for foreign exchange, and adjustment functions to represent the disequilibrium behaviour of the spot and forward exchange rates. The level of the three-month forward premium could then be derived from these two endogenous variables by the identity (a), or the spot and forward exchange rates could themselves be introduced into the banks' desired supply and demand functions. Unfortunately for the model, this cannot be done because statistics on the quantities traded in the UK foreign exchange market are not published.

The model attempts to circumvent this problem by postulating a single adjustment function to represent the complicated behaviour of the foreign exchange market. To do this, it is first assumed that the level of the spot exchange rate is fixed exogenously to the model by the demands and supplies of exporters and importers, and by the authorities. Given the level of the spot exchange rate, the level of the forward premium on foreign currency is determined by the forward rate. Although there will be a different forward rate corresponding to the maturity date of each forward exchange contract made, the model takes the three-month forward premium for the dollar vis-à-vis sterling as representative, on the assumption that substantial arbitrage tends to equalise the forward premium on different maturities. The behaviour of the different groups of transactors is not explicitly specified. It is simply assumed that they have in mind some expected level $f^e(t)$ of the three-month forward premium—formulated on the basis of current levels of interest rates in the UK, the Eurocurrencies market, and abroad, the level of the spot exchange rate, and the balance of trade; and that they enter into forward exchange commitments on the basis of these expectations. The actual forward premium is then assumed to adjust with an exponentially distributed lag to the difference between the expected and actual forward premium. In this way, the adjustment function which describes the changes in the forward premium on foreign exchange can be expressed in a way analogous to the other equations of the model as a second-order differential equation.

$$D^2 f(t) = \alpha_6 \beta_6 [f^e(t) - f(t)] - \alpha_6 D f(t) \qquad (9)$$

$$\alpha_6 \beta_6 > 0, \ \alpha_6 > 0$$

where the expected forward premium might be formed as follows:

$$f^e(t) = \gamma_{61} r_T(t) + \gamma_{62} r_F(t) + \gamma_{63} r_N(t) + \gamma_{64} x_0(t)$$

$$+ \gamma_{65}[EX - EI](t) + \gamma_{66} ER(t)$$

$$\gamma_{61} > 0, \; \gamma_{62} < 0, \; \gamma_{63} > 0, \; \gamma_{64} < 0, \; \gamma_{65} < 0, \; \gamma_{66} < 0$$

This is a highly oversimplified formulation of the complicated behaviour in the foreign exchange market, but it may serve to provide some tentative insights as to the major determinants of the forward rate. It should be noted, however, that the form of the adjustment function specified above, in which the actual forward premium adjusts to the difference between the expected and actual level, cannot be distinguished econometrically from the case in which some sector has a desired level of the forward premium and enters into the market in response to discrepancies between its desired level and the actual forward premium. This point is important because during the period from November 1964 to November 1967, the UK authorities supported the rate on forward sterling, keeping the forward premium on foreign currency down to a very small figure.[1]

The private sector

Since the securities held by the banks are traded on markets in which other sectors of the UK economy participate, a change in some other sector's holdings of certain securities may induce the banks to readjust their portfolios. If these changes involve readjustments between domestic and international holdings, short-term capital flows between the UK economy and the Eurocurrencies market will occur. Thus, although our main interest is in the portfolio of the banks, brief reference should be made to the equations of the model which specify the behaviour of the private sector in several financial markets.

The private sector's holdings of bills and local authority debt will probably respond to its excess demands for these securities, especially if it is the transactions of the banks which have the strongest influence on their yields.

$$D^2 T_2(t) = \alpha_7 \beta_7 [\hat{T}_2(t) - T_2(t)] - \alpha_7 D T_2(t) \tag{10}$$

$$\hat{T}_2(t) = \gamma_{71} r_0(t) + \gamma_{72} r_T(t) + \gamma_{73} r_N(t) + \gamma_{74} Y(t) + \gamma_{75} D_3(t)$$

where

$$\alpha_7 \beta_7 > 0, \; \alpha_7 > 0; \; \gamma_{71} < 0, \; \gamma_{72} > 0, \; \gamma_{73} < 0, \; \gamma_{74} > 0, \; \gamma_{75} > 0$$

$$D^2 N_2(t) = \alpha_8 \beta_8 [\hat{N}_2(t) - N_2(t)] - \alpha_8 D N_2(t) \tag{11}$$

$$\hat{N}_2(t) = \gamma_{81} r_0(t) + \gamma_{82} r_B(t) + \gamma_{83} r_N(t) + \gamma_{84} D_3(t)$$

where

$$\alpha_8 \beta_8 > 0, \; \alpha_8 > 0; \; \gamma_{81} < 0, \; \gamma_{82} < 0, \; \gamma_{83} > 0, \; \gamma_{84} > 0$$

---

[1] Bank of England [3], p. 39. Since the devaluation, however, the authorities appear to have allowed the forward premium on foreign currency to be determined by market forces.

10

Since the banks' holdings of UK government securities are concentrated in the short-term maturities, and since changes in their holdings of these securities are assumed to respond to their excess demand for liquid assets, the private sector is assumed to exert a dominant influence on the interest rate for long-term government stock.

$$D^2 r_B(t) = \alpha_9 \beta_9 [\hat{B}_2(t) - B_2(t)] - \alpha_9 D r_B(t) \tag{12}$$

$$\hat{B}_2(t) = \gamma_{91} r_0(t) + \gamma_{92} r_T(t) + \gamma_{93} r_B(t) + \gamma_{94} r_N(t)$$
$$+ \gamma_{95} D_3(t) + \gamma_{96} Y(t)$$

where

$$\alpha_9 \beta_9 < 0, \; \alpha_9 > 0;$$

$$\gamma_{91} < 0, \; \gamma_{92} < 0, \; \gamma_{93} > 0, \; \gamma_{94} < 0, \; \gamma_{95} > 0, \; \gamma_{96} > 0$$

The requirement that the adjustment functions of the model should respond to a single excess demand gives rise to some difficulty in specifying the level of advances. Because advances are granted on the overdraft system, and because the interest charged on advances is also tied to Bank rate, it might be plausible to assume that the level of advances is determined by the demand of the non-bank private sector. On the other hand, the fact that the authorities have sought at times to limit bank credit through quantitative restrictions on the domestic advances of both the domestic and overseas and foreign banks[1] provides a counter argument for regarding the level of advances as determined by constraints on the banks' desired supply. But the recurrent difficulties of the banks in meeting these limits suggests that an overdraft system is not conducive to this form of monetary control. Wymer [21] found that although his study covered periods of restriction, the specification of advances as demand determined was more consistent with the data than the alternative formulation. Thus the level of advances is assumed to adjust to the excess demand for overdrafts by the private sector.

$$D^2 A_3(t) = \alpha_{10} \beta_{10} [\hat{A}^d_3(t) - A_3(t)] - \alpha_{10} D A_3(t) \tag{13}$$

$$\hat{A}^d_3(t) = \gamma_{101} r_0(t) + \gamma_{102} EX(t) + \gamma_{103} I(t)$$

where

$$\alpha_{10} \beta_{10} > 0, \; \alpha_{10} > 0; \; \gamma_{101} < 0, \; \gamma_{102} > 0, \; \gamma_{103} > 0$$

Since the currency holdings of the public are neglected, the most liquid asset in the private sector's portfolio is deposits, and these are viewed as the residual asset of the private sector. Equation (14) gives an approximation to the identity which determines the level of deposits:

$$D[D_3(t)] = D A_3(t) + D[ER(t)] + C_g(t) + I_g(t) - T_g(t) \tag{14}$$
$$- D B_2(t) - D N_2(t) - D T_2(t)$$

---

[1] The non-clearing banks were brought within the scope of the quantitative limit on bank lending in the spring of 1965. Early in 1967, when the clearing and Scottish banks were temporarily released from the obligation to observe this limit, the authorities did not lift the similar restrictions on other banks. See Bank of England [2], p. 166.

The authorities

The final adjustment functions of the model represent the policy responses of the UK authorities. Since the model is primarily concerned with the effect that international factors may have on these responses, the policy instruments which the model considers are those for Bank rate and for the total stock of UK government securities. It is assumed that these policy variables are adjusted according to the difference between the level desired by the authorities and their actual current level. In setting the level of their policy instruments, the authorities will respond to targets in the domestic economy such as the rate of unemployment, the price level etc. In addition, however, in conditions of even limited capital mobility, they may choose to use these instruments to 'protect reserves' or to 'reduce the pressure on sterling'. Viewing this in the context of the transactions of the UK banks in the market for Eurocurrency deposits, it has been noted above that an increase in the banks' net Eurocurrency liabilities involves a short-term capital flow from the Eurocurrencies market into the UK economy. Such a short-term capital flow implies a spot purchase of sterling for dollars, and thus tends to increase UK official reserves of gold and foreign exchange. Since the banks will tend to increase their net Eurocurrency liabilities at times when the covered yield on sterling securities rises relative to the yield on the banks' Eurocurrency claims, it is possible for the authorities to attempt to bolster official reserves by using bank rate policy and operations in the gilt-edged market. To the extent that these changes in policy increase the differential between UK interest rates and yields abroad, they may induce short-term capital inflows which tend to increase exchange reserves.[1] Such an effort by the authorities to maintain or increase the differential between domestic and international interest rates implies that the levels of Eurocurrency interest rates, foreign interest rates, and official reserves will enter into their policy decisions.

Radcliffe [10] described changes in the Bank rate as 'the traditional weapon for protecting reserves'. For some time, however, the authorities have felt that Bank rate has little direct influence on short-term capital movements to London, and have tended to rely on its announcement effects. Thus, if the authorities wish to influence the international interest differential directly, they must reinforce bank rate changes by appropriate operations in the market for government securities in order to raise (or lower) UK yields. In this case, the authorities' desired level for the total stock of government securities (excluding official holdings) will also respond to the international factors mentioned above. It should be noted that if the UK banks cover their net Eurocurrency liabilities by operations in the forward exchange market, then it is the *covered* differential between domestic and international interest rates which will influence their portfolio behaviour. In this case, the effectiveness of the authorities' policy to alter interest rate differentials between the UK and

[1] Radcliffe [10], para. 681 to para. 707. As Radcliffe noted at an earlier stage (1958–59) of the return to convertibility, the authorities 'attach some importance to keeping London rates in line with rates in other centres [and] assume that any prolonged or marked divergence would lead to a movement of funds into or out of sterling'.

abroad will depend on the resulting changes in the sterling forward discount, or in other words, on the behaviour of the spot and forward exchange rates.

Since the stock of Treasury Bills is determined by the short-term borrowing needs of the Exchequer, no adjustment function for total bills is specified for the authorities. The level of non-official holdings of UK government securities is set in response to the excess supply of the authorities, who also determine Bank rate according to the excess of the rate over the desired level.[1]

$$D^2B(t) = \alpha_{11}\beta_{11}[\hat{B}(t) - B(t)] - \alpha_{11}DB(t) \tag{15}$$
$$\hat{B}(t) = \gamma_{111}r_B(t) + \gamma_{112}r_T(t) + \gamma_{113}ER(t) + \gamma_{114}U(t)$$
$$+ \gamma_{115}I_g(t)$$

where

$$\alpha_{11}\beta_{11} > 0, \ \alpha_{11} > 0;$$
$$\gamma_{111} < 0, \ \gamma_{112} > 0, \ \gamma_{113} > 0, \ \gamma_{114} > 0, \ \gamma_{115} > 0$$

$$D^2r_0(t) = \alpha_{12}\beta_{12}[\hat{r}_0(t) - r_0(t)] - {}_{12}Dr_0(t) \tag{16}$$
$$\hat{r}_0(t) = \gamma_{121}ER(t) + \gamma_{122}r_F(t) + \gamma_{123}f(t) + \gamma_{124}U(t)$$

where

$$\alpha_{12}\beta_{12} > 0, \ \alpha_{12} > 0; \ \gamma_{121} < 0, \ \gamma_{122} > 0, \ \gamma_{123} > 0, \ \gamma_{124} < 0$$

Market identities
The final three equations which close the model are the market identities for local authority temporary debt, bills, and UK government securities:

$$N_3(t) = N(t) - N_2(t) \tag{17}$$
$$T_3(t) = T(t) - T_2(t) \tag{18}$$
$$B_2(t) = B(t) - B_3(t) - B_4(t) \tag{19}$$

The full model is, therefore, a system of twelve adjustment functions and seven identities in which the following variables are determined: four domestic interest rates (Bank rate, Treasury Bill, local authorities, longer-term government debt); the Eurodollar deposit rate offered by UK banks; eleven domestic securities holdings; two international security holdings (G_3, E_3); and the forward discount on sterling vis-à-vis the dollar in the foreign exchange market.

3. Estimation of the model
The theoretical model can be viewed as an *a priori* hypothesis concerning the simultaneous structure of disequilibrium portfolio adjustments by the

[1] Since the authorities alter Bank rate at discrete intervals rather than continuously, it might be argued that the continuous adjustment function in (16) is inferior to a discrete formulation of the authorities' changes in Bank rate. However, since the authorities have the opportunity to alter Bank rate at weekly intervals, they can review their decision about the level of this rate more or less continuously. Further, the time interval between successive reconsiderations of the level of Bank rate is substantially less than the (quarterly) observation period of the estimated model. Thus, for purposes of estimation, the continuous specification of the Bank rate adjustment function seems to be at least as good as a discrete formulation.

UK banks and other sectors in both the international Eurocurrencies market and domestic financial markets within the UK. The purpose of the econometric work of this section is to obtain estimates of the model, and to determine whether significant relations exist between the banks' portfolio adjustments in the two markets.

Limitations on the data available, however, make it possible to estimate only a subsystem of the full model. The estimated system is derived by omitting three sets of equations from the theoretical model. In the first place, the two equations representing the policy responses of the authorities are eliminated, so that Bank rate and the total stock of government securities are exogenous to the system. The equations relating to the UK private sector's holdings of deposits and advances are also removed so that these holdings are determined outside the model. Finally, since we are not interested in the banks' behaviour towards the components of their liquid asset portfolio, the liquid assets of the banks are viewed as a single security. This allows the adjustment function for bills to be neglected, so that only the behaviour of the banks towards the level of their total liquid assets needs to be considered. These assumptions would be inappropriate if the purpose of the model were to describe the behaviour of the UK financial system itself. In the present context, however, the limited amount of data and the complexity of the system make it necessary to focus on that portion of the banks' aggregate balance sheet which is likely to be most closely related to international transactions.

The estimated model consists of seven adjustment functions and four identities which determine: the banks' holdings of liquid assets, government securities, local authority debt, net Eurocurrency liabilities to foreigners, and gross Eurocurrency claims on foreigners; UK private sector holdings of local authority debt and government securities; the interest rates on local authority debt, UK government securities and Eurodollar deposits; the forward premium on the US dollar versus sterling.

The sample period of the model extends over twenty-nine quarters from Q4 1962 to Q4 1969. The data were deseasonalised using a seasonal index of deviations of quarterly means about the mean of each variable. Following Wymer [22] a discrete time approximation which maintains the structural form of the continuous model was derived, and the estimates presented are for the approximation to the continuous system.[1] Three estimators were used:

---

[1] When the desired demand functions have been substituted into the adjustment functions, a second-order system such as the model specified here can be written generally as

$$D^2 y(t) = A_1 y(t) + A_2 D y(t) + B z(t) + u(t)$$

where D is again the differential operator, $y(t)$ is a vector of n endogenous variables, $z(t)$ is a vector of m exogenous variables, $u(t)$ is a vector of disturbances, A_1 and A_2 are matrices of order n and B is a matrix of dimension $n \times m$.

Wymer [22] has demonstrated that this continuous system can be approximated by a discrete system of the form

$$\Delta^2 y_t = \bar{A}_1 M^2 y_t + \bar{A}_2 M \Delta y_t + M^2 \bar{B} z_t + e_t$$

where the operators are

$$\Delta = \frac{1}{\delta}(1-L), \quad M = \frac{1}{2}(1+L) \text{ and } L x_t = x_{t-1}$$

two-stage least squares, three-stage least squares, and full information maximum likelihood. Only the full information maximum likelihood estimates are presented. The structural estimates of the discrete approximation to the continuous model are presented in Table 15.1. The numbers in brackets are the standard errors of the estimated coefficients.

The restriction that each adjustment equation is a function of only one excess demand is sufficient to allow the identification of the behavioural parameters. The estimates of the behavioural parameters of the approximation to the continuous system (and their standard errors) are presented in Table 15.2. In this table the estimated equations of the approximation are written using the notation of the continuous system.

TABLE 15.1. *Estimated structural model*[1]
Quarterly data: Q4 1962 to Q4 1969

(The numbers in brackets are the standard errors of the coefficients.)

1. $\Delta^2 B_3 = -5\cdot44\Delta B_3 + 5\cdot56 L_3 - 0\cdot85 E_3 + 1\cdot07 r_B + 0\cdot28 r_G - 2\cdot10 D_3$
   $(1\cdot54)\quad(1\cdot49)\quad(1\cdot76)\quad(0\cdot48)\quad(0\cdot14)\quad(0\cdot59)$

2. $\Delta^2 r_B = -5\cdot98\Delta r_B - 6\cdot77 B_2 - 7\cdot30 r_B + 2\cdot05 r_N + 5\cdot45 D_3$
   $(1\cdot03)\quad(1\cdot22)\quad(1\cdot06)\quad(0\cdot50)\quad(0\cdot85)$

3. $\Delta^2 N_2 = -5\cdot91\Delta N_2 - 0\cdot92 r_B - 1\cdot46 N_2 + 0\cdot56 r_N + 0\cdot34 D_3$
   $(1\cdot55)\quad(0\cdot27)\quad(0\cdot49)\quad(0\cdot17)\quad(0\cdot13)$

4. $\Delta^2 r_N = -2\cdot24 r_N + 28\cdot14 N_3 - 1\cdot75 r_N - 1\cdot44 f - 0\cdot34 r_G + 1\cdot30 D_3$
   $(0\cdot35)\quad(4\cdot22)\quad(0\cdot80)\quad(0\cdot50)\quad(0\cdot43)\quad(0\cdot58)$

5. $\Delta^2 r_G = -2\cdot43\Delta r_G + 6\cdot97 r_N - 6\cdot70 f - 9\cdot19 r_G - 25\cdot48 x_0 + 3\cdot45 G_3$
   $(0\cdot65)\quad(1\cdot96)\quad(1\cdot86)\quad(1\cdot82)\quad(11\cdot80)\quad(0\cdot76)$

6. $\Delta^2 F_3 = -22\cdot73\Delta F_3 + 10\cdot07 r_N + 2\cdot90 f - 3\cdot18 r_G - 157\cdot63 F_3 + 162\cdot20 G_3$
   $(37\cdot00)\quad(15\cdot46)\quad(5\cdot91)\quad(5\cdot23)\quad(251\cdot68)\quad(258\cdot39)$

7. $\Delta^2 f = -1\cdot70\Delta f + 9\cdot58 r_N - 11\cdot30 f - 8\cdot18 r_G - 72\cdot47 x_0$
   $(0\cdot71)\quad(2\cdot94)\quad(3\cdot09)\quad(2\cdot27)\quad(20\cdot35)$

8. $E_3 = F_3 - G_3$

9. $L_3 = D_3 + E_3 - N_3 - B_3 - A_3$

10. $N_3 = N - N_2$

11. $B_2 = B - B_3 - B_4$

[1] The notation for x_{0t}, a stock holding or interest rate at time t is:
$$\Delta^2 x_0 = (1-L)^2 x_{0t}; \quad \Delta x_0 = 1/2(1-L^2) x_{0t};$$
$$x_0 = 1/4(1+L)^2 x_{0t} \text{ where } Lx_{0t} = x_{0t-1}$$

The matrices of coefficients $\bar{A}_1$, $\bar{A}_2$, and $\bar{B}$ of this approximate model depend linearly on the elements of A_1, A_2 and B. Thus the discrete approximation maintains the structural form of the continuous model. The *a priori* restrictions which apply to the continuous model can also be imposed on the discrete approximation during estimation. The computer programmes which were used in the research (TRANSF for preparing the data and SIMUL for estimating the models) were written by C. R. Wymer.

TABLE 15.2. *Estimates of behavioural parameters of the approximation to the continuous system*[1]

(The numbers in brackets are the standard errors of the coefficients.)

---

1. $D^2B_3 = -5.56[\hat{L}_3 - L_3] - 5.44DB_3$ $\beta_1 = -1.02$
   $\quad\quad\quad(1.49)\quad\quad\quad\quad\quad(1.54)$ (0.18)

   $\hat{L}_3 = 0.15E_3 - 0.19r_B - 0.05r_G + 0.38D_3$
   $\quad\quad(0.32)\quad(0.08)\quad(0.02)\quad(0.05)$

2. $D^2r_B = 6.77[\hat{B}_2 - B_2] - 5.98Dr_B$ $\beta_2 = 1.13$
   $\quad\quad\quad(1.22)\quad\quad\quad\quad\quad(1.03)$ (0.13)

   $\hat{B}_2 = -1.07r_B + 0.30r_N + 0.80D_3$
   $\quad\quad(0.11)\quad(0.07)\quad(0.08)$

3. $D^2N_2 = 1.46[\hat{N}_2 - N_2] - 5.91DN_2$ $\beta_3 = 0.25$
   $\quad\quad\quad(0.49)\quad\quad\quad\quad\quad(1.55)$ (0.06)

   $\hat{N}_2 = -0.63r_B + 0.38r_N + 0.23D_3$
   $\quad\quad(0.23)\quad(0.12)\quad(0.10)$

4. $D^2r_N = -28.14[\hat{N}_3 - N_3] - 2.24Dr_N$ $\beta_4 = -12.54$
   $\quad\quad\quad(4.22)\quad\quad\quad\quad\quad(0.35)$ (2.03)

   $\hat{N}_3 = 0.06r_N + 0.05f + 0.01r_G - 0.05D_3$
   $\quad\quad(0.03)\quad(0.02)\quad(0.01)\quad(0.02)$

5. $D^2r_G = -3.45[\hat{G}_3 - G_3] - 2.43Dr_G$ $\beta_5 = -1.42$
   $\quad\quad\quad(0.76)\quad\quad\quad\quad\quad(0.65)$ (0.34)

   $\hat{G}_3 = -2.02r_N + 1.94f + 2.66r_G + 7.38x_0$
   $\quad\quad(0.61)\quad(0.61)\quad(0.46)\quad(3.99)$

6. $D^2F_3 = 157.63[\hat{F}_3 - F_3] - 22.73DF_3$ $\beta_6 = 6.94$
   $\quad\quad\quad(251.68)\quad\quad\quad\quad(37.00)$ (0.88)

   $\hat{F}_3 = 0.06r_N + 0.02f - 0.02r_G + 1.03G_3$
   $\quad\quad(0.02)\quad(0.02)\quad(0.03)\quad(0.01)$

7. $D^2f = 11.30[f^e - f] - 1.71Df$ $\beta_7 = 6.64$
   $\quad\quad\quad(3.09)\quad\quad\quad\quad\quad(0.71)$ (2.89)

   $f^e = 0.85r_N - 0.72r_G - 6.41x_0$
   $\quad\quad(0.11)\quad(0.08)\quad(0.61)$

8. $E_3 = F_3 - G_3$

9. $L_3 = D_3 + E_3 - N_3 - B_3 - A_3$

10. $N_3 = N - N_2$

11. $B_2 = B - B_3 - B_4$

---

[1] Since the coefficient of the excess demand in each adjustment function is an estimate of $\alpha\beta$ (as in the equation on p. 268) the estimate of the adjustment coefficient, β, and its standard error are given separately for each equation. The estimated rate of adjustment, α, is the coefficient of the Dy term.

TABLE 15.3. *Mean elasticities of the desired demand functions*

(The numbers in brackets in this table are the *t*-values of the elasticities.)

	r_B	r_N	r_G	f	E_3	D_3	x_0	G_3
$\hat{L}_3$	−0·34 (2·53)		−0·08 (2·20)		0·01 (0·48)	0·98 (7·44)		
$\hat{B}_2$	−0·69 (9·43)	0·19 (4·33)				0·74 (10·47)		
$\hat{N}_2$	−3·4 (2·74)	2·04 (3·13)				1·81 (2·24)		
$\hat{N}_3$		0·86 (2·13)	0·15 (0·80)	0·18 (3·18)		−0·93 (2·12)		
$\hat{G}_3$		−3·81 (3·33)	4·47 (5·13)	0·94 (3·17)			5·57 (1·85)	
$\hat{F}_3$		0·11 (2·73)	−0·03 (0·77)	0·008 (1·12)				0·96 (83·51)
f^e		3·29 (7·89)	−2·50 (9·56)				−9·96 (10·59)	

The coefficients of the desired demand functions have been converted into elasticities calculated at the means of the variables in Table 15.3.[1]

It is convenient to begin the discussion of the testing programme by considering the overall results of the structural estimates presented in Tables 15.1 and 15.2. In the discussion a variable is said to be significant if the hypothesis that the estimated coefficient of the variable equals zero is rejected at the 5 per cent level of significance. The conclusions which follow concerning the specification of the simultaneous structure of the adjustment functions and the variables which are significant determinants of the behavioural relationships apply to the sample period of the estimated model only.

On the usual statistical criteria, the structural estimates of the model are satisfactory. In the estimated structural model (Table 15.1) thirty-one of the

---

[1] Since the model is specified as linear in variables, the coefficient of each variable in a demand equation is the partial derivative of the desired demand with respect to the predetermined variable. Thus if Y is the dependent variable in a demand function and X an independent variable, an estimate of the mean elasticity is given by

$$\bar{e}_{YX} = a\,\frac{\overline{X}}{\overline{Y}}$$

where a is the coefficient of X in the equation which determines Y, and $\overline{X}$ and $\overline{Y}$ are the means of the time series of X and Y, respectively. In order to test the hypothesis that these elasticities are significantly different from zero, the numbers in brackets in this table are *t*-values rather than standard errors.

thirty-nine coefficients are significant at the 5 per cent level.[1] In the case of the estimates of the behavioural parameters of the model (Table 15.2) thirty-three of the thirty-nine coefficients are significant. The estimated elasticities of the desired demand functions (Table 15.3) are of plausible size, ranging from −3·81 to 9·96.

The first four equations of Tables 15.1 and 15.2 present the estimates of the disequilibrium portfolio behaviour of the banks and the private sector in three UK domestic financial markets: liquid assets, UK government securities, and local authority temporary debt. Equation (1) represents the adjustment of the banks' holdings of government securities in response to their excess demand for liquid assets. The estimation results of this equation indicate that the banking system sells UK securities at times when it wishes to increase its liquid asset holdings. As the estimates of the coefficients of the desired demand function for liquid assets (Table 15.2) indicate, an increase of £1 million in total deposits will lead, ceteris paribus, to an estimated increase of £0·38 million in the banks' desired holdings of liquid assets.

These estimates, therefore, imply a 38 per cent marginal liquid asset ratio for banks resident in the United Kingdom. This figure may seem somewhat high when it is recalled that the London clearing banks were required to maintain a conventional minimum liquid asset ratio of only 28 per cent during the sample period. It should be remembered, however, that the definition of the banking system used in this study includes, in addition to the clearing banks, the overseas and foreign banks and the discount houses. Virtually all of the assets in the portfolio of the discount houses are included in the definition of 'liquid assets'. Similarly, the overseas and foreign banks tend to hold a higher level of liquid assets than the domestic banks. Thus an estimate of 38 per cent for the marginal liquid asset ratio of the aggregate banking sector appears quite reasonable.[2]

The level of net Eurocurrency liabilities was included in the demand function for liquid assets in order to determine whether the banks sought to increase their holdings of domestic liquid assets at times when they were switching more Eurocurrency deposits into sterling. In most estimated models, however, there was no evidence that this was the case.

In some specifications of this equation the UK Bank rate was included as a determinant of the desired level of liquid assets, but it was never significant in the estimation results. This may reflect the high level of aggregation of the banking sector in the model. Changes in Bank rate are likely to have their main effect on the distribution of assets between the domestic banks and the dis-

---

[1] It should be noted that although the *a priori* expected signs of the coefficients of each predetermined variable are given in the theoretical model, these expected signs were not actually imposed as restrictions in the estimation of the model. Thus in several cases estimated coefficients which are statistically significant violate their *a priori* sign restrictions. The implications of this sign-switching will be considered below.

[2] For the aggregate banking sector as defined in the model, the ratio of liquid assets (cash, bills and money-at-call) to deposits was 0·47 in December 1962. By December 1969 it had fallen to 0·32. The average ratio for the sample period was 0·39.

count houses, both of which are included in the banking sector. In addition, the portfolio behaviour of the overseas and foreign banks is unlikely to be closely related to changes in Bank rate. On the other hand, the Eurocurrency rate is significant in this equation. This may indicate an overall relation between the international portfolio behaviour of the overseas and foreign banks and their domestic portfolio behaviour, but further research would be required in order to understand the exact nature of this linkage.

The second estimated equation represents the effect of the portfolio behaviour of the private sector on the yield in the market for UK government securities. In the estimated structural model, the coefficient of B_2 is significant but violates the *a priori* expected sign, while three of the other four coefficients agree with their expected sign. Since the coefficient of B_2 is used in deriving estimates of the behavioural parameters, it causes further sign-switching in the estimated demand function in Table 15.2. This counterintuitive result also occurs in the model of the UK financial system which is estimated by Wymer [21]. The quantities specified by the theoretical model are for the book value of these securities, and this does not reflect the actual market value at times when yields are changing. Nor is there any satisfactory method for deriving the correct series.

Equations (3) and (4) describe the behaviour of the private sector and the banks in the market for local authority temporary debt. Equation (3) specifies that the private sector's holdings of these securities respond to its excess demand. All the coefficients in both the desired demand and adjustment functions are significant with the correct sign.

The local authorities market is included in the model not only because it is one of the most important short-term financial markets in the United Kingdom, but also because it is this market which is likely to show a close relation to the banks' behaviour in the international Eurocurrencies market. However, the estimate of the adjustment function for the interest rate on local authority temporary debt provides no definite evidence that this interrelation was significant during the sample period. Although the Eurocurrency interest rate was a significant determinant of the local authorities rate in some versions of the estimated model, it was not found to be significant in the version for which the results are presented. Further, the coefficient of the forward premium on foreign currency, although significantly different from zero, is not consistent with its *a priori* expected sign.

The last three equations of the model represent the international portfolio behaviour of the UK banks and the adjustment of the forward premium on foreign currency. Equations (5) and (6) of the model specify the banks' adjustments to their portfolio of Eurocurrency liabilities and claims. In this study it is assumed that the banks resident in the United Kingdom are the most important international financial intermediaries in the Eurocurrencies market. This implies that the UK banks are likely to have a more direct influence over the interest rate which they pay on their Eurocurrency deposit liabilities than on the quantities which they hold.

The model specified here requires that each adjustment equation is a function of only one excess demand. Thus it could be assumed either that the UK banks adjust the acceptance rate which they pay on their Eurocurrency deposits according to their excess supply of these liabilities, or that they adjust the rate which they earn on Eurocurrency advances in response to their excess demand for these claims. Since the behaviour of the UK banks in the Eurocurrencies market has not been thoroughly investigated, neither of these alternative hypotheses can be excluded *a priori*. They are, therefore, a question which requires empirical study.

However, the absence of satisfactory time series for Eurocurrency interest rates presents difficulties for the estimation of the international portfolio behaviour of the UK banks. The theoretical model requires the acceptance rate which is paid by UK banks on their Eurocurrency deposit liabilities to overseas residents. Unfortunately, published time series are available for only one Eurocurrency interest rate—the interbank rate on Eurocurrency deposits in London. Thus the published series for the rate on Eurocurrency deposits does not correspond to the conceptual rate required by the theoretical model.

This data problem is approached as follows. Although no published data exist for the UK banks' Eurocurrency deposit or lending rates, both these rates of interest are likely to be very closely related to the London interbank rate on Eurocurrencies. This is the case because the international Eurocurrencies market is a highly competitive market in which the Eurocurrency liabilities of banks in different countries are close substitutes in the portfolios of deposit holders. Thus any excess profits resulting from an increase in the differential between the Eurocurrency deposit and lending rates of the UK banks are likely to be bid rapidly away by banks in other countries, so that the Eurocurrency deposit and lending rates will be closely related to each other and to the London interbank rate. If this argument is correct, the interbank rate could be used as a proxy for the UK banks' unobservable borrowing and lending rates in their desired supply and demand functions for Eurocurrencies. However, the sign restriction on the coefficient of this rate in the Eurocurrency equations of the estimated model could not be determined *a priori*, since it would not be known before estimating the model whether the published rate is more closely related to the UK banks' Eurocurrency borrowing or lending rate.

Thus in the estimated model the interbank rate on Eurocurrencies was used.[1] This allows several possible econometric specifications of the international portfolio behaviour of the UK banks. The choice between these alternative specifications was made on statistical grounds.

The first specification tried was that in which the Eurocurrencies rate adjusts to the banks' excess supply of Eurocurrency liabilities, while their holdings of Eurocurrency advances adjust to their own excess demand. This specification is similar to that given in (7) and (8) of the theoretical model. Implicit in this specification of the econometric model is the idea that the

[1] The Eurocurrency interest rate used in the estimation of the model was the interbank rate on three-month Eurodollars in London.

London interbank rate is more closely related to the unobservable acceptance rate on Eurocurrency deposits in London. This specification, however, did not prove satisfactory. In particular, the estimated adjustment coefficient of the interest rate equation violated its expected sign, causing further sign-switching in the estimates of the coefficients of the desired supply function for Eurocurrency deposits.

This specification was therefore rejected,[1] and in later versions of the model it was assumed that the Eurocurrencies rate adjusts to the UK banks' excess demand for these claims, while Eurocurrency deposits adjust to their own excess supply. This specification gave adjustment coefficients for both Eurocurrency equations which were both significant and consistent with their expected sign.

Since the model could not be estimated using separate series for the UK banks' Eurocurrency borrowing and lending rates it is perhaps not surprising that the interbank rate on Eurocurrencies is not significant in estimated equation (6) for their desired supply of Eurocurrency liabilities. It is interesting to note, however, that the interest rate on UK local authority debt is significant with the correct sign in both the desired demand and supply functions for Eurocurrencies. This appears to indicate that the UK banks take this domestic rate into account in determining the levels of their Eurocurrency liabilities and claims. The estimated model assumes, in effect, that the interbank Eurocurrencies rate represents the lending rate for these securities. Under this assumption the estimated coefficient of the Eurocurrencies rate in the banks' desired demand for Eurocurrency advances agrees with its *a priori* sign restriction.

The final estimated equation determines the forward premium on foreign currency. This equation gave very satisfactory econometric results (in the sense of statistically significant coefficients with the expected sign), and these results remained quite stable over different specifications of the simultaneous structure of the model. Since this equation is based on a simplified specification of the behaviour of transactors in the forward exchange market, it is somewhat surprising that it should appear to be so well determined.

The equation assumes that transactors in the foreign exchange market have some expected level of the forward premium on foreign exchange, and that the effect of their behaviour is to cause the forward premium to adjust in response to the difference between the expected and actual level. However, this specification cannot be distinguished econometrically from one in which the UK authorities intervene in the market in an effort to move the forward premium on foreign exchange toward some policy target level. In this case, the adjustment function for the forward premium on the US dollar is a policy adjustment function rather than a market adjustment function.

This distinction may be important in explaining the estimation results of equation (7). The Bank of England [2] has indicated that during twelve of the

---

[1] Another specification which was tested assumed that the banks adjust their net Eurocurrency liabilities in response to the difference between their desired and actual net-switched position. This specification did not give satisfactory results and was therefore rejected.

twenty-nine quarters in the sample period of the model, the authorities intervened in the forward exchange market in an attempt to influence the size of the covered differential between UK interest rates and yields abroad. The estimates of equation (7) in Table 15.2 indicate that the major determinants of the authorities' policy target level of the forward premium during the sample period were the Eurocurrency interest rate, the yield on local authority debt, and the spot exchange rate. The fact that the estimated coefficients of the Eurocurrency and local authorities rates in the equation for the target level of the forward premium are similar in magnitude and opposite in sign indicates that the monetary authorities intervened in the forward exchange market in order to minimise the covered yield differential in the two markets. These results are consistent with the authorities' own explanation of their behaviour.[1]

The estimates of the model in this study appear to give rise to two broader conclusions. The first is that the behaviour of UK banks in both domestic and Eurocurrencies markets can be explained quite well by econometric estimates of a discrete approximation to a theoretical model which is specified in disequilibrium and continuous time. The second conclusion concerns the relation between yields and holdings in the UK financial system and those in the Eurocurrencies market, which may arise from the banks' domestic and international portfolio behaviour.

The estimation results of the model indicate that, during the sample period, the interest rate on local authority debt and the forward exchange premium were significant determinants of the UK banks' desired supplies and demands of Eurocurrency liabilities and claims. Further, the forward exchange premium itself was found to respond significantly to changes in the levels of both domestic and Eurocurrency interest rates. However, the Eurocurrency yield and the forward premium on foreign exchange did not appear to be significant determinants of either the UK banks' demand for local authority loans, or the yield on these securities. Finally, the demand for sterling liquid assets was not significantly affected by changes in the banks' net Eurocurrency liabilities to foreigners. Thus the estimation results do not appear to provide strong support for the hypothesis that yields and holdings in UK financial markets are related to those in the international Eurocurrencies market as a result of the banks' portfolio behaviour.

Such a conclusion, however, must be regarded as rather tentative. The lack of positive statistical evidence of the existence of these interrelations could be the result of problems in the specification of the model. For example, it might be due to the aggregation of the domestic and overseas and foreign banks into a single sector. Alternatively, it may be because the highly restricted adjustment functions of the model mis-specify the complicated non-

[1] The Bank of England states: 'A comparison of the three-months' Eurodollar rate with the return on UK local authority deposits of the same term, adjusted to allow for the cost of forward cover, shows that the yields were nearly the same for most of the time up to the devaluation of sterling in November 1967. . . . This near identity of covered yields was almost entirely attributable to the fact that between November 1964 and devaluation the authorities supported the rate for forward sterling, keeping the discount to a very small figure.' See Bank of England [3].

tatonnement processes of the system. It is clear that further research is needed on these aspects of portfolio behaviour in domestic and international financial markets.

References

1. ARNDT, SVEN W. 'International short-term capital movements: a distributed lag model of speculation in foreign exchange', *Econometrica*, **36**, no. 1 (1968), 59–70.
2. BANK OF ENGLAND. 'Control of bank lending: the cash deposits scheme', *Quarterly Bulletin*, **8**, no. 2, (1968), 31-70.
3. BANK OF ENGLAND. 'The Euro-currency business of banks in London', *Quarterly Bulletin*, **10**, no. 1, (1970), 31–49.
4. BANK OF ENGLAND. 'Inflows and outflows of foreign funds', *Quarterly Bulletin*, **2**, no. 2 (1962), 93–102.
5. BANK OF ENGLAND. 'The overseas and foreign banks in London', *Quarterly Bulletin*, **1**, no. 4 (1961), 18–23.
6. BANK OF ENGLAND, 'Overseas and foreign banks in London: 1962–1968', *Quarterly Bulletin*, **8**, no. 2 (1968), 156–65.
7. BANK OF ENGLAND. 'The UK banking sector: 1952–1964', *Quarterly Bulletin*, **9**, no. 2 (1969), 176–91.
8. BERGSTROM, A. R. *The Construction and Use of Economic Models*, English Universities Press, 1967.
9. BLOOMFIELD, ARTHUR I. 'Official intervention in the forward exchange market: some recent experiences', *Banca Nazionale del Lavoro Quarterly Review*, March 1964, pp. 3–42.
10. COMMITTEE ON THE WORKING OF THE MONETARY SYSTEM, *Report*, Cmnd 827, HMSO, 1959.
11. COOPER, R. N. *The Economics of Interdependence: Economic Policy in the Atlantic Community*, McGraw-Hill, 1968, ch. 5.
12. CROOME, DAVID R. and JOHNSON, HARRY G., eds. *Money in Britain* 1959–1969, Oxford University Press, 1970.
13. GRIFFITHS, BRIAN. *Competition in Banking*, London, Institute of Economic Affairs, 1970.
14. GRUBEL, H. G. *Forward Exchange, Speculation, and the International Flow of Capital*, Stanford University Press, 1966.
15. HELLIWELL, JOHN. 'A structural model of the foreign exchange market', *Canadian Journal of Economics*, February 1969, pp. 90–105.
16. KNIGHT, MALCOLM D. 'A continuous disequilibrium econometric model of the participation of banks in Britain and the United States in the Euro-currency deposit market,' unpublished PhD thesis, University of London, 1972.
17. MUNDELL, R. A. *International Economics*, New York, Macmillan 1968, ch. 19, 'The cost of exchange crises and the problem of sterling', pp. 272–81.
18. SAYERS, R. S. *Modern Banking*, 7th edn, Clarendon Press, 1967.
19. STEIN, JEROME L. 'International short-term capital movements', *American Economic Review*, March 1965.
20. WILLETT, THOMAS D. and FORTE, F. 'Interest rate policy and external balance', *Quarterly Journal of Economics*, **83**, no. 2 (1969), 242–62.
21. WYMER, C. R. 'Econometric estimation of stochastic differential equation systems with applications to adjustment models of financial markets', unpublished PhD thesis, University of London, 1970.
22. WYMER, C. R. 'Econometric estimation of stochastic differential equation systems', *Econometrica*, 1972 (forthcoming).

A continuous disequilibrium econometric model of the domestic and international portfolio behaviour of the UK banking system: Discussion

Michael Parkin

Malcolm Knight should be congratulated on having produced a very professional piece of work in the crucially important problem area of short-run monetary dynamics in an open economy. Knight's work is a natural development of three strands of literature. The first is the earlier models (for example those by Goldfeld [3], De Leeuw [1], Norton [8] and Miller [5]) which develop essentially closed economy representations of the UK or US financial system. The second is the important work by Wymer [11] and Grossman and Dolde [4] which develops a continuous time formulation, but which again ignores the open economy aspects of the world. The third is the theoretical work on the long-run analysis of open economies, starting with Hulme and ending with recent contributions from Swoboda [9], Mundell [7] and others which emphasise the importance of the substitutability between domestic and foreign assets. The conclusion of this work is that, in a fixed exchange rate world, the closer the substitutability between foreign and domestic assets are the less effective and independent is domestic monetary policy. It therefore becomes crucial to know how substitutable domestic and foreign assets are. The natural way to attempt to gain this knowledge is to extend econometric work on national monetary systems to take a full account of the interaction between domestic and international markets.

Knight does just this. His model specifies and estimates behaviour equations in the form of differential equations for asset demands and price (or interest rate) adjustments, covering all the important financial markets in which the UK banks operate. His broad finding is that domestic and foreign assets are not very close substitutes. There are several problems with the formulation of the model though which I would like to draw attention to, some of which might be giving rise to a misleadingly low estimate of the substitution elasticities. First, the detailed microeconomic behaviour of the individual units which comprise the model are not fully spelt out. All we have are *ad hoc* propositions about the demand functions and the market price adjustment functions. This is particularly important in that it leads to certain rather serious shortcomings. One of these is the dichotomy in portfolio behaviour between domestic and foreign portfolio items. This dichotomy is especially unfortunate since one of the key questions the answer to which we would like to know, concerns the degree of substitutability between domestic and foreign assets. It does not help in the pursuit of this information simply to enter the total foreign portfolio as a constraining variable on the domestic portfolio choice. Rather, *all* the rates of return on domestic and foreign assets are needed for a correct estimation of the substitutability between them.

The second problem concerns Knight's notion of the 'residual asset' and 'residual institution'. Knight assumes, following Wymer, that an institution chooses $n-1$ of its n assets, the nth being determined residually as that necessary to balance the balance sheet. This is wholly inappropriate. The correct division of the portfolio into choice assets and exogenous assets would leave the institution choosing the values of the endogenous choice asset on the basis of expectations about the exogenous assets and yields, and there would be no 'residual asset'. The coefficients in the demand functions would reflect the fact that the choice was a simultaneous choice constrained by a balance sheet and therefore the demand functions would display appropriate Cournot and Engel aggregation properties.

Third, the postulated adjustment processes run purely in terms of adjustments, the speed of which depends upon the amount of disequilibrium in the market being adjusted. It is well known from the pure theory of adjustment costs developed by Treadway [10], and also from the empirical work of Motley [6], that this is, in general, an inappropriate adjustment specification. The adjustment of the ith asset will *a priori* and, according to Motley empirically, depend on disequilibrium in all asset markets and not just in the ith market.

We come now to the problems with the market behaviour. The market behaviour propositions concern interest rate adjustments and they all take the form of postulating that the rate of change of an interest rate will depend on the disequilibrium in that asset in the portfolio of the largest operator in the market. This seems to be an especially odd assumption since the biggest operator, as defined by the model, need not necessarily be the most powerful market operator. This will be clear when it is realised that the model has aggregates of individual firms, each individual firm being the units that operate in the market. To pick the biggest sector as that which affects the price implies that the biggest sector is the most monopolistic. This is not at all obvious. One suspects that it would have been much more appropriate to have proposed an interest rate adjustment process based on excess demand in the market as a whole.

The main message which we get from the estimates in this model if we read them uncritically is that substitution elasticities are rather low. My own guess is that this is a completely wrong conclusion and that in fact the substitution elasticities are rather high. I make this guess on the basis of the fact that the foreign asset variable picks up a very big coefficient in several equations. This suggests that there is a good deal of substitutability going on but it is not being correctly estimated owing to the mis-specification of the equations which incorporate a foreign asset volume instead of the appropriate foreign interest rate.

One would like to see most of the problems raised above taken care of in future work: this is a respectable allowance for optimising behaviour in the individual micro-units and a more appropriate specification market price adjustment processes. None of this though detracts from the importance of what Malcolm Knight has done. He has led the way in a very useful manner in the development of open economy models. What we now need is a more rigorous treatment of the underlying theory and careful estimation of the crucial parameters, so that we can begin to say something concrete about the extent to which monetary authorities in fixed exchange rate open economies have freedom of manoeuvre in pursuit of their monetary policies.

References

1. DE LEEUW, F. 'A model of financial behaviour', in *The Brookings Quarterly Econometric Model of the United States*, ed. J. C. Duesenberry, G. Fromm, L. R. Klein, and E. Kuh, Rand McNally 1965, pp. 465–530.
2. DE LEEUW, F. 'A condensed model of financial behaviour', in *The Brookings Model: Some Further Results*, ed. Duesenberry, Fromm, Klein and Kuh, Rand, McNally 1969, pp. 270–315.
3. GOLDFELD, S. M. 'Commercial bank behaviour and economic activity', Amsterdam, 1966. 'An Extension of the Monetary Sector' in *The Brookings Model: Some Further Results*, pp. 317–359.
4. GROSSMAN, H. I. and DOLDE, W. C. 'The appropriate timing of monetary policy', Brown University, 1969, (mimeo).
5. MILLER, M. H. 'An empirical analysis of monetary policy in the United Kingdom: 1954–65', unpublished PhD thesis, Yale University.
6. MOTLEY, B. 'Household demand for assets: a model of short run adjustments', *Review of Economics and Statistics*, 52, no. 3 (1970) 236–41.
7. MUNDELL, R. A. *International Economics*, New York, Macmillan, 1968.
8. NORTON, W. 'Debt management policy in the United Kingdom', *Economic Journal*, 79, no. 315 (1969) 475–94, (development of PhD thesis).
9. SWOBODA, A. 'Monetary policy under fixed exchange rates: effectiveness, the speed and proper use.'
10. TREADWAY, A. 'The multivariate flexible accelerator', Northwestern University (mimeo).
11. WYMER, C. R. 'Econometric estimation of stochastic differential equation systems', *Econometrica*, forthcoming.

Trade unions and wage inflation in the UK: a reappraisal[1]

16

D. L. Purdy and G. Zis

1. Introduction

Prominent amongst attempts to explain inflation is the view that trade union pressure on wage rates is a significant independent cause of rising prices. The recent 'wages explosion', coinciding in the UK with a relatively high level of unemployment and an incomes 'policy off' phase, has further stimulated interest in this view. The aim of this paper is to subject to critical scrutiny the empirical work in favour of this hypothesis developed in a series of articles by A. G. Hines [6, 7, 8, 9]*.

Hines argues that other writers either dismiss the possibility that unions may affect the rate of change of money wages independently of demand [13], or use unsatisfactory methods of identifying trade union pressure [11, 3]. He proposes as an index of union pushfulness the rate of change in the proportion of the labour force belonging to trade unions, ΔT_t ($= T_t - T_{t-1}$, where T_t denotes the unionised percentage of the labour force, or union density, in year t). His basic hypothesis is that ΔT_t is an indicator of union activity which simultaneously manifests itself in pressure on wage rates and in increased union membership and density. This hypothesis is tested at the aggregate and disaggregated levels by regressions of the rate of increase of money wage rates, ΔW, on the militancy variable, ΔT, for various periods since 1893 and in both simple and multiple regression analyses. The general conclusion which Hines draws from his findings is that since the period before World War I unemployment, taken as a proxy for excess demand, has become progressively less, and 'institutional' forces progressively more important in determining the rate of change of money wage rates. In particular, union pushfulness, measured by ΔT has emerged in the postwar period as a key factor in determining the pace of wage inflation.

[1] We are indebted to all members of the Inflation Workshop, University of Manchester, and would like to express our special appreciation to M. Gray, D. Laidler, M. Parkin and D. Rose for their helpful comments and guidance. Also, we are grateful to Mr G. Foster for his assistance. The responsibility for any errors is ours.

* Numbers in square brackets relate to References on p. 327.

We find the Hines hypothesis unsatisfactory on both *a priori* and empirical grounds. Other writers have been similarly dissatisfied (see [5]), and have proposed alternative indicators of union militancy such as strike frequency or the number of working days lost through strikes. None, however, has presented a systematic critique of Hines. The present study is an attempt to mount such a critique. In the next section we consider a number of qualitative objections to Hines's hypothesis, which is shown to be lacking in theoretical foundation, to be of doubtful relevance to actual union-employer bargaining in the UK, and in any case to be incorrectly specified. In section 2, we report on the consequences of adjusting the data used by Hines in his empirical work so as to put them on a basis which is both consistent and more closely in conformity with Hines's hypothesis. These adjustments make little difference to Hines's postwar results, but substantially affect his interwar findings. In section 4 we reconsider the explanatory power of the union militancy variable and show, contrary to Hines, that the contribution of this variable to the explanation of money wages is significant, but relatively unimportant.

In section 5, we investigate the assumption that changes in union militancy are adequately reflected by changes in union density. In particular we show how the existence of the closed shop and changes in the structure of employment may affect recorded changes in union density. We construct a more satisfactory measure of the change in aggregate union density which abstracts from the process of labour force reallocation, and conclude that Hines's unadjusted measure has been a poor index of union militancy in the postwar period. We further suggest how some of the observed association between ΔW and ΔT can be explained in terms of changes in the structure of employment. In section 6 we present our general conclusions. The upshot of our argument is that the case for the cost push view of inflation remains to be proven.

2. A critique of the Hines hypothesis

In this section we subject to critical scrutiny the arguments adduced by Hines to justify the use of ΔT as an index of militancy.

Hines claims several merits for ΔT as an index of militancy. It is objective and is uncorrelated with the demand for labour measured in various ways.[1] He also argues that as the T series is not dominated by its time trend, ΔT escapes Lipsey's objections [13] to the 'cost push via union strength' thesis

[1] The tests which Hines employs to demonstrate this lack of correlation, namely the simple regression of ΔT on U, current and lagged, on the Dow–Dicks-Mireaux index of excess demand pressure, and on the deviation of the index of industrial production around a straight line time trend, may be too crude to pick up the relationship between unionisation and labour market pressure. There is considerable unanimity amongst labour historians that a relationship of some sort exists between labour movement activity and both short term cyclical fluctuations and the longer periods of economic change with which economic historians are mainly concerned. See Hobsbawm 'Economic fluctuations and some social movements since 1800', Weidenfeld and Nicolson (1964).

that any such index would display a secular upward trend, implying that if union strength were an important determinant of wage changes there would have been a steady acceleration of wage and price movement over time. It should be noted that Lipsey referred to indices of union *strength*. Hines, on the other hand, speaks of the *activity* or *militancy* of unions, which is reflected in their year to year changes in membership density. It remains to be shown that a high or low degree of union *activity* is the same thing as a high or low degree of union *strength*. We deal below with the arguments adduced to support such an equivalence.

Further, Hines claims that ΔT is sensitive to all the 'considerable annual variation in the strength of the independent pressure which unions bring to bear on the rate of change of money wages'. In fact during the postwar period the level of unionisation, T, has remained on a plateau at between 39 and 41 per cent of the labour force. On Hines's own definitions and data the ΔT series cannot be said to have exhibited considerable annual variation. Between 1949 and 1961 its range was between -0.95 and $+0.60$. Even small changes in union density which are brought about by factors other than Hines-type militancy will have a marked effect on a series with such a minor degree of variability.[1]

The proposition that ΔT is an index of militancy which simultaneously manifests itself in increased union membership and in upward pressure on wage rates is not derived from any formal model of union behaviour. Nowhere does Hines spell out the objectives of the union and indicate the relative priorities which the union attaches to conflicting objectives. There is a presumption in his theory that unions aim to drive up their members' real wages by exerting pressure on money wages; that unions aim to extend the organised proportion of the labour force lying within their jurisdiction, and that the rate at which they succeed in carrying out this latter objective is a major determinant of their success in pursuing the former. Beyond this all that we have is a number of *ad hoc* rationalisations and supporting assertions, which, moreover, differ slightly in each of the papers. What follows is a compendium of all the reasons proffered by Hines to support the basic proposition that the unions' bargaining power is reflected by the rate of change of union density in any period. It should be stressed, however, that these in no way add up to a theory of union behaviour, and that without such a theory the sense in which Hines's hypothesis can be said to have contributed to the explanation of postwar inflation is at best extremely attenuated.

Hines argues that an increased rate of recruitment will make officials feel stronger and encourage them to adopt a more intransigent negotiating stance. At the same time the morale of shopfloor workers will be raised and they will become more willing to support a tougher stand by their officials, thus enhancing the potency of the strike threat. It is further argued that more intense organising activity will communicate the union's greater militancy to the employers. Then too, an extension of the union's control over a larger

[1] A large part of the work reported in the present paper is devoted to an investigation of the impact of some of these other factors on Hines's results; see section 5.

section of the labour force will directly reduce the danger that non-union competition may undermine the union's ability to support its demands by a strike or the threat of a strike.

The last reason mentioned appears to relate to the *level* rather than the *rate of change* of union density. Thus, even if non-union competition is an important factor affecting union bargaining power, which may be doubted on the grounds that the legal right of peaceful picketing is of greater value in preventing strike-breaking than the level of union density, the correct formulation of Hines's wage determination hypothesis should include T as well as ΔT. Hines confines the role of T in explaining ΔW to interperiod comparisons only, and excludes T from his regression estimates for the interwar and postwar periods considered separately.[1] An additional reason for including T as well as ΔT in the wage determination hypothesis follows from Hines's argument that more intensive union recruitment will communicate the union's greater militancy to the employers. A given value of ΔT will presumably carry more weight with employers the higher the already achieved level of union density. Hines himself suggests at one point that there may be diminishing returns to recruitment effort, so that a given ΔT indicates more militancy at high than at low levels of T.

Hines justifies the omission of employer resistance to union wage claims as an independent force in wage bargaining on the grounds that employer resistance will be permanently reduced to insignificance by the combination of a régime of administered prices with universal knowledge of the 'wage round'. Hence there is no need to qualify the evidence of increased union pressure on wage rates by reference to the state of employer resistance. It may well be the case that the employer's ability to pass on increased labour costs in higher prices without fear of losing sales has been a constant factor throughout the postwar period making for a lower *average* level of employer resistance than hitherto. It does not, however, follow that there has been no variation in the degree of employer resistance around this low average level,[2] and there is no *a priori* reason to assume that employer resistance has varied inversely with union militancy, making it unnecessary to give separate consideration to this factor.

The upshot of these assertions as to the role of the militancy variable, ΔT, is according to Hines [8], that 'a successful membership drive' is 'a necessary accompaniment of success in the wage bargain'. Hence, unions seek to increase their membership immediately before and during wage negotiations. In strict logic this conclusion does not follow. None of the reasons mentioned for associating the size of an increase in union density with an increase in bar-

---

[1] This omission is further considered in section 3 below.
[2] Taking the length of time elapsing between the date of filing and the date of settlement of wage claim as a crude index of the degree of employer resistance, the fifteen separate sets of national wage rate negotiations between the Engineering Employers Federation and the Confederation of Shipbuilding and Engineering Unions which occurred between the end of the war and the conclusion of the three-year package deal in 1964, took between two months and twelve months with a mean time taken of six months.

gaining strength entails that a membership drive is a *necessary* condition of success in wage negotiations. At most they imply that increased unionisation will be a *sufficient* condition of success. Hines fails to show that there are no other ways of improving bargaining strength.

Apart from their logical coherence the relevance of Hines's *ad hoc* rationalisations may also be questioned. Where a closed shop is in operation the arguments concerning the role of ΔT are inapplicable. An effective closed shop means that employees must become members of one of a number of specified unions, either as a condition of obtaining employment in the first place, or as a condition of retaining it once obtained. McCarthy [15] estimated that some 3·75 million workers were employed in closed shop establishments, whilst a further 1,350,000 workers were in open shops within trades where the closed shop practice predominated, and which were, therefore, likely to be subject to the 'semi-closed shop' enforced by informal sanctions. Twenty-two per cent of manual workers were covered by closed shop arrangements and these constituted 49 per cent of trade unionists in manual groups. The extensiveness of the closed shop in British industry not only limits the applicability of the Hines hypothesis; it may also seriously affect the recorded changes in aggregate ΔT.[1]

Equally, as recently as 1964 it was estimated that only 54·3 per cent of the labour force in Great Britain was employed in industries which generally do not have a union recognition problem; 27 per cent of the labour force was located in areas in which employers generally refuse to recognise trade unions; a further 11 per cent in areas with a partial recognition problem; and 7 per cent in areas in which unions have not generally tried to organise, but in which recognition problems would arise if they did [1, pp. 72–3]. Of course, unions do seek to organise in establishments where they are not recognised. One of the prime purposes of building up membership in such establishments is precisely to elicit eventual recognition. Often employers explicitly agree to grant recognition if the union or unions concerned succeed in organising a majority of their employers. As with the closed shop, the existence of a substantial recognition problem limits the applicability of Hines's arguments concerning the role of union militancy in wage bargaining. Again, since one of the determinants of the worker's decision to join a union is precisely whether or not the union is recognised by the employer, the extensiveness of the recognition problem and the discontinuous jump in union membership which is likely to follow the granting of recognition, may seriously affect recorded changes in union membership and density.

A final limitation to the applicability of Hines's hypothesis is the fact that some unions do not engage in industrywide bargaining over standard or minimum wage rates but prefer to rely instead on plant and company level bargaining. The leading white-collar unions, Draughtsmen and Allied Technicians Association (DATA) and the Association of Scientific, Technical

---

[1] The impact of changes in the proportion of the total labour force employed in the closed shop sector on recorded changes in union membership and density is examined in section 5 below.

and Managerial Staffs (ASTMS) for instance, are in this position. The Amalgamated Union of Engineering Workers (AUEW) has recently jettisoned industrywide bargaining in favour of plant bargaining. It is not clear whether a model of wage-related union militancy which is explicitly cast in terms appropriate to industrywide negotiations, can be applied without modification to cases such as these. Moreover, it is a commonplace of the literature on labour economics and industrial relations that the postwar period has seen the emergence of a substantial gap between minimum or standard wage rates agreed in official industrywide negotiations, and actual earnings in the workplace throughout many leading sectors of the economy. There are many other methods available to most unions of raising their members' effective real wages besides increasing their bargaining strength in industrywide negotiations.

It may be objected that these doubts as to the relevance of Hines's hypothesis apply to the microbehaviour of unions, whereas Hines's main empirical case is conducted at the aggregate level. Without entering the methodological controversy over the independence of macro and micro theory, the reply to this objection is simply that Hines's own supporting arguments relate to individual bargaining units. None of the above qualitative considerations is decisive against Hines. They do, however, weaken the cogency of his case. In sections 4 and 5 below we attempt to quantify some of the objections raised in this section. First, however, we must reconsider the data which Hines used to test the significance of his union militancy variable.

3. Adjustments of the data appropriate to testing Hines's hypothesis

In his initial investigations of the wage rate/union militancy relationship, Hines measured union density as the ratio of trade union membership in the UK to the labour force in Great Britain. His labour force series was the total working population, which includes on the one hand the employers, self-employed and armed forces, and on the other hand the unemployed. We re-estimated the simple regression of ΔW or ΔT after adjusting the labour force data in various ways.

Equation (1) in Table 16.1 is the equation estimated by Hines for the period 1949–61. Equation (2) places the denominator of the ratio used to measure union density on the same UK basis as the numerator. Equation (3) excludes from the denominator the employers, self-employed and armed forces, who can hardly be considered as potential candidates for unionisation. Equation (4) additionally excludes the unemployed.

The place of unemployed workers in the union militancy/wage negotiations mechanism outlined in section 2 is unclear. If unions undertake recruitment drives with a view to increasing their bargaining strength during wage negotiations, it seems more plausible to postulate that they will concentrate their energies on recruiting those who are actually in employment. Unemployed workers are dispersed and have little obvious motivation to join unions.

On the other hand, in so far as unions direct their efforts towards reducing the rate of dropout from membership, then the unemployed do become an important focus of any membership drive since the unions will want to persuade workers to maintain their membership even when they are out of work. Indeed, it is only by postulating this latter type of membership effort that any sense can be made of the Hines hypothesis as applied to the interwar period when the militancy index, ΔT, registered severe falls. For this period (when, incidentally the explanatory performance of ΔT is better than in any other period), the Hines hypothesis must presumably be that wage rates fell more or less rapidly according to the degree to which unions were successful in maintaining their membership against the prevailing downward trend. Because of this lack of clarity about the place of the unemployed, we decided to see whether it makes any difference when the potentially unionisable labour force is defined so as to exclude them.

TABLE 16.1. *Period 1949–61 = Equation estimated* $\Delta W_t = a + b\Delta T_t$

No.	a	b	$\bar{R}^2$	DW	Description
(1)	5·392	4·219 (0·975)	0·562	n.a.	Hines's results $L = TWP$ for GB
(2)	5·539 (0·545)	4·336 (1·283)	0·465	2·071*	$L = TWP$ for UK
(3)	5·599 (0·488)	3·974 (0·889)	0·613	2·239*	TWP for UK minus employers, self-employed and armed forces
(4)	5·880 (0·533)	3·482 (0·908)	0·533	2·104*	TWP for UK minus employers etc. and the unemployed

L = Labour force
TWP = Total working population
Standard errors are given in parentheses
* Indicates that the test showed no autocorrelation at the 1 per cent level

The data adjustments described above do not seriously upset Hines's results. The estimated constant term and slope coefficient are not significantly different from those estimated by Hines. Indeed, the explanatory power of the militancy variable is considerably improved when we remove the employers, self-employed and armed forces (equation 3). This is probably due to the fact that the various labour force concepts used to compute ΔT in these regressions moved in sympathy over the period in question. Suppose that the series for the 'true' labour force variable differs from Hines's series by some constant proportion α (where α may be $\gtrless 0$). Then we shall have:

$$\Delta T_t = T_t - T_{t-1} = \left(\frac{T^*}{L}\right) t - \left(\frac{T^*}{L}\right) t - 1$$

so that

$$\left[\frac{T^*}{L(1+\alpha)}\right] t - \left[\frac{T^*}{L(1+\alpha)}\right] t - 1 = \frac{1}{1+\alpha} \Delta T_t = \Delta T'_t$$

say, for $\alpha > 0$. A regression of ΔW on $\Delta T'$ would give estimates of a' and b' in the equation: $\Delta W_t = a' + b' \Delta T'_t$ where $b' = b/1 + \alpha$. We should therefore, expect Hines's estimated slope coefficient to be upwardly or downwardly biased according as the 'true' labour force series is proportionally greater or less than the series used by Hines. The results shown in Table 16.1 indicate that the bias introduced by Hines's mis-specification of the labour force variable is negligible in the postwar period.

When we turn to the interwar period we find that Hines's mis-specification of the labour force is more serious. His labour force series is based on interpolation from a straight line time trend fitted to just two observations on the total occupied population taken from the 1921 and 1931 Censuses. The derivation by linear interpolation of a series for a variable known to be influenced by fluctuations in the level of economic activity is a most dubious procedure. Moreover, the definition of the 'total occupied population' altered between these two Censuses in a way which affected the recorded change in total occupied population.[1] The concept is in any case unsatisfactory for Hines's hypothesis. It includes the unemployed and, more importantly, employers and managers and members of the armed forces. A far more satisfactory labour force statistic is provided by the series for numbers insured under the unemployment insurance scheme.[2] Equation (2) in Table 16.2 is based on a labour force variable defined as total insured employees (employed plus unemployed). Equation (3) excludes the unemployed from this total.

In contrast to our findings for the postwar period, the respecification of the labour force variable makes a considerable difference to the regression estimates. The slope coefficients in (2) and (3) are significantly lower than those obtained by Hines. When the unemployed are included in the labour

---

[1] In 1921 total occupied population was defined as total population aged twelve and over minus persons retired or not gainfully employed, whereas in 1931 the age was raised to fourteen and over owing to the institution of a break between primary and secondary education in 1926 which effectively made secondary education up to fourteen universal.

[2] 'Throughout the period following the beginning of the insurance scheme in 1911, the scheme excluded employers and workers on their own account, and also certain classes of employees, the principal of which were indoor private domestic servants, teachers with pension rights, female professional nurses, established civil servants and permanent employees in national and local government and in railway service. After 1920 the scheme covered the very great majority of manual workers and a large proportion of non-manual workers.' Ralph B. Ainsworth, 'Labour statistics' in *Sources and Nature of the Statistics of the UK*, ed. M. G. Kendall, vol i. Royal Statistical Society, 1952.

TABLE 16.2. *Interwar period 1924–38 = Equation estimated* $\Delta W_t = a + b\Delta T_t$

No.	a	b	$\bar{R}^2$	DW	Description
(1)	0·098 (0·902)	2·488 (0·061)	0·902	1·479*	Hines's results, period 1921–38
(2)	0·697 (0·239)	0·882 (0·126)	0·774	0·626	L = Total insured employees in the UK
(3)	0·534 (0·428)	0·473 (0·193)	0·265	1·120*	L = Total insured employees in employment in the UK

* Indicates that the test showed no autocorrelation at the 1 per cent probability level. For other values the test showed positive autocorrelation.

force series (equation 2) there is autocorrelation in the residuals, whilst when they are excluded the autocorrelation disappears but the proportion of variance explained by ΔT drops to less than a third of the level explained by Hines's militancy index.

What emerges from these findings is that within certain limits if one wants to use ΔT as an index of union militancy then it does not greatly matter whether the labour force series used to compute ΔT is truly representative of the potentially unionisable labour force, provided that whatever series is used is internally consistent. If Hines's hypothesis is interpreted as depending crucially on the *direction* and *rate of change* of union density, then, within limits, no great significance attaches to the precise calculation of the *level* of density at any given point in time. On the other hand if T as well as ΔT should be included in the wage determination equation as we argued in section 2, then the correct specification of the labour force becomes a matter of some importance.[1]

Moreover, even if we adopt Hines's interpretation of the militancy hypothesis the limits within which mis-specification of the labour force is irrelevant are illustrated by our findings for the interwar period. The labour force series which we used moved far less in sympathy with that used by Hines in the interwar period than in the postwar period. Thus, Hines's results are

[1] One of the defects of Hines's disaggregated study [8] is that the calculations of union density by industry are notoriously unreliable since there exists no accurate breakdown of union membership by industry. Thus, according to our calculations the level of union density in Group 4 of Hines's twelve broad industry groupings, the General Workers Group (comprising Chemicals and Allied Industries, Other Manufacturing, Bricks, Pottery, Glass and Cement, Gas, Water and Electricity, and Transport and Communications—in all nearly 20 per cent of total employees) exceeds 100 per cent in some postwar years and is unrealistically high throughout. This evident absurdity is due to the practice of including the *whole* of the membership of the two large general unions in this industry grouping together with the membership of the other unions which recruit therein.

only moderately robust in the face of modifications designed to make the data used to compute ΔT more conformable to his hypothesis.

It is also worth noting the contrasting results which follow the exclusion of the unemployed from the unionisable labour force in the two periods. One conclusion which might be drawn from this contrast is that the focus of union concern over membership is different at different levels of employment. During the large scale unemployment of the interwar period union efforts to maintain their membership among the unemployed had an importance which they have since lost in the full employment conditions of the postwar period. If this is so then the correct specification of the labour force is one which includes the unemployed.

It is worth while investigating the consequences of respecifying the labour force in the way outlined above. In Table 16.3 we present Hines's regression

Table 16.3

Equation estimated	a	b	c	$\bar{R}^2$	DW	Description and period
(1) $\Delta W_t = a + bT_t$						
Hines	25·032	−1·191		0·497	n.a.	1921–38
	(0·497)	(0·295)				L = estimated
						TOP
P & Z	−6·238	0·164		0·086	0·576	1924–38
	(4·373)	(0·108)				L = UK
						insured
						employees
(2) $\Delta W_t = a + b\Delta T_t$						
Hines	0·098	2·488		0·913	1·479*	1921–38
	(0·902)	(0·061)				L as in (1)
P & Z	0·691	0·882		0·774	0·626	1924–38
	(0·239)	(0·126)				L as in (1)
(3) $\Delta W_t = a + b\Delta T_t + cT_t$						
Hines	0·7567	2·454	−0·027	0·913	1·59*	1921–38
	(0·8951)	(0·285)	(0·176)			L as in (1)
P & Z	−6·253	0·891	0·172	0·950	2·309	1924–38
	(1·027)	(0·060)	(0·025)			L as in (1)

L = Labour force
TOP = Total occupied population
Standard errors are shown in parentheses
   *Indicates that the test showed no autocorrelation at the 1 per cent probability level. For other values the test showed positive autocorrelation

estimates for three variants of the unionisation hypothesis together with our own estimates based on modified labour force data for the interwar period. For Hines's postwar period 1949–61 the parameter estimates yielded by our regressions for each of these variants do not differ significantly from those obtained by Hines. They are not, therefore, shown separately here.

Like Hines, we found that the *level* of unionisation alone offered no explanation of ΔW (equation 1). Unlike Hines, however, we found that the level of unionisation did contribute significantly to the explanation of ΔW when both the level and the rate of change of unionisation were included together as independent variables (equation 3). Moreover, the autocorrelation found in the regression of ΔW on ΔT alone is removed when T is added as a regressor. This strongly suggests that if the unionisation hypothesis is true, the correct formulation of it is one which includes the size as well as the activity of unions, notwithstanding Hines's statements to the contrary. Hines is prepared to assign an explanatory role to T only in interperiod comparisons of wage movements, arguing that the increase in the level of union density postwar compared with prewar has been responsible for an upward shift of the $\Delta W - \Delta T$ relationship. This interpretation is convenient for the militancy hypothesis and the view that unions have acquired progressively more importance in determining the rate of change of money wages, since the insignificance of T within the postwar period cannot then be taken as contrary evidence. If, however, T *ought* to be included in the correct formulation of the militancy hypothesis, then its insignificance within the postwar period, which, of course, is due to its extremely small variability, weakens the view that union militancy has been an important independent cause of wage inflation.

Moreover, Hines's arguments concerning the role of T in comparisons of wage movements between the postwar and interwar periods can be questioned. He found that the regression line for a simple regression of ΔW on ΔT was both steeper and higher in the postwar period than in the interwar period. He offers two alternative explanations for the increase in the slope coefficient. The first is that there is an upper limit to the extent of unionisation and the more closely this limit is approached the smaller are the returns in terms of increasing union density to a given outlay of recruitment effort by the unions. Hence a given change in union density indicates more militancy at high than at low levels of density. It is difficult to reconcile this proposition with the fact that the large unions have not in the postwar period shown any tendency to grow more slowly than average (if anything they have grown faster), even when account is taken of growth by amalgamation. Moreover, the militancy-ΔT relationship may, as we noted in section 2, be upset by the discontinuous changes in union membership and density which are likely to accompany the granting of recognition or the extension of the closed shop. Hines's alternative explanation, which in his disaggregated study [8] seems to be preferred, is that in the postwar period a leader-follower relationship has operated across different bargaining units, with the result that a given increase in unionisation concentrated in the leading sector becomes associated with a higher rate of increase in the aggregate wage index. For this second explanation to be valid a connection would have to be shown between the emergence of a leader–follower relationship after the Second World War and the increase in the level of unionisation postwar as compared with prewar. If the argument is that unions in follower sectors have been able to emulate the wage increases achieved in the leading sector because they have reached higher levels of density than before the war, this merely strengthens the case for formulating the militancy hypothesis in terms of both T and ΔT. In any case the choice of the 'General Unions' sector comprising Transport and Communications, Gas, Water and Electricity and a number of other heterogeneous industries, for the role of leading sector appears bizarre.

The explanation Hines offers for the increase in the intercept of the regression line for the postwar period is that the postwar rise in the level of union density reflected the organisation of previously unorganised workers. Wage rates in these sectors were pushed up and there was a once for all increase in the general level of wage rates. This explanation would be consistent with an upward shift in the $\Delta W - \Delta T$ relationship of a temporary nature only. Once the level of unionisation stabilised again after the organisation of previously unorganised workers, any alleged impact which this might have on the constant term of the regression would be expected to disappear. In order to obtain a permanent shift of the regression line it would have to be shown that a permanent increase in the level of unionisation would permanently raise ΔW, not W.

The hypothesis that the coefficient on ΔT has undergone a permanent increase since the war is not borne out when the postwar period of observation is extended up to 1969. In Table 16.4 we present estimates of two variants of the unionisation hypothesis first for the whole period 1949–69 and then for each of the subperiods 1949–59 and 1960–69. For the whole period the coefficient on ΔT was not significantly different from that estimated by Hines for the interwar period (see Table 16.2), though it is significantly higher than our estimate. When we consider each of the subperiods separately not only is the coefficient on ΔT significantly reduced for the most recent period but it also becomes completely insignificant.[1] This result holds for both variants of the unionisation hypothesis. Furthermore, the result most favourable to Hines (equation 1, period 1949–59) is achieved only with a very large constant term, and we have already seen that his rationalisation of the increase in the constant term since the interwar period is consistent with only a temporary upward shift of the regression line. In short, neither of the unionisation variables appears to have been doing much work in explaining ΔW. Before this conclusion can be accepted, however, the explanatory power of the unionisation variables must be re-examined in the context of a full wage

---

[1] The insignificance of the militancy variable for the 1960s receives support from one of Hines's own estimates [9]. In a wage equation fitted to annual data for the 'policy on' periods, most of which occurred during the 1960s, the 't' statistic on the coefficient of ΔT is 1·11. It should also be noted that when ΔW is computed by the first central difference method and annual average data used the coefficient on ΔT becomes significantly greater than zero in the subperiod 1960–69 but is still lower than in the subperiod 1949–59.

determination equation. It is to this question that the next section is addressed.

TABLE 16.4

Equation estimated	a	b	c	$\bar{R}^2$	DW	Period
(1) $\Delta W_t = a + b\Delta T_t$						
	5·557	2·568		0·412	1·850*	1949–69
	(0·364)	(0·663)				
	6·092	4·051		0·607	2·197*	1949–59
	(0·594)	(0·999)				
	5·579	0·791		0·047	2·363*	1960–69
		(0·658)				
(2) $\Delta W_t = a + b\Delta T_t + cT_t$						
	1·384	2·546	0·096	0·382	1·883*	1949–69
	(15·274)	(0·685)	(0·353)			
	15·843	4·229	−0·220	0·561	2·208*	1949–59
	(42·812)	(1·315)	(0·997)			
	30·844	1·318	−0·598	0·058	2·307*	1960–69
	(56·211)	(1·362)	(1·330)			

In each equation the labour force used to calculate T and ΔT was defined as UK Total Working Population minus Employers, Self-Employed and Armed Forces

* Indicates that the test showed no autocorrelation at the 1 per cent probability level

4. A reconsideration of the explanatory power of Hines's hypothesis

In his 1964 paper Hines reports on the estimation of a three-equation sub-system of the economy in which ΔW, ΔP and ΔT are simultaneously determined. The model is fitted to data for the whole period from 1921 to 1961 excluding the war years. The wage equation tested is:

$$\Delta W_t = a_0 + a_1\Delta T_t + a_2 T_t + a_3\Delta P_t + a_4\Delta P_{t-1} + a_5 U_t$$

Both Ordinary Least Squares and Two Stage Least Squares methods of estimation result in firm coefficients on the unionisation variables.[1]

Thomas and Stoney [18] have shown that considered as a stochastic

[1] The similar estimates which Hines reports in his 1971 paper derived from quarterly data for the postwar period alone can be discounted. The observations on T and ΔT are derived by linear interpolation from the semi-annual observations used by Lipsey and Parkin [14]. But these observations were themselves obtained by linear interpolation from the annual observations. Hines, therefore, has inadvertently produced a series with only one true observation in four!

difference equation system, the Hines model is dynamically explosive. Godfrey [5] has argued that this property makes it difficult to interpret Hines's original estimates and suggests that the model may be mis-specified. Our present concern is with the comparative explanatory power of the unionisation variables in the wage equation above.

A number of problems relating to data and definitions of variables immediately arise. First, the adjustments described in the previous section to the data used to compute T and ΔT have been maintained in what follows. The labour force statistics used are for the UK and exclude the employers, self-employed and armed forces, but include the unemployed. For the interwar period figures for total insured employees (employed plus unemployed) are used. Second, whereas Hines used the GDP price deflator to compute ΔP for the years 1921–58 supplemented by the retail Price Index for 1959–61, we have used the Retail Price Index throughout on the grounds that this is more appropriate in a model of wage determination. Third, in Hines's model unemployment is entered linearly. There seems to be little justification for this. If the true relationship between ΔW and U is non-linear, then even though a linear approximation may be tolerable within the interwar and postwar periods separately, it will not be appropriate for the two subperiods together. Consequently we have entered the unemployment variable in its reciprocal form. Further, we did not place a lag on unemployment, as Hines did implicitly. Fourth, Hines's wage series consists of end-December figures for an index of hourly wage rates. ΔW_t is defined as:

$$\left[\frac{W_t}{W_{t-1}} - 1\right].100$$

His price series on the other hand consists of annual averages. ΔP_t is defined as:

$$\frac{\frac{1}{2}(P_{t+1} - P_{t-1})}{P_t}.100$$

Two difficulties arise here. On the one hand, the denominators of these two percentage rates of change represent different base lines, the one end-December, the other mid-year. For consistency, ΔW_t should either have been computed from annual averages of monthly figures and defined similarly to ΔP_t, or defined as:

$$\Delta W_t \equiv \frac{(W_t - W_{t-1})}{\frac{1}{2}(W_t + W_{t-1})}.100$$

On the other hand, the use of the first central difference method for calculating only ΔP_t introduces a greater degree of smoothing in this variable than in ΔW_t. To achieve consistency with regard to the base line and to eliminate this differential degree of smoothing we have used a wage series consisting of annual averages of monthly figures for hourly wage rates and have defined ΔW as

$$\Delta W_t \equiv \frac{\frac{1}{2}(W_{t+1} - W_{t-1})}{W_t}.100$$

D. L. Purdy and G. Zis

TABLE 16.5

Equation no.	Constant	T_t	ΔT_t	ΔP_t	ΔP_{t-1}	U^{-1}_t	$\bar{R}^2$	DW	Period
		Estimates of coefficients on							
(1)	−3·634 (1·594)	0·127 (0·053)	0·562 (0·145)	0·078 (0·102)	0·126 (0·081)	−11·043 (11·631)	0·903	2·350*	1924–38
(2)	16·446 (9·858)	0·332 (0·247)	1·179 (0·406)	0·347 (0·149)	0·080 (0·148)	2·878 (1·607)	0·700	1·220†	1949–69
(3)	−0·813 (2·433)	0·032 (0·060)	0·398 (0·189)	0·299 (0·127)	0·111 (0·096)	5·389 (1·037)	0·900	1·061	1924–38 1949–69
(4)	−0·565 (0·835)		0·554 (0·180)	0·168 (0·130)		15·405 (10·660)	0·825	1·583*	1924–38
(5)	3·142 (0·789)		1·289 (0·398)	0·300 (0·129)		1·912 (1·382)	0·701	1·260†	1949–69
(6)	0·422 (0·273)		0·388 (0·180)	0·392 (0·105)		5·723 (1·010)	0·899	1·110†	1924–38 1949–69
(7)	−2·319 (2·454)	0·096 (0·083)		0·506 (0·903)		−12·893 (19·924)	0·709	1·268†	1924–38

(8)	17·095 (9·325)	−0·358 (0·227)		0·638 (0·129)	2·090 (1·728)	0·578	0·751	1949–69
(9)	−0·382 (2·362)	0·021 (0·058)		0·554 (0·073)	4·443 (0·919)	0·885	1·044	1924–38 1949–69
(10)	0·249 (1·036)			0·505 (0·092)	4·513 (13·151)	0·701	1·323*	1924–38
(11)	2·464 (0·941)			0·564 (0·124)	1·134 (1·683)	0·543	0·637	1949–69
(12)	9·444 (0·287)			0·560 (0·075)	4·515 (0·884)	0·888	1·066	1924–38 1949–69
(13)	−4·962 (1·443)	0·115 (0·035)	0·642 (0·142)	0·107 (0·101)		0·894	1·935*	1924–38
(14)	9·866 (7·991)	−0·141 (0·191)	1·121 (0·418)	0·417 (0·144)		0·678	0·966†	1949–69
(15)	−1·417 (3·212)	0·070 (0·079)	−0·115 (0·222)	0·826 (0·103)		0·802	0·636	1924–38 1949–69

* indicates no autocorrelation at the 1 per cent level
† indicates that the test was inconclusive
For other values there was positive autocorrelation
Standard errors are shown in parentheses

For the Two Stage Least Squares estimates reported below a few other minor alterations to Hines's data and definitions have been made. For consistency with the definitions of ΔW and ΔP the rate of change of import prices, ΔM, and the rate of change of productivity, ΔX, were calculated by the first central difference method. Our productivity index refers to GDP per man year rather than industrial production per man year. Finally in the union militancy equation the level of real profits, π, was entered with a lag of one year.

We first estimated a number of different specifications of the basic wage determination equation by Ordinary Least Squares, imposing different lags on the price variable and systematically omitting one variable at a time. In general the results were not affected by the length of lag on ΔP, nor by the inclusion of both ΔP_t and $\Delta P_{t-1/2}$ or ΔP_{t-1} as regressors. Our main findings are summarised in Table 16.5.

The unemployment variable was consistently insignificant in the interwar period and the postwar period considered separately, but consistently significant for the two subperiods combined. This latter result is not due to the clustering of the observations on ΔW and U in the two subperiods, as unemployment exhibited great variability in the interwar period, albeit around a much higher average level than postwar. T was significant at best only in the interwar period and even then its coefficient was very small, indicating, for instance, that a change of ten percentage points in the level of union density would be needed to bring about an increase in the rate of change of money wages by one percentage point. Contrary to Hines's results T does not become significant when the data are pooled: see equations (3), (9) and (15). Taken together these findings suggest that U rather than T has acted as the shift variable in the wage equation, which accords with the common sense notion that the persistence of relatively full employment since the war has provided a platform for wage inflation, even though the relationship between U and ΔW has not been close within the postwar period. It is noteworthy that when T is excluded from the equation for the combined periods neither the proportion of explained variance nor the size and significance of the parameter estimates are noticeably affected (equation 6), whereas when U is excluded positive autocorrelation is introduced and the coefficients on ΔT and ΔP are considerably affected (equation 15). It should also be noted that Hines [6] does not succeed in establishing the clear superiority of T over U as a shift variable. On his own results the proportion of variance explained is almost exactly the same whether U or T is used.[1] Moreover the coefficient on ΔT is almost exactly the same when T is replaced by U, whilst the correlation between T and U is very poor.

Our findings also indicate that ΔT is a significant explanatory variable.[2]

[1] For the period 1923–38 and 1949–61, for $\Delta W = a + bT + cT$ $R^2 = 0.804$ while for $\Delta W = a + bT + cU$ $R^2 = 0.786$.

[2] ΔT was consistently insignificant in the subperiod 1949–61 (not shown in Table 16.5) when included together with ΔP_t and U^{-1}. There are, however, too few observations in relation to the number of parameters to be estimated for much weight to be attached to this result.

When ΔT is excluded from the equation (equations 7–12) there is positive autocorrelation in the residuals, whilst the proportion of explained variance is somewhat, though not drastically reduced in each of the subperiods. Two further points, however, stand out. First, when unemployment is excluded as a regressor, not only is there positive autocorrelation in the equation estimated for the pooled data (equation 15), but also ΔT becomes completely insignificant and has the wrong sign. This and the previous findings relating to unemployment are totally at variance with Hines's assertion that the inclusion in the wage equation of a proxy for excess demand adds nothing to the equation's predictive power. Second, although the coefficient estimates on ΔT show some tendency to rise as between the two subperiods, they are consistently lower than those obtained by Hines, with values of roughly 0·6, 1·2 and 0·4 for the interwar postwar and pooled data respectively compared with 2·0, 3·2 and 2·0 found by Hines.

Since ΔT has exhibited little variability in the postwar period the conclusion appears inevitable that although it has had a significant independent influence on ΔW its importance has been greatly overrated. In Fig. 16.1 the relative unimportance of ΔT is vividly illustrated by comparing the ΔW predicted from the actual values of ΔT alone with both the actual ΔW and the ΔW predicted from the actual values of all the independent variables in equation (5) of Table 16.5.[1]

TABLE 16.6. *Two Stage Least Square estimates for the combined periods 1925–38 and 1950–69*

(1) $\Delta W_t = -1\cdot930 + 0\cdot060 T_t + 0\cdot441 \Delta T_t + 0\cdot123 \Delta P_t$
$\qquad$ (2·758) (0·069) $\quad$ (0·185) $\qquad$ (0·167)
$\qquad + 0\cdot232 \Delta P_{t-1/2} + 5\cdot582 U^{-1}{}_t$
$\qquad$ (0·162) $\qquad\quad$ (0·964)
$\qquad \bar{R}^2 = 0\cdot930 \qquad$ DW $= 1\cdot000$

(2) $\Delta P_t = -0\cdot185 - 0\cdot021 \Delta X_t + 0\cdot236 \Delta M_{t-1/2} + 0\cdot677 \Delta W_t$
$\qquad$ (0·280) (0·115) $\qquad$ (0·031) $\qquad\quad$ (0·069)
$\qquad \bar{R}^2 = 0\cdot036 \qquad$ DW $= 1\cdot586*$

(3) $\Delta T_t = 10\cdot626 - 0\cdot258 T_{t-1} + 0\cdot403 \Delta P_{t-1/2} - 0\cdot0004 \pi_{t-1}$
$\qquad$ (1·624) (0·039) $\qquad$ (0·059) $\qquad\quad$ (0·0003)
$\qquad \bar{R}^2 = 0\cdot724 \qquad$ DW $= 1\cdot192†$

* Indicates that the test showed no autocorrelation at the 1 per cent level
† Indicates that the test was inconclusive
For other values the test showed positive autocorrelation
Standard errors are in parentheses

[1] The ΔW predicted from this equation for 1970 was 10·38 compared with an actual ΔW of 11·03. ΔT registered an increase of 3·27 percentage points in this year and accounted for just under half of the predicted increase in wages.

These conclusions are further borne out by the results of the Two Stage Least Squares estimates reported in Table 16.6. T is insignificant; U^{-1} is significant; and the coefficient on ΔT is significant but again much lower than that found by Hines, (0·4409 compared with 1·5945). The coefficients on the two price variables are surprisingly low and neither is significant separately. They are, however, jointly significant. Thus, even if it is accepted that ΔT is a faithful indicator of union militancy it certainly cannot be maintained in the light of the findings reported in this section that ΔW can be predicted almost entirely from unionisation variables. There are, moreover, considerable grounds for doubting that ΔT does reflect what it is supposed to reflect as we shall show in the next section.

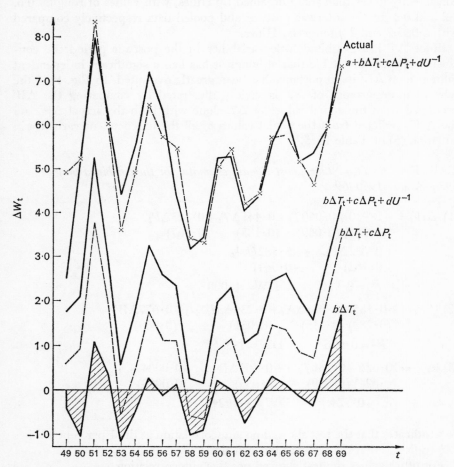

FIG 1.   Points marked $\times$ are the ΔW_t predicted from the equation

$$\Delta W_t = 3\cdot1423 + 1\cdot2893\,\Delta T_t + 0\cdot2998\,\Delta P_t + 1\cdot9121\,U^{-1}{}_t$$

The shaded area ▨ **represents the independent influence of ΔT_t on ΔW_t**

5. The measurement of union militancy

The variable ΔT is subject to a number of influences which make it a most imperfect measure of union militancy. On the one hand changes in ΔT may occur quite independently of variations in union militancy; on the other hand, ΔT may fail to pick up the possible influence of union militancy on wage rates because the effect of union militancy on ΔT is offset by the effects of the other factors which influence ΔT. In this section we investigate two such other influences on ΔT, the institution of the closed shop and changes in the structure of employment.

McCarthy [15] defines the closed shop as 'a situation in which employees come to realise that a particular job is only to be obtained and retained if they become and remain members of one of a specified number of trade unions'. It is clear that an increase or decrease in the numbers employed in establishments where a closed shop already operates may automatically raise or lower total union membership and, given the total labour force, union density, without necessarily indicating any change in union militancy. If changes in union density are to be taken as reflecting changes in the strength of union militancy, then we must be able to separate out those changes in T which are solely the result of changes in the proportion of the total labour force employed in what we may call 'the closed shop sector' from those changes which are the result of changes in the density of trade union organisation outside the closed shop sector. This can be done if we define

$$T = \lambda_c . 100 + (1 - \lambda_c) \left[\frac{T^* - L_c}{L - L_c} \right]$$

where $\lambda_c = L_c/L$, the proportion between the number of workers in closed shops, L_c, and the total labour force L;

T = aggregate union density;

T^* = the total number of workers belonging to trade unions.

At the same time any extension of the jurisdictional boundaries of the closed shop area of the economy arising from successful union demands for the establishment of a closed shop, will again automatically increase total union membership and, given the labour force, union density. In this case λ_c will rise, not because of any reallocation of the labour force as in the previous case, but because the closed shop boundaries have been enlarged so as to embrace a larger proportion of the labour force given its existing allocation. It might be argued that such an extension of the closed shop could be regarded as a specific manifestation of union militancy. But even if we grant this, changes in aggregate union density measured simply as the ratio of total trade union membership to the labour force, will still remain an imperfect indicator of union militancy. Suppose a union is aiming at 100 per cent unionisation of the relevant labour force, and to this end sustains a constant degree of militancy year after year with regularly repeated demands for a closed shop. We may expect that union's density series will show relatively small increases for the years preceding its final victory on the closed shop issue, followed by a large jump in the year of victory itself, followed by zero changes thereafter. In such a case the impact of the eventual establishment of a closed shop on the union's membership and density will be out of all proportion to the degree of militancy displayed during that year.

There are, then, two distinct types of closed shop impact to be investigated: the static impact arising from changes in the proportion of the labour force employed within given jurisdictional boundaries covered by closed shop arrangements; and the dynamic impact arising from any extensions of these jurisdictional boundaries. Unfortunately it is extremely difficult to estimate either type of impact with any precision, mainly because there are many trades in which the closed shop operates in some establishments but not in others, and the available data simply do not allow accurate estimates of closed shop coverage to be made. We have, however, been able to provide an illustrative estimate of the static effect of the closed shop on aggregate union membership and density.

The most accurate and comprehensive account of the extent of the closed shop in Britain is given by McCarthy [15], whose findings have been closely followed here. According to McCarthy the closed shop is overwhelmingly an institution found among manual workers. The following sections of the labour force were singled out from the total area affected by the closed shop as described by McCarthy and constitute what may be called the 'central closed shop sector'. They each satisfy the following criteria of selection:

(a) they relate to manual workers only;
(b) they each cover a relatively large number of workers;
(c) they all fall into McCarthy's categories of trades which are either 'comprehensively closed' or 'mainly closed'.

Collectively these sections covered nearly 80 per cent of the total number of workers estimated by McCarthy to have been subject to the closed shop at the beginning of the 1960s. The remainder consist of Co-operative workers and other non-manual groups, or of sections which are individually relatively small, or of sections which are widely dispersed throughout the 'mainly open' trades.

Industrial/Occupation area (manual workers only)	Numbers estimated to be subject to the closed shop in 1961
1. Coal mining	605,500
2. Oil refining	23,100
3. Sea transport	56,100
4. Docks	68,000
5. Railway workshops	65,000
6. Road passenger transport	100,000
7. Engineering and electrical goods (including vehicles except railway vehicles)	1,200,000

8. Shipbuilding and ship repair   157,900
9. Iron and steel manufacture   210,000
10. Textiles   110,000
11. Newspapers, periodicals and general printing   194,300
12. Construction craftsmen   100,000

Total   2,889,900

The total numbers of manual workers in each of these areas were estimated for 1948 and 1961. The numbers affected by the closed shop in each area in 1948 were then calculated on the assumption that the proportion between the number of workers subject to the closed shop and the total number of manual workers in each area was the same in 1948 as in 1961. This assumption is a very crude approximation to the assumption that jurisdictional boundaries of the closed shop in the 'central closed shop sector' remained unchanged throughout the period 1948–61. On this basis the labour force in the 'central closed shop sector' rose from 2,815,600 in 1948, to 2,889,900 in 1961, which, however, as a proportion of total employees constituted a fall from 13·6 to 12·5 per cent. This relative decline is partly due to the fact that the 'central closed shop sector' contains a number of declining industries (notably coal mining, shipbuilding and textiles) whose falling shares of total employment more than offset the rising shares of the expanding industries contained within this same sector (notably engineering and printing). Chiefly, however, the decline can be attributed to a fall in the number of manual workers as a proportion of total employees within each industry.

The relative decline of the 'central closed shop sector' automatically reduced aggregate union density below what it would otherwise have been. Thus aggregate density in 1948, calculated according to the formula given above, was 45·16 per cent. Assuming an unchanged union density outside the 'central closed shop sector' in 1961, the redistribution of the labour force away from the 'central closed shop sector' would have produced an aggregate union density of 44·46 per cent. Superficially this decline of 0·70 of a percentage point appears negligible. If the decline had occurred at an even pace throughout the period, aggregate density would have fallen by just over 0·05 of a percentage point each year, other things being equal. When, however, it is remembered that Hines's militancy variable ΔT had a range of only $-0·92$ to $+0·85$ with a mean value of $-0·19$[1] the static impact of the closed shop appears somewhat less than negligible. If we define ΔT_c as the change in union density arising solely as a result of the static impact of the closed shop, and ignore the possibility that extensions of the jurisdictional boundaries of the closed shop might also affect aggregate density figures, then the appropriate specification of the militancy variable for Hines's hypothesis would be $\Delta T_m = \Delta T - \Delta T_c$, where ΔT is the unadjusted change in union

[1] These figures relate to ΔT calculated on the basis of the labour force defined as UK total working population minus employers, self-employed and armed forces.

density as used by Hines. When account is taken of the likelihood that ΔT_c varies from year to year, there is no reason to suppose that ΔT_m and ΔT will be closely correlated. If they are not, then the adoption of this more refined measure of union militancy ought to affect the simple correlation found by Hines between union militancy and the rate of change of money wage rates. If the Hines hypothesis is correct the explanatory power of union militancy should be improved.

Unfortunately the approximations involved in estimating a series for ΔT_c are too rough to enable such a refined measure of union militancy to be constructed, especially in view of the small orders of magnitude involved. However, the static impact of the closed shop is merely a particular instance of the more general case involving the redistribution of the labour force amongst industries with different degrees of union organisation. Since union densities differ in different industries it is entirely possible for aggregate density to change without any change in density levels within each industry if there are shifts in the structure of employment. As Hines [8] himself notes:

$$T_t = \sum_{i=1}^{n} \frac{L_i}{L} \cdot \frac{T^*_i}{L_i}$$

where L_i/L denotes the ith industry's share of the total labour force and T^*_i denotes the number of trade union members in the ith industry. It follows that:

$$\Delta T_t = \sum_{i=1}^{n} \frac{L_i}{L} \Delta \left(\frac{T^*_i}{L_i} \right) t + \sum_{i=1}^{n} \frac{T^*_i}{L_i} \Delta \left(\frac{L_i}{L} \right) t$$

$$+ \sum_{i=1}^{n} \Delta \left(\frac{L_i}{L} \right) t \, \Delta \left(\frac{T^*_i}{L_i} \right) t$$

The measure of union militancy appropriate to Hines's hypothesis is one which abstracts from changes in the distribution of the labour force. Setting

$$\Delta \left(\frac{L_i}{L} \right) t = 0 \text{ for all } i$$

the expression reduces to:

$$\Delta T_t = \sum_{i=1}^{n} \frac{L_i}{L} \Delta \left[\frac{T^*_i}{L_i} \right] t = \Delta T_{mt}$$

For convenience we shall refer to ΔT_m as a 'pure militancy index', since it measures the change in aggregate union density arising solely from changes in union density within each industry, such changes being weighted by the (constant) share of the labour force in each industry. Similarly setting

$$\Delta \left[\frac{T^*_i}{L_i} \right] = 0 \text{ for all } i$$

we may define

$$\Delta T_{et} = \sum_{i=1}^{n} \frac{T^{*}_i}{L_i} \Delta \left[\frac{L_i}{L}\right] t$$

which measures the change in aggregate union density arising solely from changes in the structure of employment when union densities in individual industries are held constant.

Series for ΔT_m and ΔT_e were calculated for the interwar period and postwar period (up to 1961). Corresponding to this division of the year to year changes in union density into two components is a similar division of the annual *level* of union density. At any given time the prevailing level of union density is the resultant of two forces: on the one hand the changes in union density within each industry, on the other the changes in the distribution of the labour force amongst industries with differing density levels, which have occurred over all previous time since the beginning of trade unionism. We cannot, of course, estimate the effects of these forces. We can, however, take the density existing at any arbitrary point in time and then calculate (*a*) what the level of union density would have been had the distribution of the labour force remained the same as it was in the base period; and (*b*) what the level of union density would have been given the labour force reallocation which actually occurred but holding density within each industry constant. Denoting these two forces as T_m and T_e respectively we have:

$$T_0 = T_{m_0} + T_{e_0}$$

where T_0 is the actual level of density in the base period.

$$T_t = T_{m_t} + T_{e_t}$$

$$T_{m_t} = T_{m_0} + \sum_{i=1}^{t} \Delta T_{m_i}$$

$$T_{e_t} = T_{e_0} + \sum_{i=1}^{t} \Delta T_{e_i}$$

$$\therefore \quad T_{e_t} = T_0 - T_{m_0} + \sum_{i=1}^{t} \Delta T_{e_i}$$

The equation: $\Delta W_t = a_0 + a_1 \Delta T_t + a_2 T_t$ may now be written as:

$$\Delta W_t = a_0 + a_1 \Delta T_{m_t} + a_2 \Delta T_{e_t} + a_3 T_{m_t} + a_4 T_{e_t}$$

$$= a_0 + a_1 \Delta T_{m_t} + a_2 \Delta T_{e_t} + a_3 \left[T_{m_0} + \sum_{i=1}^{t} \Delta T_{m_i}\right]$$

$$+ a_4 \left[T_0 - T_{m_0} + \sum_{i=1}^{t} \Delta T_{e_i}\right]$$

which estimates as

$$\Delta W_t = b_0 + b_1 \Delta T_{m_t} + b_2 \Delta T_{e_t} + b_3 T^{*}_{m_t} + b_4 T^{*}_{e_t}$$

where $b_0 = a_0 + (a_3 - a_4) \, T_{m_0} + a_4 T_0$

$b_i = a_i \quad i = 1, \ldots, 4$

$$T^*_{m_t} = \sum_{i=1}^{t} \Delta T_{m_i}$$

and

$$T^*_{e_t} = \sum_{i=1}^{t} \Delta T_{e_i}$$

With this more refined definition of the union militancy variables we retested the basic unionisation hypothesis, regressing ΔW first on ΔT_m and T_m and then on all four unionisation variables ΔT_m, ΔT_e, T_m and T_e. The results are shown in Table 16.7. The performance of the militancy variables alone is poor. Though both are significant in the interwar period, neither is significant in the postwar period and T_m has the wrong sign. For the two sub-periods combined the $\bar{R}^2$ is well below that obtained by Hines (0·52 compared with 0·91) and there is positive autocorrelation in the residuals. The inclusion of the two structural variables T_e and ΔT_e makes no difference to these results for the two subperiods, when both are insignificant, but for the combined data both become significant and the autocorrelation found in the previous case disappears.

These results are consistent with the following interpretations. First, although there may be some justification for using the unadjusted ΔT series as an indicator of union militancy in the interwar period, the same is not true of the postwar period. Inspection of the series for ΔT, ΔT_m and ΔT_e reveals that in the interwar period ΔT exhibited considerable variability with a range of $-3·06$ to $2·95$ and that its movement is dominated by the movement of ΔT_m. The values of ΔT_e are small by comparison and except in one year, always negative, which reflects the sharp decline of the relatively densely unionised industries such as mining and textiles during this period. In the postwar period, however, not only is the variability of ΔT slight, but also its movement is by no means dominated by the movement of the 'pure militancy index' ΔT_m. Between 1955–56, 1956–57, 1959–60, and 1960–61 the two series moved in opposite directions and six out of thirteen years the indices had opposite signs (ΔT negative, ΔT_m positive and vice versa). Thus in the interwar period the unadjusted index of union militancy is relatively less distorted by changes in the structure of employment. Moreover, it is not, perhaps, surprising that the union militancy variables perform relatively well in the interwar period. The 1920s and 30s were years of immense flux in the fortunes of trade unionism. The decline in unionisation which began in the years immediately after the collapse of the boom which followed the First World War was turned into a rout with the defeat of the General Strike which persisted through the years of deep depression. The tide was turned with the beginning of the slow economic recovery about 1933 and in the following years unionisation made rapid advances until by the end of the decade the unions' precollapse strength had almost been restored. It is altogether more

TABLE 16.7

Equation no.	Constant	Estimates of coefficients on				$\bar{R}^2$	DW	Period
		T_m	ΔT_m	T_c	ΔT_c			
(1)	1·218 (0·262)	0·153 (0·040)	0·723 (0·083)			0·881	1·461*	1924–38
(2)	5·068	−0·184 (1·297)	1·335 (1·071)			−0·027	1·127†	1949–61
(3)	4·371 (0·531)	0·520 (0·109)	0·630 (0·283)			0·519	0·411	1924–38 1949–61
(4)	0·697 (0·534)	0·227 (0·038)	0·552 (0·088)	−0·470 (0·243)	0·970 (0·973)	0·937	2·079*	1924–38
(5)	3·827 (1·574)	−1·442 (1·592)	2·429 (1·347)	1·467 (1·495)	2·453 (3·644)	0·008	1·120†	1949–61
(6)	4·952 (0·412)	0·112 (0·122)	1·132 (0·237)	1·482 (0·383)	3·538 (1·666)	0·753	1·513*	1924–38 1949–61

* Indicates that the test showed no autocorrelation at the 1 per cent level
† Indicates that the test was inconclusive
For other values the test showed positive autocorrelation
Standard errors are shown in parentheses

plausible to regard a continuous sequence of negative values for ΔT followed by a continuous sequence of positive values as reflecting a deterioration or improvement in union bargaining strength. There is considerable evidence that periods of *major* expansion or contraction of union activity can effect the course of money wages (see [17]).[1]

Second, the significance of the 'structural' variables in the combined data may reflect the contrasts in the experience of structural change between the two subperiods. In both subperiods the trend in the industrial pattern of employment was running against trade unionism. The unions' traditional bases in industries such as mining, textiles and steel, were undergoing secular decline, whilst the sectors whose share of total employment was expanding were on the whole the least well organised. However, in the interwar period this adverse trend was especially marked as the best organised sectors were more than normally hit by heavy unemployment. This is reflected in the fact that ΔT_e was negative in all but one of the interwar years. If there had been no change in the union density within each industry the changes in the structure of employment which occurred would have produced a decline of 4·26 percentage points in aggregate union density. In these conditions wages in the densely unionized declining sectors were under exceptional downward pressure. By contrast in the postwar period (up to 1961) although the decline of the high density sectors continued, it did so at a pace which was more gentle overall and also more uneven, occasionally becoming temporarily retarded and even reversed. Thus ΔT_e for the postwar years exhibits fluctuations around a very slightly downward trend. With no change in industry density levels changes in the structure of employment between 1949 and 1961 would have produced a fall in aggregate union density of only 1·29 percentage points. These conditions provided a permissive environment for wages in the declining sectors to keep pace with the general upward movement. If this interpretation is correct then the differential impact of structural change in the two periods would account for some part of the association between the unadjusted unionisation variables and ΔW via the association between ΔW and our structural variables ΔT_e and T_e.

These interpretations are consistent with the results obtained when the 'pure militancy' and 'structural' variables are included with U^{-1} and ΔP_t as regressors (see Table 16.8). Thus ΔT_m continues to be insignificant for the postwar period (equations 2 and 5). ΔT_e is not significant in the presence of U^{-1} for the combined data (equation 6). The differential impact of structural change in the two subperiods referred to above reflects the contrasting unemployment experiences of the interwar and postwar periods. It is also worth noting that the low values of the coefficient on ΔT unadjusted, reported in section 4, are reflected with ΔT_m.

The Two Stage Least Squares estimates of the Hines three equation subsystem were repeated using the 'pure militancy' variables, T_m and ΔT_m, instead of the unadjusted unionisation variables, T and ΔT. The results are reported in Table 16.9. In the wage equation the level of unionisation T_m is insignificant; U^{-1} is significant; and the coefficient on ΔT_m is significant but

TABLE 16.8

| Equation no. | Constant | Estimates of coefficients on | | | | $\bar{R}^2$ | DW | Period |
		ΔT_m	ΔT_e	ΔP_t	U^{-1}			
(1)	$-0 \cdot 364$ (0·856)	$0 \cdot 508$ (0·182)		$0 \cdot 211$ (0·128)	$11 \cdot 194$ (10·772)	$0 \cdot 809$	$1 \cdot 259$	1924–38
(2)	$1 \cdot 099$ (1·471)	$0 \cdot 870$ (0·606)		$0 \cdot 386$ (0·150)	$4 \cdot 245$ (2·684)	$0 \cdot 626$	$1 \cdot 139$	1949–61
(3)	$0 \cdot 057$ (0·252)	$0 \cdot 434$ (0·151)		$0 \cdot 295$ (0·090)	$6 \cdot 412$ (0·920)	$0 \cdot 925$	$1 \cdot 817^*$	1924–38 1949–61
(4)	$-0 \cdot 550$ (0·796)	$0 \cdot 506$ (0·168)	$2 \cdot 477$ (1·422)	$0 \cdot 192$ (0·119)	$20 \cdot 075$ (11·192)	$0 \cdot 838$	$1 \cdot 453$	1924–38
(5)	$0 \cdot 335$ (1·355)	$0 \cdot 162$ (0·650)	$-3 \cdot 870$ (1·999)	$0 \cdot 604$ (0·174)	$3 \cdot 730$ (2·377)	$0 \cdot 711$	$1 \cdot 730^*$	1949–61
(6)	$-0 \cdot 005$ (0·322)	$0 \cdot 420$ (0·161)	$-0 \cdot 341$ (1·064)	$0 \cdot 307$ (0·091)	$6 \cdot 410$ (0·938)	$0 \cdot 922$	$1 \cdot 847^*$	1924–38 1949–61

* Indicates no autocorrelation at the 1 per cent level
† Indicates that the test was inconclusive
For other values the test showed positive autocorrelation
Standard errors are shown in parentheses

again substantially lower than that found by Hines. As before the price variables are not significant separately but they are jointly significant.

What the findings of this section show is that there are considerable grounds for doubting that Hines's unionisation variables provide in general adequate indicators of union militancy. Moreover, when these variables are adjusted to take account of structural changes in the labour force, just one of the factors which may affect the recorded level and changes in the level of union membership independently of the degree of union militancy, their explanatory power, far from improving, in some respects actually deteriorates.

TABLE 16.9. *Two Stage Least Squares Estimates for the Combined Periods 1925–38 and 1950–61*

(1) $\Delta W_t = 0 \cdot 558 + 0 \cdot 081 T^m{}_t + 0 \cdot 474 \Delta T^m{}_t + 0 \cdot 055 \Delta P_t$
$\quad\quad (0 \cdot 360)\ (0 \cdot 054) \quad\ (0 \cdot 132) \quad\quad (0 \cdot 127)$
$\quad\quad\quad + 0 \cdot 200 \Delta P_{t-1/2} + 6 \cdot 368 U^{-1}$
$\quad\quad\quad (0 \cdot 118) \quad\quad\ (0 \cdot 792)$
$\quad\quad\quad \bar{R}^2 = 0 \cdot 963 \quad\quad \text{DW} = 1 \cdot 670^*$

(2) $\Delta P_t = -0 \cdot 232 + 0 \cdot 063 \Delta X_t + 0 \cdot 239 \Delta M_{t-1/2} + 0 \cdot 682 \Delta W_t$
$\quad\quad (0 \cdot 318)\ (0 \cdot 148) \quad\ (0 \cdot 363) \quad\quad (0 \cdot 082)$
$\quad\quad\quad \bar{R}^2 = 0 \cdot 930 \quad\quad \text{DW} = 1 \cdot 668^*$

(3) $\Delta T_m = 10 \cdot 054 - 0 \cdot 40 T^m{}_{t-1} + 0 \cdot 355 \Delta P_{t-1/2} - 0 \cdot 004 \pi_{t-1}$
$\quad\quad (2 \cdot 074)\ (0 \cdot 050) \quad\ (0 \cdot 079) \quad\quad (0 \cdot 0005)$
$\quad\quad\quad \bar{R}^2 = 0 \cdot 6108 \quad\quad \text{DW} = 1 \cdot 2312\dagger$

* Indicates that the test showed no autocorrelation at the 1 per cent level
† Indicates that the test was inconclusive
Standard errors are shown in parentheses

6. Conclusions

We have shown that the leading empirical case in support of the union-strength interpretation of postwar inflation is extremely unsatisfactory. It is theoretically weak, being based on no more than *ad hoc* rationalisations of empirical associations, which are in many cases individually dubious and together imply a specification of the wage rate/militancy relationship different from that actually tested by Hines. The Hines case is empirically weak on several grounds. The data used to measure changes in union density were badly selected, and, in particular, the use of an improved labour force series has been shown to make a substantial difference to Hines's regression estimates for the interwar period. Further, Hines's postulation of a permanent increase in the coefficient on ΔT in the postwar period is unfounded, the simple association between ΔW and ΔT having disappeared altogether during the

1960s. In addition a retesting of Hines's complete wage determination equation on the basis of improved data and consistent definitions of variables reveals that the explanatory power of the militancy variables is considerably less than Hines claims, and also that the level of unemployment cannot be ignored in comparisons of wage movements between the interwar and postwar periods. Finally doubt has been cast on the use of ΔT to represent union militancy at all. In particular such factors as the closed shop and the process of labour force reallocation have been shown to have an effect on aggregate union density, which, in the postwar period at least, has been large by comparison with the actually recorded changes in union density. Moreover, when the ΔT series is adjusted so as to abstract from the aggregation effects of labour force redistribution, the explanatory power of the union militancy variables is substantially weakened. Some plausible interpretations of the observed association between ΔT unadjusted and ΔW have been suggested.

We have not set out to refute all possible variants of the cost push via union strength thesis. In particular the inference cannot be drawn from our study that 'unions do not matter'. A large part of our case against Hines has been that his proposed index of union militancy is seriously deficient. It remains entirely possible that some more satisfactory index may be devised which will succeed in explaining more than a minor part of the movements in money wage rates, and which is theoretically well grounded. What can, however, be asserted on the basis of the results presented here is that Hines's version of the union strength thesis is unacceptable.

Year	ΔW_t	T_t	ΔP_t	$\Delta P_{t-1/2}$	U_t	ΔT_{m_t}	T_{m_t}	ΔT_{e_t}	T_{e_t}	ΔX_t	π_t	$\Delta M_{t-1/2}$
1924	1·18	48·98	0·89	0·28	10·33	0·95	0·95	0·43	−0·43	3·79	876·4	1·97
1925	0·58	47·73	−0·29	0·0	11·28	−0·80	0·15	−0·33	−0·76	0·74	830·6	−0·65
1926	−0·73	44·67	−2·68	−0·56	12·56	−2·46	−2·31	−0·07	−0·83	−0·75	758·0	−4·67
1927	−1·18	41·74	−0·92	−2·23	9·72	−2·51	−4·82	−0·47	−1·30	1·45	891·7	−4·29
1928	−0·89	40·45	−0·91	−3·25	10·82	−0·92	−5·74	−0·15	−1·45	0·0	924·1	−0·72
1929	−0·45	40·17	−3·44	−0·60	10·43	−0·13	−5·87	−0·27	−1·72	0·72	984·2	−4·35
1930	−0·15	39·03	−4·87	−3·89	16·00	−0·92	−6·79	−0·08	−1·80	−0·71	973·2	−12·70
1931	−1·65	36·20	−4·14	−6·13	21·25	−2·82	−9·61	−0·18	−1·98	−1·47	919·0	−16·98
1932	−2·17	34·69	−3·17	−4·05	22·05	−1·32	−10·93	−0·22	−2·20	1·47	840·1	−10·87
1933	−0·47	34·09	−1·47	−1·45	19·93	0·31	−10·62	−0·27	−2·47	2·86	977·2	−3·49
1934	0·47	35·42	1·45	0·35	16·74	0·72	−9·92	−0·07	−2·54	2·08	1139·3	2·33
1935	1·71	37·27	2·14	1·39	15·51	2·06	−7·86	−0·07	−2·61	2·74	1288·6	4·44
1936	3·03	39·70	4·17	2·38	13·11	2·88	−4·98	−0·21	−2·82	0·66	1445·0	6·38
1937	3·51	42·65	3·62	4·30	10·83	3·41	−1·57	−0·22	−3·04	−1·35	1500·0	5·88
1938	1·84	43·53	1·29	1·56	12·88	−0·06	−1·63	0·04	−3·00	0·0	1394·0	0·94
1949	2·52	44·84	3·39	3·85	1·63	−0·37	−0·37	0·28	0·28	3·25	1843·0	7·09
1950	5·27	44·03	6·56	3·86	1·63	−0·87	−1·24	0·10	0·38	1·90	2054·3	9·38

Year												
1951	8·01	44·88	8·96	7·94	1·32	0·72	−0·52	0·06	0·44	0·0	2203·2	15·91
1952	6·13	45·17	5·48	7·95	2·16	−0·02	−0·54	0·14	0·58	1·27	1822·7	2·24
1953	4·40	44·25	2·00	3·35	1·78	−0·34	−0·88	−0·19	0·39	3·05	1887·5	−6·49
1954	5·50	43·83	3·29	2·49	1·46	−0·30	−1·18	−0·20	0·19	2·38	2045·0	−2·04
1955	7·20	44·04	4·88	4·43	1·21	−0·25	−1·43	0·08	0·27	1·16	2250·3	2·25
1956	6·30	43·94	4·12	4·33	1·30	0·25	−1·18	−0·15	0·12	1·16	2160·0	2·20
1957	4·36	44·03	3·28	3·77	1·55	0·16	−1·02	−0·03	0·09	1·70	2191·4	−0·48
1958	3·18	43·17	1·78	2·73	2·25	−0·70	−1·72	0·01	0·10	2·25	2078·6	−3·45
1959	3·47	42·46	0·83	0·87	2·28	0·46	−1·26	−0·38	−0·28	3·26	2252·9	1·54
1960	5·23	42·63	2·19	1·23	1·73	0·41	−0·85	−0·27	−0·55	2·11	2499·0	0·51
1961	5·28	42·64	3·71	3·43	1·63	−0·20	−1·05	−0·06	−0·61	1·04	2360·0	−0·51
1962	4·06	42·07	3·01	3·62	2·13					2·06	2252·8	0·0
1963	4·36	41·90	2·60	2·28	2·62					3·50	2528·0	2·03
1964	5·61	42·15	3·92	3·30	1·75					2·88	2772·5	2·22
1965	6·29	42·24	4·26	4·43	1·50					1·89	2770·1	1·21
1966	5·15	42·14	3·16	3·80	1·61					2·31	2507·8	0·96
1967	5·37	41·88	3·56	3·04	2·52					3·60	2483·1	3·10
1968	5·90	42·33	4·98	4·24	2·53					3·45	2626·8	5·88
1969	7·71	43·64	5·78	5·37	2·53					2·10	2497·9	4·87

326   D. L. Purdy and G. Zis

Data sources

Hourly rates of wages:	*British Labour Statistics: Historical Abstract* 1886–1968; *Department of Employment Gazette*, H.M.S.O. (For period 1924–38, June of each year figures used.)
Labour force figures:	*British Labour Statistics: Historical Abstract* 1886–1968; *Monthly Digest of Statistics*, H.M.S.O.
Trade union membership:	*British Labour Statistics: Historical Abstract* 1886–1968; *Department of Employment Gazette*, H.M.S.O.
Unemployment (total register):	*British Labour Statistics: Historical Abstract* 1886–1968; *Monthly Digest of Statistics*. H.M.S.O.
Retail prices (all items):	*British Labour Statistics: Historical Abstract* 1886–1968; H.M.S.O. *The British Economy: Key Statistics* 1900–70. H.M.S.O. (For period 1924–38, June of each year figures used.)
Imports average values:	*The British Economy: Key Statistics* 1900–70. H.M.S.O.
Output per man (GDP):	*The British Economy: Key Statistics* 1900–70. H.M.S.O.
Profits (Companies):	*The British Economy: Key Statistics* 1900–70. H.M.S.O.
Price deflator:	R. G. Lipsey and M. D. Steuer in *Economica* 1961; OECD Main Economic Indicators.

References

1. BAIN, G. S. 'Trade union growth and recognition', Research Paper no. 6, Royal Commission on Trade Unions and Employers' Associations, London, 1964.
2. BURTON, J. *Wage Inflation*, Studies in Economics, London, Macmillan, 1972.
3. DICKS-MIREAUX, L. A. and DOW, J. C. R. 'The determinants of wage inflation: United Kingdom 1946–56', *Journal of the Royal Statistical Society*, Series A, 1959.
4. ECKSTEIN, O. and WILSON, T. A. 'The determinants of money wages in American industry', *Quarterly Journal of Economics*, Vol. 76, 1962, pp. 379–414.
5. GODFREY, L. 'The Phillips curve: incomes policy and trade union effects', in *The Current Inflation*, eds. H. G. Johnson and A. R. Nobay, Macmillan, 1971.
6. HINES, A. G. 'Trade unions and wage inflation in the United Kingdom, 1893–1961', *Review of Economic Studies*, 1964.
7. HINES, A. G. 'Unemployment and the rate of change of money wage rates in the United Kingdom 1862–1963: a re-appraisal', *Review of Economics and Statistics*, 1968.
8. HINES, A. G. 'Wage inflation in the United Kingdom 1948–1962 a disaggregated study', *Economic Journal*, 1969.
9. HINES, A. G. 'The determinants of the rate of change of money wage rates and the effectiveness of incomes policy' in *The Current Inflation*, eds. Johnson and Nobay, 1971.
10. HOBSBAWM, E. J. E. *Labouring Men: studies in the history of labour*, Weidenfeld and Nicolson, 1964.
11. KLEIN, L. R. and BALL, J. R. 'Some econometrics of the determination of the absolute level of wages and prices', *Economic Journal*, 1959.
12. LIPSEY, R. G. 'The relation between unemployment and the rate of change of money wage rates in the United Kingdom 1862–1957', *Economica*, 1960.
13. LIPSEY, R. G. *An Introduction to Positive Economics*, 2nd Ed. Weidenfeld and Nicolson, 1963.
14. LIPSEY, R. G. and PARKIN, J. M. 'Incomes policy: a re-appraisal', *Economica*, 1970.
15. MCCARTHY, W. E. J. and BLACKWELL, *The Closed Shop in Britain*, 1964.
16. PHILIPPS, A. W. 'The relation between unemployment and the rate of change of money wage rates in the United Kingdom', *Economica*, 1958.
17. PHELPS-BROWN E. H. 'The long-term movement of real wages', *The Theory of Wage Determination*, ed. J. T. Dunlop, Macmillan, 1966.
18. THOMAS, R. L. and STONEY, P. J. 'A note on the Dynamic Properties of the Hines Inflation Model', *Review of Economic Studies*, 1970.

Trade unions and wage inflation in the UK. A reappraisal: Discussion

B. J. McCormick

Good hypotheses are so hard to come by in economics that it is a little disappointing to see one which Clive Jenkins and Professor Hines espouse treated so roughly. So even if Messrs Purdy and Zis are correct in their views as to the facts, can we retain the hypothesis by setting it against different facts? Is it really the case that Professor Hines has led Purdy and Zis to look at the wrong facts?

But first, what is the theory underlying the hypothesis? Standard texts on labour economics or industrial relations are not much help. There seem to be two theories in the literature. One which goes back to Marshall and the Webbs is based on the elasticity of derived demand. The usual question is: in what circumstances can a trade union raise the wages of its members without losing them their jobs? Now a variant of this is: what increase in membership will secure and maintain a wage increase? So we have here a coincidence of increasing wages and membership. But note that the answer strongly depends upon the determinants of the elasticity of derived demand of which excess demand is a symptom.

The second theory is a little more difficult to pin down but it is a kind of satisficing model which is perhaps a better explanation of wage followers since it leaves undetermined the satisfying wage. What does emerge, however, out of such a theory is a model which might explain the behaviour of unions in the 1950s when the links between wages and prices were still affected by wartime controls and the mentality of people accustomed to operating in such markets.

But having attempted to explain union behaviour, we are still left with the behaviour of workers, employers and governments. Hines's model leaves out all three. A worker's willingness to join a union may be affected by the level of organisation—the degree of security against victimisation—rather than the wage increase. Employer resistance may be influenced by Government attitudes to inflation and unemployment.

In looking at the postwar period Purdy and Zis, and most other critics, have emphasised the small amount of variation in union membership; so small as to be accountable by other factors than wage movements. However, if we look at the numbers of unions then we notice a marked fall. There has, especially in the 1960s, been a merger movement which has probably been accompanied by wage pressure as a form of persuasion. I would regard this phenomena as the more promising field for testing Hines's hypothesis, though it would need to be related to plant wages rather than industry collective bargaining.

On the subject of industrywide collective bargaining, Purdy and Zis mention the development of wage drift and plant bargaining as criticisms of the Hines's hypothesis. There is however a more fundamental objection and that is the fact that in collective bargaining it is common for coalitions of unions to negotiate with employers. Hence it would be extremely difficult to identify which union was responsible for the wage increase. Here, as elsewhere, a little knowledge of the institutional arrangements for collective bargaining would have helped.

Turning to the interwar period, it is not clear from Hines's hypothesis whether in conditions of unemployment there is a trade off between wages and unemployment. What probably happens is that while a union may hope to maximise the wage bill, the downward pressure on wages caused by work-sharing causes a split in the membership with the ultimate expulsion (unemployment) of some. Now in these situations the attitude of those in jobs to those unemployed may be interesting as Purdy and Zis observe. Perhaps the union devotes some of its finances to unemployment pay, though this could have been true only of the craft unions, e.g. the printers.

I turn finally to the testing carried out by Purdy and Zis. Many of their changes in definitions and measurement of data are I think desirable. There is, however, one notable exception. They say of unemployment: 'We did not place a lag on unemployment, as Hines did implicitly' (p. 307). In a field where data can be bent to suit all tastes it is a pity that they did not set out their reasons for so crucial a change. But this is a small blemish in an excellent paper.

The rate of interest in a
state of economic flux[1]

17

P. N. Mathur

1. Introduction

In an economy experiencing steady growth, the rate of new investment might
well be pushed to the point in the investment demand schedule where the
marginal productivity of the new invested capital is equal to the market rate
of interest. This result has been shown to hold also in the case of balanced
growth with Harrod–Neutral embodied technological progress. However,
in other environments, the rate of interest may hardly effect the rate of new
investment. The results of empirical studies have been well summarised by
Schackle [6]* a decade ago.

> In an economy with fast obsolescence rate . . . the powerlessness of interest
> rates within the ordinary range of 2 to 8 per cent per annum, to influence the
> demand price of near horizon equipment by undergoing any change of a size
> which may be supposed to occur within months, is a matter of plain arithmetic.
> The ineradicable uncertainty of enterprise, the nearness of horizons thus im-
> posed, the powerlessness of the changes in the interest rate, are all intimately
> bound together. . . Most of the investors want their investment to pay for itself
> within a few years.

And as such, total amount of new investment is autonomous of the interest
rate. I have called such a state of the economy as 'a state of economic flux'.
  The interest rate as a phenomenon pre-dates industrial economy. Historically it has been known to exist far back into the past. However, in such cases
it must have been primarily determined by what has been called the consump-
tion-loan model of interest. This is qualitatively a different phenomenon
from the interest rate in an industrial society rather than a different model of
the same reality. It may be referred to as a primitive interest rate. There is

[1] I am indebted to my colleagues in the Economics Department of the University
College of Wales, and to various scholars attending the Conference whose incisive
comments have proved of invaluable help in writing this. I would particularly like to
mention the names of Professor Graham L. Rees, Mr L. J. Williams, Mr J. Kitchen,
Mr J. R. Edwards and Mr D. Law, in this connection.

* Numbers in square brackets relate to References on p. 342.

no guarantee that a primitive interest rate will be a positive quantity—it may be negative, zero or positive, in accordance with the demand and supply of the funds for consumption.

The classicist had, primarily, a stationary model of the economy for exact analysis. In a stationary state the population was constant and so was the total output, total capital and the rest of the economic variables. The essential classical method consisted of comparative analysis of different stationary states derived on the basis of differing economic parameters, and no theory could have been developed for moving from one state to another. With such an analytical framework the concept of extra capital creation in the whole economy is not very meaningful and therefore no interest rate of different type to the primitive interest rate could have existed—even if the economy was an industrial one. In fact, as we now know from the Golden Rule of Growth theory, even if more capital than the optimum is invested and the economy is constrained to keep it up, there would have been less *per capita* consumption than otherwise possible. This would imply a negative marginal productivity. Thus we find Schumpeter [5] maintaining that in equilibrium real interest is always zero and that the interest we find in the market during circular process is not something of any significance other than that of consumption loan, as he fully realised the implications of the stationary economy.

The difficulty has arisen because the interest rate has been made as one of the major pillars of the neoclassical theory of distribution. It cannot sustain that weight under the stationary assumption. This has been almost jocularly demonstrated by P. Sraffa [7]. He moves smoothly from one price configuration to another through the whole range of technologically possible interest rates in a stationary economy, with the assumption of only labour and capital as constraining factors in the economy, and shows that interest rate can be arbitrarily determined; demand plays no part in determining the price system for production structure can be adjusted to it.

The situation is different in a steadily growing economy, in that the whole economy will be growing at the rate of growth of population. Then production, consumption and stocks remain constant in relation to population over the years. Then capital accumulation will be at the same rate as the rate of growth of population, and society will be saving at the same rate in relation to the stocks. Thus, we get a concept of social rate of interest which is equal to the rate of growth of population when the 'golden rule' of accumulation is prevailing.

The theories developed in the context of the stationary economy or the economy experiencing steady growth could be applied to any of the modern economies experiencing a high degree of innovational activity only under certain assumptions about that technical progress. Certain special types of technological progress have been found to be particularly amenable to it. For instance, that having disembodied technical change implying that capital equipment is something like a Meccano set—which can be rebuilt with new specifications, according to economic necessity.

However, Mrs J. Robinson and W. E. G. Salter [4] have taught us to think of an economy where the technology is embodied in the equipment. The equipment or fixed capital embodies the technology of the time when it was newly installed. This technology remains the same up to the time it is scrapped. The technological progress in the economy comes about by the installation of new equipment—embodying better techniques. At a particular moment of time equipment installed at different past dates will be simultaneously working, having, of course, different productivities.

In understanding the working of a short-run economy, we can neglect the embodiment of technological change in the relevant equipment only at the cost of relevance. Thus, in the state of flux there will be a spectrum of technologies of different productivities working simultaneously, and new investment will be autonomous, depending on changing visions of economic possibilities.

In all the work that has been done during the last decade on embodied technological change, total capital has been taken as embodied. No distinction is made between the fixed capital and the working capital portions of it. However, while fixed capital embodies the technological change, working capital is malleable and can be easily transferred from one technology to the next, being renewable in each cycle. So, in reality, the capital should not be considered as 'putty-clay', malleable before formation and unchangeable after it is formed into equipment, but should be considered as 'putty-putty' and 'putty-clay' where working capital is always of the nature of putty rather than of clay.

The intention of the present paper is to examine the implication of introducing working capital in the model for embodied technological progress. An attempt is made to analyse some influences of the interest rate exhibited in economies which are in a state of flux. It has been shown that in such a case, interest rate plays a role in allocating scarce working capital to processes of different vintages similar to that played by wage rate in the allocation of labour. Thus, it shares with wage rate the thankless task of exhibiting the obsoleteness of certain production processes of older vintage in the economy and thus is one of the main tools of technological transformation.

2. A simplified model of the economy with embodied technological progress

The model developed below is basically of Keynesian type, where the new investment to be done in the current year (t) is exogenously determined. It may be decided by the entrepreneurs, government agencies etc. Apart from this, the economy has got *in situ* various amounts of fixed capital equipment belonging to different vintages. Each vintage capital equipment has got a technologically determined output, employment and associated requirements for working capital; let us call them by: $y(v)$, $n(v)$ and $m(v)$, respectively.

To be able to concentrate on the complications introduced by the introduction of working capital, we are assuming in what follows that the technological progress is at such a fast rate that all the later techniques are preferable to the earlier ones, irrespective of the current wage–interest rate relationships. Thus, if an equipment of T years of age is working, all the equipment of less than T years of age will be working also.[1]

The autonomous or exogenous investment in the current period will be the fixed investment plus the concomitant working capital to go with it. However, the total new saving required to be done from the current production would be less than this amount. Because simultaneously some other capacity would be becoming obsolete and would be releasing the savings embodied in its working capital. It will not be able to do so for the fixed capital if there is something left of it physically which technically is capable of continuing its previous role in production. The various accounting devices used for taking care of obsolescence are monetary devices to apportion this loss appropriately and do they not affect the reality of the effective abandonment of some productive power embodied in the fixed capital equipment, while no such loss is sustained in the case of working capital that was working with it, unless some works are abandoned while in progress, which is rare.

The amount of fixed investment done in the current period will determine the amount of savings required. This amount will be equal to the amount of fixed investment plus the amount of working capital required to work that fixed investment, minus the amount of working capital that will be released by equipment which is currently becoming obsolete. If the oldest machines now in use are T years old and the equipment of the age between $(T+\delta)$ and T is to become obsolete, then the amount of working capital released will be that which was working with that equipment.

The output of the equipment on the margin of obsolescence will provide the wages for the persons engaged on it, as well as the interest for the working capital that it employs. It need not provide the interest on the fixed capital, as it has zero opportunity cost, being on the margin of obsolescence. Thus, the difference between the productivity per employed person of T-year old equipment and the current wage rate will be the interest rate on its associated per person working capital.

It may be noted that in this vintage model the output of a given vintage is fixed. Any capital of a given vintage either produces to the full capacity or does not produce at all. There is no scope of partial utilisation of capacity of any particular vintage. This assumption helps us to abstract from problems of underutilisation due to monopoly or similar restrictive practices etc.

In the following, to get at essentials, we have examined an economy which has only one commodity serving indifferently as a fixed capital good, working

---

[1] This assumption is designed so as not to divert the attention to the peropheral problem of reswitching of techniques with changing interest rates. In the latter case the ranking of techniques with respect to profitability, may differ with different interest rates and will not be the same, as that with respect to time. The main arguments can nevertheless be applied even in that case, provided we go on rearranging various capacities according to the rank appropriate to the interest rate. However, in the text only the pedagogically easier and much more likely case is considered where the two rankings, viz. that according to profitability and that in accordance with time of installation are the same.

capital good, and a consumer good. It is measured unambiguously in current physical units. However, fixed capital already embodied in equipment in previous periods is not commensurate. It cannot be unambiguously measured in current physical units of the commodity. However, for the current decisions we do not require its measurement. We only require to know its current characteristics, viz. how much output per unit of time it can help produce and how much labour and working capital it requires to be associated with itself in the process.

3. A short descriptive digression

It is difficult to visualise on one commodity model. But it keeps life simple by doing away with the pricing problem. Nor is it as unnatural as it sounds. After all, by a well-known theorem formulated by J. R. Hicks [1], if, throughout the period of analysis the relative prices of different commodities do not change, they can be regarded as a single commodity. The fixed price method of analysis is essentially a single commodity model, and quite a bit of macro-analysis falls under this category.

Nevertheless, let us try to visualise an economy producing only 'corn'. In its production some fixed capital is used, say 'bullocks', which are really converted 'corn'. Apart from that working capital is required for 'seed' and and 'feed'. That is also in the form of 'corn'. Different techniques consist of different breeds of 'bullocks' having different working capacities, feeding requirements and possibly different amounts of 'corn' embodied in themselves. We assume that the entrepreneur can only get the breed of the current vintage which is better than all previous ones. With the existing 'bullocks' his option is either to keep them working with necessary cooperating factors of production or not to feed them nor take any work from them. He takes this decision only at the harvest time, so that all the working capital invested in 'seed' or 'feed' is back in liquid form at that time. There will be no special problem if he takes the decision not to use a 'bullock' only when the 'bullock' is dead. For by then he would have used all the potentialities of his fixed asset. But if he takes the decision to abandon it even during the 'bullock's' lifetime he is writing off some technically useful, though not economically useful asset. Then this decision must be governed by economic considerations.

The decision to invest in the 'bullocks' of latest vintage is mostly taken by sets of entrepreneurs other than those who will be forced by economic circumstances to close a portion of their business, and thus may be taken not to be governed by their decision to close down. Further, in a state of flux it is autonomous of the interest rate. Thus it is exogenous to the variables in the economy we are considering.

Further, when an entrepreneur decides to close down one enterprise as uneconomic, the 'bullock' associated with it is, of course, obsolete. However, its associated working capital is available to him in the form of 'corn'. If there is no net dissavings involved, they must be transferred to those who can make use of the same for productive investment. To visualise this aspect we may envisage that all 'corn' which is not consumed has to be stored at a central place, of entrepreneurs who have decided to make new investment also place their demand for the total 'corn' required for fixed capital formation, as well as for working capital, to their 'store manager'. If any business is closed, all the 'corn' that was being utilised as working capital in it thus also goes in the same store. The 'store manager' is required to see that the ingoing and outgoing of the stores exactly match. For this he has got two instruments, that is, he can set up a wage rate and an interest rate. We have to find out how that 'store manager' would behave in the circumstances. First, when he has also to maintain full employment, and second when no such policy requirements are imposed on him. We want to know, in both cases, whether he has complete freedom of fixing the interest rate and the wage rate, or whether he can arbitrarily fix one, or none. Further, in the former case, is there any restriction imposed by technological considerations on the range of values that he can choose?

4. Model in a full employment economy

Let $y(v)\,dv$ be the gross output of the capital of vintage v installed during the period $(v, v+dv)$. Similarly, let $m(v)\,dv$, $n(v)\,dv$ be the corresponding working capital and labour requirements, w and r be the wage rate and short term interest rate, respectively, and T be the age of the oldest machine in working use. From our assumption that the vintage model is such that if capital of vintage T is working then all younger ones will be working too, and the machines on the verge of obsolescence are just able to pay the wages on the labour employed by them and interest on the working capital necessary for their production, the younger machines must be earning some quasirent over and above their payments for wages and interest on working capital. We shall first deal below the determination of various economic variables in conditions of full employment and then discuss what we can say about unemployment equilibrium.

When there is a full employment, summing the labour required of machines of different vintages, the age of the oldest machinery in use will be given by:

$$L= \int_{+T}^{0} n(v)\,dv - N \tag{1}$$

where L is the total labour force in the economy and N is total employment. Summing the output of different machines, the total production (Y) is given by:

$$Y= \int_{+T}^{0} y(v)\,dv \tag{2}$$

and similarly, total working capital (M) by:

$$M= \int_{m}^{0} m(v)\,dv \tag{3}$$

This is depicted in Fig 17.1.

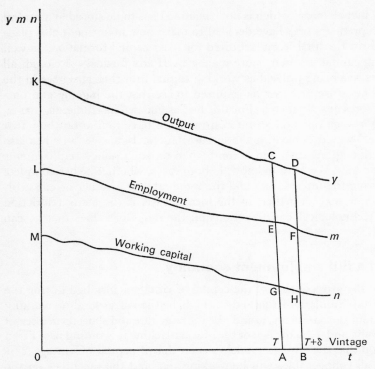

FIG 17.1.   Technological relations in a vintage model

Thus in Fig 17.1 we represent given technological information. The vintage of existing capital is represented on x-axis. The ordinate represents all the three technologically given specifications in their respective units; y gives the output, m the working capital requirements, and n the labour requirements of the total fixed investment done at any past period. Fixed capital is not represented, as once it is embodied all information about it is given by the above three technological characteristics (of course, assuming no scrap value).

The assumption about the technological progress is that if the capital of vintage (T) is not obsolete, all the capitals of the less older vintages will also not be obsolete. Therefore, the total output in that case will be given by the area OACK, total employment by OAGM and total working capital in the economy by OAEL.

The production of the capital of the oldest vintage, $y(T)$ should just provide for the wages of the workers working on it and interest on the working capital used with it; therefore, $y(T) = wn(T) + rm(T)$. The output of subvintage capital $y(v < T)$ will be able to provide some quasirent over and above the wages and interest on its working capital. It is this quasirent which should pay the entrepreneur for his enterprise as well as the returns to the fixed capital invested. This will last until this capital comes on the verge of obsolescence. At that moment the quasirent on this will disappear; which means that wage and/or interest rates will rise so much as to claim the whole of the product of that vintage. Thus, wages and/or interest rates rise when older capital becomes obsolete. This relationship between wage rates, interest rates and the oldest working vintage is illustrated in Fig 17.2.

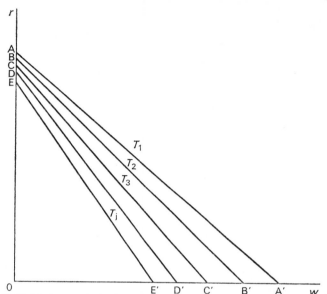

FIG 17.2.   Relationship between wages and interest rates with vintages

Each line in this diagram like AA′, BB′, CC′ ... depict the relationship between wage rate W and interest rate r, for different values of the age of the capital on the verge of obsolescence (T), they may be called the iso-vintage curve (4). The farther out the line, the lower the obsolescence age and vice versa. Here $T_1 < T_2 < T_3 \ll T_j$. Thus the knowledge of any two given technological conditions, is sufficient to give the value of the third, e.g. we need know only T and r, and the value of W will be determined by the technical conditions, as depicted in Fig 17.2, or equation (4).

Following M. Kalecki and N. Kaldor [3], savings in the economy may be assumed to be determined as proportionate to factor incomes. Letting S_c, S_d and S_w as proportions saved out of quasirents, interest incomes and wages, then total savings will be equal to:

$$S = s_c Y - (s_c - s_d) rM - (s_c - s_w) WN \qquad (4)$$

where Y, M and N denote total production, total working capital and total employment. As shown in Fig 17.1, they obviously depend on the vintage on the verge of obsoleteness, viz. T.

Substituting the value of W from above, we get:

$$S = \left[s_c Y - (s_c - s_w) \frac{N}{n} y \right] - \left[(s_c - s_d) M - (s_c - s_w) \frac{mN}{n} \right] r$$

$$(4')$$

It may be seen that both the quantities inside the bracket are dependent on vintage T only.

Figure 17.3 draws these curves in ST dimension for the various given values of r.

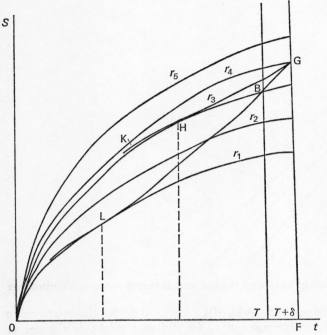

FIG 17.3.   Iso-interest saving-vintage curves

For given T higher the r, higher the savings as normally $(s_c - s_w)mN$ should be greater than $(s_c - s_d)Mn$. Where $s_c = s_d$ this is obviously true. Further, total savings increase with increasing T, as it increases the income of all the three classes.

Total autonomous investment in the economy is given. This consists of autonomous fixed investment, investment in the working capital necessary to go with it, and other autonomous expenditure, if any. Let this be given by FG on Fig 17.3. If the total fixed capital being used up to the last period cannot be manned, the fixed capital of the oldest vintage will become obsolete. The working capital engaged with it will be released for new investment. Therefore, the new investment necessary will not be equal to FG but less. Analytically:

$$I = A - \int_{T+\delta}^{T} m(\nu)\,d\nu \tag{5}$$

where A is the autonomous investment and I is the new investment required.

In accordance with the relation 1 (or Fig 17.1) the total labour force may only be sufficient now to man the capital of vintages up to T. Then the total investment requirements in accordance with the relation (5) will be TB in Fig. 17.3. We also see that, in order that the savings are equal to investment, the interest rate should be only r_3. Corresponding to point B in Fig 17.3, the wage rates get determined from Fig 17.2 (relation 4) and output levels from relation 2 (Fig 17.1).

Thus we see that full employment of a vintage capital model where several techniques of production exist simultaneously, imply a short term interest rate dependent upon the exogenous demand for investment, history of past investment and propensities to save out of various factor incomes, and it is completely determined out of non-monetary considerations. Further, this formulation is not dependent on any long-term considerations.

5. Situation in unemployment equilibrium

In a case where there is no full employment, the exact value of interest rate becomes indeterminate. Various values of short-term interest rates can coexist with a given level of autonomous investment. However, once the value of short-term interest rate is fixed, both the age of capital of oldest vintage, as well as the wage rate gets determined. Thus, in general, the economy regains one degree of freedom, which may be used in moving towards full employment. It will be seen that any such movement will be a movement towards higher interest rates and use of greater vintages. As greater vintages are less productive, this implies a proportionately higher squeezing of the wage rates. The reduction in wage rates should also compensate for the higher quasirents payable as a consequence of working of the older vintage capital.

There may come about one very interesting case that is worth noting. If the new investment curve becomes tangent to any constant interest saving curve, that interest rate becomes the minimum below which the saving investment identity cannot be satisfied. Thus, if the investment curve is GHK which is tangent to the constant interest saving curve r_3, r_3 becomes the minimum possible interest rate.

Thus, we see from $(4')$, for constant r, and remembering (1), (2) and (3):

$$\frac{\delta s}{\delta T} = s_w y - (s_c - s_w) N \frac{\mathrm{d}}{\mathrm{d}T} \frac{(y)}{n}$$

$$+ \left\{ (s_a - s_w) m + (s_c - s_w) N \frac{\mathrm{d}}{\mathrm{d}T} \frac{(m)}{n} \right\} r \tag{6}$$

This will be always greater than zero as $s_w Y$ and $(s_a - s_w)m$ are positive and $\mathrm{d}/\mathrm{d}T(y - mr)/(n)$ will be negative, as this is the rate of change of wage rate with changing vintages and constant interest rate.

Equation (6) gives us the marginal rate of savings per unit of time with respect to the changing vintages of the oldest fixed capital being utilised, and when the rate of interest has been kept constant. It consists of two parts. First it gives the marginal savings from the marginal income and is given by $s_w y + (s_a - s_w) mr$. The second portion $-(s_c - s_w) N(\mathrm{d}/\mathrm{d}T)(y - mr)/(n)$ represents the effect of the changes in the distribution of income in wage rates, consequent to this marginal utilisation, on the total savings from the rest of the income. The older the vintage used the less the marginal productivity, and thus given interest rate, it implies lesser wage rates. This has the distributional effect of increasing the quasirents and as we may expect a higher saving rate from quasirents than wages, this effect will also be towards increasing the size of savings.

On taking second partial derivative of saving function with respect to T, keeping r constant, we get:

$$\frac{\delta^2 s}{\delta T^2} = s_w \frac{\mathrm{d}y}{\mathrm{d}T} + (s_a - s_w) r \frac{\mathrm{d}m}{\mathrm{d}T} - (s_c - s_w) \frac{\delta^2}{\delta T^2} \frac{(y - mr)}{n} \qquad (7)$$

Normally we expect new capacity, as well as working capital requirements, to work it to increase over time, implying that the older the vintage the less it will be. So normally both $\mathrm{d}y/\mathrm{d}T$, as well as $\mathrm{d}m/\mathrm{d}T$ should be negative. $\delta^2/\delta T^2 (y - mr)/(n)$ being the rate of the decrease of the wage rate is expected to be positive.[1] Thus we can expect $\delta^2 s/\delta T^2$ to be negative in most of its range, showing that the marginal savings with increasing vintages decline, giving the shape of iso-interest saving curve, as shown in Fig 17.3.[2]

We have seen above that the investment requirements also change, in accordance with the age of the oldest vintage capital in use. This relationship is given in equation (5). From this we get the slope of the investment requirement curve at vintage T as equal to $m(T)$. For a given interest rate (r) this investment requirement curve may not meet the iso-interest curve at all, or it may touch it at a single point or it may meet it at two points of intersection.

In the first case the economy may have to increase the rate of r to be able to meet the commitments of autonomous investment if at all possible. In the second case, where the two curves touch each other, the rate of wages gets

---

[1] To concretise let us assume that near the appropriate margin y, m and n are all decreasing exponentially with increasing vintage at rate η, μ, and ν respectively. Then:

$$\frac{\mathrm{d}}{\mathrm{d}T} \left(\frac{y - rm}{n} \right) \equiv \frac{\mathrm{d}}{\mathrm{d}T} w = (-\eta y + \mu rm + \nu nw)/n$$

which will be negative as our assumption about technical progress implies that η is greater than both μ and ν and we know that $y = rm + nw$. Further:

$$\frac{\mathrm{d}^2}{\mathrm{d}T^2} \left(\frac{y - rm}{n} \right) \equiv \frac{\mathrm{d}^2}{\mathrm{d}T^2} w = \frac{1}{n} (\eta^2 y - \mu^2 rm - \nu^2 nw)$$

$$- \frac{1}{n^2} (-\eta y + \mu rm + \nu nw)$$

which is the sum of two positive terms.

[2] From the relationship (4'), we see that the surmise given in the text will hold only in the general case where $(s_c - s_w)N/n$ is greater than $(s_c - s_a)M/m$ for the relevant values of T.

In the abnormal case of T where they are equal, the savings will be invariant to changes in the interest rate. In the most unlikely perverse case, the model will be giving the upper rather than the lower limit of the possible interest rate.

uniquely determined, as well as the oldest vintage to be used and concomitant output, working capital in use, and employment. In the last case there is the choice of two values for vintages with a given interest rate. Thus, we see that given an investment and the specifications of the economy that we are discussing we get a lower limit to the possible short-term interest rates, this lower limit is given by that interest rate for which the iso-interest saving curve just touches the investment-vintage relationship given in equation (5). Within certain limits it may be possible to have a higher interest rate and still satisfy the conditions of the model. However, the interest rate cannot fall below the lower limit set. At this point the interest rate is given by the value of r, which makes $\delta s/\delta T$ equal to m. That value is:

$$
r = \frac{m - s_w y + N(s_c - s_w)\,\dfrac{\mathrm{d}}{\mathrm{d}T}\left(\dfrac{y}{n}\right)}{m(s_d - s_w) + (s_c - s_w)\,N\,\dfrac{\mathrm{d}}{\mathrm{d}T}\left(\dfrac{m}{n}\right)} \tag{8}
$$

We have seen in this paper that in a one-commodity model with vintage capital, it is not necessary that there should be always full employment. In a case where there is unemployment there is a wide range of choice of the combination of rate of interest and wage rates, which together determine the level of employment and output. However, there is a lower limit below which an interest rate technically cannot fall. Further, it also tells us the listing of the equipment that will be used for any particular unemployment situation. As I pointed out before, a single commodity model is equivalent to a fixed price macro model of an economy, which means that if we assume no flexibility of the relative prices in a macro model, the above analysis helps us towards the understanding of the following problems:

(a) The economic mechanism which helps in technological transformation of an economy and determination of obsoleteness of a capital good or process in a not fully-employed economy. The traditional theory has put all this weight on the rising wages and thus on the paucity of available labour. However, this cannot explain the technological advance, so often noticed during times of depression etc.

(b) It gives an alternative explanation of the stickiness of the rate of interest downwards under certain conditions to the well-known liquidity trap.

(c) Further, there has been a widely felt, but seldom expressed, difficulty of translating macro underemployment equilibrium situations in micro terms. When a macro model gives the total output to be produced by the economy, it has no mechanism to allocate the unused capacity to various firms. In practice we may have to assume a sort of local monopoly or partial monopoly power for each firm to explain the phenomenon of wide distribution of unemployed capacity under such situations. The model above throws light in the direction in which we can look, to make this transition to micro behaviour even in a competitive world.

12]

References

1. HICKS, J. K. *Value and Capital*, Oxford, 1939, p. 313. See also *Capital and Growth*, Oxford, 1965, p. 78.
2. KALECKI, M. *Essays in the Theory of Economic Fluctuations*, London, 1939, pp. 59–60.
3. KALDOR, N. 'Alternative theories of distribution', *Review of Economic Studies*, Vol. 23, 1955–56, pp. 94–100.
4. ROBINSON, J. *The Accumulation of Capital*, London, 1956.
   SALTER, W. E. G. *Productivity and Technical Change*, Cambridge, 1960.
5. SCHUMPETER, J. A. *The Theory of Economic Development*, 1911.
6. SHACKLE, G. L. S. 'Recent theories concerning the nature of interest', *Economic Journal*, June 1961, Vol. 71, pp. 248–49.
7. SRAFFA, P. *Production of Commodities by means of Commodities*, Cambridge 1960.

The rate of interest in a state of economic flux: Discussion

L. Fishman

We are indebted to Professor Mathur for calling our attention to two major theoretical questions that remain unanswered in growth theory, and for an interesting attempt to solve them both at a stroke. It is a pity that the solution does not appear to come off. The two problems are the nature of capital under conditions of technical progress and the role and nature of the pure rate of interest in growing economies. His solution is to bring in working capital as the malleable capital element and thereby allow marginal adjustments in 'capital' (i.e. working capital). We can thus have a Salter type embodied technical progress model, and still have malleable 'capital' (i.e. working capital). Assuming well behaved functions and Keynesian type savings and investment relationships, the interest rate is determined on the margin by the return on malleable working capital—although the model is not closed. The assumptions that permit the major problems to be avoided are made explicit in the paper:

1. 'The model has only one commodity serving indifferently as a fixed-capital good, working capital good, and a consumer good. It is measured unambiguously in physical units . . . fixed capital already embodied in equipment in previous periods is not commensurate but need not be measured.'
2. 'We are assuming . . . that the technological progress is at such a fast rate that all the later techniques are preferable to the earlier ones, irrespective of the current wage-interest rate relationships.' Thus the problems of reswitching are really assumed away by the model and it is not clear that the addition of working capital into the model adds much more than a touch of realism.

Several questions present themselves. First, is working capital the bridge we want to use to link capital theory to the 'real-world' interest rate? It is true that probably more loans to business are made for working capital purposes than for any other, but is not this a rather weak reed on which to build the entire interest rate edifice? And although it is true that working tends to be more liquid than other forms of embodied capital, much of it will still be very much embodied in inventories of one type or another or kept in purely monetary form, in which case it hardly qualifies as the fount of productivity. A second group of questions arise from the nature of the assumptions. If it is the assumptions that do permit our problems to be solved, then should we not emphasise and discuss the validity of the assumptions, and not concentrate on the relevance of the results?

Analytics of choice in fiscal policy[1]

18

M. Wolfson and A. Rayner

Introduction

The recent anxiety of economists and public officials engaged in macro-economic planning contrasts sharply with the complacency they expressed only a few years ago. Macroeconomic direction of the economy was once taken to be achievable by standard, well understood instruments of monetary and fiscal policy. Yet the target variables often seem to respond perversely in magnitude and even in direction.

There have been a number of explanations of this development. One approach amounts to a rejection of the Keynesian paradigm altogether. It has been suggested that it be replaced by a tale of rampant monopoly by some economists, and by perfect competition and the quantity theory of money by others. A second explanation, which is within the paradigm, supposes the economy to have a natural harmonic period, which, when operated on by governmental impulses of the 'right' periodicity, takes on an increasing amplitude in its fluctuation. Quite often, these harmonic swings may conflict with the intention of the authorities.

Without evaluating the validity of these explanations, or attempting to equal the thoroughness with which they have been worked out, we offer a simpler sort of explanation which is well within the traditional apparatus. We have dealt with only a bit of the problem, but our intimation is that similar methods might be applied to other aspects of control policy.

Our purpose is to explore the non-linear nature of the fiscal policy choices which are open to governments. By definition the fiscal policy instruments are government expenditure and taxes. In practice the choice is expressed as an amount of government expenditure combined with a suitable tax *rate*. The introduction of the tax rate, rather than the money tax take, into an otherwise linear model, has non-linear implications. The magnitude and often the

[1] The authors are grateful for the kind assistance and comments of L. Johansen (Oslo), A. D. Brownlie (University of Canterbury), E. Ames (State University of New York), E. McCann (University of Canterbury), J. Farrell (Oregon State University). The shortcomings of this paper ought to be assigned solely to the authors and not to their friends and associates.

direction of the effect of the fiscal instruments on the variables representing policy goals will alter with the magnitudes of the instruments.

A practical question of interest to the planner is: how nearly linear and well-behaved is the system within the ranges of the variables that are likely to be experienced? Is the response to a change in a fiscal instrument likely to alter much in magnitude or direction? One approach to these questions is by building large scale realistic models of economies (e.g. in [4])*. While this approach may give the planner more meaningful numbers to work with, it has the disadvantage that the workings of the non-linearities and indeed singularities become too complex to be considered in general, analytical, form.

Since the non-linearity emerges from even an extremely simple macro-economic model, it is possible to trace its effects in an unsophisticated Keynesian model, which we consider in the first part of this paper. The model is estimated for New Zealand, the United Kingdom and the United States, in order to give examples of the numerical magnitudes of the parameters that appear in the analytical expressions. The second part of the paper extends the model slightly, although it remains extremely simple compared with most modern macro-models. Even this small increase in the size of the model makes the analytic expression of the workings of the non-linearities become complex. This model is estimated for the same three countries to analyse the extent of the non-linearity for some actual values of the parameters and to allow us to show the effect of enlarging the model on its non-linearity. It is, of course, not suggested that this second model is an accurate statement of the options open to the governments, or always even statistically significant for every coefficient estimated in the way that Evans' results are intended to be. But it does suggest some kinds of outcomes that might not have been anticipated by the authorities. That is to say, the estimates are intended to be illustrative, rather than the basis for forecasting.

The models are both of a Keynesian, comparative static nature. For the purpose of the exercise we restrict the government to fiscal policy instruments, although some possible monetary implications of the fiscal policy appear in the more complex model.

The fiscal policy instruments are related by the government's budget identity,[1] $D \equiv G - tY$, where D is the budget deficit, G government expenditure, Y national income and t the proportional tax rate. In general G and t will be used as the instruments of government policy, and are therefore exogenous to the model, while D is determined endogenously along with Y and certain other variables. (We will examine later, as a byproduct, the non-linear trade-off relationship between D and t for fixed G.)

The first model treats investment as exogenous, and assumes a closed economy. We postpone any discussion of the money market and the method

---

[1] The implications of the budget restraint have been explored by others, notably by Carl F. Christ [2, 3]. These papers are not however, concerned with the non-linearity we investigate, nor do they use a partly empirical approach as is done here.

---

*Numbers in square brackets relate to References on p. 358.

of financing the deficit until the second model. This is possible because we assume that investment, consumption and government expenditure are not affected by interest rates or real balances. The second model treats investment as endogenous and introduces a money market and a foreign trade sector. Both models are further simplified by working entirely in money terms and not considering the determination of the price level.

Model 1

This model is limited to three endogenous variables, national income (Y), consumption (C) and the budget deficit (D). There are therefore three equations:

$$Y \equiv C + I + G \tag{1}$$

$$C = c(1-t) Y + a \tag{2}$$

$$D \equiv G - tY \tag{3}$$

where I is exogenous investment. The first and third relations are identities, while the second is the behavioural consumption function. In this behavioural equation, as well as in those that appear in model 2, we assume that the relation is determinate, rather than stochastic, for analytical simplicity.

The structural form of the model[1] in matrix notation is:

$$\begin{bmatrix} -1 & 1 & 0 \\ c(1-t) & -1 & 0 \\ -t & 0 & -1 \end{bmatrix} \begin{bmatrix} Y \\ C \\ D \end{bmatrix} + \begin{bmatrix} 1 & 1 & 0 \\ 0 & 0 & a \\ 0 & 1 & 0 \end{bmatrix} \begin{bmatrix} I \\ G \\ 1 \end{bmatrix} = 0 \tag{4}$$

By matrix inversion[2] and multiplication we obtain the reduced form:

$$\begin{bmatrix} Y \\ C \\ D \end{bmatrix} = \frac{1}{1-c(1-t)} \begin{bmatrix} 1 & 1 & a \\ c(1-t) & c(1-t) & a \\ -t & (1-c)(1-t) & -ta \end{bmatrix} \begin{bmatrix} I \\ G \\ 1 \end{bmatrix} \tag{5}$$

If the matrix in the reduced form (5) did not contain variables, then its elements would directly show the effect of changes in the exogenous variables on the endogenous ones; the matrix elements would be the impact multipliers. However, since the reduced form is non-linear, the impact of a change in one exogenous variable will depend on the value of others.[3] Thus, the coefficient of the items of autonomous expenditure in the first equation of the reduced form are the usual Keynesian income multiplier, $1/1 - c(1-t)$, whose value depends upon the tax rate variable.

---

[1] The approach used in this paper is similar to that shown in [6, ch. 3].

[2] Because the first matrix in (4) contains the variable t, it may become singular. Therefore the reduced form (5) is not defined where $t = 1 - 1/c$.

[3] This could be shown more directly by taking total derivatives of reduced form (5) and showing dY, say, as a function of dI, dG and dt. The coefficients of the latter derivatives would not all be constants.

In particular we can use the reduced form to show the non-linear impact of the policy instruments, G and t. To focus on this we fix I at some value. Then each equation in (5) expresses an endogenous variable in terms of the two policy instruments. The three dimensional relationships given by these equations can be graphed using contours for fixed values of the endogenous variables. We term these iso-contours. There is a family of iso-contours for each endogenous variable, obtained by varying its value. In Fig. 18.1 we have graphed some of these contours. They show how a government has to make compensating changes in G and t to keep each of the target variables constant and, further, how changes in G and t affect the levels of the target variables. Needless to say, both the domain and range of these functions must be limited in practice to economically meaningful intervals.

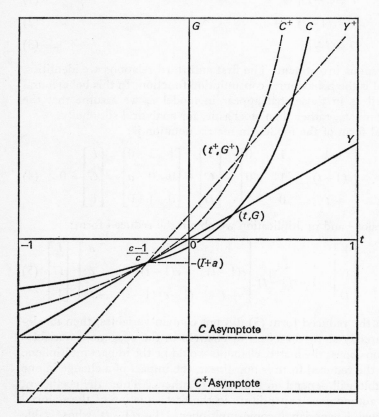

FIG 18.1.   Iso-income and consumption contours for model 2

(a) An iso-income contour is a straight line of the form $G = (cY) t + \{(1-c) Y - (I+a)\}$, for the income level Y. Each member of a family of contours passes through the common point $t = -(1-c)/c$, $G = -(I+a)$ and has slope cY. Thus, in the non-negative quadrant, a greater value of Y implies an iso-income contour above and to the left of that for a lower level of income. In the figure, therefore, $Y^+ > Y$.

(b) Iso-consumption contours are rectangular hyperbolas of the form $\{G+(C+I)\}\{t-1\}=(a-C)/c$. For any income greater than zero, C exceeds a when $t < 1$ and $c > 0$, so that the right hand side of the equation is negative; one branch of the hyperbola opens to the upper left and the other to the lower right. Only the upper left branch is shown since it alone is of economic significance, the other branch involving $t > 1$ and $G < 0$.

The asymptotes are $t=1$ and $G=-(C+I)$. The former is common to all iso-consumption contours, while the latter falls with increasing consumption. The family of iso-consumption contours pass through one common point which is the same as that for the iso-income contours. Therefore, for values of t greater than $-(1-c)/c$, an iso-consumption contour associated with a higher level of consumption is above and to the left of that for a lower level; contours $C^+ > C$ in the relevant part of Fig. 18.1.

(c) Iso-deficit contours on the G-t plane coincide with the iso-consumption contours, and are therefore not shown in Fig. 18.1. From the structural form of the model, it can be shown that $D=((1-c)/c)C-I-(a/c)$. Since I is fixed,

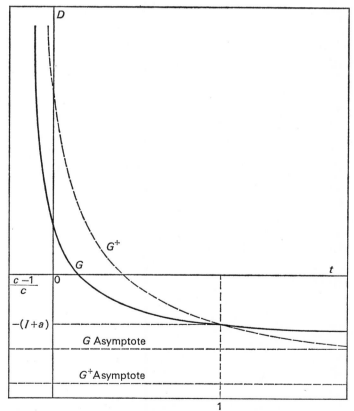

FIG 18.2.   Deficit-tax rate frontier: model 1

a fixed value of C implies unvarying D. Note however, that a given percentage change in C will result in a different percentage change in D.

The intersection point of the iso-contours for the actual values of each of the endogenous variables for any one year, will have as its coordinates the tax rate and government expenditure of that year. Ordinary realistic considerations will restrict such points to some subsection of the non-negative quadrant.[1]

In general the government has at its disposal both the G and t instruments of fiscal policy. Suppose now that the authorities decide upon a certain expenditure G. This expenditure can be financed by a set of tax rates. Corresponding to each value of t there exists a unique value of D, given by the last line of the reduced form (5). Thus for each G there is a subset of D and t values that are consistent. We call this set the deficit-tax rate frontier. It is a rectangular hyperbola of the form:

$$\left\{t+\frac{1-c}{c}\right\}\left\{D+\frac{1}{c}\left(I+a+(1-c)\,G\right)\right\}=\frac{1-c}{c^2}\,(I+a+G)$$

The frontier is shown in Fig. 18.2 for two different values of G.

The asymptotes are $t=(1-c)/c$ and $D=(-1/c)\,(I+a+(1-c)\,G)$. The t asymptote is common to all frontiers, and the D asymptote falls with increasing G. Since the constant is positive, one branch opens to the upper right and the other to the lower left. There is a common point for all the frontiers where the tax rate is 100 per cent and a budget surplus which is equal to the sum of the autonomous expenditures $I+a$. For any non-confiscatory tax rate less than 1, increased government expenditure lifts the frontier, so that $G^+ > G$.

Of the three countries studied, we display the estimated iso-contours and D–t frontier for the United States only, for brevity and because it has the most nearly closed economy. Fig. 18.3 gives iso-contours within the relevant ranges of t and G. The particular form of these lines was obtained from an estimate of the structural form and therefore of the parameters that appear in the reduced form. Details of the estimates and the estimating procedure are given in the appendix.

The analysis thus far has been in deterministic terms. However, as noted earlier the behavioural relationships are in reality stochastic, even if one knew the true value of the parameters of the model. The estimation process introduces a further stochastic element, because we have to use estimates of the parameters rather than their true values. To present the model in deterministic form requires that we use predicted values of the endogenous variables rather than their true values. This will also ensure that the iso-lines for a particular year, intersect at the actual values of G and t for that year.

One of our purposes was to display the non-linearity of the choices available to the authorities in any one given year, even when based on this simple model. We selected 1968. Fig. 18.3 shows iso-contours ($Y68$, $C68$) for the

[1] The common intersection of all the iso-contours is at the point of singularity of the matrix in (4) referred to in note 2 on p. 336. The singularity implies that the solution for the endogenous variables is not unique.

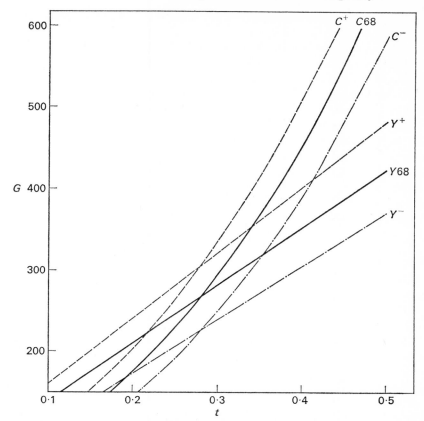

FIG 18.3.   Iso-contours US: model 1

1968 values of income and consumption, given the 1968 value of investment. We also show contours for income and consumption 10 per cent above (Y^+, C^+), and below (Y^-, C^-), the 1968 levels. We continue to hold investment unchanged, since it is a fully exogenous variable. As noted above, iso-deficit contours are not shown since they coincide with the iso-consumption contours.

Figure 18.4 shows deficit-tax rate frontiers for the 1968 value of G, and G plus and minus 10 per cent ($G68$, G^+, G^-). In the case of the D–t frontier the introduction of the stochastic element into the analysis is overcome by showing the predicted, rather than the actual, deficit on the vertical axis. In that year G was \$270·7 billion, the tax rate 0·2831, and the predicted deficit \$7·4 billion.

On the basis of the simple model we see that government expenditure could have been financed with a balanced budget by increasing the tax rate to 0·30. Alternately it would have been possible to balance the budget by reducing government expenditure by just under 10 per cent, although the original data shows that the deficit was in fact 2·73 per cent of government expenditure. The reason why the latter had to be decreased by a greater

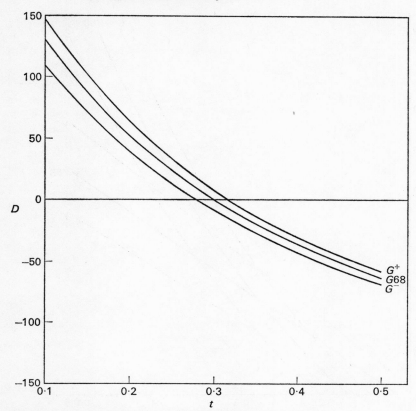

FIG 18.4.   Deficit-tax rate frontier US: model 1

amount than the deficit stems from the multiplier effect of the reduction of government expenditure on income and therefore tax receipts. We can see from Fig. 18.3 that either reducing G by 10 per cent with fixed t, or raising the tax rate to 0·30 with fixed G causes income and consumption both to fall by less than 10 per cent.

An interesting feature of this analysis is that there is an increasing marginal rate of substitution of D for t, as t decreases.[1] To finance a given government expenditure, the authorities must move along a single frontier. The implications of further changes in t for income and consumption can be seen by again referring back to Fig. 18.3. It is clear from Fig. 18.4 that a second increase of the tax rate from 0·30 by an equal amount, with G remaining unchanged, will give rise to a smaller absolute change in the deficit. Moreover, from the fact that there is an asymptote at $D = (-1/c)(I + a + (1 - c)G)$, it follows that it is impossible, by simply increasing the tax rate, to ever get a

[1] We could show this in general analytic form by finding dD in terms of dI, dG and dt, setting dI and $dG = 0$, and thus obtaining the slope of the D–t frontier, dD/dt. This is negative and increasing with t.

larger budget surplus than this absolute value of D without moving to the unrealistic left section of the hyperbola.

Model 2

We slightly enlarge the model to make investment endogenous and treat an open economy. Will an increase in the realism of the model lead to a substantial increase in the non-linear effects or drastically alter the estimated iso-contours?

Investment is made endogenous by adding a simple investment function of the form:

$$I = gY + fr + ht + I_0 \tag{6}$$

where r is the rate of interest which is assumed to be endogenous in this model. The contribution to the demand for gross investment I of induced investment and replacement of capital consumption is approximated by the first term. The coefficients f and h show the amount that investment is influenced by changes in the rate of interest and the tax rate. We expect g to be positive, and f and h to be negative.

The rate of interest being endogenous, we have to include the money market. Instead of assuming that the total supply of money is exogenous, some of the deficit is taken to be financed by the creation of new money, so that the supply of money is in part determined by the deficit. We assume that the government acts to neutralise the effect of the balance of payments on the money supply. The money supply (L) function is thus:

$$L = L_{-1} + vD + w \tag{7}$$

where L_{-1} is the stock of money existing at the beginning of the period.

The parameter v indicates the increase in the money supply that results from a unit deficit. It can be expected to be positive. Its absolute value will depend upon the proportion of the deficit that is financed in this way, as well as on the size of the bank multiplier. The remainder of the deficit is borrowed from the public and has no effect on the money supply. We continue to ignore the influence of deficit finance on other sectors; thus we do not allow for the effects of public borrowing or interest rates on consumption.

The demand for money is taken as the sum of speculative and transactions demands and is therefore a function of r and Y. After rearranging the equation we obtain:

$$r = qL + kY + p \tag{8}$$

We would expect the coefficient q to be negative and k to be positive. In the period under review, it is hardly likely that the money market was in a liquidity trap, so we may approximate the speculative demand as a single, downward-sloping, straight line.

This second model also takes foreign trade into account in the real sector. Exports E are assumed to be exogenous and imports M are determined by:

$$M = mY + n \tag{9}$$

The marginal propensity to import, m, is expected to be positive. The balance of payments is $E-M$.

To complete Model 2 we have the same consumption function and budget identity as in the first model, but the national income identity becomes:

$$Y \equiv C + I + G + E - M \tag{10}$$

Combining our seven equations, the structural form of the model becomes:

$$
\begin{bmatrix}
-1 & 1 & 0 & -1 & 1 & 0 & 0 \\
c(1-t) & -1 & 0 & 0 & 0 & 0 & 0 \\
-t & 0 & -1 & 0 & 0 & 0 & 0 \\
m & 0 & 0 & -1 & 0 & 0 & 0 \\
g & 0 & 0 & 0 & -1 & 0 & f \\
0 & 0 & v & 0 & 0 & -1 & 0 \\
k & 0 & 0 & 0 & 0 & q & -1
\end{bmatrix}
\begin{bmatrix}
Y \\ C \\ D \\ M \\ I \\ L \\ r
\end{bmatrix}
+
\begin{bmatrix}
1 & 1 & 0 & 0 \\
0 & 0 & 0 & a \\
1 & 0 & 0 & 0 \\
0 & 0 & 0 & n \\
0 & 0 & 0 & I_0 + ht \\
0 & 0 & 1 & w \\
0 & 0 & 0 & p
\end{bmatrix}
\begin{bmatrix}
G \\ E \\ L_{-1} \\ 1
\end{bmatrix}
= 0 \quad (11)
$$

The reduced form is:

$$
\begin{bmatrix}
Y \\ C \\ D \\ M \\ I \\ L \\ r
\end{bmatrix}
=
\frac{1}{\substack{1+m-c(1-t) \\ -g-fk+tvfq}}
\begin{bmatrix}
1+vfq & 1 & fq & \pi_1^1 + \pi_1^2 t \\
c(1-t)(1+vfq) & c(1-t) & cfq(1-t) & \pi_2^1 + \pi_2^2 t + \pi_2^3 t^2 \\
\substack{m-g-fk \\ +(1-c)(1-t)} & -t & -fqt & \pi_3^2 t + \pi_3^3 t^2 \\
m(1+vfq) & m & mfq & \pi_4^1 + \pi_4^2 t \\
\substack{g+fk+vfq\{m \\ +(1-c)(1-t)\}} & g+fk-tvfq & fq\{m+1-c(1-t)\} & \pi_5^1 + \pi_5^2 t + \pi_5^3 t^2 \\
\substack{v\{m-g-fk \\ +(1-c)(1-t)\}} & -vt & m+1-g-fk-c(1-t) & \pi_6^1 + \pi_6^2 t + \pi_6^3 t^2 \\
\substack{k+qv\{m-g \\ +(1-c)(1-t)\}} & k-qvt & q\{m+1-g-c(1-t)\} & \pi_7^1 + \pi_7^2 t + \pi_7^3 t^2
\end{bmatrix}
\begin{bmatrix}
G \\ E \\ L_{-1} \\ 1
\end{bmatrix}
$$

(1?)

where: $\pi_1^1 = a - n + I_0 + f(wq+p) \qquad \pi_1^2 = h$

$\pi_2^1 = a(m+1-g-fk) - nc + I_0 c + fc(wq+p)$

$\pi_2^2 = avfq + nc - cI_0 + ch - fc(wq+p)$

$\pi_2^3 = -ch$

$\pi_3^2 = n - a - I_0 - f(wq+p) \qquad \pi_3^3 = -h$

$\pi_4^1 = am + n(1-g-fk-c) + mI_0 + mf(wq+p)$

$\pi_4^2 = n(c+vfq) + mh$

$\pi_5^1 = (a-n)(g+fk) + \{m+1-c\}\{I_0 + f(wq+p)\}$

$\pi_5^2 = vfq(n-a) + h(m+1-c) + cf(wq+p) + cI_0 \qquad \pi_5^3 = ch$

$\pi_6^1 = w(m+1-g-fk-c) \qquad \pi_6^2 = v(n-a-I_0-fp) + cw$

$\pi_6^3 = -vh$

$\pi_7^1 = k(a-n+I_0) + (m+1-g-c)(wq+p)$

$\pi_7^2 = qv(n-a-I_0) + hk + c(wq+p) \qquad \pi_7^3 = -hvq$

The reduced form can once more be used to show the effect of policy instruments G and t by iso-contours for each endogenous variable for given values of the fully exogenous variables. This version is clumsier to manipulate, but we can see that the relationships still fall into two general classes:

(a) *Linear*. In the cases of iso-income and iso-import contours, G is a linear function of t, and therefore the iso-contours are straight lines. Since from equation (9) M is constant if Y is invariant, the two iso-contours coincide. It is always possible to compute the value of imports for any income.

(b) *Conic sections*. The remaining five iso-contours all have non-zero co-efficients for the Gt and t^2 terms. They therefore belong to the class of non-linear conic sections. From inspection of the reduced form (12) we see that all the conic sections in model 2 have the same general form. After normalising to make the coefficient of Gt unity:

$$Gt + \alpha t^2 + \beta G + \gamma t + \delta = 0 \qquad (13)$$

This is an hyperbola whose centre is $t = -\beta$, $G = 2\alpha\beta - \gamma$. Its major axis is at angle ϕ with the horizontal where $\tan 2\phi = 1/\alpha$. Its asymptotes are $t = -\beta$ and $G = -\alpha t + (\alpha\beta - \gamma)$. The orientation of the hyperbola depends on the sign of $-(\beta\gamma - \alpha\beta^2 - \delta)$ which is the constant after translation of the axes to the centre.

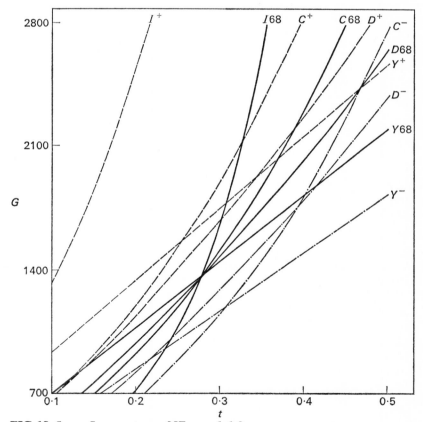

FIG 18.5.   Iso-contours NZ: model 2

Now, recall that a family of iso-contours is obtained by altering the value of the appropriate endogenous variables in the reduced form (12). Inspection of the common coefficient of all the endogenous variables in the reduced form shows that such alterations only affect γ and δ. A striking result follows. The first asymptote is a fixed vertical line for an entire family of iso-lines, while the second has unvarying slope.

In general, the coefficients in (13) are complicated combinations of the parameters of the structural form. However, it can be seen from the coefficients of t^2 in (12) that the parameter h will always appear multiplicatively in the numerator, but not in the denominator, of α. Therefore when h is zero, (13) reduces to a rectangular hyperbola whose asymptotes are parallel to the coordinate axes. This is the case whenever investment is not affected by the tax rate, as for example in Model 1.

As stated above, we are interested in examining how the extension of the model has increased the relevance of the singularities and non-linearities. Where the reduced form is hyperbolic, the extent of the non-linearity in the iso-contours will depend on three things: (i) the closeness of the centre of

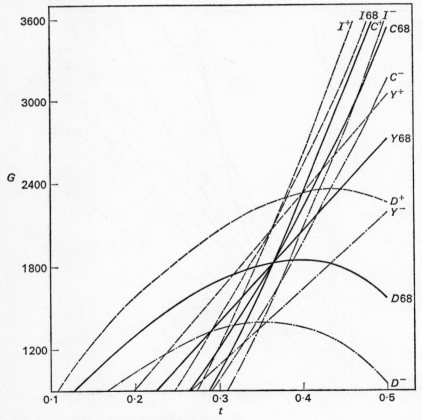

FIG 18.6.   **Iso-contours UK: model 2**

the hyperbola to the realistic range of G and t, (ii) the narrowness of the angle formed by the asymptotes and (iii) the possibility of a sign change in the constant for different iso-values of the endogenous variables. These three things depend in general upon the coefficients of equation (13) which in turn depend upon the parameters of the structural form. This second model is too complex to make it worthwhile to give general analytical expression to the dependence of the non-linearity on the parameters. Therefore we look at the problem empirically, by using the estimates of the parameters for the three countries which are given in the appendix, and observing the change in the iso-contours.

Figures 18.5–7 show, for each of the three countries, iso-income (and hence iso-import) lines, and iso-consumption, iso-deficit and iso-investment hyperbolas. We have not shown the money market iso-contours for L and r, to simplify the figures and because these are less likely to be of policy significance. The iso-contours are shown for the predicted 1968 values of the endogenous variables. Further contours are generated by taking the 1968 values plus and minus 10 per cent for income and consumption, and plus and minus 20 per

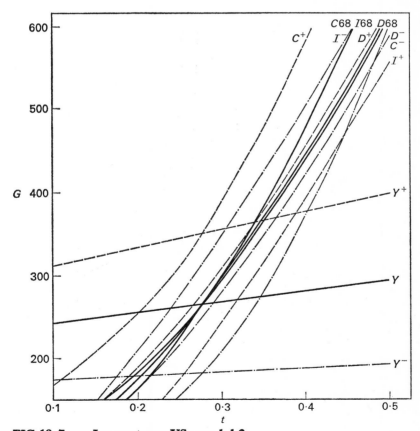

FIG 18.7.   Iso-contours US: model 2

cent for investment, since this latter has larger fluctuations. The iso-deficit contours vary around the 1968 value by absolute amounts appropriate to each country ($100 million for NZ, £1 thousand million for the UK and $10 thousand million for the USA). Iso-deficit and iso-consumption contours do not coincide in this second model, since investment is no longer exogenous.

While the iso-import contours follow the iso-income lines exactly, the value of imports associated with the 10 per cent change in income used to generate the latter will not differ by 10 per cent from the 1968 imports figure. The actual value for imports can be obtained from Y and the estimated structural form in the appendix. It should be noted that one iso-import line is also an iso-balance-of-payments-line, since exports are exogenous.

In the case of the United States all three hyperbolas are reasonably linear in the range of G and t values of policy significance. However, a disconcerting feature is the insensitivity of income to changes in the tax rate. This is, in part, explained by the perverse behaviour of investment, which apparently increases with the tax rate and compensates for the reduced consumption. Too much should not be made of this since the sign of the estimated parameter h contradicted prior expectations. Further, as is discussed in the appendix,

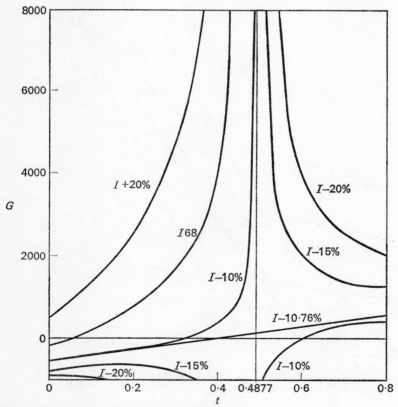

FIG 18.8.   Iso-investment NZ: model 2

the coefficient was not significant, even though it was large and thus had a considerable influence on I.

As an example of the form of the hyperbola, consider the US iso-consumption contour for 1968. The coefficients in terms of equation (13) are: $\alpha = 729$, $\beta = -1$, $\gamma = 245$ and $\delta = 67$. The centre is at $t = 1$, $G = -1703$. The contour has asymptotes $t = 1$ and $G = -729t - 974$. The second of these has negative slope, but is rather flat when taking the scale of the figure into account. The constant is -1041, orienting this hyperbola 'northwest and southeast'.

United Kingdom income is clearly more responsive to tax rate changes; investment reacts in the expected direction and has significant coefficients. All the UK relationships are linear, or approximately so, with the striking exception of the iso-deficit contours. The 1968 iso-deficit contour has coefficients: $\alpha = -12873$, $\beta = 1 \cdot 099$, $\gamma = 8318$ and $\delta = 27$. The hyperbola has centre at $t = 1 \cdot 099$, $G = 19977$; the asymptotes are $t = 1 \cdot 099$ and $G = 12873t + 5829$. The constant is 6380. While the centre is well outside the relevant range of G and t, the second asymptote is positively sloped and very steep. Moreover the sign of the constant means that the hyperbola is squeezed

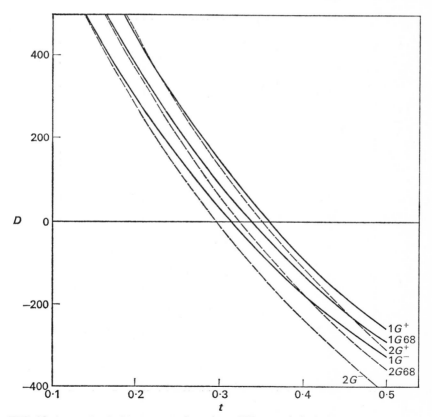

FIG 18.9.   Deficit-tax rate frontiers NZ: models 1–2

within the quadrant which is in the narrow angle between the asymptotes. Hence the shape of the hyperbola in the figure.

The shape of the iso-deficit contours implies that the UK deficit-tax frontier also takes on a distinctive shape as a consequence of these parameters. For a fixed governmental expenditure, successive increases in tax rates initially reduce the deficit, and then larger t values increase it again. Furthermore, for any given deficit, there exists a maximum level of government expenditure consistent with the system.

New Zealand presents the most interesting result, because the centre of the hyperbola for the iso-investment family is within the relevant range of G and t values, and also the sign of the constant term determining orientation of the hyperbola is sensitive to the value of I. Thus, for the family of investment contours the coefficients are: $\alpha = -1466$, $\beta = -0.4877$, $\gamma = 5.8166I - 2656$ and $\delta = 2.3091I - 1854$. The centres are at $t = 0.4877$, $G = 4086 - 5.8166I$. Putting in the 1968 value of I, the G coordinate is $G = -346$. With a smaller value of I, the G coordinate becomes positive and clearly moves to within the relevant range. The asymptotes are $t = 0.4877$ and $G = 1466t + (3371 - 5.8166I)$, the second of which is rather flat and of positive slope. The

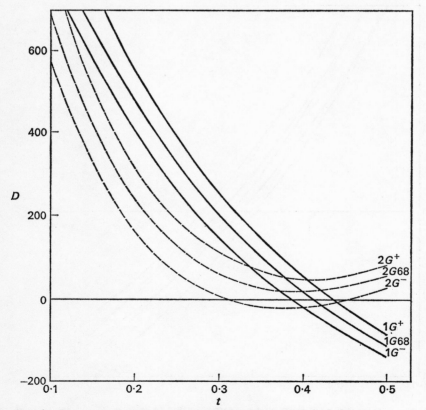

FIG 18.10.   Deficit-tax rate frontiers UK: models 1-2

constant is $3498 - 5{\cdot}1459I$. This is negative at the 1968 value of I, but becomes positive when I is less than 680, which is only 10·76 per cent lower than the 1968 value. At this stage, the hyperbola shifts into the other quadrant. At $I=680$, the constant term vanishes and the hyperbola degenerates to the asymptotes themselves.

The result of this instability is that only small sections of the iso-investment contours appear on Fig. 18.5. To illustrate more fully the shape and behaviour of the family of contours Fig. 18.8 is given for a wider range of values of G, t and I.

Investment in New Zealand exhibits both changes in the sign of response to changes in t and G, as well as discontinuous alteration in the marginal rate of substitution between these instruments, as t increases past the singularity at the vertical asymptote $t=0{\cdot}4877$.

Figures 18.9–11 show the D–t frontiers for the three countries. Each figure contains the frontier for government expenditure of 1968, plus and minus 10 per cent, for models 1 and 2 (i.e. $1G68$, $1G^+$ etc.). As before, the vertical axis measures the predicted deficit, which will in general not be the

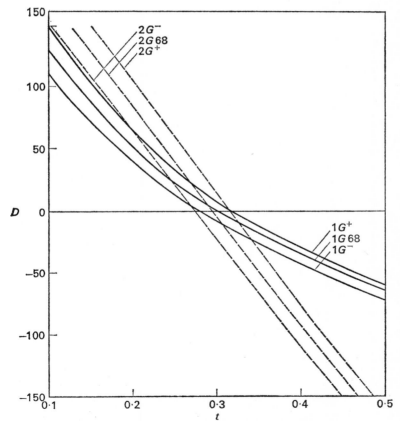

FIG 18.11.   Deficit-tax rate frontiers US: models 1–2

same in the two models for the 1968 value of t. Showing the frontiers for the two models on one figure allows one to see the effect of widening the model on the alternative methods of financing the fixed government expenditure.

In Fig. 18.10 the deficit tax frontier of the United Kingdom for Model 2 yields a really startling result, when taken in conjunction with the contours in Fig. 18.6. The deficit is close to its minimum value, at the 1968 tax rate and government expenditure. It would be possible to reduce the deficit very slightly by a fairly large increase in t, but Fig. 18.6 shows that this would have disastrous consequences for C, Y and I. Any further increase in t would then only increase the deficit.

Conclusion

It is certainly the case that most of the relations we have examined, while in general non-linear, have turned out to be approximately linear for the estimated values of the parameters in the three countries. While the majority of them are hyperbolas, within the range of G and t instruments relevant to policy makers they could have been well approximated by straight lines.

Experienced and practical men of affairs in government, might then be led to feel justified in anticipating that by restricting themselves to small changes in the G and t instruments, roughly proportional changes would ensue in income, consumption and so on. In fact, as New Zealand investment and UK deficits show most dramatically, this is not always the case. Only the income relationship was strictly linear even in the first simplest model. And, as the second model shows, for certain critical values the direction as well as the magnitude of the response may be subject to sudden shifts. In this second model, although the structural form does not contain any new non-linearities, those that were present already in Model 1 become more pervasive and influential. The larger the size of the model, and therefore of the matrix that is inverted to obtain the reduced form, the greater is the chance for the non-linearities to interact with one another and with the otherwise linear relations. We conclude that instability is not simply an artifact of simplifications introduced to ease the labours of model builders. Introducing more variables and equations in order to make the model more realistic will not eliminate a disturbing feature which follows from the nature of the fiscal instruments themselves. The fiscal authorities may be led by experience to act in a way that brings about results that were not part of their original intention.

Appendix

(a) Estimating procedures and data

For the purpose of estimation we introduce explicit, well-behaved, random error terms into the models at the appropriate places. The estimates are obtained by an instrumental variable technique similar to two stage least squares (2SLS). It is not possible to apply 2SLS directly, since the reduced forms of the models are more or less complex non-linear functions of the exogenous variables. Thus the ordinary least squares estimate of the linear reduced form, the first stage of 2SLS, is not appropriate.

Suppose, nonetheless, we perform a linear ordinary least squares regression of the endogenous variables on all the exogenous variables, and then use the predicted values from this regression as instrumental variables in an estimate of the structural form, exactly as in the case of 2SLS. The estimate thus obtained by behaving as if the reduced form were linear, is identical to that of 2SLS, where the reduced form is in fact linear.

The instruments used in this technique are appropriate, since, (i) they are independent of the error terms in the structural form, because they are linear combinations of exogenous variables which are assumed to be independent of the errors, and (ii) they are clearly not independent of the true values of the endogenous variables, because they are related, albeit in a non-linear fashion, in the reduced form. The estimates are therefore consistent.

Further, their asymptotic covariance matrix is identical to that of proper 2SLS. To see this we need only observe that the asymptotic covariance matrix of the 2SLS estimator is in fact derived from that of an instrumental variable estimate where the predicted values of the endogenous variables are proper instruments (see [5, p. 332]). Because our estimator has the same asymptotic covariance matrix as that of a proper 2SLS estimator, we can simply use the estimate of this matrix obtained on the assumption we were using proper 2SLS.

In the case of the money supply equation, a variation of this procedure is used starting with an ordinary least squares regression of $L - L_{-1}$ on the value of D obtained from the linearised first stage. This regression gives the estimated parameters. The true value of D is then used to obtain residuals and the standard error of v. Lastly, the true value of L_{-1} and D are used to predict L, find residuals and therefore to find the R^2 explanation of the variance of L.

The values of R^2 and the standard errors for the estimates of the structural form were on the whole satisfactory. However, in order to obtain the various iso-contours, the estimated parameters had to be substituted into the true non-linear reduced form. It should be appreciated that the accuracy of the estimate of the reduced form obtained in this fashion is not the same as that of the structural form. A better procedure for estimating the reduced form would have been to estimate it directly, non-linear as it is, and subject to the restriction imposed by the over-identified structural form. This task was not undertaken, since the purpose of the exercise was simply to get reasonable values of the structural form parameters.

The models were estimated for each country based on data for the years 1952 to 1968. Throughout, monetary units are millions of dollars for New Zealand, £10 million for the UK, and billions of dollars for the US. Interest rates are expressed in percentages, while tax rates are written as a proportion.

Definitions of the national income variables followed standard national procedures, with the following exceptions. Investment was limited to gross investment by the private sector. Money supply included quasi-money. Tax receipts included local government taxes and income from government corporations. The tax rate was the quotient of the tax receipts divided by national income. Government expenditure included local authority spending, transfers and gross investment by the non-private sector. Interest rates were the yields on long term government obligations.

The deficit was obtained from the budget identity—government expenditure minus taxes. National income was likewise obtained from an accounting identity, and therefore varied between the models. National income in the simple model of the closed economy was construed to exclude the balance of trade component. In both the complex and simple models, we included transfer payments in income, to be able to analyse money flows.

(b) Estimates

Table 18.1 gives the estimates of the parameters, equation by equation, for the two models and for each country.

TABLE 18.1. *Estimates of the structural forms*

1. The consumption function

$$C = c(1-t)\,Y + a$$

	NZ			UK			USA		
c (s.e.c.)	a	R^2		c (s.e.c.)	a	R^2		c (s.e.c.)	a	R^2

Model 1

NZ			UK			USA		
0·7121	116·51		0·8298	31·49		0·7925	4·48	
		0·9954			0·9960			0·9985
(0·0131)			(0·0141)			(0·0081)		

Model 2

0·7462	74·28		0·8357	8·88		0·7865	3·89	
		0·9901			0·9968			0·9989
(0·0201)			(0·0127)			(0·0071)		

2. The import function. Model 2 only

$$M = mY + n$$

NZ			UK			USA		
m (s.e.m.)	n	R^2	m (s.e.m.)	n	R^2	m (s.e.m.)	n	R^2
0·1795	198·55		0·1815	92·83		0·0534	−5·30	
		0·9046			0·9714			0·9701
(0·0156)			(0·0083)			(0·0025)		

3. *The investment function.* Model 2 only

$$I = gY + fr + ht + I_0$$

	g (s.e.g.)	f (s.e.f.)	h (s.e.h.)	I_0	R^2
NZ	0·2620	−165·36	781·08	245·39	0·9283
	(0·0455)	(90·67)	(1302·0)		
UK	0·1113	19·53	−2114·54	474·92	0·9562
	(0·0380)	(27·10)	(697·92)		
USA	0·4258	−107·41	2308·38	−343·01	0·1180
	(0·6507)	(252·17)	(6008·45)		

4. *The money supply function.* Model 2 only

$$L = L_{-1} + vD + z$$

NZ			UK			USA		
v (s.e.v.)	z	R^2	v (s.e.v.)	z	R^2	v (s.e.v.)	z	R^2
0·9601	−16·92	0·9936	1·1365	17·47	0·9855	0·8619	21·78	0·9882
(0·2178)			(0·6011)			(0·6522)		

5. *The money demand function.* Model 2 only

$$r = kY + qL + p$$

	k (s.e.k.)	q (s.e.q.)	p	R^2
NZ	0·004516	−0·009867	8·085	0·7874
	(0·001737)	(0·004233)		
UK	0·002760	−0·004158	2·871	0·8820
	(0·000929)	(0·002247)		
USA	0·020475	−0·023390	0·262	0·9372
	(0·006728)	(0·009635)		

TABLE 18.2. *Numerical estimates of the reduced form and predicted endogenous variables for 1968 values of I, E and L_{-1} where appropriate*

Income

NZ	Model 1	$Y(0\cdot2879+0\cdot7121t)=781+G$	$\hat{Y}=4455$
	Model 2	$Y(0\cdot9181+2\cdot3127t)=2\cdot5665G+781t+3300$	$\hat{Y}=4508$
UK	Model 1	$Y(0\cdot1702+0\cdot8298t)=444+G$	$\hat{Y}=4826$
	Model 2	$Y(0\cdot1806+0\cdot9280t)=0\cdot9077G-2115t+1344$	$\hat{Y}=4322$
US	Model 1	$Y(0\cdot2075+0\cdot7925t)=131\cdot0+G$	$\hat{Y}=928\cdot5$
	Model 2	$Y(2\cdot0403+2\cdot9519t)=3\cdot1654G+2308t+1135$	$\hat{Y}=919\cdot9$

Consumption

NZ	Model 1	$C(0\cdot2879+0\cdot7121t)=0\cdot7121(1-t)\,G-473t+589$	$\hat{C}=2411$
	Model 2	$C(0\cdot9181+2\cdot3127t)=1\cdot9151(1-t)\,G-583t^2+1025t+2531$	$\hat{C}=2985$
UK	Model 1	$C(0\cdot1702+0\cdot8298t)=0\cdot8298(1-t)\,G-343t+374$	$\hat{C}=2579$
	Model 2	$C(0\cdot1806+0\cdot9280t)=0\cdot7586(1-t)\,G+1767t^2-2883t+1124$	$\hat{C}=2304$
US	Model 1	$C(0\cdot2075+0\cdot7925t)=0\cdot7925(1-t)\,G-100\cdot3t+104\cdot7$	$\hat{C}=532\cdot7$
	Model 2	$C(2\cdot0403+2\cdot9519t)=2\cdot4896(1-t)\,G-1816t^2+934\cdot0t+901\cdot0$	$\hat{C}=523\cdot2$

Deficit

NZ	Model 1	$D(0\cdot2879 + 0\cdot7121t) = 0\cdot2879(1-t)\,G - 781t$	$\hat{D} = 147$
	Model 2	$D(0\cdot9181 + 2\cdot3127t) = -0\cdot2538Gt + 0\cdot9181G - 781t^2 - 3300t$	$\hat{D} = 117$
UK	Model 1	$D(0\cdot1702 + 0\cdot8298t) = 0\cdot1702(1-t)\,G - 444t$	$\hat{D} = 79$
	Model 2	$D(0\cdot1806 + 0\cdot9280t) = -0\cdot1643Gt + 0\cdot1806G + 2115t^2 - 1344t$	$\hat{D} = 24$
US	Model 1	$D(0\cdot2075 + 0\cdot7925t) = 0\cdot2075(1-t)\,G - 131\cdot0t$	$\hat{D} = 7\cdot4$
	Model 2	$D(2\cdot0403 + 2\cdot9519t) = -0\cdot2135Gt + 2\cdot0403G - 2308t^2 - 1135t$	$\hat{D} = 11\cdot0$

Imports

NZ	Model 2	$M(0\cdot9181 + 2\cdot3127t) = 0\cdot4607G + 599t + 775$	$\hat{M} = 1008$
UK	Model 2	$M(0\cdot1806 + 0\cdot9280t) = 0\cdot1647G - 315t + 261$	$\hat{M} = 866$
US	Model 2	$M(2\cdot0403 + 2\cdot9519t) = 0\cdot1690G + 107\cdot62t + 49\cdot82$	$\hat{M} = 43\cdot8$

Investment

NZ	Model 2	$I(0\cdot9181 + 2\cdot3127t) = -0\cdot3976Gt + 0\cdot1939G + 583t^2 + 1056t + 737$	$\hat{I} = 762$
UK	Model 2	$I(0\cdot1806 + 0\cdot9280t) = 0\cdot0152Gt + 0\cdot1333G - 1767t^2 - 339t + 287$	$\hat{I} = 356$
US	Model 2	$I(2\cdot0403 + 2\cdot9519t) = -0\cdot4623Gt - 1\cdot1955G + 1816t^2 + 1333t + 181\cdot1$	$\hat{I} = 119\cdot4$

368	**M. Wolfson and A. Rayner**

The consumption, import, and money demand functions all show estimated coefficients of the expected sign and are of a high level of significance. The money supply function coefficients are of the expected sign, but of a lower level of significance. The investment function is the least satisfactory. The best fit was obtained for the UK where the coefficients of Y and t are of the expected sign and highly significant. The estimate of f is positive rather than negative, but not significantly different from zero. New Zealand also shows a satisfactory fit with coefficient of Y positive and highly significant. The estimate of f is of the expected sign and reasonably significant, while that of h has unexpected sign, but is not significant.

The estimate of the investment function for the USA is very unsatisfactory. This is largely a result of the perversity of the 2SLS procedure. The value R^2 from a 2SLS regression of I on Y alone is 0·95, while the introduction of r has reduced this to 0·12. The reason is that the second stage regression of I on the predicted values of Y and r produced a coefficient of r which was large in terms of influence on I, but insignificant at that stage. The predicted values of r and Y were then replaced with the true values to obtain residuals and thus the standard errors and R^2. The differences between the predicted r and its true value, combined with its large coefficient, led to large values for the residuals and hence the bad fit for the equation. While we could have re-estimated the equation using ordinary least-squares, it seemed hard to justify this procedure statistically.

Fortunately, the striking results we obtained were for countries other than the USA and therefore could not have resulted from this one rather freakish equation.

Table 18.2 gives the numerical estimates for most of the reduced form for 1968 values of I in case of Model 1, and E and L_{-1} in the case of Model 2. Estimates of money and rate of interest equations are omitted as explained in the text. The table also gives the predicted 1968 values for the endogenous variables. Substitution of these in the appropriate equations gives the iso-contours.

References

1. AMES, EDWARD. *Incomes and Wealth*. Holt, Rinehart & Winston, 1969.
2. CHRIST, CARL F. 'A short-run aggregate demand model of the interdependence and effects of monetary and fiscal policies with Keynesian and classical interest elasticities', *American Economic Review*, 57, no. 2 (1967).
3. CHRIST, CARL, F. 'A simple macro-economic model with a government budget restraint', *Journal of Political Economy*, 76, no. 1 (1968).
4. EVANS, M. K. 'An econometric model of the Israeli economy, 1952–65', *Econometrica*, 38, no. 5 (1970).
5. GOLDBERGER, ARTHUR S. *Econometric Theory*, Wiley 1964.
6. KLEIN, L. R. and EVANS, M. K. *Econometric Gaming*, New York, Macmillan, 1969.

Analytics of choice in fiscal policy: Discussion

P. N. Junankar[1]

1. Introduction

This Rayner–Wolfson (R–W) paper is an interesting empirical study of a small macroeconomic model which embodies a government budget constraint. The pioneering work in this field was done by Carl Christ [3]. The primary concern of R–W is to explore the non-linearities in fiscal policy choices facing a government. The models they investigate are simple Keynesian comparative static underemployment models with a *fixed* price level: the first of a closed economy with exogenous investment and (implicitly) no bonds, and the second of an open economy with endogenous investment and a bond market. I shall confine my remarks to the theoretical implications of the R–W paper.

2. A comparison with Christ's paper

Christ has shown that the introduction of a government budget constraint in simple Keynesian models implies that the *method* of financing the government's expenditure affects our conventional multipliers. R–W show explicitly that the multipliers do not have constant coefficients but depend on the values of the instrumental variables. But unlike Christ they treat the monetary implications of fiscal policy in a cavalier fashion (I will return to this later). Christ works out impact multipliers under different assumptions and also shows that the long run multiplier equals the inverse of the marginal tax rate. R–W seem to concern themselves simply with showing that non-linear choices exist between instrumental variables. In fact they find, for the simple models estimated, linear approximations seem to be justifiable for the UK and the USA.

3. A critique of R–W paper

The *first* criticism I have of the R–W paper is that it is a static model with a *fixed* price level. In this context why does the government not choose a

[1] I would like to thank Sean Murray for his help in writing this. He is, of course, not to blame for any misrepresentations.

zero tax rate, a value of government expenditure (*G*) to get full employment and let the money supply accommodate? Since the main point of introducing a government budget constraint is to study the monetary implications it seems desirable to make the price level endogenous. It is customary for discussants to suggest extensions, but it seems to me some gesture needs to be made towards dynamising the model.

Second, although R–W have discussed the alternative choices available to the government they do not embed their results in a Tinbergen–Theil framework to study *which* of the alternative combinations is optimal.

The third and final criticism I have of the R–W paper returns to my earlier remark on the cavalier treatment of the monetary implications of fiscal policy. Model 1 completely ignores the financing decision and implicitly there are no bonds in it. Model 2 has a mis-specified government budget constraint: it is identical to that of model 1 without bonds. In this model government expenditure can be financed by taxes, printing money or by issuing bonds. But if the government issues bonds then *it increases its expenditure by the amount of the interest payments on them.* Sean Murray has shown in a paper as yet unpublished [1], that the introduction of this latter term changes many of the usual results.

In the light of the above comments perhaps R–W ought to have confined themselves to estimating multipliers *à la* Christ.

Conclusions

Let me conclude by saying that this is, to my knowledge, the first comparative study of the empirical implications of introducing a government budget constraint in macroeconomic models. I hope that more work will be done in this field as a result of the R–W paper.

Reference

1. MURRAY, S. 'Financing the government's budget deficit' (mimeograph).

Manipulating demand for money[1]

19

Maxwell J. Fry

1. Introduction

A public sector deficit can be financed by increasing the money supply. There are three concomitant measures which a government can take to increase the resulting flow of resources to the public sector and reduce the subsequent inflation: first, increase the proportion of the money supply backed by government rather than private assets; second, shift the demand for money so that more is demanded at every level of income; third, increase the income and decrease the cost elasticities of demand for money. This paper considers some techniques used to manipulate demand for money in Iran, Pakistan and Turkey for this purpose.

The literature on inflationary finance has shown that in the long run revenue obtained in this way reaches a maximum at some finite rate of money expansion. It has also been suggested that the revenue-maximising rate of money increase is frequently deflationary rather than inflationary. However, this essay is confined to short-run analysis and does not address itself to the problems of designing optimum long-run strategies of public finance. The welfare costs of inflationary finance have also received considerable attention in the literature since the issue was reopened by Bailey in 1956 [2].* Although no attempt has been made here to measure these, the conclusion is reached that they have been high enough to affect quite substantially the rate of economic growth.

Programmes of planned economic development in the underdeveloped countries have generally been accompanied by significant increases in public expenditure. Even with accelerated rates of economic growth, public revenue has failed to increase as fast as expenditure. The consequent deficit typically has to be financed, in an underdeveloped country lacking a capital market, through foreign aid (defined throughout to include all grants and loans from abroad) and/or increases in the money supply. The latter can take the form of

[1] The research reported in this paper constitutes part of a forthcoming monograph entitled Money, Growth and Development Planning in Iran, Pakistan and Turkey. I would like to thank the Social Science Research Council for its financial support.

* Numbers in square brackets relate to References on p. 384.

government borrowing from the central bank or from the commercial banks; in both cases this leads to an increase in the money supply and similar effects on the level of demand [25, p. 526]. These produce inflationary pressures and a deteriorating balance of payments situation. Attempts are often made to minimise the inflation generated in this process.

Foreign exchange controls, maximum interest rates, high reserve requirements, etc., can be imposed to increase the flow of resources to the public sector [33]. The introduction of policies of this kind produce a phenomenon closely akin to financial repression so frequently discovered in underdeveloped countries and strongly criticised by Western economists (e.g. [8, 10, 31, 40]). However, this form of financial control is not aimed at repressing all financial development, but rather at encouraging financial institutions which can be made to provide a large proportion of their funds to the public sector and discouraging those which cannot. Such financial control might be termed financial restriction as opposed to financial repression.

Successful financial restriction would be exemplified by a higher proportion of funds from the financial system being transferred to the public sector and three effects on the demand for money, namely, a rightward shift in the function, higher income and lower cost elasticities of demand. All three effects enable a greater public sector deficit to be financed at a given rate of inflation.

The resort to inflationary finance springs from an inherent over-optimism on the part of government authorities regarding increases in public revenue. Plans are formulated in the following vein:

> If revenues can be raised as a percentage of national income, and if the percentage of revenues saved can also be increased over time, then general government may be able to finance its own capital formation and even contribute to the capital needs of public enterprises. This is the picture set forth hopefully in most planning documents [39, p. 541].

Typically, these hopes are not realised, one major reason for this being ignorance of the extent to which financial transfers to the public sector must increase to meet the planned expenditure [13, chs 6 and 7]. The result is 'a growing tendency . . . to resort to borrowing from commercial and central banks' [39, p. 542].

The choice of Iran, Pakistan and Turkey for this study springs from their common membership in the Regional Cooperation for Development (RCD) which was established in 1964 with the object of setting up

> a strong regional group . . . to initiate and participate in measures for facilitating concerted action for the economic reconstruction of this region, for raising the level of this region's economic community and for maintaining and strengthening the economic relations of the countries of this region both among themselves and with other countries of the world [38, p. 3].

Since then a number of steps have been taken towards achieving these aims, e.g. joint industrial projects, trade facilities, banking and insurance services, communications, etc. However, neither a common market nor a monetary union, both mentioned at the RCD's inauguration, has been established. In fact, comparing achievements with the very ambitious programme outlined in 1964 has led to growing scepticism in the efficacy of the RCD [16]. Intra-regional trade has remained virtually non-existent [4]. However, UNCTAD prepared a classified report in 1971 which has, apparently, put forward proposals for increasing such trade. The ministerial meeting held in Isfahan during August 1971 ended on a particularly optimistic note, perhaps largely as a result of the Shah's renewed enthusiasm [24]. Furthermore, the recent secession of East Pakistan and hostilities with India has produced a strong desire in Pakistan for closer links with her western neighbours.

This paper reports on some preliminary research constituting part of a larger study on the financial aspects of economic cooperation within the RCD. A prevalent view encountered in Iran maintains that closer association with Pakistan and Turkey would be detrimental to the rial. This fear springs from the obvious overvaluation of both the rupee and the Turkish lira. It appears unlikely that any significant steps in the direction of further integration will take place until some general measures towards reducing economic controls, particularly in the field of foreign trade, have been instigated in Pakistan and Turkey. This paper attempts to shed some light on the link between many such controls and one of the causes, namely, large public sector deficits.

2. A bird's eye view of economic development in the RCD since 1950

Table 19.1 presents estimates of the annual percentage growth rates in GNP. It is evident that development in Iran, Pakistan and Turkey during the two decades since 1950 has been somewhat uneven. A common characteristic in the pattern of economic growth is that it accelerated in all three countries during the 1960s. Although the factors contributing to the increased growth rates differ, the stagnation of the 1950s appears to stem from the same cause, namely, reduced ability to import.

Oil nationalisation in Iran, which occurred in 1951, resulted in the immediate closure of the oilfields and refinery production for three years, thus starving Iran of foreign exchange revenue from by far her most important export [3, pp. 162–4]. Imports remained below their 1951 level until 1954, [21], and no economic growth occurred. The increase in imports between 1954 and 1960 was paralleled by an increase in the rate of economic growth to an estimated annual rate of 5 per cent [3, pp. 58–9].

The 1960s have experienced an unforeseen upsurge in oil revenues; between 1960 and 1970 the value of imports trebled [20, 21]. This was accompanied by liberal foreign trade policies, the encouragement of foreign investment, a boom in consumer durables and sufficient funds to enable the Plan expenditures to be revised upwards. Growth in the 1960s accelerated to over 10 per cent p.a. by the early 1970s.

Pakistan suffered a considerably more dramatic reduction in imports:

13

TABLE 19.1. *Percentage rates of growth in real GNP*

	Iran	Pakistan	Turkey
1951	0·0	0·0	15·3
1952	0·0	2·9	8·6
1953	0·0	6·3	11·1
1954	0·0	0·5	−9·1
1955	0·0	−0·3	7·7
1956	5·0	6·0	6·8
1957	5·0	0·8	6·3
1958	5·0	1·4	11·8
1959	5·0	4·3	4·3
1960	4·7	5·2	2·4
1961	4·7	5·9	0·6
1962	5·6	3·5	6·4
1963	5·4	8·3	7·7
1964	8·6	4·5	4·9
1965	9·3	4·7	4·5
1966	7·8	5·0	10·3
1967	11·7	7·5	6·2
1968	9·6	5·7	6·5
1969	10·3	6·3	6·3
1970	10·3	1·4	5·7

Sources: Iran: 1950–59 from J. Bharier, *Economic Development in Iran, 1900–1970* (London, Oxford University Press, 1971), pp. 58–9; 1959–70 from Bank Markazi Iran, *Annual Report and Balance Sheet, 1971* (Tehran: Bank Markazi Iran, 1971), Table 2, p. 116.
Pakistan: Central Statistical Office, Government of Pakistan, *Monthly Statistical Bulletin*, 1956–71.
Turkey: State Institute of Statistics, *National Income, Total Expenditure and Investment of Turkey, 1938, 1948–1970* (Ankara: State Institute of Statistics, 1971), Table 1, pp. 10–11.

their level in 1954 fell below half the peak achieved during the Korean boom in 1951. Imports did not exceed their 1951 level until 1960 [20, 21]. Private investment fell throughout the 1950s because of the scarcity of foreign exchange [17, 23]. The shortage of foreign exchange can be attributed both to the decision not to devalue the rupee with sterling in 1949 (this led to an embargo on Pakistani imports by India) and a 'mildly excessive' rate of monetary expansion given this exchange rate policy [41, p. 638]. What growth there was occurred in the embryonic industrial sector in which profits of 50–100 per cent, a result of the highly protected consumer goods market established to curtail imports, were reported [9, p. 5]. Domestic savings has been closely correlated with the level of imports [37, p. 9; 23, pp. 505–15]. The upsurge in imports during the 1960s, due in the main to a substantial increase in foreign aid, was accompanied by increasing domestic savings and hence a compounded increase in investment. Economic development over the 1960s resulted from both industrial and agricultural growth, a reversal in the policy of agricultural repression occurring in 1959 when a price support programme was introduced and investment encouraged [9, p. 4].

Turkey also experienced declining imports from 1952 to 1958, the 1952 level not being reached until 1962 [21]. This decline was caused by rapidly increasing public sector expenditure; large deficits resulted and price controls were established to limit the ensuing inflation. The latter had two effects, the first being to drive private enterprises out of business, the second to produce large operating deficits in the State Economic Enterprises which were then financed through increases in the money supply. Thus, the anti-inflationary price controls added fuel to the inflationary fire [27, ch. 1]. Domestic inflation had a dramatic effect on the balance of payments. Exchange controls had to be tightened and under and over-invoicing discouraged by minimum price controls for exports and maximum prices for imports. The price controls on exports simply dried up the already waning export industry. The shortage of foreign exchange resulted in very low rates of capacity utilisation in industry as shortages of raw materials occurred [7, p. 7]. The price support for agricultural products administered by the Soil Products Office did increase acreage sown, but yields fell. Meanwhile, exports of agricultural commodities by the Soil Products Office could only take place at prices well below the support price and it was obliged to engage in massive borrowing from the Central Bank [27, ch. 2].

The 1960s present a much brighter picture. Iran experienced an industrial boom and the 'White Revolution'. Pakistan obtained large amounts of foreign aid and developed both industry and agriculture. Turkey, after a revolution in 1960, started a programme of planned economic development, increased exports and received unforeseen foreign exchange in the form of remittances from workers in Germany [11, p. 15]. Foreign aid was considerably higher than it had been during the 1950s, despite the fact that it fell far short of the amount hoped for by the planners [12, p. 315].

Tables 19.2, 19.3 and 19.4 present a summary of movements in the money supply, prices and velocities of circulation in the RCD countries over the past two decades. Money supply narrowly defined ($M1$—defined as currency in circulation plus demand deposits) has increased at approximately the same rates in Iran and Pakistan and at a faster rate in Turkey. High-powered money and money broadly defined ($M2$—adds time deposits to $M1$) has increased during the 1960s faster in Iran and Turkey than in Pakistan.

Given that Iran experienced faster growth in real GNP during the 1960s the differences in the average rates of inflation reported in Table 19.3 are quite predictable. Rates of inflation have declined noticeably in Iran, risen slightly in Pakistan and fallen slightly in Turkey. However, because the Turkish indices were calculated with large weights attached to official prices controlled by law over the 1950s the actual rate of inflation during that decade was probably considerably understated [27, ch. 2].

TABLE 19.2. *Money supply and high-powered money*

		M1	M2	HPM
IRAN				
(Billions of rials, end of April)	1951	13·4	—	—
	1961	39·1	52·5	23·3
	1971	93·0	232·1	88·8
Average annual	1951–61	10·71%	—	—
rates of change	1961–71	8·64%	14·87%	13·38%
PAKISTAN				
(Millions of rupees, end of	1950	3209	3437	2143
December)	1960	6676	7769	4451
	1970	15775	23059	9327
Average annual	1950–60	7·33%	8·16%	7·28%
rates of change	1960–70	8·60%	10·87%	7·38%
TURKEY				
(Millions of Turkish lira, end of	1950	1594	1774	1059
December)	1960	9256	10044	5033
	1970	35268	44171	19573
Average annual	1950–60	17·57%	17·34%	15·59%
rates of change	1960–70	13·38%	14·81%	13·57%

Sources: Iran: *Bank Markazi Iran Bulletins*, 1–10, 1960–71.
          Pakistan: *State Bank of Pakistan Bulletins*, 1949–71.
          Turkey: *Türkiye Cumhuriyet Merkez Bankası Aylık Bulteni*, 1960–71.

Consistently higher rates of inflation in Turkey might be expected to have been associated with faster velocities of circulation; the reverse findings shown in Table 19.4 seem paradoxical. However, higher *per capita* income in Turkey might result in lower velocities if the income elasticities of demand for money are greater than one. To eliminate this possible income effect, the average annual continuously compounded rates of change in velocities are given in the second part of Table 19.4. During the 1960s the rate of deceleration in velocity using M1 has been considerably more marked in Turkey than in Iran or Pakistan. Velocity using M2 has fallen faster in Turkey than in Pakistan but not as fast as it has in Iran. The more rapid growth in income, together with the sharp reduction in the rate of inflation, might account for this rapid fall in $V2$ in Iran. The only way to test this hypothesis is to estimate demand for money functions.

3. Demand for money: preliminary estimates

Exploratory work is reported in this section on econometric estimates of demand for money functions in Iran, Pakistan and Turkey for the 1960s. Elsewhere, definitional problems involved in such analysis have been dis-

TABLE 19.3. *Average rates on inflation*

		INFLATION 1 based on wholesale price indices	INFLATION 2 based on GNP implicit deflators
IRAN	1951–61	4·6	5·0
	1961–70	1·6	1·3
	1951–70	3·1	3·2
PAKISTAN	1950–60	2·6	2·5
	1960–70	3·2	2·8
	1950–70	2·9	2·7
TURKEY	1950–60	9·7	9·8
	1960–70	4·8	4·9
	1950–70	7·2	7·4

Sources: Iran: 1950–59 from J. Bharier, *Economic Development in Iran, 1900–1970* (London: Oxford University Press, 1971), Table 3, pp. 46–7 and pp. 58–9; 1959–70 from Bank Markazi Iran, *Annual Report and Balance Sheet*, 1971 (Tehran: Bank Markazi Iran, 1971), Tables 1 and 2, pp. 115–16 and *Bank Markazi Iran Bulletin*, 10 (55), May–June 1971, pp. 150–1.
Pakistan: Pakistan Institute of Development Economics, *A Measure of Inflation in Pakistan*, 1951–60 (Karachi: Pakistan Institute of Development Economics, Monograph No. 4, 1961), Table 1, p. 5 and *Central Statistical Office Monthly Statistical Bulletin*, 1956–1971.
Turkey: United States Agency for International Development, *Economic and Social Indicators—Turkey*, 1967–1971 (Ankara: United States Agency for International Development, 1967–71 and State Institute of Statistics, *National Income, Total Expenditure and Investment of Turkey*, 1938, 1948–1970 (Ankara: State Institute of Statistics, 1971), Table 1, pp. 10–11.

cussed [13, ch. 5] and refinements to the data included. Here, results using the most readily available comparable data are given. The equation

$$\log M^d = b_0 + b_1 \log Y + b_2 i^*$$

has been estimated where M^d represents *per capita* real money holdings, Y *per capita* real GNP and i^* the expected rate of inflation.

Two expected inflation series have been calculated, the first based on an adaptive model, the second on an extrapolative one. A comparison of the two by Turnovsky found that the former gave slightly better results in the USA [42]. Weights for the adaptive model were arbitrarily chosen as follows:

$$i_t^* = 0\cdot36i_t + 0\cdot252i_{t-1} + 0\cdot1784i_{t-2}$$

$$+ 0\cdot12348i_{t-3} + 0\cdot08812i_{t-4}$$

A third series combining both adaptive and extrapolative models was then constructed. Here, it was assumed that higher weight would be placed on the

TABLE 19.4. *Velocities of circulation*

		V1	V2	VHPM
IRAN	1951	10·4	—	—
	1961	8·4	6·1	12·6
	1970	8·5	3·6	9·8
PAKISTAN	1950	6·8	6·3	10·6
	1960	5·5	4·7	8·5
	1970	5·4	3·6	9·2
TURKEY	1950	6·9	6·2	10·1
	1960	5·7	5·3	10·8
	1970	4·5	3·7	8·3

Average annual percentage rates of change in velocities of circulation

		V1	V2	VHPM
IRAN	1951–61	−2·8	—	—
	1961–70	+0·2	−5·9	−2·8
	1951–70	−1·2	—	—
PAKISTAN	1950–60	−2·1	−2·9	−2·2
	1960–70	−0·1	−2·6	+0·8
	1950–70	−1·1	−2·8	−0·7
TURKEY	1950–60	−2·0	−1·7	+0·7
	1960–70	−2·3	−3·7	−2·7
	1950–70	−2·1	−2·7	−1·0

$$V1=\frac{Y}{M1} \qquad V2=\frac{Y}{M2} \qquad VHPM=\frac{Y}{HPM}$$

where *HPM* is high-powered money

Sources: Same as Tables 19.1 and 19.2

extrapolative expectations the clearer the trend in the rates of inflation over the past five years. The equation

$$i_t = a + bt$$

where t runs from −4 to 0 is used to predict inflation between $t=0$ and $t=1$. If the regression produces an R^2 of one then the extrapolative model is used, if the R^2 is zero then the adaptive model is chosen. In all other cases the expected rates of inflation produced by the extrapolative and adaptive models are weighted by R^2 and $(1-R^2)$, respectively, and then summed.

The results presented in Table 19.5 and Fig 19.1 must be interpreted with due regard to the arbitrariness of the weighting patterns used. Further work may justify more confidence in them. Some comfort can be taken from the fact that similar estimates to these have been produced in much more elaborate econometric work on Turkey [1]. A virtue might perhaps be made of the fact that the results reported were the only ones produced; there can be no accusation of data-mining.

For the remainder of this paper attention is focused on attempts to explain the differences in the demand estimates for the three countries. Had data been available, the explanations given might have been subjected to econometric testing. The search for good quantitative proxy variables for financial restriction has so far failed, although it continues. Work is also in progress to estimate demand functions for the 1950s; parameter estimates are expected to differ from those produced for the 1960s in a predictable fashion given that economic policies pursued in the 1960s were so different from those followed in the 1950s.

TABLE 19.5. *Income and cost-elasticities for the demand for money*

$$\log M^d = b_0 + b_1 \log Y + b_2 i*$$

IRAN

(1961–71) $\log M1 = -3\cdot07 + 1\cdot10 \log Y - 2\cdot26i*$

        t $(6\cdot6)\ (22\cdot7)$ $(3\cdot2)$

        $\bar{R}^2 = 0\cdot98$

        $DW = 0\cdot90$

PAKISTAN

(1960–70) $\log M1 = -2\cdot48 + 1\cdot14 \log Y - 1\cdot29i*$

        t $(5\cdot4)\ (14\cdot4)$ $(4\cdot9)$

        $\bar{R}^2 = 0\cdot96$

        $DW = 1\cdot82$

        $\log M2 = -8\cdot00 + 2\cdot12 \log Y - 0\cdot90i*$

        t $(12\cdot2)\ (18\cdot9)$ $(2\cdot4)$

        $\bar{R}^2 = 0\cdot98$

        $DW = 1\cdot44$

TURKEY $\log M1 = -4\cdot18 + 1\cdot38 \log Y - 0\cdot34i*$

(1960–70) t $(4\cdot6)\ (10\cdot2)$ $(2\cdot0)$

        $\bar{R}^2 = 0\cdot97$

        $DW = 2\cdot11$

        $\log M2 = -6\cdot49 + 1\cdot75 \log Y - 0\cdot35i*$

        t $(6\cdot9)\ (12\cdot6)$ $(2\cdot1)$

        $\bar{R}^2 = 0\cdot98$

        $DW = 2\cdot36$

13*

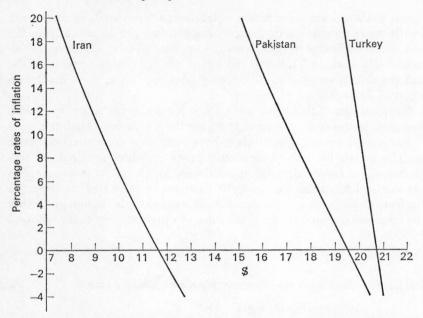

FIG 19.1.   Demand for money (*M*1) at a *per capita* income of $100

4. Financial restriction

During the 1960s Turkey has been to the greatest, Iran the least, lengths to engage in financial restriction. Iran's development plans have been financed from oil revenues; these have considerably exceeded expectations. Since 1955 domestic resources for development in Pakistan have been matched almost equally by foreign aid. Nevertheless, inflationary finance has been used in excess of levels planned. A programme of planned economic development for Turkey was inaugurated in 1962; a massive transfer of resources from private to public sectors was required to achieve planned targets. Given that foreign aid fell far short of that upon which the Plan was based [13, ch. 6], heavy reliance on inflationary finance was not surprising. In all three countries, however, public investment consistently failed to meet planned targets. One of the indications of the extent to which financial restriction has existed in Pakistan and Turkey is the difference between maximum interest rates under which the banks are obliged to operate and the return on capital; in Turkey the shadow rate of return was estimated in the mid-1960s at 20 per cent [30, p. 538] and in Pakistan at 12–15 per cent [36, p. 97]. Maximum interest rates on bank loans were $10\frac{1}{2}$ per cent in Turkey throughout the 1960s and averaged around 7 per cent in Pakistan.

The first glaring paradox in an examination of financial restriction in the RCD countries is the observation that the growth in banking since 1950 has been spectacular. It must, therefore, be remembered that the financial control for inflationary finance is not synonymous with indiscriminate measures to prevent all financial development, but consists of measures which promote financial channels providing a seignorage to the public sector and curtail those which do not. With the degree of severity varying in the predictable way, the authorities have imposed maximum interest rates, advance limits, bank nationalisation and reserve requirements on both banks and non-banks in all three countries. Furthermore, non-institutional lending is illegal in Turkey.

Controls have made banking highly lucrative. Indeed, the legally determined interest rate spread in Turkey is so large that bank branches have mushroomed in some of the most unlikely places [13, ch. 6]. In all three countries the rise particularly in time deposits within the past decade has been substantial. The banking habit has been encouraged through directives on the location of bank branches to persuade people to substitute financial claims for unproductive tangible assets, such as gold and jewellery. Provided these financial claims are then partially backed by government liabilities more funds are made available to finance its deficit. It may well be easier to persuade people to finance the government in this indirect manner rather than to do so directly.

Simply encouraging people to hold bank deposits, perhaps by making banking excessively lucrative, appears to be a much less costly way of financing a public sector deficit than maintaining an over-valued currency and operating exchange controls. However, McKinnon has recently argued that the importance of financial development in the process of economic development (and thus the costs of financial repression) has been grossly underestimated [31]. He supports this contention in two ways: first by presenting a model of a fragmented capital market in which marginal rates of return on investment cannot be equalised and second by illustrating his proposition with a sample of successful (Japan, Germany, Taiwan, Korea) and unsuccessful (Chile, Argentine, Brazil, Philippines, India, Turkey) countries. Success is measured by the record of growth in *per capita* income. The significant aspect of his model is that in it physical capital and money become complements rather than substitutes. His examples show that velocity of circulation is much lower (and therefore real money balances higher) in the successful countries than in the unsuccessful ones. Higher velocities in the unsuccessful countries is attributed to financial repression, a situation in which the rate of interest is held below the free market rate, foreign exchange controls exist and the capital market is deliberately fragmented by government policies. This conclusion is supported by, among others, Friedman:

> In developing countries a major source of future development is an improved financial structure. In every country which is developed the financial institutions have played a major role in assuring a wide distribution of capital funds, in assuring the efficient utilisation of capital, in assuring the availability of capital to people who do not themselves have the wealth. And the effect of imposing a special pattern on the financial institutions is to prevent them from serving that very important function [10, p. 709].

Despite frequent criticism of measures constituting financial restriction no quantitative estimates on their costs have yet been produced. Neither have explanations for the prevalence of this phenomenon in underdeveloped countries abounded. One attempt to provide the latter has been made here.

5. Exchange control[1]

Exchange control can be defined as a system under which foreign exchange is rationed by devices other than price. It therefore implies the existence of an overvalued domestic currency. These are frequently encountered in underdeveloped countries. Although there are several strong reasons for maintaining an overvalued currency, a few can be identified with attempts to minimise inflation. If in the absence of foreign exchange controls substitution of foreign exchange for domestic currency and foreign securities for domestic securities to avoid the inflationary tax or obtain securer investment opportunities took place, velocity would rise and thus a given public sector deficit would produce greater inflation. A second effect of overvaluation is to tax exports and hence redistribute income. Where exports are mainly primary products the redistribution can be expected to flow from the rural to the urban sectors of the community. If the latter have higher propensities to save in financial form a given public sector deficit will produce less inflation. A third effect of overvaluation is to reduce the size of the balance of payments deficit (foreign savings) in terms of the domestic currency and to increase public sector savings. Although this is simply a statistical effect without any influence on the total availability of resources it does disguise transfers to the public sector. As Cooper points out: 'A roundabout way of accomplishing a controversial objective will often succeed where direct action would fail, because it obscures, perhaps even from the policy-makers themselves, who is really benefiting and who is being hurt' [6, p. 11].

The effect of exchange control on public sector revenue is evident through the tariff revenues received. One of the major problems of public finance in underdeveloped countries, however, is the income inelasticity of tax revenues. Tariffs exemplify this since they encourage import substitution and so a reduction in the volume of imports.

A further anti-inflationary device, used to the greatest extent in Turkey, which can be employed when the domestic currency is overvalued is import pre-deposits. Under such arrangements, a certain proportion of the value of the import has to be deposited in local currency before import licences, etc., are granted, only to be released again after the import has cleared customs. In this way, money can be sterilised for considerable periods by delaying the import licence and foreign exchange disbursements.

Throughout the 1960s foreign exchange controls have continuously been relaxed in Iran. By 1971 the free market foreign exchange rate fluctuated only marginally from the official rate [32]. The system of pre-deposits, however, has been maintained for the explicit purpose of sterilising importers' funds [32].

In contrast to the Iranian experience, Pakistan's exchange regulations

[1] Unless otherwise specified, details on exchange controls operated in all three countries over the period have been taken from [19].

appear to have become increasingly complex. Since 1949 when Pakistan did not devalue with sterling on the grounds that the supply of exports was price inelastic, the rupee has been continuously overvalued. Pre-deposit schemes have been introduced at various times and licensing has featured throughout the period. Foreign exchange controls were tightened after the Korean boom ended and devaluation took place in 1955. In 1959 the Export Bonus Scheme was introduced establishing a system of multiple exchange rates. This scheme was supplemented by the Performance Licensing Scheme introduced in 1961 and modified in 1964 [18, 28]. With these has developed a very elaborate system of exchange control. Several studies have attempted to estimate the extent of overvaluation and its effects. The estimates of overvaluation range from 30 to 90 per cent [22, 34, 35].

The Turkish lira has been devalued twice over the past two decades, the first occasion being in 1958 after several crisis years from 2·8 to 9·0 Turkish liras to the dollar, the second in 1970, again in the face of acute balance of payments problems and international pressure, to 15·0 Turkish liras to the dollar [15]. Despite these devaluations the Turkish lira has remained overvalued. On the assumption that all imports are competitive the lira was overvalued by 40 per cent in the mid-1960s; on a conservative estimate of the extent to which some imports are complementary the overvaluation was estimated at 95 per cent [30, p. 540]. The foreign exchange regime in Turkey has made use of most of the devices falling under the heading of exchange control. The severity of the licensing controls during the 1950s can in part be judged from the extent to which evasion occurred. Calculations of Turkey's balance of payments using trading partner accounts suggest that considerable over and under-invoicing took place despite the price controls on both imports and exports mentioned earlier. Furthermore, after 1956 a complicated system of 'switch deals' with Eastern European countries became common [27, ch. 2]. By 1956, '*Ad hoc* measures had gone so far that various individual regulations were mutually inconsistent, while the losses entailed in exporting were such that only the Government or semi-official agencies were exporting' [27, ch. 3]. During the late 1960s pre-deposits became an important weapon in the import regime's armoury. Prior to the devaluation in 1970 pre-deposits constituted 40 per cent of the money supply and were immobilised for 50–60 weeks [14, Table 1, pp. 88–89].

Costs of overvaluation have been estimated for Turkey and found to be substantial [26, 27]. In fact, an inverse relationship appears to have existed in Turkey over the past two decades between a five-year moving average incremental capital-output ratio and the degree of trade liberalisation [27, ch. 9]. The explanation suggested is that capacity utilisation has fluctuated violently with changes in the foreign trade regime.

6. Conclusion

Exchange control and financial restriction in the RCD countries have been in greatest evidence when pressures on public finance have existed (1950s in Iran, 1950s and 1960s in Pakistan and Turkey). Despite rapid economic growth in Iran during the 1960s exchange controls were reduced.

Financial restriction and exchange controls have been costly and difficult to enforce. Nevertheless, in Turkey where they have been most ardently pursued velocity of circulation was lowest, income elasticity of demand for money high and cost elasticity low. In addition, a sizable proportion of the resources of the financial system was placed at the disposal of the public sector.

This leads to the final question: Has financial restriction accelerated or retarded economic growth? A negative relationship seems to have existed in the RCD countries, lower growth during the 1950s being associated with a period of greater financial restriction. However, concomitant with counter-movements in these variables were distinctive swings in the pattern of foreign trade. Thus, a time series relationship is difficult to isolate. On the other hand, a cross-country comparison during the 1960s also produces a negative relationship between growth and the degree of financial restriction, highest growth and least financial restriction being observed in Iran. Given Iran's exceptional success in increasing her revenue from oil these results are again impossible to accept as unqualified evidence in support of the generally held view that financial restriction impedes growth; for that, a much larger sample would be needed. Estimates using a 22-country sample are being run as this preliminary report goes to press.

References

1. AKYÜZ, Y. 'Money and inflation in Turkey 1950–1968', unpublished PhD thesis, University of East Anglia, 1971.
2. BAILEY, M. J. 'The welfare cost of inflationary finance,' *Journal of Political Economy*, 64, no. 2 (April 1956), pp. 93–110.
3. BHARIER, J. *Economic Development in Iran 1900–1970*, Oxford University Press, 1971.
4. CENTRAL STATISTICAL OFFICE, GOVERNMENT OF PAKISTAN, *Pakistan's Trade with Iran & Turkey and Industrial Production*, Karachi: Central Statistical Office, 1971.
5. COOPER, R. N. 'An assessment of currency devaluation in developing countries', in *Government and Economic Development*, ed. G. Ranis, Yale University Press, 1971, pp. 472–513.
6. COOPER, R. N. *Currency Devaluation in Developing Countries*, Princeton University, Essays in International Finance no. 86, 1971.
7. ECONOMIST INTELLIGENCE UNIT, *Quarterly Economic Review: Turkey*—No. 24, November 1957.
8. EMERY, R. F. *The Financial Institutions of Southeast Asia: A Country-by-Country Study*, Praeger, 1970.
9. FALCON, W. P. and STERN, J. J. 'Pakistan's development: an introductory perspective', in *Development Policy II—The Pakistan Experience* ed. W. P. Falcon and G. F. Papanek, Harvard University Press, 1971, pp. 1–7.
10. FRIEDMAN, M. 'Monetary policy for a developing society', *Bank Markazi Iran Bulletin*, 9, no. 54 (March–April 1971), pp. 700–12.
11. FRY, M. J. 'The Turkish Lira', *International Currency Review*, 2, no. 2 (May 1970), 13–17.
12. FRY, M. J. 'Turkey's first five-year development plan: an assessment', *Economic Journal*, 81, no. 322 (June 1971), pp. 306–26.
13. FRY, M. J. *Finance and Development Planning in Turkey*, Leiden: Brill, 1972.
14. FRY, M. J. and İLKIN, S. 'Devaluation of the Turkish lira', *The Turkish Yearbook of International Relations*, 1968, pp. 82–95.

15. FRY, M. J. and İLKIN, S. 'The devaluation of the Turkish lira', *International Currency Review*, **2**, no. 6 (January 1971), pp. 28–31.

16. HALE, W. M. and BHARIER, J. 'CENTO, RCD and the northern tier: a political and economic appraisal,' *Middle Eastern Studies*, forthcoming.

17. HASAN, P. *Deficit Financing and Capital Formation: the Pakistan experience 1951–59*, Pakistan Institute of Development Economics, Karachi, 1962.

18. HECOX, W. E. 'The export-performance licensing scheme', *Pakistan Development Review*, **10**, no. 1 (Spring 1970) 24–49.

19. INTERNATIONAL MONETARY FUND, *Annual Reports on Exchange Restrictions*, 1950–71.

20. INTERNATIONAL MONETARY FUND, *Direction of Trade*, 1960–71.

21. INTERNATIONAL MONETARY FUND, *International Financial Statistics*, 1950–71.

22. ISLAM, A. I. A. 'An estimation of the extent of over-valuation of the domestic currency in Pakistan at the official rate of exchange, 1948/49–1964/65', *Pakistan Development Review*, **10**, no. 1 (1970), 50–67.

23. ISLAM, N. 'Foreign assistance and economic development: the case of Pakistan', *Economic Journal*, **82**, no. 325s (1972) (Supplement), 502–30.

24. *Kayhan International*, Tehran daily newspaper, 22–26 August 1971.

25. KESSEL, R. A. and ALCHIAN, A. A. 'Effects of inflation', *Journal of Political Economy*, **70**, no. 6 (1962), 521–37.

26. KRUEGER, A. O. 'Some economic costs of exchange control: The Turkish Case', *Journal of Political Economy*, **74**, no. 5, (October 1966), pp. 466–80.

27. KRUEGER, A. O. 'Turkey's foreign trade and economic growth', Minnesota University, mimeographed manuscript, 1971.

28. LEWIS, S. R. *Pakistan: industrialization and trade policies*, Oxford University Press, 1970.

29. LEWIS, S. R. and HUSSAIN, S. M. 'Relative price changes and industrialization in Pakistan: 1951–1964', *Pakistan Development Review*, **6**, no. 3 (Autumn 1966), pp. 408–31.

30. MARTENS, A. 'The two-gap theory of development reconsidered with special reference to Turkey', *European Economic Review*, **1**, no. 4 (1970), 512–45.

31. MCKINNON, R. I. 'Capital in a theory of economic development', Stanford University, photocopied manuscript, 1971.

32. MEMARZEDEH, A. 'Monetary policy and foreign exchange control', Paper presented at the CENTO Symposium on Central Banking, Monetary Policy and Economic Development, Izmir 5–12 April 1971, EC/20/CB/D15.

33. NICHOLS, D. A. 'Some principles of inflationary finance', *Journal of Political Economy*, forthcoming.

34. PAL, M. L. 'The determinants of domestic prices of imports', *Pakistan Development Review*, **4**, no. 4 (Winter 1964), 597–622.

35. PAL, M. L. 'Domestic prices of imports in Pakistan: extensions of empirical findings', *Pakistan Development Review*, **5**, no. 4 (1965), 547–85.

36. PAPANEK, G. F. and QURESHI, M. A. 'The use of accounting prices in planning', in *Organisation, Planning and Programming for Economic Development*, New York: United States Papers Prepared for the United Nations Conference on the Application of Science and Technology for the Benefit of the Less Developed Countries, vol. 8, 1963.

37. PLANNING COMMISSION, Government of Pakistan, *The Fourth Five Year Plan 1970–75*, Islamabad: Planning Commission, 1970.

38. RCD SECRETARIAT, *Regional Cooperation and Development among Iran, Pakistan and Turkey: establishment of aims; progress of activities*, Tehran: RCD Secretariat, 1969.

39. REYNOLDS, L. G. 'Public sector saving and capital formation', in *Government and Economic Development* ed. G. Ranis, Yale University Press, 1971, pp. 516–52.

40. SHAW, E. S. 'Capital scarcity and financial policy in economic development', *Bank Markazi Iran Bulletin*, **8**, no. 47 (Jan.–Feb. 1970), pp. 565–73.

41. SOLIGO, R. 'Monetary Problems of Pakistan', *Journal of Political Economy*, **75**, no. 4–ii (August 1967), 635–50.

42. TURNOVSKY, S. J. 'Empirical evidence of the formation of price expectations', *Journal of the American Statistical Association*, **65**, no. 332 (Dec. 1970) 1441–54,

Manipulating demand for money: Discussion

A. R. Nobay

As is well established, inflation is a form of taxation which is borne by holders of money, and the resort to such a means of finance by governments results in welfare costs. Bailey and others have attempted to calculate the 'maximum desirable rate of inflation' by equating the marginal revenues from the tax with the marginal welfare costs. Recently, this issue has been revisited by Friedman [1], who finds that from estimates of the demand for money function for several underdeveloped countries, the actual rate of inflation experienced by these economies far exceeds those rates which yield the greatest amount of purchasing power to the fiscal authorities. This, he attributes to political myopia on the part of the fiscal authorities.

A corollary to the 'new view' of money would, of course, suggest a seductive avenue, whereby the authorities given these high rates of inflation could nevertheless maximise their revenues by imposing quantitative restrictions on a whole range of assets which would otherwise be substitutes for money, or more precisely government debt. Such an approach has recently been put forward by Nichols [2], as a counter to Friedman. This simple, but hitherto neglected proposition amounts to saying that the authorities are able to influence the key variables in the demand for money function, in contrast to the generally accepted notion that the demand for real cash balances is endogenously determined.

It is within this context that Fry attempts to examine financial regulations and restrictions imposed by Iran, Pakistan and Turkey, in the course of their development financing. He presents an overview of economic development in these economies at a fairly rapid pace, and this should provide those interested in this area with a useful reference point on the subject. On this part of the paper I have very little to say, except to note a possible contradiction—if as is stated, 'the stagnation of the 1950s appears to stem from the same cause, namely, reduced ability to import', how does one reconcile the statement a little later that Turkey's declining imports were caused by rapidly increasing public sector expenditure, unless if somehow public expenditure had a significantly larger propensity to import? Perhaps this section suffers from the pace at which the strands of argument are carried out.

As the title suggests, the essence of the paper is an attempt to evaluate governments' efforts to manipulate the demand for money. Two specific aspects are examined—exchange controls and financial restrictions. Friedman, it will be recalled, concludes that the authorities' myopically *tolerate* inflation in excess of their revenue maximising rates, whereas Nichols, whose propositions this paper seeks to consider, proposes measures to maximise governments' revenues *given* the rates of inflation that these countries experience. It seems to me that given fixed exchange rates, the inflation rate should more correctly be regarded as being exogenous. However, one notes that Fry variously interprets the measures which Nichols proposes in order to maximise revenue in a somewhat different light—that of minimising the inflation generated by government deficit financing. This clearly raises analytical issues which require careful analysis.

Fry begins his analysis of inflationary finance by accepting the proposition that the welfare costs have been 'high enough to affect quite substantially the rate of economic growth'. However, this line of reasoning is somewhat short-lived, as the introductory section on inflationary finance in practice, proceeds to redefine restrictions such as foreign exchange controls, maximum interest rates, high reserve requirements etc., not as financial repression, as would McKinnon and Friedman, but as a form of financial restriction aimed at 'encouraging financial institutions which can be made to provide a large proportion of their funds to the public sector and discouraging those which cannot'. I stress that this distinction is not a semantic one, but is crucial in an evaluation of the welfare implications of such financial controls. The paper does not deal with such issues and this would seem to be a pity as one cannot really evaluate the effects of financial controls without reference to this aspect of inflationary finance. The analysis is further open to a number of other criticisms. I propose to consider these below.

Fry rightly notes Cooper's point that political factors play a large part in maintaining an over-valued currency. It would follow, therefore, that exchange controls are applied primarily in order to maintain the over-valued rate, and not to manipulating the demand for money, as is subsequently suggested —the effects, if any, on the demand for money are purely incidental and not consciously sought for. Then too, the assertion that there are several reasons for maintaining an over-valued currency is a strong one, and in my view is not satisfactorily substantiated. As a case in favour of maintaining an over-valued currency, it is asserted that there arises a redistribution of income from the rural to the urban sectors of the community. The merits of such a redistribution are not at all clear to me. On the contrary, one could point to the fact that often, development efforts centre around the agricultural sector, and such a redistribution does not elicit the required supply responses from that sector with consequent effects upon development.

It is suggested that controls have made banking highly lucrative, from which it is concluded that this is a simple way of encouraging people to hold time deposits. Whilst one can find reasons for accepting the first proposition, there is very little in any analysis to suggest that people will be encouraged to hold time deposits. A simple but nevertheless important point to make is that increased monetisation of these economies will result in larger amounts of government debt being absorbed, but it clearly does not require, and neither does it follow, that monopoly profits by banks induce larger holdings of time deposits by individuals. Also, the framework which enables higher interest rates in underdeveloped economies to dramatically increase the supply of funds and consequently generate demand inflation is somehow unrealistic —even in developed economies, despite the presence of alternative earning assets, we are yet to find large interest elasticities in demand for money functions. In any case, this model is implicitly rejected by the author in the empirical result presented as interest rates do not appear in the demand functions.

Whilst appreciating that the empirical results are somewhat preliminary, they clearly do not support the hypothesis examined in the paper. One confusion that seems to be maintained is equating the price of money in the sense of the purchasing power of money, with the opportunity cost of holding real money—i^*, calculated as it is in a somewhat eccentric way, is equated with the cost of holding money. What happens to the usual homogeneity postulate in the demand for money? Clearly, what is required is a well specified demand for money model using cross-sectional and dummy variables, and even here numerous specification problems need to be considered—in particular, one needs to account for the differences in monetisation between countries and over time. The detailed institutional and other knowledge which Fry has on these economies would be an asset in formulating such a testable model.

A major difficulty a discussant faces with this paper is that a number of important issues are tackled simultaneously without a clear reference point to a framework or model. It is possible therefore that my comments are misdirected and derive from my own confusion, particularly as I understand the paper to be part of a larger study on this subject. However, subsequent discussion will tell. The subject matter which Fry introduces us to is a fascinating and important one, integrating as it does monetary policy, inflationary finance and economic development and we must clearly thank him for having presented us with such a thought provoking paper.

References

1. FRIEDMAN, M. 'Government Revenue from Inflation', *Journal of Political Economy*, July 1971.
2. NICHOLS, D. A. 'Some principles of inflationary finance'. *Journal of Political Economy*. Forthcoming.

Index of names

(Italicised numbers indicate starting page of author's paper included in this volume.)

Kraus, Marvin, 16n.
Krüger, A. O., 385
Krzyzaniak, M., 33
Kurz, M., 232, 236, 242

Labordère, Marcel, 219
Laidler, D. E. W., *65*, 294
Lancaster, K., 112, 135
Law, D., 330
Lawrence, T. E., 217
Layard, Richard, *170*, 188, 192n., 212
Leibenstein, H., 154
Leuin, V. I., 223
Leontief, W. W., 52, 58, 59
Lewis, S. R., 385
Lind, R. C., 114–15, 116
Lipsey, R. G., 112, 135, 232, 241, 295–6, 306n., 327
Little, I. M. D., 156, 160n., 161, 161n., 163
Littlewood, J. E., 94, 109
Llewellen, Wilburg, 144, 154
Lloyd George, David, 219, 222
Lumsden, K. G., 187
Lydall, H. F., 98n., 102n., 106, 109

Malinvaud, E., 1, 116–17, 135
Marglin, S. A., 156, 161n.
Marris, Robin L., 144, 154
Marshall, Alfred, 217, 221, 241
Martens, A., 385
Mathur, P. N., *320*, 343–4
Maunders, K., 139n.
Mayne, Margaret, 243n., 257
Meade, James, 188, 223
Means, G. C., 143, 154
Melchior, Carl, 223, 224
Meltzer, A. H., 260
Memarzedeh, A., 385
Merrett, A. J., 33
Metcalf, David, 188, *192*, 211, 212–14
Metcalfe, J. S., *50*, 60, 63–4
Mill, John Stuart, 91, 107n., 193
Miller, M. H., 25n., 33, 125, 257, 261, 293
Mills, F. C., 1n., 3, 10, 15
Milne, P. S., 139n.
Mirrlees, J. A., 62n., 64, 90, 90n, 92, 92n, 93–7, 102–4, 106, 108, 109, 112n., 135, 156, 160n., 161, 161n., 163, *167*
Modigliani, F., 125
Moggridge, D. E., 224
Mohring, H., 1n.
Monsen, R. Joseph, 151n., 154
Monti, Mario, 256, 261
Morningstar, M., 188
Mossin, J., 117, 125n., 135
Motley, B., 292, 293
Mundell, R. A., 290, 293
Murray, S., 369
Musgrave, R. A., 19n., 33, 107n., 109
Muth, R., 1n., 3, 12n., 15, 82, 84
McCann, E., 345n.

McCarthy, W. E. J., 313–15, 327
McCormick, B., 202n., 210, *328*
McCulloch, J. R., 90
McFadden, D., 35n., 36n., 47
McKeachie, W. J., 188
McKean, Ronald N., 150–1, 154
McKenzie, L. W., 47, 47n.
McKinnon, R. I., 381, 385, 387

Nelson, P., 200, 210
Neuberger, E., 188
Nevin, E. T., 160n.
Newhouse, J. P., 188
Nichols, Don, 385, 386, 388
Nicholson, R. J., *85*, 139, 147, 151, 152, 154
Nikaidô, H., 61–70
Nobay, A. R., 261, *386*
Norton, W. E., 257, 261, 293

Ohlin, Bertil, 50, 51n., 62
Ostroy, J. M., 234, 242

Pal, M. L., 385
Paldam, M., 84
Papanek, G. F., 385
Pareto, V., 93, 97–8, 98n., 108, 111
Parkin, J. M., 17n., 50n., 90n., 263n., *291*, 294, 306n., 327
Patinkin, Don., 233, 241
Pauly, Mark V., 142, 143–5, 147, 154
Peacock, A. T., 139, 154, 188
Pearson, K., 103n., 109
Perkin, H., 196, 197, 198n., 211
Peters, W., 17n.
Phelps, E. S., 41, 45
Phelps-Brown, E., 327
Phillips, A. W., 327
Pigou, A. C., 91, 92, 96, 106, 109
Plato, 107
Polch, J. J., 246n.
Polya, G., 94n., 109
Prais, S. J., 84
Prest, A. R., 105, 109, 188
Purdy, D. L., *294*, 328–9

Quirin, G. D., 141n., 154
Qureshi, M. A., 385

Radner, Roy, 113, 136, 231, 234, 236, 242
Rawls, J., 105, 109
Rayner, A. C., *345*, 369–70
Reading (Lord), 225
Reddaway, W. B., 212
Reder, M., 202n., 211
Rees, Graham L., 330
Rees, J. A., 115n., 136
Rees, R., *110*, 112n., 115n., 119n., 136
Reid, M. G., 81, 84
Reynolds, L. G., 385
Ricardo, David, 59
Richardson, R., 200n., 211

Index of subjects